Understanding Counterinsurgency

D1567611

This textbook offers an accessible introduction to counterinsurgency operations, a key aspect of modern warfare.

Featuring essays by some of the world's leading experts on unconventional conflict, both scholars and practitioners, the book discusses how modern regular armed forces react, and should react, to irregular warfare. The volume is divided into three main sections:

- Doctrinal origins: analyzing the intellectual and historical roots of modern Western theory and practice;
- Operational aspects: examining the specific role of various military services in counterinsurgency, but also special forces, intelligence, and local security forces;
- Challenges: looking at wider issues, such as governance, culture, ethics, civil-military cooperation, information operations, and time.

Understanding Counterinsurgency is the first comprehensive textbook on counterinsurgency, and will be essential reading for all students of small wars, counterinsurgency and counterterrorism, strategic studies, and security studies, both in graduate and undergraduate courses as well as in professional military schools.

Thomas Rid is a visiting scholar at the Shalem Center in Jerusalem, and a non-resident fellow at the Center for Transatlantic Relations in the School for Advanced International Studies, Johns Hopkins University.

Thomas Keaney, Colonel, USAF (Retd), is associate director of strategic studies at the Johns Hopkins University School of Advanced International Studies.

Understanding Counterinsurgency

Doctrine, operations, and challenges

Edited by
Thomas Rid and Thomas Keaney

LONDON AND NEW YORK

First published 2010
by Routledge
2 Park Square, Milton Park, Abingdon, Oxon, OX14 4RN

Simultaneously published in the USA and Canada
by Routledge
270 Madison Avenue, New York, NY 10016

Routledge is an imprint of the Taylor & Francis Group, an informa business

Typeset in Times New Roman
by Keystroke, Tettenhall, Wolverhampton
Printed and bound in Great Britain
by TJ International Ltd, Padstow, Cornwall

British Library Cataloguing in Publication Data
A catalogue record for this book is available from the British Library

Library of Congress Cataloging-in-Publication Data
Understanding counterinsurgency : doctrine, operations and challenges / edited by
Thomas Rid and Thomas Keaney.
        p. cm.
    Includes bibliographical references and index.
1. Counterinsurgency. I. Rid, Thomas. II. Keaney, Thomas A.
U241.U53 2010
355.02'18--dc22   2009044225

ISBN10: 0–415–77764–X (hbk)
ISBN10: 0–415–77765–8 (pbk)
ISBN10: 0–203–85237–0 (ebk)

ISBN13: 978–0–415–77764–3 (hbk)
ISBN13: 978–0–415–77765–0 (pbk)
ISBN13: 978–0–203–85237–8 (ebk)

Contents

Notes on contributors   vii
Acknowledgments   x
List of abbreviations   xi

1   **Understanding counterinsurgency**   1
    THOMAS KEANEY AND THOMAS RID

PART I
Doctrine   9

2   **France**   11
    ETIENNE DE DURAND

3   **Britain**   28
    ALEXANDER ALDERSON

4   **Germany**   46
    TIMO NOETZEL

5   **United States**   59
    CONRAD CRANE

PART II
Operational aspects   73

6   **Army**   75
    PETER MANSOOR

7   **Marine Corps**   87
    FRANK HOFFMAN

8   **Airpower**   100
    CHARLES J. DUNLAP, JR

9   **Naval support**   114
    MARTIN N. MURPHY

10 **Special forces**   128
    KALEV I. SEPP

11 **Intelligence**   141
    DAVID KILCULLEN

12 **Local security forces**   160
    JOHN NAGL

PART III
Challenges   171

13 **Governance**   173
    NADIA SCHADLOW

14 **Culture**   189
    MONTGOMERY McFATE

15 **Ethics**   205
    SARAH SEWALL

16 **Information operations**   216
    ANDREW EXUM

17 **Civil-military integration**   230
    MICHELLE PARKER AND MATTHEW IRVINE

18 **Time**   242
    AUSTIN LONG

19 **Counterinsurgency in context**   255
    THOMAS RID AND THOMAS KEANEY

    Suggested further reading   261
    Index   267

Contributors

Alexander Alderson, Colonel, British Army, is director of the British Army's Counter-insurgency Centre. He has operational experience from Northern Ireland, the Balkans, and Iraq, and in 2009 rewrote British COIN doctrine. He is a visiting fellow at the University of Oxford, successfully completed a PhD in modern history, and has published widely on counterinsurgency.

Conrad Crane is the director of the US Army Military History Institute. He has authored or edited books and monographs on the Civil War, World War I, World War II, Korea, and Vietnam, and has written and lectured widely on airpower and landpower issues. He was the lead author for The Army/US Marine Corps Field Manual, *Counterinsurgency*, which was released in December 2006.

Charles J. Dunlap, Jr, Major General, has served 34 years in the US Air Force. He is a distinguished graduate of the National War College and author of the 2008 monograph *Shortchanging the Joint Fight? An Airman's Assessment of FM 3-24 and the Case for Developing Truly Joint Doctrine.*

Etienne de Durand is director of the Security Studies Center at the Institut français des relations internationales in Paris. He also is a professor at the Institut d'etudes politiques de Paris and the Collège interarmées de défense, as well as the author of numerous articles and monographs on strategy and military affairs in France and the United States.

Andrew Exum is a fellow with the Center for a New American Security and a combat veteran of the wars in both Afghanistan and Iraq. He returned to Afghanistan to serve as a civilian advisor to General Stanley McChrystal in 2009 and is the founder of the counterinsurgency blog Abu Muqawama.

Frank Hoffman is research fellow at the Potomac Institute for Policy Studies, Arlington, Virginia. His professional experience includes 30 years of public service as a Marine infantry officer and as a national security consultant to the Department of Defense, the Defense Advanced Research Projects Agency (DARPA), the Marine Corps, the Joint Forces Command and the intelligence community. He is the author of numerous articles and one book, *Decisive Force of War* (Praeger, 1996).

Matthew Irvine is a graduate of Wake Forest University with a degree in History and Middle East and South Asia Studies. His research focuses on US defense policy, modern conflict, and the Middle East. He is a graduate student at the American University School of International Service.

Thomas Keaney, Colonel, USAF (Retd), is associate director of strategic studies at the Johns Hopkins University School of Advanced International Studies. He has served as chairman of the department of military strategy at the National War College, forward air controller in Vietnam, and B-52 squadron commander. Among his recent publications is *War in Iraq: Planning and Operations* (Routledge, 2007), edited with Thomas Mahnken.

David Kilcullen has served in counterinsurgencies in Southeast Asia, Iraq, Afghanistan, Pakistan, and Africa. He was special advisor to the Secretary of State in 2007–8, senior counterinsurgency advisor to Multi-National Force-Iraq in 2007, and chief counterterrorism strategist at the State Department in 2005–6. He is the author of *The Accidental Guerrilla* (Oxford University Press, 2009) and principal author of the *US Government Counterinsurgency Handbook* (2008).

Austin Long is an assistant professor at Columbia University's School of International and Public Affairs. He was previously an associate political scientist at the Rand Corporation. His work has been published in *International Security, Survival, The International Journal of Intelligence and Counterintelligence, The American Interest, The Journal of Cold War Studies*, and by the Rand Corporation.

Peter Mansoor, Colonel, US Army (Retd), is the General Raymond E. Mason, Jr Chair of Military History at the Ohio State University. His military career included two tours in Iraq, involving service as a brigade commander (2003–4) and as executive officer to General David Petraeus (2007–8). He is the author of *Baghdad at Sunrise: A Brigade Commander's War in Iraq* (Yale University Press, 2008).

Montgomery McFate is currently the senior social scientist for the US Army's Human Terrain System. Previously, she worked at the US Navy's Office of Naval Research and the Rand Corporation's Intelligence Policy Center. Dr McFate received a BA from the University of California at Berkeley, a PhD in anthropology from Yale University, and a JD from Harvard Law School. She was a member of the team that produced The US Army/ Marine Corps Field Manual, *Counterinsurgency*.

Martin N. Murphy is a senior fellow at the Center for Strategic and Budgetary Assessments (CSBA) in Washington, DC, where he writes on all aspects of naval warfare. He is the author of *Small Boats, Weak States, Dirty Money: Piracy and Maritime Terrorism in the Modern World* (Columbia University Press, 2009).

John Nagl is the president of the Center for a New American Security. A retired army officer who served in both wars in Iraq, Dr Nagl is the author of *Learning to Eat Soup with a Knife* (University of Chicago Press, 2005) and was on the writing team that produced The US Army/Marine Corps Field Manual, *Counterinsurgency*.

Timo Noetzel is a research group leader at Konstanz University, a fellow of the Stiftung Neue Verantwortung, Berlin, and senior policy advisor to the chairman of the Munich Security Conference. He was poltical advisor to the ISAF Regional Commander North in 2007, participated as an observer in COMISAF's strategic assessment in 2009 and subsequently served as an advisor to the Allied Joint Force Commander. He holds a BA (Hons) in Politics from the Queen's University of Belfast and an MPhil and a Dphil from St Antony's College, Oxford. His work has been published in *Survival, International Affairs, Contemporary Security Policy*, and other journals.

Michelle Parker is a USAID foreign service officer on sabbatical as an international affairs fellow with the Council on Foreign Relations. Her recent publications focus on the civilian side of counterinsurgency operations, including *Reconstruction Under Fire: Unifying Civil and Military Counterinsurgency* from the Rand Corporation.

Thomas Rid is a visiting scholar at the Shalem Center in Jerusalem, and a non-resident fellow at the Center for Transatlantic Relations in the School for Advanced International Studies, Johns Hopkins University. He has published widely on strategy and political violence. His most recent book is *War 2.0* (Praeger, 2009).

Nadia Schadlow is a senior program officer in the International Security and Foreign Policy Program of the Smith Richardson Foundation in Westport, Connecticut. She is also a frequent guest lecturer at West Point and served on the Defense Policy Board between September 2006 and June 2009. Dr Schadlow is author of "War and the Art of Governance" (2003, *Parameters* 33(3), 85–94).

Kalev I. Sepp teaches at the US Naval Postgraduate School in Monterey, California. He served as deputy assistant secretary of defense for special operations, and as a US Army Special Forces officer in combat in Panama and El Salvador. A graduate of Harvard University, he wrote the 2005 *Military Review* article "Best Practices in Counterinsurgency" while serving in Iraq.

Sarah Sewall teaches public policy at the Harvard Kennedy School of Government. She served as deputy assistant secretary of defense and senior foreign policy advisor to Senate majority leader, and led the national security agency review process for the Obama Transition. She wrote the introduction to The US Army/Marine Corps Field Manual, *Counterinsurgency*.

Acknowledgments

Counterinsurgencies are long wars. Success, in particular, takes time. That, we found out, is also true for books on counterinsurgency. The idea to edit a volume on counterinsurgency of general interest goes back to the summer of 2007, to a conference in Paris, organized by the Institut français des relations internationales. Etienne de Durand and his team—notably Philippe Coquet and Thomas Rid—brought together doctrine development teams from the armies of the United States, France, Britain, and Germany for a two-day workshop. This would not have been possible without the help of Françoise Thomas. Many but not all of the book's authors attended the conference in Paris.

This project would not have been possible without the contributors' enthusiastic dedication and potent energy. Some hold or held positions of responsibility in government, industry, or academia. Others even played active roles in ongoing operations. All wrote their chapters in addition to a grueling workload. Therefore, first and foremost we would like to thank the authors of this volume for their hard work and their patience in getting the book to press. We would like to thank General David Petraeus for his interest and his help in reviewing Conrad Crane's chapter on US counterinsurgency doctrine. We also thank Janine Davidson, Gian Gentile, and H.R. McMaster for their support along the way.

Thomas Rid would like to express gratitude, first, to Dan Hamilton and his staff at the Center for Transatlantic Relations at the Nitze School for Advanced International Studies, Johns Hopkins University, for a familiar institutional home and the fabulous Calouste Gulbenkian Fellowship, and second, to Mike van Dusen, Samuel Wells, and Lucy Jilka at the Woodrow Wilson Center for International Scholars for their extraordinary support during the summer of 2009. Finally he would like to express gratitude to the Fritz Thyssen Foundation. Etienne de Durand would like to thank Emma Broughton, Corentin Brustlein, Pierre Chareyron, and Marc Hecker for their help.

A special thank you goes to the phenomenal Matt Irvine for his most helpful hand in the final phases of the book.

Finally we would like to thank our editors at Routledge, Andrew Humphrys and Rebecca Brennan, for their constructive counsel and their endurance.

Thomas Rid and Thomas Keaney
Jerusalem and Washington

Abbreviations

ALN	Armée de Libération Nationale (Algeria)
ANA	Afghan National Army
ANP	Afghan National Police
AQI	Al-Qaeda-Iraq
ARVN	Army of Vietnam
CAC	Combined Arms Center
CDEF	Centre de Doctrine d'Emploi des Forces
CENTCOM	US Central Command
CERP	Commander's Emergency Response Program
CIA	US Central Intelligence Agency
COIN	Counterinsurgency
CORDS	Civil Operations and Revolutionary Development Support
CPA	Coalition Provisional Authority
DGR	Doctrine de la Guerre Révolutionaire
FARC	Revolutionary Armed Forces of Colombia
FLN	Front de Libération Nationale (Algeria)
FM 3-24	The US Army/Marine Corps Field Manual, *Counterinsurgency*
FOB	Forward Operating Base
HTS	Human Terrain System
IDF	Israel Defense Forces
IED	Improvised Explosive Device
IMOD	Iraq Ministry of Defense
INS	Israel Navy Ship
IRGC	Iranian Revolutionary Guard Corps
ISAF	International Security Assistance Force
ISR	Intelligence, Surveillance, and Reconnaissance
JSOC	US Joint Special Operations Command
LTTE	Liberation Tigers of Tamil Eelam
MACV	Military Assistance Command, Vietnam
MNF-I	Multi-National Force-Iraq
MRF	Mobile Riverine Force
NATO	North Atlantic Treaty Organization
NGO	Non-Governmental Organization
OAS	Organisation de l'Armée Secrète
OEF	Operation Enduring Freedom
OIF	Operation Iraqi Freedom

OSS   Office of Strategic Services
PRT   Provincial Reconstruction Team
RAF   UK Royal Air Force
SOF   Special Operations Forces
TRADOC   US Army Training and Doctrine Command
UAV   Unmanned Aerial Vehicle
UNAMA   United Nations Assistance Mission to Afghanistan
UNOSOM   United Nations Operations in Somalia
USAID   US Agency for International Development
USMC   United States Marine Corps
VC   Viet Cong

1 Understanding counterinsurgency

Thomas Keaney and Thomas Rid

Not long ago, "counterinsurgency" was an odd and obscure word. In March and April 2003, the United States armed forces pushed into Baghdad with breathtaking speed. Saddam Hussein's conventional military formations were defeated in a tough but swift battle and his dictatorship was ended. Senior US decision makers, both civilian and military, expected to leave Iraq soon and victorious, but an unexpected enemy crossed their plans. Iraqis and a small number of foreign fighters, not wearing uniforms, began to harass coalition forces with AK-47s, so-called improvised explosive devices—today the well-known IEDs—and suicide attacks. Small-scale, unconventional attacks kept rising. The Pentagon was reluctant to acknowledge that the war was not over, but was instead entering a more vicious and entirely unexpected phase. In mid-June 2003, General John Abizaid, who came in as the new head of US Central Command, took a hard look at the emerging type of war: "guerrilla tactics," he proclaimed "is a proper way to describe it in strictly military terms." This acknowledgment of reality spiraled the general's first briefing into the big news. In subsequent months, the US and its allies would find themselves more and more engaged, not only in combating these "tactics" but also having embarked in counterinsurgency warfare and all that accompanied it: new doctrine, new enemies, an alien population, a different way to use military power on land, in the air, and at sea, unfamiliar intelligence gathering, training of local forces, trials of local governance, unexpected cultural hurdles, ethical dilemmas, propaganda challenges—all while time was running out. Basically, the US military attempted to understand counterinsurgency while fighting a counterinsurgency: an undertaking akin to redesigning and refitting a race car, and teaching the driver new routines, all while speeding along the course.

The US military quickly found itself squeezed between two pressure plates: one at home in Washington—where Congress and a skeptical public were increasingly concerned by the mounting human losses and returning veterans, many of whom were irreparably maimed both physically and psychologically—and one in Iraq's cities and streets, where increasingly sophisticated roadside bombs shattered hopes of swift success. To make a gloomy situation worse, the political reasons for invading Iraq were more and more discredited. No weapons of mass destruction were found, and Saddam's connections to the perpetrators of 9/11 turned out to be fabricated, although al-Qaeda then took root between the Tigris and Euphrates as the situation there initially deteriorated under American occupation. At the end of April 2004, the Abu Ghraib prison scandal broke, turning into an iconic humiliation of American power. By 2006, a number of different and increasingly sophisticated groups confronted the US forces: Ba'athists, nationalists, Shia militias of various loyalties, Salafists, and foreign fighters. The weapons and tactics they used grew equally sophisticated; most importantly an array of constantly evolving IEDs, a signature weapon of modern insurgencies. The roadside bombs were psychologically crippling, as soldiers, hampered in their ability to fight back against an invisible enemy, took entirely unpredictable but calamitous hits as they traveled Iraq's roads "mounted or dismounted," in vehicles and on foot patrols. Then, in 2007, a major scandal involving neglect and unsatisfactory conditions at Walter Reed Army Medical Center broke, accompanied by tumultuous press coverage, adding to the woes of the US armed forces. America seemed to ask its volunteer force to do the worst job, and then treated the veterans in the worst way when they came home. The war in Iraq had turned dark and grim, almost apocalyptic.

But even more than that, Iraq was not the only battlespace that kept American forces and their allies occupied. The war in Afghanistan was simmering on low heat while the world's attention was captivated by the invasion of Iraq and its aftermath. But as the insurgency took off in Iraq, Afghan resistance against foreign troops at the Hindu Kush intensified as well. New and nasty IED tactics began to seep from Baghdad's suburbs to Helmand's valleys, aided by the Internet and foreign jihadists. The initially successful resistance of Iraq's militants inspired Afghanistan's insurgents. As a consequence, America and its NATO allies found themselves in similar situations: they also increasingly attempted to transplant successful counterinsurgency tactics and methods—developed and tested on the job in Iraq—from the one theater to the other.

It is against this dim and nearly hopeless background that the seemingly unshakable determination and the steep learning curve of the US land forces has to be viewed. Throughout the wars, many American newspapers published a small box with names of those who died fighting, two or three almost every day, sometimes more: mostly privates, specialists, and corporals; sometimes sergeants or master sergeants; more rarely junior officers; very rarely senior officers. The many injured do not even make the news. The courageous men and women who adapted to counterinsurgency warfare under such adverse conditions deserve the utmost respect and admiration of any informed observer, no matter their opinion on the reasons for or against both wars—including those who read or even write about the war, often from a safe distance.

In the years after 2004, a conceptual reorientation of gigantic proportions took place inside the US armed forces. Countless articles were published on counterinsurgency—and the subject was explored in government reports, in presentations, speeches, press articles, on sharp-worded blogs, and in a vast number of books and essays. Counterinsurgency, the "graduate level of war," naturally required a multidisciplinary approach in scholarship and practice: historians, political scientists, strategists, area specialists, anthropologists, socio-logists, as well as military officers and journalists, tackled the subject from a multitude of angles. The debate's range of ideas and the number of its publications, as a result, has assumed almost encyclopedic proportions.

It is within this ferment of activity that this book has emerged, with two goals: first, to provide a starting point for students as well as practitioners in understanding counter-insurgency; and, second, to make that starting point available to America's allies in the Atlantic Alliance and beyond. Fortunately, we were able to find among the book's contributors many of the most productive thinkers on counterinsurgency, as well as some of the most influential political and military advisors. The authors also represent a broad disciplinary background and bring first-hand experiences from many regions and conflicts to the table. Most contributors, it should also be noted, are American and write from a predominantly American perspective. Therefore the book—just like its subject—is focused on developments driven by the United States more than by its European or other allies. Not least to bridge gaps between the allies, the book is designed as an entry point into the debate, not as an exit or summary, or even an assessment of it. It is with this focus and intent that this book proceeds, with the text organized along a chronological structure.

The first part of the book covers the doctrinal, intellectual, and—to a more limited extent—the historical origins of today's counterinsurgency thinking in NATO's four most significant land forces.[1] The experiences of America's European allies are, at closer inspection, at the intellectual and historical epicenter of the counterinsurgency debate. The former colonial empires, especially France and Britain, can look back on a multiplicity of imperial conflicts, both when the erstwhile European empires conquered their new possessions, when they tried to maintain them, and most notably when they lost almost all of them in a series of wars of decolonization that brought independence to a large number of countries. These campaigns were often drawn-out operations—one prominent example is the war in Algeria of 1954 –62—and the armies defense establishments were not only fighting, but, like today, debating and trying to understand the counterinsurgencies they found themselves in. There is therefore much to be learned from European colonial history, and the counterinsurgency debate has borrowed heavily from these historical examples.

France's counterinsurgency doctrine, therefore, is the subject of the first chapter. The French experience with counterinsurgency began with the conquest of Algeria in 1830, when a number of mountainous insurgencies battled the European conquerors for more than a dozen years. Etienne de Durand argues that France's experience with counterinsurgency was rich and diverse, perhaps more so than that of any other European nation. De Durand traces the doctrinal origins back to the three "wise men": Thomas-Robert Bugeaud, Joseph-Simon Galliéni, and Hubert Lyautey. He looks for the major lessons and "non-lessons" of the colonial and decolonization period, and to what extent they are still relevant in the twenty-first century. De Durand analyses the doctrines of *guerre révolutionnaire* and *arme psychologique* and puts them into their appropriate strategic and political context—the result can be read as a warning of the hidden perils of protracted counterinsurgency operations.

Britain has an equally wealthy experience with "small wars." Alexander Alderson, one of the United Kingdom's leading doctrine writers, traces the influences of Britain's towering figures of counterinsurgency thinking: Colonel Charles Callwell's *Small Wars*, General Sir Charles Gwynn's *Imperial Policing*, Sir Robert Thompson's *Defeating Communist Insurgency*, and Brigadier Frank Kitson's *Low Intensity Operations*. He highlights three fundamental characteristics: the use of minimum force, civil-military cooperation, and tactical flexibility—as well as the British Army's cultural predisposition toward learning and adaptation. Alderson discusses three cases: Malaya, 1948–60; Northern Ireland 1969–2007; and Aden 1963–8.

Germany never was a notable colonial power. Perhaps this explains the near absence of classic writings on counterinsurgency—as opposed to light infantry tactics—by any well-known German military thinker. More significantly, the Bundeswehr, the army of the modern Federal Republic, was formed under the profound impact of World War II, when the misdeeds of the Wehrmacht were still fresh, and not only in living memory but in the memory of the new army's senior officers. More than perhaps any other modern army, the German military —and even more so the German public—had an ambiguous relationship to the use of force. The unspoken, tragic reminder was indefinitely present: the last time Germans used the force of arms, the outcome was catastrophe. Only in the past dozen years or so has Germany began to develop a "normal" relationship to the use of military force, yet still—and rightly so—observed by a rigorously skeptical public and Parliament. In an environment of population-centric operations, Germany's caution, although sometimes counterproductive, may have a beneficial side effect. Timo Noetzel examines the recent evolution of counterinsurgency thinking and doctrine in the Bundeswehr. Not unlike what happened with the US and British forces, a more stress-intensive operational environment seems to be pushing counterinsurgency lessons from the bottom up, sometimes against the political and cultural resistance of the military establishment in Germany.

The United States, in several ways, had to tie these different historical lessons together as it was updating its own counterinsurgency doctrine in 2006. As America's land forces faced a disorienting counterinsurgency environment in Iraq, a number of officers turned to European and colonial experiences in similar situations and eagerly absorbed counterinsurgency theory. The doctrinal outcome of an intense process of learning under fire was the famous Field Manual, *Counterinsurgency* (FM 3-24). Conrad Crane provides an insider's account of the drafting and development process and puts the document, its application, and the controversy it generated into context.

The second part of the book deals with various operational aspects of counterinsurgency warfare. Each chapter looks at the role of the different services—after all, most military activity continues to be structured, funded, trained, and often deployed along service lines, not just jointly. Consequently, the various military services have different views and even different methods they apply to counterinsurgency campaigns. Service perspectives are certainly singular; the Royal Air Force will have a different view of its role in counterinsurgency than the German Luftwaffe. All insurgencies are ultimately based on land, and almost always lack the resources to acquire sophisticated weapons systems, let alone an air force or a navy—yet from the counterinsurgent's perspective, all services have a role in counterinsurgency, and each service has to come to terms with a specific set of opportunities and challenges. Some of these operational features are shared across the Atlantic Alliance.

The Army, given its size and expertise, is the most involved of the armed forces in counterinsurgency. Peter Mansoor argues that, whether used in an enemy-centric or a population-centric strategy, ground forces are vital to the conduct of counterinsurgency warfare. He analyses the Army's wide range of tasks in ground war "among the people": for instance, in securing population centers and lines of communication, force protection, sustainment activities; but also in offensive operations to clear enemy safe havens and targeted raids to kill or capture insurgents. Finally, Mansoor highlights an often neglected but highly important responsibility: ground forces are charged with running detention facilities in a legal and humane manner.

The Marine Corps, in the United States, is an impressive force that complements the Army and sometimes competes with it. But the Marines, more than the Army, have a longstanding reputation for their skillful mastery of small wars. The famous *Small Wars Manual*, published in 1940, epitomizes this skill. Frank Hoffman explores how the Marines learned—and sometimes forgot—the tough lessons of counterinsurgency, and how the Corps' historical experiences influence the way America's smaller land force deals with the complex insurgencies of the twenty-first century.

Airpower has long been a critical, if somewhat controversial, element of counterinsurgency operations. Charles Dunlap, one of the US Air Force's top thinkers on irregular warfare, argues that no single component of the armed forces can defeat twenty-first century insurgencies. But more so: in practice, Dunlap writes, the surge of ground forces has been accompanied by a surge in airstrikes in both Iraq and Afghanistan in recent years ("the use of airpower has skyrocketed"). Modern technology, Dunlap argues, should not be dismissed prematurely. The central elements of airpower—flexibility and versatility—make it uniquely suited for counterinsurgency.

Naval support may be critical for a counterinsurgency—and even for an insurgency. Martin Murphy points out that scholars of insurgency and counterinsurgency have often concentrated on what happens in jungles and cities. As a result they have neglected both the maritime aspect of insurgency and naval support for counterinsurgency. All counterinsurgency campaigns conducted since 1945, he argues, have been undertaken in the certain knowledge that navies remain in control of sea lines of communication stretching back to home. Murphy asks, what are the strategic and policy implications of the use of naval power in counterinsurgency? He responds that naval involvement for counterinsurgency depends, not unlike land-based operations, on accurate intelligence, an intimate understanding of the operational environment, and a willingness to endure and persist. The argument is illustrated with brief empirical accounts of several campaigns.

Special forces are another critical operational element of counterinsurgency warfare. Kalev Sepp, one of the very few scholar-practitioners of that discipline, outlines the particular roles of special forces in counterinsurgency environments. The more irregular the threats and operations of the future, the more important special forces will likely become. "SOF," as these units are sometimes called in jargon, are carefully selected personnel who tend to be older, more experienced, more resilient, physically tougher, and more independent than the larger body of soldiers. They are highly trained in a number of unconventional skills, among them "contingency languages," which they need to penetrate and survive in denied areas. Sepp considers the role of technology, education and training, languages, and intelligence. He concludes by suggesting a to-do list to improve allied SOF—and with a word of caution.

Intelligence is essential in counterinsurgency. David Kilcullen argues that intelligence officers in unconventional operations among the people are not unlike their counterparts in conventional warfare: they are engaged in "something akin to ethnography." Fieldwork participant observation, as well as qualitative and quantitative data, describes both the physical and social environment. Kilcullen calls the environment "ethnography from hell." With the focus, complexity, and identification of friend and foe blurred, extrapolating from one source to the organization behind it poses great difficulty. In these circumstances, Kilcullen identifies six pathologies that may inhibit the counterinsurgent's ability to operate optimally: a preference for quantitative methodological rigor over qualitative local knowledge; a tendency to focus on threats to the force rather than threats to the local population; a tendency to misinterpret cultural signals; a Eurocentric conception of state building; a preference for input rather than outcome; and a vulnerability to loss of situational awareness through rotation issues.

Local security forces ultimately enable sustainable stability and functioning governance. John Nagl outlines the role of trainers and advisors to local security forces, the "professors" of the graduate level of war. He argues that advisory efforts are an extremely valuable force multiplier in counterinsurgency, allowing intervening forces to leverage relatively small numbers of their own forces to increase dramatically the effectiveness of local forces, while simultaneously enhancing the legitimacy of the host nation government. Nagl identifies some of the lasting principles of success for this most difficult—and most important—part of counterinsurgency warfare. These principles may help future intervening powers to apply strategic leverage to the defeat of an insurgency through the application of responsive indigenous forces.

Governance and political progress, not just progress with local security forces, remains vital for long-term success in counterinsurgency. Government capacity and competence, to be sure, are also much more difficult to achieve than a more secure environment. The counterinsurgent, Nadia Schadlow argues, must tackle the tougher job of restoring basic government services and administrative structures at the local and national levels. The instrument to achieve these goals are "governance operations"—those activities that aim to establish or re-establish basic local and national government services in order to rebuild a population's confidence in its government. Schadlow provides historical examples that illustrate the central role of governance operations in counterinsurgency campaigns and examines a number of contemporary strategic and operational challenges.

Culture is a most important element that permeates almost all activities in irregular warfare. Montgomery McFate asks why understanding sociocultural dynamics is so critical for a counterinsurgency. A recognition that culture matters, and that the counterinsurgency is population-centric rather than enemy-centric, she points out, has been incorporated into official documents. But improved doctrinal documents do not automatically translate into improved operational practice. Many deeper lessons and reforms remain to be implemented, as McFate illustrates by providing a wealth of examples and experiences. One is that information about the local population is necessary but not sufficient: a commander must have dedicated, expert staff members to assist him or her in understanding the concrete operational and tactical relevance of local, specific sociocultural knowledge. Furthermore, cultural knowledge is not limited to improving the interaction with the neutral population, but also with the enemy: understanding the organizational structure of an insurgent group allows counterinsurgent forces to neutralize it more effectively. The risks of "ethnocentrism" and of not getting culture right are dire: a failure to understand the local political system and local political culture may result in counterinsurgent forces inadvertently escalating the conflict or becoming an unwitting proxy of a particular political group, McFate warns.

Ethics is more central in unconventional war. The counterinsurgent's efforts are often shaped in response to the enemy's goals and tactics, and this tendency presents a set of unique challenges to the counterinsurgent and the government forces. The counterinsurgent has to deal with a "moral asymmetry": he or she will be held responsible for the effects not only of his or her own actions, but also for those of the enemy. A foreign power, Sarah Sewall argues, therefore faces two central conundrums when it conducts counterinsurgency abroad: it cannot guarantee the justness of its cause and can only seek to ensure the justness of its military actions by assuming greater risk. Assumptions and claims about morality and value, Sewall illustrates, permeate an insurgency and its suppression in unequal ways. The ethical imperative becomes an operational one, as the counterinsurgent's *cause* must be perceived by the local population as moral and worthy of support. The justification also matters to the citizens and electorate of the counterinsurgent's own country, and the conduct of the struggle—its moral syntax—may shape its outcome in a decisive way. Mission success, "not normative niceties," forces the counterinsurgent to fulfill moral obligations. Sewall closes by pointing to some tough challenges ahead.

Information Operations, not unrelated to ethical aspects, also present the counterinsurgent with an unpleasant asymmetry. Andrew Exum points out that information operations, for conventional armies, tended to be designed to support combat operations, not vice versa. For insurgent groups, by contrast, the opposite applies: guerrilla groups have made effective use of the new information technologies, such as the Internet and cell phones—as well as of old information "technologies" such as posters, night letters, and word of mouth—to conduct armed propaganda campaigns. Exum, consequently, highlights the disconnect between the counterinsurgent's theory and the insurgent's practice. The most elaborate doctrine and the most sophisticated debates on the subject are more likely to be found among Western counterinsurgent forces, which have the resources to invest in theory. The most impressive and the most innovative *practical* use of information operations, by contrast, can be found among insurgents—and Exum illustrates his point by looking at one of the most successful and nimble insurgent groups: Hezbollah, the Lebanese militant group and political force.

Civil-military integration is essential to wars amongst the people. Without civilian political and development efforts, the long-term goals of counterinsurgency will prove illusive. In Afghanistan, the provincial reconstruction team emerged as a model to integrate civilian specialists with military personnel while forward deployed. This concept grew into a multinational concept of development and assistance and was used throughout both Afghanistan and Iraq, and it was adopted and adapted by many of America's allies. Michelle Parker and Matthew Irvine highlight many of the structural challenges facing civilians in a military environment, including integrating civilians into the military command structure, effectively allocating interagency resources toward common goals and developing comprehensive goals for all personnel. The durability of the PRT concept and its adaptation to new challenges highlight the innovative benefits embodied in this critical test of civil-military integration.

Time, finally, is a crucial factor in all forms of warfare, although its role varies across the spectrum of conflict. Time, remarkably, has very rarely been analyzed as a separate category of strategy—yet, particularly in protracted irregular wars, time might be decisive for victory or defeat. Austin Long analyzes the role of time across the spectrum of conflicts, and across the levels of war. An appreciation of both the tactical and strategic aspects of time in counterinsurgency, Long argues, is critical to an overall understanding of the course of a conflict. Failure to incorporate these two aspects of time into counterinsurgency campaign planning, "like attempting to run a marathon as a sprint," could ultimately doom the effort.

Before giving the word to the authors, a couple of points should be mentioned. First, a word on terminology: several terms are used to describe war that is not fought between two or more conventional armed forces. If at least one side involves units or commandos that are not composed of professionally organized, trained, and uniformed soldiers, these fighters are—in one of the most minimalistic descriptions—called unconventional or irregular; sometimes the confrontations between such unequal forces is called "asymmetric." All these terms are minimalistic because they make no political statement, and because both sides may agree on them. But thereafter, terminology itself becomes part of the conflict: both sides describe themselves positively and the opponent negatively. It is either the "occupier" against the "resistance," or the "government" against "terrorists"—legitimacy, the prize in such population-centric wars, resides in terminology and language, in the way each side describes itself and its opponents. Everybody who is engaged in counterinsurgency, either as a scholar or practitioner, should be aware of the terminological quicksand they are navigating. Then there is another aspect to terminology: what today is called counterinsurgency had different names in the recent and distant past. Some of these names and labels are increasingly out of fashion today, and rightly so: low-intensity conflicts, "military operations other than war," but also peace operations, peace enforcement, small wars, stability operations, or, depending on the *casus belli*, humanitarian interventions. Other expressions are: revolutionary wars, insurrections, or rebellions. Attempting to draw a clear line between different phenomena and kinds of conflict, we believe, is of very limited utility. Often it only serves to delineate one academic debate from another—for those in the conflicts, whether they suffer or shoot or both, the difference is less obvious.

Second, it is important to note in clear terms what the objective of this book is not. *Understanding Counterinsurgency* does not attempt to summarize what has become a vast debate. Its goal can only be to provide a glimpse at some of the debate's most important aspects. The book is designed to help the student of asymmetric wars to understand the complex matter at hand, and it does so mostly from the perspective of the strong, not the weak. Both those planning to engage in counterinsurgency and those who write about it should understand it first; and, we hope that they find this book useful.

And finally we feel it is important to highlight that counterinsurgency is not without its vocal critics. Some of these criticisms are briefly presented in these pages (see Chapter 5). Some criticize that the focus on counterinsurgency causes an army to lose its conventional fighting skills, with dire long-term effects. Or, that the investment in such training does not justify the return. Others find that specializing in counterinsurgency could lead to more counterinsurgency. Such criticisms are noted, but not fully explored, as that subject calls for a book with a substantially different focus. It is with these qualifications that this exploration of counterinsurgency now proceeds.

Notes

1   The choice of cases is not to belittle the impressive efforts of smaller allies, such as Canada, Australia, the Netherlands, Italy, or Poland, to name only a few. France was chosen as an example mainly because French counterinsurgency theorists had such a critical role in reshaping the American learning experience. Britain was included because it is America's most important ally in Iraq and Afghanistan, and because British theorists of counterinsurgency are among the most important. Germany was chosen not just because it is Europe's largest country and the homeland of Carl von Clausewitz, but also because the Bundeswehr is—after the British Army—the largest troop contributor to NATO's Afghanistan mission.

Part I
Doctrine

2 France

Etienne de Durand

We do not learn;
and what we call learning
is only a process of recollection.
Plato, *Meno*

The French military shuns the expression *contre-insurrection*, or counterinsurgency. Yet its historical experience with "war amongst the people" has been rich and diverse, perhaps more so than that of any other European country. In fact, its experience has been so diverse that it would probably be misleading to speak of a French counterinsurgency "school," with the implied consistency and continuity that such an expression carries. From the early colonial conquests to the decolonization wars in Indochina and Algeria in the 1950s and 1960s, up to the military interventions of the 1990s, elements of continuity can be identified at the institutional level, and even more so in terms of military culture. Some French military units perceive themselves as being part of a colonial tradition to this day, and they perpetuate this tradition with pride. Rather than a French counterinsurgency school per se, various currents and individualities proved influential but never succeeded in rallying the whole military institution behind them.

The French experience with counterinsurgency really began with the conquest of Algeria in 1830, when a number of mountainous insurgencies battled the European conquerors for more than a dozen years. France's experience with colonial counterinsurgency also ended in Algeria, more than 130 years later, in 1962. The Evian accords that recognized Algeria's independence also marked the abrupt end of the French colonial and counterinsurgency experience. What followed, which was not unlike what was witnessed in the United States after the Vietnam War, was a thorough reorientation of French national security toward the Cold War and its demands, especially nuclear deterrence. Despite the rupture of 1962 and its fallout, particularly the political censorship that was imposed in the wake of the failed 1961 coup, some of this experience with colonial warfare and counterinsurgency has informally shaped the practices, doctrines, and culture of the French military up to the present day. What remains to be seen beyond the French military, however, is whether and to what extent the lessons of the colonial and decolonization periods are still relevant today.

The empire and a new army model

Understanding the French doctrine and practice of counterinsurgency in the twentieth and twenty-first centuries requires that their colonial roots be scrutinized and put into perspective. In this journey to the past, two episodes and three figures stand out: the conquest of Algeria and the golden age of imperialism at the end of the nineteenth century on the one hand; Bugeaud, Galliéni, and Lyautey on the other. Together, they had a lasting, if limited, impact both on French strategic thinking and on the French tradition of counter-insurgency.

Despite a long history of small wars and a rich collection of writings on *"la petite guerre"* well before the nineteenth century and the conquest of Algeria, French military thinking was mostly preoccupied with continental warfare up to the end of the Napoleonic wars and again from 1871 to 1914. Guaranteed first by the Quadruple Alliance against France and then by the Concert of Europe, the long peace that for the most part prevailed in Western Europe between 1815 and 1870 helps explain—together with the domestic weakness of the Bourbon and Orléans dynasties and their subsequent desire for prestige—the French imperial forays in Algeria and elsewhere which laid the basis for the second French colonial empire. For the most part, these imperial adventures and the resulting empire were not planned for; therefore, their importance and resulting implications for French military culture would surface only progressively.

Algeria itself was something of a chance beginning. It began as retaliation against Barbary piracy and evolved, following a number of stages, into a fully-fledged campaign of conquest fueled by domestic politics: King Louis-Philippe needed glory to solidify his regime, born out of the 1830 revolution but facing significant opposition from legitimists and republicans alike. Neither the population, nor the military, nor the government itself had expected such a long series of campaigns and the resulting conquest.

Another such chance beginning, which was to have an enduring influence on subsequent French military thought on irregular war, was the conflict between Thomas-Robert Bugeaud, a veteran of the Battle of Jena and the Spanish Peninsular campaigns, and Abd el-Kader of Mascara, the highest authority in Algeria in the 1830s, when it was still largely independent despite the small French presence that had followed the 1830 intervention. Also a former member of Parliament and a famous agricultural innovator, Bugeaud would influence many generations of colonial officers, right up to World War II.[1] The soldier-politician was named governor-general of Algeria—in effect commander-in-chief—in December 1840.

Bugeaud relied on his first-hand experience of the Spanish guerrillas during the Napoleonic Wars, thus replicating in Algeria both the savagery so prevalent in Spain and the small-war tactics the *Grande Armée* developed there, but also using the smarter tactics pioneered by Marshal Suchet in Aragon—probably the only successful example of pacification in the Peninsula. This explains both the extreme brutality of the conquest, and the constant efforts to understand indigenous politics and rally the tribes. On the one hand, Bugeaud never hesitated to target the population directly through *razzias*, a French raiding tactic, which deprived it of its livelihood or resulted in the capture and forced relocation of women and children. French troops would routinely resort to extreme measures, literally smoking out rebel groups hidden in caves (*enfumades*) or starving them to death through a systematic scorched earth policy, and even engaging in occasional massacres. Tactically, Bugeaud insisted on breaking up the large formations, reducing reliance on firepower and conventional maneuvers so typical of the continental theater and mindset, always stressing mobility and local initiative over artillery, heavy baggage, or pre-planned maneuvers. Rather than mounting large-scale cordon and sweep operations, he organized battalion-sized mobile detachments (*colonnes mobiles*) that were to emulate the rebels' mobility, go deep into contested zones, and remain on the move as a means of constantly harassing the enemy—this practice would be reinstituted in Indochina and Algeria and dubbed *nomadisation*.

On the other hand, Bugeaud also instituted the *bureaux arabes*, an organization headed by a civilian "human terrain specialist" of sorts and in charge of mapping the political terrain, administering the local population, including its socioeconomic needs, and linking back with the military so as to ensure that operations would fit in the local context. The *razzias* were thus the flip side of the *bureaux arabes*, as Bugeaud always strove to associate conquest and "colonization" (especially agricultural colonization), meant here as development. This innovative and successful heritage was to be directly claimed by his most famous successors, Galliéni and Lyautey.

The wise guys

Joseph-Simon Galliéni and his pupil Hubert Lyautey played an important role in using and refining some of Bugeaud's methods, perhaps even in civilizing them. Like no others, the two marshals symbolize, to this day, a golden age of imperialism and for a remarkably successful period of the colonial army.

Galliéni helped achieve the pacification of Tonkin and had an important impact on modern Madagascar, where he served for nine years from 1896 to 1905. When the general arrived in Madagascar, he energetically changed the doctrine and operational employment of his forces. The "first preoccupation" of his units, he ordered, would henceforth be to "bring back the population's calm and its confidence." Outposts, he decreed, "must be organized defensively, so that the remaining security rear guards are as weak as possible." Galliéni ordered a show of force in all directions and at all hours to "give the inhabitants a real idea of our military power and to be able to inspire their confidence in our protection."[2] Lyautey, for his part, was instrumental in the semi-colonization of Morocco and its subsequent evolution. Today he is buried next to Napoleon in the Hôtel des Invalides, and visitors can note the reverential Arabic scriptures on his sarcophagus. Taught by Galliéni, he proved as adept as his master at pacifying entire regions, but would also theorize on the best practices of French colonization and their military implications. In his *Lettres du Tonkin et de Madagascar*, he explains at length the oil spot method, understood as a complex political-military maneuver conducted at the grassroot level but extendable to the entire theater. He also analyzes how the overall logic of colonial conquest falls under the strategic rubric of *pacification*, which profoundly differs from military conquest as traditionally practiced and understood. While in the latter military success on the front brings about political concessions or surrender at the national level, pacification works essentially the other way round: political support through social and administrative work at the local level makes it possible to achieve enduring success at the tactical military level.

As Galliéni put it: "the most fertile method is that of the oil spot, which consists of progressively gaining territory in the front *only after* organizing and administering it in the rear."[3] This method finds of course a direct echo in later thinkers such as Galula and can also be linked to the contemporary doctrine of NATO in Afghanistan, with its "shape, clear, hold, build" formula.[4] The latter seems rather less convincing as it describes a sequential process, whereas the oil spot method argues for a dynamic and integrated model. As practiced by both Galliéni and Lyautey and theorized by the latter, the oil spot model is decidedly population-centric: securing the population, organizing it socially and economically, and marginalizing the "rebels" must go hand in hand all along. This model also integrates from the onset what we would today call the civil and military dimensions.

As Lyautey explains, capturing a village does not mean the same thing when it is held by enemy regulars, representing a mere geographical objective in a conventional campaign, and when its alien population must be subjugated and rallied. In other words, since the social and political dimension of colonial conquest is as important as its military aspect, *pacification* must rely on a constant and subtle mix (*dosage*) of both coercion and consent. The former can be obtained through shows of force, capture of rebels, strict control of the population; the latter relies on the cooptation of local elites ("govern with the mandarin and not against the mandarin"), social works spreading the material advantages of modern civilization, and even missionaries. As "political action is by far what matters most," the country and its inhabitants should be handled with tact and consideration as far as possible, and destruction considered as a last resort.[5]

In light of the peculiarities of military life in the colonies, it is only logical that Lyautey put such an emphasis both on the officer's social and administrative role in the colonies (which he develops in his *Le Rôle social de l'officier*) and on the distinctive ethos of the military units engaged in colonization. To him, the "*colonial*" is "a special being no longer civilian or military, but simply colonial." Because of the "political and moral responsibilities" that go with the position, the best officers should go to territorial command, stay there for a while and be exempted from the rotation system.[6] That is also the reason why Galliéni and Lyautey are somewhat critical of the *bureaux arabes*, headed by special corps of military cadres dedicated to administration and therefore divorced from operations. Rather than two parallel authorities, they favor unity of command, "identity of military command and territorial command," as the best way to ensure "the combined action of force and politics."[7] It follows that substituting the regular or metropolitan army to the *coloniaux* is simply impossible, as illustrated by the failure of the first French attempt at pacifying Madagascar, undertaken with such units in 1896.

It was during the late nineteenth century that the *Armée d'Afrique*, officially known as the 19th Army Corps, came into existence as a distinct military organization. Based in Algeria, it was centered on the Foreign Legion and indigenous units led by French officers (*spahis*, *goumiers*, *zouaves*, and *tirailleurs algériens*). Predating the *Armée d'Afrique*, marine infantry and artillery regiments (*marsouins* and *bigors*) made up the other part of the colonial forces. First called marines as an extension of the Navy, they became attached to the Army during the colonial period and were renamed *régiments coloniaux*. The colonial regiments, forming an Army within the Army, with its own traditions and identity, are known today as *régiment d'infanterie de marine* (RIMA). This distinct branch of the Army has always managed, like the Foreign Legion, to form a small and yet influential mafia, keen on preserving its identity and advancing its institutional position. Unsurprisingly tensions have occasionally flared up, and continue to do so, between the regulars or line units (today the "metro" as in metropolitans) and the *coloniaux*.

This illustrates a larger point: colonial warfare and imperial endeavors are never neutral, as they tend in the long run to affect the military from within and also to disrupt civil-military relations. Beyond interbranch rivalries, this kind of warfare is indeed bound to affect the military's ethos and to lead them to differ in significant ways from Huntington's model of "objective control"; sometimes even leading to some degree of "subjective control," with the colonial military meddling in politics, at least at the local level.[8] This form of military specialization does not only reflect that between colonial war and "industrial war," to use Rupert Smith's term, but has also proved a necessary condition of success for most imperial powers throughout history. French colonial effectiveness depended on it as much as the British hold on India relied on the Indian Army, which consisted of local troops led by British officers who spent half of their lives in the country. Beyond the oil spot, the selective brutality, or even the cunning, of commanders such as Lyautey, this is probably the key lesson to be drawn from the French colonial experience: it is by going native, by speaking the language(s), and by developing an intimate knowledge of the human terrain that European officers were able to manipulate local politics and social dynamics effectively. The process, it should be noted, took several decades.

Pacification as a sideshow

That said, a few caveats are in order as well. Despite its many accomplishments, French colonial warfare should be regarded neither as a series of unmitigated successes nor as the dominant paradigm it never was. There were several serious setbacks to the French colonial enterprise, such as, the slow and difficult pacification of Tonkin between 1885 and 1896 against the "Black Flags" and other "pirates." Furthermore, most of these insurgent movements were local and loosely organized, and on the whole poorly equipped, both at the material and ideological levels, to resist French forces that were themselves limited in terms of resources and political support at home. Before 1890 and the emergence of a significant colonial lobby in Paris, most colonial conquests were rather small-scale affairs led by opportunist officers and adventurous explorers who faced only sporadic resistance.

When this was not the case, as against Abd el-Kader in Algeria, French colonial campaigns were not just successful applications of Galliéni's oil spot method, but included significant brutality, sometimes in a very focused way—as when Galliéni had local nationalist leaders in Madagascar put on trial and executed—sometimes on a scale that defies comparison with any contemporary war involving a Western democracy. The *razzia*, agian, was a permanent companion of the *bureau arabe*: in fact the two methods were created as a pair and benefited from each other.[9] As the "oil spot" and "organization on the march" largely failed during the conquest of Morocco, Lyautey himself had to resort to the tried and true method of *razzia*.[10] But to claim, like Douglas Porch, that the theories of Galliéni and Lyautey were mostly an attempt at advancing the colonial army's bureaucratic position vis-à-vis the regular army and were a response to domestic conditions, a "public-relations exercise with the French people" aimed at assuaging opposition to colonization, is going too far.[11] As Porch himself admits, since colonial warfare was more political than military, "the essential problem of the French colonial army was . . . how to keep European military practices out of the colonies."[12] Besides, Morocco notwithstanding, the soft approach to pacification worked in several instances; the realities of implementation should therefore not be allowed to obscure the interest of the doctrine and its inner consistency.

Finally and most importantly, the colonial enterprise and its associated tactics and military practices were always regarded at best as a secondary endeavor or a derivative, at worst as a dangerous diversion, especially after the French defeat in 1870 at the hands of Prussia.[13] Throughout France's centuries-long experiment with European warfare, it was continental warfare—read: big war—where glory, victories, but also military careers, innovations, doctrine, structures, and traditions, were made. In this respect, colonial brilliance and imperial expansion were also the operational and political stepchildren of an army that had suffered a major defeat at the hands of its German neighbor and that had in the process relinquished its hold, if not its claim, on the Napoleonic legacy.[14]

These caveats prompt the following question: how relevant really were those colonial experiences for what was to come next, the decolonization conflicts? It was partly by answering this question—basically accepting the tactical teachings of the colonial era but proclaiming its strategic irrelevance—that the French counterinsurgency school came into distinct being.

The "centurions": from guerre révolutionnaire to arme psychologique

Among Western nations, France felt the earliest and the hardest the impact of revolutionary warfare after World War II. In reaction to this, in Indochina especially, the French military developed a coherent, indeed brilliant if also at times deeply flawed, body of thought and best practices. Half of it, at the tactical and operational levels, is still relevant and indeed has informed, through Galula and Trinquier, counterinsurgency doctrine everywhere in the Western world. The other, strategic half, can seem at first glance to be merely an intellectual curiosity, and as such of limited interest and best left to historians. However, if properly analyzed, it is highly relevant to contemporary operations.

The 1950s and 1960s probably stand out as the only moment in which there existed something that could be called a French counterinsurgency school of thought, i.e. a coherent and systematic attempt at distilling and disseminating the lessons learned in Indochina, so as to apply them in Algeria. Though practitioners like generals Jacques Massu and Marcel Bigeard tend to be as famous if not more so in France, Charles Lacheroy, Roger Trinquier, and David Galula are now the most widely recognized theorists of a movement that also included at the time figures such as Jacques Hogard, Maurice Prestat, Lucien Poirier, Jean Nemo, or Souyris. Most of them held at the time mid-level ranks, from captains to colonels, implying that the high command never fully engaged in counterinsurgency—this general truth was violated only in a few notable exceptions such as General André Beaufre, whose contribution to counterinsurgency theory tends to be neglected.[15]

Two common misconceptions should be exposed and dispelled. First, and despite his recent but posthumous fame thanks to a number of US officers, Galula was always a marginal figure in France: even though his recommendations and teachings have a lot in common with those of Trinquier, he cannot be regarded as representing the "French counterinsurgency school" but has rather essentially been "re-imported" back to France through the high profile his writings acquired after 2006. The French "school" differs from counterinsurgency orthodoxy as defined in retrospect by Galula in several important aspects, in a nutshell: its anticommunist obsession, its emphasis on control rather than consent—of which more later— and its frequent reliance on very coercive measures.[16] Accordingly, Lacheroy should probably be regarded as the real foundational figure of the French "school," while Trinquier proved its most influential and enduring one thanks to his book, *Modern Warfare*. Second, the French rarely if ever used expressions such as "insurgents" or counterinsurgency, referring rather to "rebels," "subversive warfare," and "revolutionary warfare"—*Doctrine de la guerre révolutionnaire* or "revolutionary warfare doctrine" (DGR) tended to predominate at the time. To this day, "insurrection" is thought of as a spontaneous uprising, occurring generally in an urban setting with the support of the people, while *rébellion* refers to an armed attempt at seizing power, planned and organized by an active minority.

Though training and teaching centers existed, in Indochina, Paris, or Algeria, these military thinkers did not make up a formal school with a body of thought codified in a series of doctrinal documents. Apart from a few doctrinal documents such as the TTA 117, authored by Hogard, most of their prolific production appeared as articles in the *Revue d'information militaire* or the *Revue de défense nationale*.[17] Beyond the agreed upon importance of revolutionary warfare as a radical innovation, their production also exhibited significant divergences—regarding, for instance, the continued relevance of colonial practices, the exact reach of communist ideology, or the balance needed between control and consent.[18] All told, it was less than a school of thought or a doctrine and more than just an ongoing debate. In truth, they were rather a generation united by common experience and a similarity of individual paths.

Most of them had, broadly speaking, the same background. Militarily, they often came from the *regiments coloniaux* or the Foreign Legion; had fought in World War II, sometimes as *résistants* or commandos (Jedburghs); served in Indochina and in Algeria as mid-level officers, and were thus directly exposed to combat.[19] Beyond the colonial heritage and the succession of military campaigns, they belonged to a generation traumatized by the twin experience of total war and defeat. From the memories of World War I, then World War II, and eventually to Indochina, total war informed and colored everything, displacing other, more limited forms of war, like the Korean war, as incomplete, frustrating failures. For this generation of French officers, the trauma of 1940 was a defining moment and a painful memory, and they proved ideologically committed to restoring national greatness and to defend in particular the *Union française* or Empire against all aggressions, overt or covert, however distant from metropolitan France. If Indochina proved enraging enough, with the lackluster political support and meager resources provided by Paris, the defeat could at least be explained away by these very factors, along with the proximity with Maoist China and the lack of Allied involvement. That the same story could repeat itself in Algeria, however—part of France itself at the time and the cradle of the French empire—was simply unacceptable, and this goes a long way to explaining why half of these centurions ended up as rebels themselves, first in the failed coup attempt of 1961 and then as *Organisation de l'Armée Secrete* (OAS) agents.[20] For all these reasons, most of the Trinquier generation saw themselves—the enemies they fought, and the wars they were engaged in—as substantively different from those of the colonial era. Accordingly, the remaining analysis will be focused on the most important figures of the French counterinsurgency movement in its purest form, such as Lacheroy and Hogard, who also happen to be less accessible than Galula or Trinquier because their writings have not been translated into English.

The nature of the revolutionary problem

To describe how the French perceived revolutionary warfare, it seems fitting to begin with Lacheroy, who was in many respects the foundational figure of the French counterinsurgency movement in its most radical form, and who lectured about DGR for almost a decade in theater as well as at the Ecole supérieure de guerre (War College). In one such conference, given in 1958 at the Centre d'instruction à la pacification et contre-guérilla, he endeavors to explain the real nature and the working mechanisms of revolutionary warfare. First, Lacheroy begins with the misunderstood originality and effectiveness of revolutionary warfare, which is *not* small war or guerrilla warfare under another name, but the truest and most accomplished form of total war, which is why this "lateral war," so low in intensity in its first stages that it seems innocuous enough, displaces the other forms of warfare, whether high-intensity operations or nuclear war.[21] In fact, "In Indochina, as in China, as in Korea, as elsewhere, we note that the strongest seems defeated by the weakest." The key to this apparent paradox resides precisely in the difference between the guerrilla approach as mere tactic and revolutionary warfare as comprehensive strategy: the latter's overriding purpose is to control the "rear," the population. As Lacheroy puts it, "the number one problem is to control populations that are used to support a war that takes place amongst them. He who holds or takes them has already won."[22] "The system of parallel hierarchies" is what allows this control of the population, with a first hierarchy made of associations (e.g. youth associations), a second one based on territorial divisions, and finally the hierarchy of the communist party, also known as the "OPA," the enemy *political and administrative organization*. All this ensures the "control of the bodies," itself a necessary precondition to the "control of the souls": i.e. the moral and ideological reorientation of the population, completed through the widespread use of *action psychologique*, a body of "moral techniques" such as indoctrination, *auto-critique*, and denunciations, aiming at organizing, supervising, and mobilizing the population through generalized surveillance from within. That some French officers had had to endure these techniques in Vietminh jails only made those men all the more impressed by them. Incidentally, Lacheroy insists that control of the "bodies" is a necessary precondition to that of the souls. In other words, and this is valid for both insurgents and counterinsurgents, rallying the population behind a given ideal is pointless if it is left unprotected. Security and control always trump "hearts and minds" and consent.

In its perfect form, as practiced by Mao or the Vietminh, revolutionary warfare unfolds in five phases, but can also be encountered in degraded forms, as was the case in Algeria. First, as Lacheroy puts it, "in the beginning, there is nothing" but a few determined people who are going to create a problem or magnify a given society's "internal contradictions," to use the Marxist language of the period, resorting to terrorism and propaganda at all levels. The second phase consists of targeted assassinations of low-level authority figures, so as to terrorize the population and cut it off from the central government, thus achieving "the complicity of silence." Then comes the third phase, with the introduction among the people of political commissars and other ideological leaders, and in parallel the appearance of the first armed groups; it is generally at this late stage that the armed forces are first brought in. The fourth phase witnesses greater specialization within the civilian component of the rebellion and the development of armed elements into larger, more organized groups at the provincial level. The fifth and final phase simply completes the process by keeping and building upon the previous elements: the rebels now enjoy a three-tier military, with guerrillas, provincial units, and regulars, as well as a fully fledged shadow government, active throughout the country.

Faced with such a thorough and systematic strategy that relies upon the *total* mobilization of the population across all lines of operations, counterinsurgents have no choice, according to the centurions, but to reciprocate and engage in a total war of their own.

An integrated and total approach

Building on their understanding of the revolutionary warfare practiced by the Vietminh as something profoundly innovative, proponents of DGR endeavored first to adapt tactics and operations, then to change the Army's structures and even its whole culture, so as to promote an ambitious strategy of counter-subversion and pacification. Overall, their tactical innovations proved much more successful than the deeply flawed strategic vision some of them embarked upon.

It should be noted upfront that most of the mistakes made by the US in Iraq were also made by the French in Indochina and even in Algeria, since the DGR mafia did not always prevail within the Army. To list but a few of these common mistakes: a defensive and reactive posture articulated around large, FOB-like bases; offensives designed around massive but ineffective cordon and sweep operations or shows of force; "humanitarian" actions designed to win "hearts and minds" but disconnected from the security situation, and therefore ineffective, if not downright counterproductive. But the French proved also willing and able to learn from their mistakes; to adapt, emulate, or counter enemy tactics and adjust their own operations accordingly, redefining accepted terms and concepts as needed or crafting new ones.

Counterinsurgency operations were for instance described as *guerre en surface*, which does not mean "surface war" or ground combat, but is contrasted with *guerre de front* and refers to the total absence of fronts, of columns, or other familiar military forms. Notwithstanding self-contained events and battles like Dien Bien Phu, the French military relearned an old lesson at the hands of the Vietminh, namely that insurgency warfare is a war of small posts fought everywhere in theater but won nowhere, as the enemy presents no clear and attainable vulnerabilities, no physical centers of gravity at which to strike. Thus *guerre en surface* occupies the middle, operational ground between guerrilla tactics and revolutionary war as the overall enemy strategy.[23] Hogard especially goes into some detail as to the requirements of each level.[24]

At the tactical level, he advocates a "system of small posts" favoring the development of regional and even local expertise among officers.[25] Unless a six to one numerical advantage, actionable intelligence, and follow-up long-term presence and "clear" operations can be obtained, cordon and sweep operations (*bouclage*) should be shunned altogether. Having units out in the field and constantly moving, called the "whirlwind technique" (*tourbillon*) or *nomadisation*, is much preferable, provided pacification can be conducted immediately thereafter. The best strategy is to entrust to local units, trained and resourced for it, the mission of constantly protecting the population and harassing the guerrillas thanks to locally obtained intelligence.[26] When neither of these methods is possible, relocating isolated populations and creating "forbidden zones" is the only option.[27] In practice, French forces in Algeria combined a grid of local forces (*quadrillage*) with mobile units, either airmobile elite units such as paratroopers or *commandos de chasse*. The main purpose of the latter was to emulate their enemy's mobility, following a specific, company-sized insurgent unit wherever it went, so as to "tag" it and make the insurgents constantly insecure in the field. Has this ever been done on a significant scale in either Iraq or Afghanistan? More generally, locally recruited units, *harkas*, GAD, and others,[28] represented up to 40,000 troops at the peak of the war and remained for the most part loyal and committed until De Gaulle made it clear that independence was underway.

At the operational level, Hogard insists on a principle that is counter-intuitive for the military: "Operations should be conducted only when they support the general policy of pacification; they are otherwise harmful."[29] Accordingly, controlling the main axes should only take place when it is the first step to completely controlling the surrounding zone (*contrôle en surface*), which leads him to conclude on the continued relevance of the oil spot policy ". . . at almost all levels, provided the slick is not extended too fast."[30] In practice, the French did not systematically apply those principles for quite some time, until General Challe in 1959–61 implemented a west to east systematic sweep along the pacification principles: shape and clear first; then clear, hold, and build.

At the strategic level, the DGR theory stresses the need to separate the insurgent from the population and weaken his hold on it, not only physically but also politically, by delegitimizing his action and countering his propaganda. To operationalize the strategy, the proponents of DGR maintain that the insurgent's integrated political-military action and his attempt at mobilizing the masses require a response *in kind*. In Hogard's words:

> The goal to be reached [is] to *destroy the rebel political-military organization* that ensures revolutionary control over a varying part of the population. To do so and ensure success, we must substitute our infrastructure to that of the enemy [which in turn requires] the intimate collaboration of all, civil servants, the police, local authority figures, and the military.[31]

Successful pacification, especially of the active kind, which involves the population in its own defense, therefore requires that two fundamental principles be followed. First must take place a complete integration of all available means along all lines of operation so as to empower *action psychologique* and control the population, "bodies" as well as "souls": indoctrinating and organizing people into official associations (thus compromising them in the eyes of the *Front de Libération Nationale* (FLN)) is seen as key to real pacification.

In parallel, the military must accomplish a paradigmatic shift in the way it organizes, trains, and fights. As Lacheroy also stresses, command structures must be stable, benefit from a high degree of autonomy and develop a true local expertise on the *milieu* in which they operate. More importantly, there has to be "an undisputed supremacy of the territorial over the operational."[32] In other words, the local units in charge of a given sector or region must always prevail over the intervention units and theater reserves; the latter must be the "servants" of the former. The overriding imperative of controlling the population through *action psychologique* and *guerre psychologique* (defensive and offensive information operations, including propaganda, manipulation, etc.) necessitates the creation of a political and information deputy alongside the commander at all levels; this deputy and the *5e bureau* in general must have a say in decisions at least equal to that of the operations chief.[33] At the lower levels, training and education must be thoroughly changed and adapted, by emphasizing small units—if possible special operations forces—over big ones, and most importantly by reversing modern habits and putting the best and brightest in infantry instead of technological branches. Or, to sum it all up in Lacheroy's unmistakable language:

> revolutionary war can't be waged with an Army organized in divisions; revolutionary war can't be waged with a peacetime administration; revolutionary war can't be waged with the Habeas Corpus [or any other example of a peacetime legal framework].[34]

Partially implemented in Algeria in 1957 and 1958 under Salan, this action plan generated a lot of tensions even within the military. First, among the *coloniaux,* some had remained unconvinced as to the "control of the souls" promised by *action psychologique*, preferring instead to try and win the hearts of the Muslim population through classic humanitarian aid and economic development, *à la* Lyautey. Created in 1955, the resulting *Sections Administratives Spécialisées,* or SAS, proved indeed quite valuable in rallying the population and providing intelligence.[35] Moreover, the "tyranny" of the DGR proponents and their *5e bureaux* was put to an abrupt end when De Gaulle, skeptical vis-à-vis both the method and the war in general, came to power in 1958; with the full backing of the President and the conventional military, subsequent operations like the Challe plan re-assumed a more classic form and focused on enemy guerrillas, while DGR was first abandoned and then banned after the aborted coup of 1961.

All told, even though the military "results" were obtained through a lot of hesitations and reversals, as well as much blood and treasure, French military thinkers and practitioners of the 1950s, and the DGR *doctrinaires* especially, proved adept at understanding revolutionary warfare, developing appropriate responses to it, and challenging traditional military culture accordingly. Overall, except for the most controversial aspects of *action psychologique*, most of the tactical and operational innovations they pioneered proved to be sound ones. Indeed, most of the Petraeus "innovations" experienced in Iraq or advocated in FM 3-24 were routinely practiced in Algeria, and then in the late stage of the Vietnam War, from the focus on the population to the SAS or the Civil Operations and Revolutionary Development Support (CORDS). In purely operational terms, the Battle of Algiers, the battle on the borders (*bataille des barrages*), and the Challe plan all proved successful, so much so that the ALN was in dire straits in 1960, and some of its leaders were trying to negotiate surrender.

Ideological overreach

Yet there are no such things as "pure operations": Algeria was an altogether different story at the strategic and political level. There is no doubt that the DGR school had a strategically sound understanding of revolutionary warfare: first as a total war in terms of ends, means, and commitment; second as only superficially akin to traditional guerrilla and small wars of the past. Partisans of *action psychologique* were also keenly aware that revolutionary warfare was informed through and through by politics and ideology. Finally they understood that the traditional logic linking tactical success and strategic victory did not necessarily apply, and that some tactical moves, however successful, would prove detrimental strategically and had been thought as such by the insurgent. They took revolutionary warfare very seriously indeed and regarded it as a new, fully fledged form of war that had displaced conventional and perhaps even nuclear conflict—Trinquier calls it intentionally *la guerre moderne*, which the English translation "modern warfare" captures only partially.

At the same time, the DGR school's understanding of the political dimension was deeply flawed, both locally and vis-à-vis the homeland. First the visceral anticommunism and obsession with subversion must be underlined as defining features of the French counterinsurgency school and this is echoed in most of their writings.[36] The prevalence of that obsession led them to conveniently explain away local grievances as the root causes of the insurgencies they were facing. They especially missed the nationalist dimension of these conflicts, which they tended to regard as secondary or even illusory—it was simply the old communist trick of infiltration and *noyautage* of the local nationalist parties played all over again.

Next comes their complete misunderstanding of the political dynamics at home. Since their enemy was waging a *total war* across all lines of operations, they endeavored to reciprocate in kind (hence the use of all sorts of coercive measures up to torture), all the while assuming, wrongly as it turned out, that French public opinion would concur. But the very methods used, because of their brutality, contributed to both the alienation of the Algerian population and the disgust and eventual disinterest of the French population. What had been but barely acceptable in Indochina, a distant conflict involving only regulars who were complaining at the time about the lack of support back home, became intolerable in Algeria, where the use of draftees and the proximity with the homeland provoked a much stronger involvement of the French people in a conflict that had itself become much more savage, with the full implementation of *guerre psychologique*.

By the same token, they completely failed to understand that the decolonization wars, even in Algeria, did not threaten metropolitan territory and therefore would not, in all probability, be perceived by the public as a *total war encompassing vital interests*. Worse, the linkage they tried to draw between the homeland and the colonies rested on the wrongheaded notion, widespread in military circles, that a world revolution was on the move, whose success overseas would pave the way for its outbreak in Europe. In its ultimate implication, this perspective regarded revolutionary warfare less as a new form of war than in reality as the armed stage of a global communist conspiracy.[37] Beyond the ideological context, however, the DGR proclivity for a totalitarian approach to war replicated in many respects trends that had already been present during the colonial period.[38]

Finally—and here blame should also be squarely laid at the political decision makers' doorsteps—they utterly failed to articulate a political strategy, or even a political message, attractive to the local populations, which is also why the conspiracy theory was so attractive as a Freudian rationalization of sorts. At another level, this lack of a political and strategic direction, the consecutive fact that the French military was able to operate in a relative political vacuum, and the natural tendency of this kind of war to move away from Huntington's model of "objective control" in civil-military relations largely set the stage for the failed coup of 1961 which itself completed the process of delegitimizing the war effort and the counterinsurgency doctrine more generally.

In this respect, the French school not only proved unable to prevent the loss of the empire and defeat in Algeria, but its excesses resulted in its teachings and proposals being rejected *en masse*. With the end of the Algerian War, the termination of OAS, and the following purges ordered by de Gaulle, *guerre révolutionnaire* and *action psychologique* became thoroughly discredited, while the defense reform displaced counterinsurgency in favor of nuclear deterrence. More generally, the widespread use of torture in Algeria, not to mention the dubious roles played by some veterans of *guerre révolutionnaire*, like Paul Aussaresses, as advisors to 1970s South American military dictatorships generated such opprobrium as to render the whole Algeria business something of a taboo within the military and society at large.

From vestige to revival

At the institutional and official level, the French military has recently, and in a way by chance, rediscovered its own counterinsurgency tradition, through its involvement in Afghanistan and the posthumous international fame of Galula, brought about by General Petraeus and FM 3-24. At the more informal level of military culture, however, the French colonial tradition managed to grow roots that were deep enough to ensure its muted survival up to this day.

The preservation of this heritage owes much, of course, to the continued existence of the Foreign Legion, and the *regiments coloniaux*, renamed *infanterie* or *artillerie de marine*, as well as to the large military presence and strategic influence that France kept in its former African colonies throughout the Cold War. Though generally of a low-level nature, this postcolonial presence involved from time to time the direct use of force, either in discrete actions, as in Kolwezi in 1978, or through lasting military deployments (such as the *opération Epervier* against Libya in Chad during the 1980s). These missions were typically carried out by paratroop or light infantry units, most of them professionalized Foreign Legion or ex-colonial regiments. In 1983, these regiments were put together in the *Force d'Action Rapide* (FAR), thus becoming institutionally distinct from the *Armée d'Allemagne* focused on territorial and NATO defense and based on conscription. Once again the old distinction between the metropolitan and the "overseas" army had been resurrected. The FAR units thus kept alive their colonial heritage in a low-key manner, in the form of military traditions, tactical best practices and, most importantly, knowledge of the human terrain in Africa and the habit of overseas operations.

This small-scale heritage received a boost with the end of the Cold War and the ensuing sea change in the international system. The absence of a direct threat on French territory for the first time since the Franco-Prussian War, combined with the military's mixed performance in the Gulf War, and the requirements of the peacekeeping tours in Yugoslavia, all led to President Chirac's decision to suspend conscription in 1996 for the first time since 1870. The stabilization of Bosnia and Kosovo, as well as recurring interventions in the midst of African crises, required large and regular troop rotations, which in turn made the professionalization of the military mandatory. Besides, French leaders had come to recognize that the capacity to participate in large-scale overseas interventions had displaced nuclear deterrence as the new coin of international influence in the post-Cold War era.

At the doctrinal and intellectual level, the evolution has also proved uneven. With nuclear deterrence and the prospect of major war receding in the background, the involvement in the Balkans appeared as a radical break, leading the French military to regard peace operations as the new norm. By making a distinction at the time between "coercion" and "mastery of violence," and with most crises calling for the latter, the French military in the 1990s almost came to accept as a doctrine the reduced saliency and relevance of military force—some prominent general officers and military thinkers were even leaning toward the obsolescence of war as a policy instrument, somewhat prefiguring Rupert Smith's thesis.[39] It is no wonder, therefore, that *The Utility of Force* received such a warm welcome in Paris, when General Vincent Desportes, then head of the Centre de Doctrine d'Emploi des Forces (CDEF), the French Army's TRADOC, took the initiative to have it translated from English to French. By the same token, one book by a French author that had in the meantime grown into a classic treatise of the theory of war in the modern era was finally translated in 2008, again thanks to the general's initiative: David Galula's *Counterinsurgency Warfare*. The history of French and American mutual influence and borrowings with respect to counterinsurgency has thus come full circle.[40] Until today, however, the stabilization approach *à la* Rupert Smith and the writings of the colonial school have proved vastly more influential in the French military than Galula or the "centurions."

General Smith's influence is quite palpable in Army doctrine, as illustrated in some of the highest-order publications—for instance, the capstone document FT-01 entitled "Gagner la bataille, conduire à la paix—Les forces terrestres dans les conflits aujourd'hui et demain"— down to operational-level documents such as "Doctrine d'emploi des Forces Terrestres en stabilisation." Essentially, the French Army notes that contemporary operations take place amongst the people in three distinct, though somewhat overlapping phases: intervention, stabilization, and "normalization." Within this framework, coercion initially predominates then rapidly recedes in the stabilization phase, while "mastery of violence"—later to be split up between *sécurisation* and *assistance*—progressively gains in importance, to be eventually replaced by reconstruction in the normalization phase. Since the use of force is no longer able to deliver the strategic objective, but can only set the stage for it—or "create a condition," as Rupert Smith has it—stabilization is characterized as the decisive phase of the entire operation, when the political process of reconciliation can gain traction and lead to peace, provided it is properly conducted and in cooperation with all relevant actors.

Obviously, this doctrinal framework has been colored by the crises of the 1990s and the experience of peacekeeping or peace enforcement in a chaotic environment made up of various non-state, warring parties. As such, it does not deal directly with insurgencies or rebellions, in the sense of politically organized and fundamentally hostile guerrillas. It is therefore only recently, with the wake-up call of Afghanistan, that the Army has decided to tackle the counterinsurgency issue per se, leading to the publication of its "Doctrine de contre-rébellion" (FT-13). What is immediately striking about this text is the way it tries to reclaim the French counterinsurgency heritage, while simultaneously distancing itself from the most controversial aspects of it. This it manages to do by carefully circumscribing this heritage to the tactical level. The text is divided in three parts: the first is devoted to understanding the specific context of counterinsurgency and defining the main notions; the second part deals with the management of the population and how to secure and protect it from the rebellion; and the third part focuses on a variety of tactics that can be used to destroy the armed groups.

FT-13 opens on a refrain familiar to the counterinsurgency specialist: the population is the main stake—securing it and restoring a sense of normalcy are required to get from it the necessary political support and intelligence tips. Tactical successes do not add up to victory, as the political dimension always takes precedence over the operational one. What matters most are intelligence and knowledge of the human terrain; strict respect of human rights, the laws of armed conflict, and local laws, which are at the core of the operation's legitimacy; media engagement and cultural awareness that minimize frictions and counter the insurgents' propaganda. At the tactical and operational levels, FT-13 ventures into similarly well-charted waters, noting the uselessness of large cordon and sweep operations, and the need for permanent or stable points of contact with the population, or stressing the importance of helping the government, building and training local forces, and finding the right military and cultural balance between dispersion in outposts and concentration in large bases.

But the text is also original in several respects, ranging from definitions to tactics. First, counter-rebellion is characterized as the most coercive variant of *sécurisation* (securing), a tactical "mode of action" that is mostly prevalent in the stabilization phase; whereas classic coercion (offensive and defensive operations) predominates in the intervention phase, and assistance in the normalization phase. Comprising specific tactics such as lock-down, curfew, sweep, and harassment operations, counter-rebellion, therefore, is *not* the equivalent of US or British counterinsurgency, which is much broader in scope and more or less corresponds to stabilization in French doctrinal parlance—it is also a way of reminding the reader of the French originality and intellectual independence in this field.[41] Focused on neutralizing the enemy armed organization, which involves securing the population and separating it from the rebels, counter-rebellion takes place within a larger interagency and international framework that specifies the objectives and the limits of military action—this larger framework has not yet been formalized in a joint doctrinal document. Operationally, FT-13 explicitly takes inspiration from French traditions and best practices, quoting Lyautey and extolling the virtues of the oil spot method as the most fitting stabilization tool, given the reduced numbers with which modern Western forces have to operate, but also quoting Trinquier, Galula, and the Algerian tactic of *nomadisation*.[42]

Several important elements are lacking or barely tackled, however, from the numbers and resources required in counterinsurgency to the implications of the multinational frameworks prevailing today. Almost nothing is said either of the fight against the enemy's *organisation politico-administrative*, especially its leadership, intelligence, and propaganda and logistical cadres. Likewise, counter-propaganda is described as having the effect of disaggregating the rebellion, creating rifts within it, and isolating the populations from the rebels, yet the text provides almost no detail on *opérations militaires d'influence* and does not say whether and to what extent they should be linked to the *action psychologique* of old. While the doctrine says little on the subject, it seems that in the field the French military is not averse to using "psyops," though it stops short of what the Americans call "kill or capture operations." More generally, no clear lessons are drawn from past French experience with counterinsurgency, even though both Galula and Trinquier are quoted, leaving the reader to wonder what part exactly of this mixed heritage is claimed explicitly or implicitly. This absence of an overall and explicit assessment of the French colonial and counterinsurgency schools might even be regarded as damaging to FT-13, as it seems to amount to an oblique and uneasy endorsement of the centurions' legacy, even though the text tries to frame counterinsurgency within international and national legal contexts. In all fairness, this doctrinal document seeks to skirt partisan politics and high-end ideological debates in order to focus on the tactical teachings of French military experience in Africa, Indochina, and Algeria.

Accordingly, the document stays within very prudent bounds and avoids dwelling too long on the thorniest issues such as propaganda, *action psychologique,* detainee operations, or counterintelligence. The most noteworthy weakness is the missing link between policy and strategy: though it would have been difficult anyway to include this dimension in full in an Army doctrinal document, the text too often substitutes the formal bow to the legal framework to an indepth analysis of the political, ethical, and legal aspects of counterinsurgency.

All told, FT-13 is a good and useful doctrinal document, as it was meant to be, but is far from an intellectual overhaul of the French colonial and counterinsurgency traditions. The uneasiness palpable here and there in this text is also evidence enough that the French military institution, though engaged for more than a decade in a series of serious reforms and adaptations, has not yet fully come to terms with the ghosts of the past.

Lessons and non-lessons

These uneasy omissions are not limited to French strategic circles. The contemporary counter-insurgency debate also tends to be sightless in one eye: on the operational level, partly thanks to General Petraeus, it heaps praise on David Galula's writings and French counterinsurgency doctrine in general, the influence of which has increased markedly in the wake of the war in Iraq. But on a strategic level, the lessons to be gleaned from the French experience are as neglected as they are important and pertinent at the strategic, political, and institutional levels.

Tactical brilliance and doctrinal innovations are for naught if the enterprise is flawed at the strategic level—this is especially true in irregular warfare, in which the political dimension predominates so much that no military move, however local or insignificant, can be safely isolated from its political context. Similarly, the strategic and political piece is not a mere set of techniques (such as *action psychologique*), however ingeniously applied. In other words, ideology and politics cannot be solved by, or disaggregated into, governance, no matter how well conducted the latter is.

The all-encompassing nature of irregular warfare calls for a broad understanding of counterinsurgency that tries to "seamlessly" integrate all lines of operations. In turn, this all-encompassing, integrated approach often creates the illusion among the military that they are waging a total war, responding in kind to their enemy. However, with the possible exception of Israel, Western nations engage in counterinsurgency for limited stakes, which leads to inevitable tensions between what the military thinks is required on the ground, in terms of methods or resources, and what the population is ready to accept back home. By the same token, the inescapable implication of the military in politics, both in theater and at home, tends to generate tensions in civil-military relations: the military sometimes resists being drawn into a "dirty war" or demands too much latitude, while the civilians in administration and government are reluctant to accept the delegation or centralization of authority under the military or the methods that the latter sometimes advocates (forced population movements, coercion, etc.).

These difficulties are magnified with militaries relying on conscription. Irregular warfare in distant places is therefore best suited to an all-volunteer, specialized or at least "oriented" force, such as colonial units, with a real interest for and investment in the region. In this respect, the colonial generation of French thinkers of irregular warfare, which had to make do with limited resources and political support over a long period of time, still has much to teach us—perhaps even more than the centurion generation, at the strategic level.

On a final note, counterinsurgency aptly illustrates that armies, like people, never actually learn but simply remember. More precisely, some cultural reflexes and attitudes are preserved as long as they are useful, but the main lessons tend to be forgotten, especially after a traumatizing episode, and are therefore rediscovered anew every time—see the case of the US after Vietnam and in Iraq. It is therefore high time that Western militaries institutionalize the lessons to be drawn from past and present counterinsurgency experiences, however distasteful, and strive to hold on to them by integrating them once and for all in military education. One could do far worse than to read Lyautey these days.

Notes

1 Thomas Rid, "The 19th Century Origins of Counterinsurgency Doctrine," *Journal of Strategic Studies*, 2010, forthcoming.
2 Etat-major, 2e bureau, Tananarive, instructions, 1 October 1896. Reproduced in Frédéric Hellot, "La Pacification de Madagascar," *Journal des Science Militaires*, Vol. 75, No. 10 (1899), 49–50.
3 Joseph-Simon Galliéni, *Neuf ans à Madagascar*, Paris: Librairie Hachette, 1908, p. 326, emphasis added.
4 David Galula, *Pacification in Algeria 1956–1958*, Santa Monica, CA: Rand Corporation, 1963 (2006), p. 274: "once the selected area is pacified, it will be possible to withdraw from it an important share of our means and to assign them to neighboring areas, thus spreading an oil slick on the water."
5 Lyautey quoting Galliéni, in Hubert Lyautey, "Du rôle colonial de l'armée," *Revue des Deux Mondes* (1900), 16.
6 Ibid., 4, 9.
7 Ibid., 7, 16.
8 See Samuel Huntington, *The Soldier and the State*, Cambridge, MA: Harvard University Press, 1957.
9 Thomas Rid, "Razzia. A Turning Point in Modern Strategy," *Terrorism and Political Violence*, Vol. 21, No. 4 (2009), 617–35.
10 Douglas Porch, "Bugeaud, Galliéni, Lyautey: The Development of French Colonial Warfare," in Peter Paret (ed.), *Makers of Modern Strategy*, Princeton, NJ: Princeton University Press, 1986, pp. 391–3.
11 Ibid., pp. 387, 394.
12 Ibid., pp. 399, 404.
13 Douglas Porch, *The March to the Marne. The French Army 1871–1914*, Cambridge: Cambridge University Press, 1981. Porch, "Bugeaud, Galliéni, Lyautey." Jean Gottmann, "Bugeaud, Galliéni, Lyautey: The Development of French Colonial Warfare," in Edward Mead Earle (ed.), *Makers of Modern Strategy*, Princeton, NJ: Princeton University Press, 1943, pp. 234–59.
14 Porch, "Bugeaud, Galliéni, Lyautey." See also Jean-Charles Jauffret, "Les Armes de 'la plus grande France,'" in Guy Pedroncini (ed.), *Histoire militaire de la France: tome III. De 1871 à 1940*, Paris: PUF, 1992.
15 Peter Paret, *French Revolutionary Warfare from Indochina to Algeria*, New York: Praeger, 1964. André Beaufre, *Introduction à la stratégie*, Paris: Economica, 1985.
16 See the useful comparison between Trinquier and Galula in "De Galula à Petraeus: l'héritage français dans la pensée américaine de la contre-insurrection," *Cahier de la recherche doctrinale*, Centre de doctrine d'emploi des forces, May 7, 2009.
17 TTA 117—"Instruction provisoire sur l'emploi de l'arme psychologique," authored in July 1957 by (then) Major Jacques Hogard.
18 Michel Goya, "Le peur et le coeur. Les incohérences de l'action militaire française pendant la guerre d'Algérie," *Stratégique*, Nos. 93–6 (2009), makes that case regarding Algeria and the diverging currents within the French military.
19 Regarding the interesting connections between the French and the Americans on counterinsurgency, see Elie Tenenbaum, "L'influence française sur la stratégie américaine de contre-insurrection, 1945–1972," MA thesis, IEP de Paris, July 2009 (unpublished).
20 See Jean Lartéguy, *Les mercenaires*, Paris: Pocket, 1963, for a good description of the atmosphere of the 1950s in the French officer corps. See also Lartéguy's novels on Algeria: *Les centurions* (1963) and *Les prétoriens* (1964).
21 "... nous n'aurons peut-être pas de guerre atomique, ... nous n'aurons peut-être pas de guerre conventionnelle, mais des guerres révolutionnaires, hélas, nous en aurons beaucoup, nous en avons déjà; nous ne faisons que cela." Charles Lacheroy, 2nd Conference entitled "Principes de la riposte à la guerre révolutionnaire" (Principles of Response to Revolutionary War), 1957.
22 "Le problème n° 1 c'est celui de la prise en main de ces populations qui servent de support à cette

guerre et au milieu desquelles elle se passe. Celui qui les prend ou qui les tient a déjà gagné." Charles Lacheroy, 1st conference entitled "Leçons de l'action Viet-Minh et communiste en Indochine" (Lessons from Viet-Minh and Communist Actions in Indochina), 1957. Note that the thesis and very expression used by Rupert Smith, "war amongst the people," are already present in this text, and even more explicitly in Jean Nemo, "La guerre dans le milieu social," *Revue de défense nationale* (May 1956): "The Army lives among the population, 'in the crowd'. . ." (616); "War 'in the crowd' makes that crowd and its opinion the real stake" ("La guerre 'dans la foule' fait de cette foule et de son opinion le veritable enjeu," 221).

23 H. Martin, "Guérilla, guerre en surface et guerre révolutionnaire," *Revue militaire d'information* (August 1957), 9. See also Nemo, "La guerre dans le milieu social," 620–1, who contrasts *action en surface* conducted by local guerrillas and *guerre en surface*, which requires the intervention of the Vietminh's regular units.

24 Jacques Hogard, "Le soldat dans la guerre révolutionnaire," *Revue de défense nationale* (February 1957), 211–27.

25 Ibid., 213.

26 Ibid., 221–2.

27 See Roger Trinquier, *La guerre moderne*, Paris: Economica, 2008 (1st edn 1961), pp. 65–81.

28 GAD stands for *groupe d'auto-défense* (self-defense group); *harka* refers to minor fights and by extension to small fighting groups. Essentially, GAD and *harkas* (along with *mokhaznis* and *groupes mobile de police rurale* or GMPR), were local, irregular auxiliaries led by French officers. Created in 1956–7, these units had local defense for their main mission, though some of them had more specialized roles: *mokhaznis* were created to protect *sections administratives spéciales* (SAS, specialized CIMIC units), and *harkas* were progressively entrusted with more offensive missions, being often incorporated within *commandos de chasse*.

29 Hogard, "Le soldat dans la guerre révolutionnaire," 220: "Les Opérations n'ont d'intérêt que dans la mesure où elles favorisent la politique générale de pacification; elles sont néfastes dans le cas contraire."

30 Ibid., 215, 218–19.

31 Ibid., 215: "Le but à atteindre a été défini: *détruire l'organisation politico-militaire rebelle* qui assure le contrôle révolutionnaire sur tout ou partie de la population. Pour y parvenir et pour assurer nos succès, il faut substituer notre infrastructure à celle de l'ennemi [ce qui implique] la collaboration intime de tous, fonctionnaires, policiers, notabilités locales, militaires."

32 Lacheroy, "The Response to Revolutionary War." See also Hogard, "Le soldat dans la guerre révolutionnaire," 217–18, 224.

33 *5e bureaux* have no modern equivalent in modern headquarters, as their responsibilities would be divided between J2 (civil-military actions or CIMIC), J9 (intelligence), and Special Forces (psychological operations).

34 "On ne fait pas une guerre révolutionnaire avec une armée endivisionnée; on ne fait pas une guerre révolutionnaire avec une administration de temps de paix; on ne fait pas une guerre révolutionnaire avec le Code Napoléon," Lacheroy, "The Response to Revolutionary War."

35 Goya, "Le peur et le coeur." "Là où les SAS voulaient conquérir les cœurs, les 5e bureaux recherchent la domination des esprits."

36 Paul Villatoux, "L'institutionnalisation de l'arme psychologique pendant la guerre d'Algérie au miroir de la guerre froide," *Guerres mondiales et conflits contemporains*, No. 208 (2002). As the author shows, the fear of subversion predates the Cold War but was singularly reinforced but the strength of the Communist Party in France at the time and the violent strikes that it organized in 1947.

37 See among others Jacques Hogard, "Guerre révolutionnaire ou révolution dans l'art de la guerre," *Revue de défense nationale* (December 1956).

38 Porch, "Bugeaud, Galliéni, Lyautey," 406.

39 Loup Francart and Jean-Jacques Patry, *Maîtriser la violence*, Paris: Economica, 2002 (1st edn 1999). Patrice Sartre, "Comprendre les crises violentes pour les maîtriser," in Paul Quiles, Alexandra Novosseloff, et al., *Face aux désordres du monde*, Paris: Les Portes du monde, 2005.

40 Elie Tenenbaum, "L'influence française sur la stratégie américaine de contre-insurrection, 1945–1972."

41 Centre de Doctrine d'emploi des Forces "Doctrine de centre-rébellion" (FT-13), Paris, January 2009, p. 9.

42 Ibid., p. 24.

3 Britain

Alexander Alderson

The British Army's principal military experience is of irregular, not regular, warfare.[1] Although the British Army had to be "capable of fighting a war of the first magnitude while simultaneously being ready to engage in wars of smaller dimensions,"[2] it was from the small wars, which Charles Callwell defined as "operations of regular armies against irregular, or comparatively speaking irregular, forces,"[3] that its experience and an extensive literature came.[4] The Army's small wars experience remains a powerful influence in shaping its character, identity, sense of history, doctrine, and its general approach to operations other than general war.[5]

Yet despite a once evident prowess in small wars—when it "excelled in small-unit, antiguerrilla warfare [and] other aspects of counterinsurgency"[6]—the British Army has not produced much in the way of formal counterinsurgency doctrine. Even at the height of the colonial problems in the 1950s and 1960s, the United Kingdom did not produce a general theory of counterinsurgency—"There was no official publication," one prominent historian pointed out.[7] Bespoke doctrine was written for the campaigns in Malaya and Kenya, and lessons from elsewhere were assimilated into official publications such as *Keeping the Peace*,[8] but the development of general doctrine had to wait until the 1990s, when the Army established a more formal approach to its development. British thinking evolved into doctrine.[9] This has the advantage of allowing experience to be analyzed and assimilated. But doctrine that lags too far behind the operational environment risks becoming irrelevant. "In the absence of literature on the subject," General Sir Charles Gwynn noted in 1934, "tradition becomes the only means of broadcasting experience, and tradition is apt to be based on experience limited to a small number of cases." Yet, Gwynn was careful to add, tradition "has its dangers."[10]

British doctrine has been shaped by a remarkable range of influences: government policy, lessons from campaigns, and unofficial theories drawn from personal experience. Policy shapes the sort of war the government wants, and the way in which it is conducted. In Britain's case, policy underpins the principle of minimum force, which this chapter will examine further. Policy also determined the various approaches taken by British forces: on the one hand it was responsible for the long-term strategy followed in Northern Ireland, on the other, for the minimalist, very successful approach taken in Oman.[11] Experience from the many campaigns informed both formal doctrine, through the assimilation of lessons learned, and the analysis and theories offered by practitioners. Together, they shaped an approach that is marked by three fundamental characteristics: the use of minimum force, civil-military cooperation, and tactical flexibility.[12] But this is not the full story.

Tactical flexibility is part of a much broader function of learning and adaptation. How an army learns from experience and adapts to changing circumstances is determined to a great extent by its general approach to education and training. Small wars and insurgencies present particular problems, and armies that learn and adapt have tended to meet with greater success than those that do not.[13] The British Army has traditionally been culturally attuned to small wars, and has learned and adapted instinctively as a result. Practically, the British Army has emphasized learning and adapting—for example, in Malaya, Kenya, and Northern Ireland—but this approach has not always been emphasized in its doctrine.

All practitioners and theorists underline the special role that intelligence plays in counter-insurgency. Good intelligence is without doubt "one of the greatest battle-winning factors" in counterinsurgency warfare.[14] In counterinsurgency the traditional top-down flow of intelligence is reversed. Much depends on an intelligence organization adapting to this change—building the picture from routine information, and finding ways to overcome the difficulties that insurgencies present. For example: insurgents tend not to be conspicuous except in what they do; the distinction between a legitimate political organization and militant activists may be blurred; and gathering intelligence from the population may threaten its rights, liberties and hence its support.

This last aspect of obtaining information from the population—human intelligence—has been a key element of the British approach to counterinsurgency. Its doctrine has long recognized a clear link between how force is used and the relationship between security forces and the population among which it operates: the greater the level of trust, the better the flow of information. That information plus, as British doctrine identifies, "surveillance or the reports from routine police or army patrols [and time]-consuming collation of detail and painstaking analysis may then prove the key to unraveling important aspects of the insurgent's activity."[15]

The four fundamentals of minimum force, civil-military cooperation, intelligence, and learning and adaptation provide the framework against which this chapter will examine the historical and intellectual origins of British small wars theory. It will look at how the four themes became inextricably interwoven into the British approach by theory, experience, and doctrine. This chapter examines present doctrine to establish what the British approach to counterinsurgency is, before examining the importance of policy for shaping the minimum use of force. Space limits discussion to the four principal British theories that have influenced this approach: Colonel Charles Callwell's *Small Wars*, General Sir Charles Gwynn's *Imperial Policing*, Sir Robert Thompson's *Defeating Communist Insurgency*, and Brigadier Frank Kitson's *Low Intensity Operations*.[16] Three campaigns are then evaluated against the four fundamentals to identify their impact on the overall outcome, and, subsequently, on doctrine: Malaya 1948–60, an example of success; Northern Ireland 1969–2007, the most recent; and Aden 1963–8, an unsuccessful campaign. The chapter concludes by examining the extent to which the British approach remains relevant.

A British approach

The British approach to counterinsurgency is explained in the Army Field Manual, *Counter-Insurgency Operations*. Published in July 2001, it was the latest in a line of pamphlets to wrestle with the challenges of applying military force in revolutionary wars, internal security problems, and insurgencies.[17] It had no joint doctrine equivalent. The pamphlet describes an approach based on minimum force, civil-military relations and the preeminence of intelli-gence. The pamphlet makes clear that there "has never been a purely military solution to revolution; political, social, economic and military measures all have a part to play in restor-ing the authority of a legitimate government."[18] This echoes General Sir Frank Kitson's conclusion that:

there can be no such thing as a purely military solution because insurgency is not primarily a military activity. At the same time there is no such thing as a wholly political solution either, short of surrender, because the very fact that a state of insurgency exists implies that violence is involved which will have to be countered to some extent at least by the use of legal force. Political measures alone might have prevented the insurgency from occurring in the first place, . . . [but] once it has taken hold, politics and force, backed up by economic measures will have to be harnessed together for the purpose of restoring peaceful conditions.[19]

Despite "changes in circumstances or merely intellectual fashion," *Counter-Insurgency Operations* declares that insurgency and counterinsurgency are essentially about "the battle to win and hold popular support, both at home and in the theatre of operations."[20] This means breaking the link between the insurgent and the people by the application of those "military, paramilitary, political, economic, psychological and civil actions taken by the Government to defeat insurgency."[21] To do this, counterinsurgency must be politically led and cross-government in approach. However, *Counter-Insurgency Operations* also urges caution: there is no British template for counterinsurgency, and there is no "general antidote to the problem of insurgency."[22] Each response has to be different because each insurgency is different; each has to be put in the right context by careful analysis of the problem and the sensible application of principles.[23] Kitson pointed out the logical consequences of this insight: "if you had eighty different insurgencies, there were eighty different ways to defeat them."[24]

The Ministry of Defence defines doctrine as "the fundamental principles by which military forces guide their actions in support of objectives. It is authoritative, but requires judgment in application."[25] Principles are therefore important. Those explained in *Counter-Insurgency Operations* are "derived partly from experience and partly from the works of General Kitson and Sir Robert Thompson"[26]; their value is widely recognized, and they continue to provide a sound basis for analysis.[27] As Bob Cassidy notes:

> Although the halcyon days of British counterinsurgency operations came to an end with the Malayan Emergency in the 1960s, the examples of Northern Ireland and Oman indicated that the principles on which its approach to counterinsurgency was founded are as valuable now as then.[28]

Policy

The British approach is often characterized by the principle of minimum force.[29] But what is minimum force, and why is it so important to the British approach? *Counter-Insurgency Operations* explains that it means "No more force may be used than is necessary to achieve a legal aim. The amount used must be reasonable and it must not be punitive. Directly the aim is achieved no more force may be used."[30] This does not mean "do not use force," because not using enough force may fail to protect the soldier or those whom he is protecting. Similarly, excessive force may be illegal. The use of either—too much force or not enough— is equally wrong.

The principle can be traced back in military publications as far back as the 1912 edition of the *Manual of Military Law*, which established the relationship between the civil authorities and the armed forces, and the legal use of force when restoring law and order. It made the distinction between a riot—when only that force necessary to restore law and order could be used—and insurrection, where the authority of the Crown was challenged directly and "the law permitted 'any degree of force necessary.'"[31]

It was General Dyer's actions at Amritsar, in the Punjab, on April 13, 1919, that forced clarification. Dyer believed he faced an insurrection, and was therefore justified in the use of lethal force. He therefore ordered soldiers to open fire on some 10,000 unarmed protestors, killing 379 and wounding over a thousand. Widespread outrage followed; martial law had to be imposed, Dyer was relieved of command, and Indian nationalist politics reached a turning point. Lord Hunter's enquiry into events at Amritsar concentrated on the legal distinction between rioting and insurrection and concluded that both Dyer's decision to order his troops to fire on the crowd without warning, and for those troops to continue to fire as the crowd dispersed, were unjustified.[32] The British government confirmed Hunter's findings. The direction it issued established minimum force as a cornerstone of the British approach in small, internal wars:

> The principle which has consistently governed the policy of His Majesty's Government in directing the methods to be employed, when military action in support of civil authority is required, may be broadly stated as using the minimum force necessary. His Majesty's Government are determined that *this principle shall remain the primary factor of policy* whenever circumstances unfortunately necessitate the suppression of civil disorder by military force within the British Empire.[33]

The Army found the whole process institutionally bruising. It was divided over the way Dyer was dealt with, and the minimum force policy did nothing to ameliorate inevitable tensions between the Army and the civil authorities, which were now to monitor more closely military actions operating under their control. Nevertheless, "the inter-war army came to argue that military force was a weapon of discrimination and restraint,"[34] qualities that added authority to the Army's position, and provided a benchmark against which its actions could be judged. Minimum force became "a pragmatic response to dealing with insurgents and terrorists . . . the vital ingredient in separating both of these from their support base."[35]

Limitations of policy: aerial policing

One solution to the problem of maintaining expensive garrisons across the empire was a proposal from the Royal Air Force to swap airpower for manpower. The defeat of a Dervish revolt by airpower in Somalia in 1919 proved it had merit,[36] and in 1921 Winston Churchill, then colonial secretary and a former secretary of state for air, agreed that "the RAF should assume the dominant role in policing Iraq, that overall command of British forces there should be given to a senior RAF officer, and that the present establishment in Iraq be increased from five air squadrons . . . to eight." [37]

"Bombing without occupation" was devised to maximize the "demoralization engendered in the tribesman by his feelings of helplessness and his inability to reply effectively to the attack."[38] Operations in Iraq between 1922 and 1932, where the RAF had the right people, troops, authorities, and equipment, provided further evidence it worked, and so the concept was used elsewhere across the empire. By the time the 1936 Arab Revolt broke out in Palestine, problems had emerged—not simply those of limited resources. Gwynn concludes that:

air action could not render assistance to the civil power in the task of maintaining internal order, and armoured cars also had their limitations . . . One must conclude that *the achievements of the Royal Air Force in Iraq had not been thoroughly analysed,* and that the Government in its desire for economy had formed an over optimistic estimate of the potentialities of the new arm.[39]

Palestine proved to be the turning point for aerial policing, principally because of concerns about meeting the levels of discrimination and proportionality. The RAF's proposal of dropping "one 250-pound or 500-pound bomb in each village that speaks out of turn . . . [because the] only thing the Arab understands is the heavy hand, and sooner or later it will have to be applied"[40] was rejected. Tight restrictions were imposed on the use of close air support within 500 yards of habitation, and air operations limited to patrolling open country-side, and to dealing with targets flushed out by ground operations—tasks at which it excelled.[41] But the limitations of air power were recognized. Thus the British "were willing to forego the military advantages of the aeroplane in order to preserve the principle of minimum force,"[42] and soldiers and police were once again to provide the most effective means of protecting the population.

Theory

Although not doctrine in any formal sense, Colonel Charles Callwell's *Small Wars* is generally agreed to be the start point for British irregular warfare writing. First published in 1896, it identifies and addresses the problems a modern, regular army faced when dealing with irregular adversaries: poor intelligence, the difficulty of designing a strategy and applying it through operational art and tactics, communications, logistics, and security. Not much has changed.

Callwell's framework for operations divided a troubled area into sectors, each held at key locations by strong points and block houses, from which highly mobile columns could then patrol the area and close with the enemy. His framework can be recognized in later campaigns in the Frontier Provinces, Malaya, Oman, Northern Ireland, and now Afghanistan. Although Callwell acknowledged there should be "a limit to the amount of license in destruction,"[43] his methods fall well short of any notion of minimum force. His intention was to drive an insurrection to failure by depriving the enemy, and the local population among which it lived, of the means to survive.[44] Despite his acknowledgement that "the laws of regular warfare do not sanction"[45] his methods, he considers them necessary to bring about the enemy's defeat. However, to dismiss Callwell because of the brutality of his language and his approach ignores the value of his still relevant observations about the inherent difficulties of small wars:

> the conditions of small wars are so diversified, the enemy's mode of fighting is often so peculiar, and the theatres of operations present such singular features, that irregular warfare must generally be carried out on a method totally different from the stereotyped system. The art of war . . . must be modified to suit the circumstances of each particular case. The conduct of small wars is . . . an art in itself, diverging widely from what is adapted to the conditions of regular warfare, but not so widely that there are not in all its branches points which permit comparisons to be established.[46]

The implication is clear: small wars cannot to be approached in the same way as conventional conflict. There are similarities, but the differences are profound enough to demand specific training and preparation, in order that soldiers "know what nature of opposition they must expect, and should understand how best to overcome it."[47] The experience of campaigns since has only served to reinforce this point, and it is one that Gwynn and Kitson both examine in greater detail.

Charles Gwynn's *Imperial Policing* (1934) is a gem of analysis and "informal" doctrine. The challenges of the minimum-force policy, particularly in terms of discrimination and proportionality, are themes that run throughout. Writing in the shadow of the Amritsar massacre, and in keeping with Callwell's view of small wars and regular-irregular conflict, Gwynn analyzes ten campaigns from 1919 to 1931,[48] "to illustrate military action achieving its result with the minimum exercise of force."[49] Far from being a dated period piece, Gwynn's emphasis on the intrinsic difficulties the soldier faces in dealing with a deepening insurgency, when the civil policy is more conciliatory than confrontational, has much contemporary relevance. In particular he examines the paradoxes the use of force creates:

> The admixture of rebels with a neutral or loyal element of the population adds to the difficulties of the task. Excessive severity may antagonise this element, add to the number of the rebels, and leave a lasting feeling of resentment and bitterness. On the other hand, the power and resolution of the Government forces must be displayed. Anything which can be interpreted as weakness encourages those who are sitting on the fence to keep on good terms with the rebels.[50]

Gwynn developed four principles he believed should underpin the Army's actions, and the methods it could legitimately and effectively use to support the civil police and the civil administration.[51] His principles were, first, that questions of policy remain vested in the civil Government and, even when the military authorities are in full executive control, the policy of the government must be loyally carried out. Second, that the amount of military force employed must be the minimum the situation demands. Third, that firm and timely action would be needed to discourage further disorder. And finally that close cooperation between civil and military authorities is required. In this last principle, Gwynn made clear that the task of restoring order did not rest with the Army alone. While unity of command, close cooperation and mutual understanding between the civil authority and the military were and remain important, the civil authority had to retain overall responsibility. As Iraq and Afghanistan show, counterinsurgency operations are much more difficult to undertake when the host country's government's infrastructure has failed, or when that government does not have the capacity to respond fully to the problem. This issue was one which Kitson would re-examine 40 years later.[52]

Gwynn's critical analysis of British interwar campaigns brings *Imperial Policing* to life, and he uses these campaigns to substantiate the principles and approach he develops. But it is his astute analysis of the challenges of the minimum-force policy that makes his contribution so important. He refers to it in each case study, highlighting an important dilemma: how to balance the use of force against its longer-term adverse consequences. Excessive force, he notes, risks alienating the population and damaging the flow of information: "the extent to which the intelligence service can obtain information depends greatly on the attitude adopted towards the loyal and neutral population."[53] This, Gwynn highlighted, risks delaying the re-establishment of normal conditions. On the other hand, not being forceful enough may weaken the government's authority. The challenge of balancing the use of force with longer-term campaign objectives remains difficult to resolve.

Sir Robert Thompson provided the third major influence. His book *Defeating Communist Insurgency* became part of what one historian described as the British Army's "obsession with Malaya."[54] The episode continued to shape the Army's institutional memory for an entire generation. Thompson saw the development and conduct of the Malayan campaign first hand, beginning as staff officer (civil) to Lieutenant General Sir Harold Briggs, author of the decisive Briggs Plan, and later as permanent secretary of defence in the Malayan administration. In 1966, after leading the British Advisory Mission in South Vietnam, Thompson published *Defeating Communist Insurgency*, in which he focused primarily on governmental rather than military responsibilities. Thompson recognized that an insurgency is, primarily, "a war for the people [therefore without] a reasonably efficient government machine, no project or programme, in the context of counterinsurgency, will produce the desired results."[55]

Defeating Communist Insurgency was, as Beckett observes, "undeniably influential in the British Army's belated recognition of the need to codify its counterinsurgency practice given the increasing prevalence of the global insurgent challenge since 1945."[56] Thompson's principles "became the centrepiece for British Army thinking"[57] after they were incorporated into the 1969 publication *Counter-Revolutionary Operations*.[58] His insistence that counter-insurgency required a political response that balanced social, economic, administrative, police, and military efforts[59] clearly influenced the British principles of "political primacy and political aim," "coordinated government machinery," and "longer term post-insurgency planning."[60]

Thompson's four-stage operational concept of "clear, hold, winning, won" was intended to restore security and governance to an insurgent area. It started with the assumption that the government had a plan and had met his fourth and fifth principles. Intelligence-led military operations first cleared insurgents from an area, after which population-control measures could then be imposed over the cleared area to protect the population and to isolate insurgents. Good governance would then be introduced to win the population's support, to re-establish governmental authority, and to build confidence in the government's ability to meet the needs of the population. The area could then be declared as "won" at the point when control measures were lifted.[61] This model accords with that which David Galula proposed,[62] the "clear, hold, build" approach described in the US Army's FM 3-24,[63] and, since February 2007, the "clear, control, retain" model used successfully by US forces in Iraq.[64]

Counter-Insurgency Operations developed Thompson's concept and suggested for the first time in British doctrine that future counterinsurgency operations would take place in an expeditionary context, in unfamiliar circumstances, "working in support of a foreign government."[65] Thompson's principles and his approach can be seen clearly in the approach described in 2001: secure a base area, establish a firm forward operational base, secure a controlled area, consolidate the controlled areas, and continue the extension of controlled areas. Like Thompson, *Counter-Insurgency Operations* (2001) did not begin to address the broader, more fundamental problems that expeditionary counterinsurgency now faces, such as host-country sovereignty and perceptions of legitimacy. This was something Frank Kitson would examine five years later.

In 1971, Brigadier Frank Kitson completed a defence fellowship at Oxford to examine how to "make the Army ready to deal with subversion, insurrection and peace-keeping operations during the second half of the 1970s."[66] Kitson drew from his own experience in Kenya, where as a young captain he had set up a district intelligence section. His experience fighting the Mau Mau shaped his ideas on how usable intelligence should be created in counterinsurgency. His subsequent experience in Malaya, Oman, Cyprus, and Northern Ireland confirmed his views.

Kitson published his thesis in 1972 as *Low Intensity Operations*: his carefully considered approach melded his professional experience and the intellectual rigor of the Oxford Common Room. The result was the most important *military* contribution to British understanding of counterinsurgency in the twentieth century. *Low Intensity Operations* met with considerable approval from within the Army, and the book was to remain the mainstay of the Army's counterinsurgency education and staff training for the next 20 years. Kitson believed that irregular warfare and insurgency was the most likely form of conflict, despite the large-scale threat posed by the Warsaw Pact. To meet the challenge of low-intensity operations, the Army would need to make considerable changes to its structure, capabilities, and system for education and training. Central to Kitson's approach is the recognition that "wars of subversion and counter-subversion are fought, in the last resort, in the minds of the people."[67] The result was a focus on the means by which public opinion could be shaped and on the need for intelligence obtained from the population.

Kitson noted how regular, conventionally trained battalions struggled to adapt to the demands of counterinsurgency. He concluded that the conventional military mindset was wholly unsuited for developing and using intelligence effectively.[68] He recognized that the conventional military approach, which looks for certainties such as key enemy formations, equipment, or headquarters, and which tends to depend on technical intelligence-gathering, did not work in counterinsurgency. It produced units that expected "whatever intelligence organization existed to provide pinpoint information regarding the whereabouts and future intentions of enemy groups so that soldiers could be put into contact with them."[69] Kitson believed that intelligence had to be built from the mass of routine information produced by patrols and day-to-day contact with the population. Understanding the normal pattern of life was critical so that unusual activity or potential threats could be identified and dealt with.

Kitson expanded his theories in *Bunch of Five*, published in 1977. There, like Callwell and Thompson, he proposed a framework for the planning and conduct of counterinsurgency that was comprised of four principles:

> coordinating machinery at every level for the direction of the campaign, arrangements for ensuring that the insurgents do not win the war for the minds of the people, an intelligence organisation suited to the circumstances, and a legal system adequate to the needs of the moment.[70]

A government working within this framework would be able to use force in support of its counterinsurgency objectives without damaging its position. To operate outside the framework, Kitson concluded, it would be "highly probable that the use of force will do more harm than good."[71]

Callwell and Gwynn recognized that training and education underpin successful counterinsurgency, but Kitson went much further. He put learning and adaptation on a par with the need for an effective intelligence system and the principle of minimum force. That Kitson placed such emphasis on education and training is indicative that it is the one fundamental aspect most easily forgotten, and the hardest to recover once a campaign is underway. As a counterbalance, Kitson proposed an education and training system focused on "*attuning men's minds* to cope with the [counterinsurgency] environment."[72] Kitson believed that officers must be "taught how to put a campaign together using a combination of civil and military measures to achieve a single government aim [and] teaching them the value of non-military ways of harming the enemy."[73] This meant that they had to understand something of the practical difficulties they would face, where the problem was made more difficult because so many of the people who will be most influential in determining success or failure are not in the armed forces at all. They are the politicians, civil servants, local government officials and police, in the area where the insurgency is taking place, and . . . *that may be in someone else's country*.[74]

Kitson's final important contribution was the short section he provided that dealt with sovereignty, with being in *someone else's country*. His observations are prescient. First, he emphasized that the guiding principle for allies countering insurgency together was

> to retain and regain the allegiance of [the host nation's] population. If this is borne in mind, it at once becomes evident that the way in which the ally's help is delivered is as important as the help itself, the main thing being that the host nation should be seen to be at the centre of the picture.[75]

The ally's interest must always take second place, the host country must have the "properly ordered system for prosecuting the war," the ally must be able "to coordinate all its aid in such a way that an individual person can represent it on the host nation's supreme council," and the ally must be represented at "every level on the host country's committee or staffs [to] feed in military, police or civil aid or advice of any sort."[76] Kitson's model neatly balances the sovereign rights of the host country with the need for coordinated government machinery and the establishment of a complementary mechanism to coordinate and integrate British or allied support. A similar approach was followed during the Oman campaign, where British intelligence, psychological operations, civil aid, and military support were integrated into the Omani Government's plan.[77]

Experience

Three counterinsurgency operations had an important impact on the British Army: Malaya, Northern Ireland, and Aden. The 1948–60 Malayan Emergency is one of Britain's most closely analyzed small wars. This should not be surprising. It was, after a slow start, a success. The government eventually reorganized to unify its efforts, it introduced a comprehensive plan to address the emergency as a whole, and the Army overhauled its training and tactics to make them relevant to the problem. As a result, the communist insurgency was countered, and Malaya independence took place in line with British government intentions.

In campaign terms, Malaya shows the value of a civilian-led command system at each level of government. When the emergency was first declared in 1948, the police commissioner was in overall command, with the armed forces supporting the civilian police. Early results were disappointing, owing in part to poor intelligence and poor coordination. In April 1950, a new post of director of operations was created to unify civil and military efforts. The first director was Lieutenant General Sir Harold Briggs. He immediately formed a committee system at every level of government to integrate all emergency efforts and to ensure that the security forces continued to support the civil power. Briggs also took a deliberate, long-term approach,[78] a point reflected in *Counter-Insurgency Operations'* principle of longer-term post-insurgency planning:

> Merely providing for the military defeat of insurgents does not in any way end the government requirement to make suitable longer term plans to enhance the economic

and social aspects of its population and to ensure that the political causes of the insurgency have been eliminated and overcome by effective planning.[79]

When terrorists murdered the High Commissioner, Sir Henry Gurney, in 1952, General Sir Gerald Templer was appointed as both high commissioner and director of operations. Combining both responsibilities under Templer's forceful leadership provided the catalyst the campaign needed. He quickly galvanized the campaign, and he insisted that all civil, military, and police agencies cooperated fully. The results fully reinforced Gwynn's principle of close civil-military cooperation. This principle, and the importance of an overall campaign director equipped with the necessary authorities, remains central to British doctrine.[80] Experience has shown that this is a most difficult condition to achieve in practice.

At the tactical level, Malaya demonstrates the importance of specialist counterinsurgency training, which used doctrine written specifically for the campaign. Militarily, the campaign got off to a poor start. Daniel Marston describes how the Army had to re-learn how to operate in the jungle, having discovered its large-scale "jungle-bashing" tactics were unsuitable when fighting an insurgency.[81] The chain of command instigated ways to refocus and retrain troops for jungle operations. Specialist long-range patrol groups were formed, and the Jungle Warfare School (JWS), established to teach standardized jungle tactics, proved a great success.[82] The tactical results vindicated the approach taken. Richard Stubbs observed that by the end of 1952,

> with rapidly moving intelligence, the security forces were able to frame localities where insurgents were known to be operating, flood the area with patrols, and set ambushes of their own rather than be ambushed. The [insurgents were] steadily pushed back onto the defensive and its numbers reduced.[83]

The JWS kept abreast of developments in the field, developed relevant tactics, and in 1952 published its own doctrine. This was *The Conduct of Anti-Terrorist Operations in Malaya (ATOM)*.[84] It was based on the accumulated knowledge of JWS instructors, and it provided detailed information on the country, the insurgency, emergency powers, training, and jungle operations and tactics. The framework of operations it identified echoed Callwell: framework operations to provide routine day-to-day activities such as patrols, cordons and searches, and ambushes; mopping-up operations to "complete the destruction and prevent revival" of communist terrorists; conducting deep-jungle operations to deny terrorists the opportunity to rest and retrain; and state priority operations and federal priority operations "to exploit opportunities in specific areas."[85]

Well written, relevant, and with full endorsement from General Templer, *ATOM* quickly became highly regarded, and it was the basis for *Keeping the Peace*, published in 1969.[86] Of particular note is the migration of the *ATOM* and JWS ideas from Malaya to Kenya during the 1952–6 Mau Mau rebellion, where General Erskine had *A Handbook on Anti-Mau Mau Operations*[87] published, and he directed units to "undertake courses at the East Africa Battle School [where] fieldcraft, jungle tactics and the correct use of native trackers and war dogs are taught."[88] More recently, the US military followed suit with the COIN Center for Excellence at Taji in Iraq in 2006.

The Army's deployment to Northern Ireland in August 1969 to help re-establish order amidst widespread Catholic–Protestant sectarian violence, marked an important shift from the colonial setting "to internal security in a domestic context."[89] Operations over the next 38 years provided the present generation of senior officers with much of its counterinsurgency experience. Although largely a domestic problem, Northern Ireland inevitably shaped the Army's view of counterinsurgency best practice: an emphasis on intelligence, restraint and minimum force, training and adaptation, and civil-military cooperation reflected through the Army's task of *supporting* the Royal Ulster Constabulary. These are themes reflected strongly in *Counter-Insurgency Operations* and its 1995 predecessor.[90]

The British government eventually dealt with the Provisional Irish Republican Army and its offshoots, on criminal, not political terms. Bombings and shootings were dealt with as crime scenes, and soldiers were trained to be forensically aware, and to understand the importance of preserving evidence so that terrorists could be pursued through the courts. This distinction between operations in Northern Ireland—Military Assistance to the Civil Power (MACP), guided by directives and orders, not doctrine—and wider counterrevolutionary warfare is reflected in the doctrine of the time. The 1977 edition of *Counter-Revolutionary Operations*,[91] first published in 1969, makes no reference either to ongoing operations in Northern Ireland, or MACP in general. Instead, it lays out an approach reminiscent of Malaya in its tactics and committee structures. In many ways this should not be surprising because, as Beckett and others note, many British troops cut their teeth in Malaya. What is surprising is the number of early mistakes it made. Sir John Kiszely considers that these would have been avoided if experience from previous campaigns had been applied properly. Instead, the Army showed "seemingly unqualified initial support for a highly partisan police force, internment without trial, and large (up to brigade-size) cordon-and-search operations on very limited intelligence, often at the expense of the hearts-and-minds campaign."[92] Nevertheless, from about 1972 when the Army formalized pre-tour training, Northern Ireland provides evidence of how the Army learned and adapted to the complex, dynamic political environment, and an ever-evolving and very capable enemy.

The Army first deployed to Northern Ireland organized for conventional operations, equipped with Saracen and Pig wheeled armored personnel carriers, very few helicopters, and little public order equipment and training. By 2007, the operations had evolved. Military and police coordinated effectively; the Army had a capable organic intelligence and surveillance capability; units at every level routinely planned and executed complex joint operations with the police, army, air force, and specialist agencies; routine tactics were based on bespoke specialist organizations; and the Army used specialist equipment, particularly for search, surveillance, counter-IED, and public order operations.[93]

This adaptation was supported by an equally responsive and effective training program, run by the Northern Ireland Training and Advisory Team (NITAT). NITAT's creation had an effect that was as important as that of the JWS in Malaya. NITAT's teams of hand-picked, experienced instructors would visit deploying units to run specialist training. Units would then complete training on urban close-quarter battle ranges and patrol training areas at Hythe in Kent, and then rural operations, which concentrated on foot patrolling, airmobile operations, and observation and surveillance skills in Norfolk.

By the mid-1980s, military operations had three roles—providing reassurance to the population, deterring acts of terrorism and public disorder, and the attrition of terrorists—and took one of three forms: covert, framework, and surge operations. A comprehensive pocketbook, similar to *ATOM*, contained all the planning data, tactics, and reports needed to conduct operations on the ground. The primary focus was intelligence gathering, principally through sophisticated police and Army covert operations. Framework operations provided the supporting infrastructure, and a visible presence on the streets to reassure the public and deter terrorism. Finally, surge operations reinforced framework operations by using mobile, predominantly helicopter-borne, reserves to respond to incidents or during periods of heightened tension, such as marching season. The similarities between this, the Callwell framework, and Malaya are obvious.

Aden provides an interesting counterpoint to Malaya and Northern Ireland. Its lessons are worth noting, not because they challenge conventional wisdom, but because they reinforce it. British strategy addressed none of the fundamentals of counterinsurgency successfully, in part or as a whole. There was no unified civil-military command, no effective intelligence (Brigadier R.C.P. Jeffries, the last brigade commander in Aden, considers "no [internal security] operations have ever before been carried out with so little operational information"[94]), no formalized predeployment training package,[95] and from 1966 only the bleak prospect of withdrawal to look forward to. Despite the final departure being almost perfectly executed, the overall campaign in Aden marked the low point of the British approach to counterinsurgency.

Britain had no easy options. As long as it needed the port of Aden to safeguard its oil supplies, Britain had to resist the rising tide of Arab nationalism in the region. This meant conducting an increasingly active counterinsurgency campaign in the colony, and in the protectorates that surrounded it. Plans for the smooth transition of power to the Federation of South Arabia were undermined by an increasing sense of Arab nationalism fueled by Egypt, by a frontier war with Yemen, and by an unsatisfactorily slow process of constitutional and political reform. All three exacerbated civil unrest and transformed previously limited tribal disputes into radicalized struggles against British imperialism.[96]

The British decision in 1966 to withdraw completely by 1968 removed any remaining rationale for its counterinsurgency campaign, and military operations concentrated on protecting immediate British interests. While the timetable for withdrawal was developed, the power struggle between opposing insurgent groups intensified,[97] further destabilizing the situation. Although Britain conducted a reasonably orderly withdrawal of its forces, none of the preconditions for transfer of authority, which had been established and achieved in Malaya, was met: the insurgencies were still gaining in strength, the Federation Armed Forces were not ready for security responsibilities, no competent government existed to take power, and the British support for the nascent Arab administration was removed.[98] Unsurprisingly, the Protectorate collapsed less than a year after the British departed.

Aden left little impact on counterinsurgency thinking except in the tactics for urban operations. The 1969 edition of *Counter-Revolutionary Operations* provided guidance on public order and riot control, based on the bitter struggles that took place in Crater. This guidance was applied on Northern Irish streets in the form of mass arrests, the use of teargas, and the use of armored cars. These methods had such significant drawbacks when used on the streets of the United Kingdom that they quickly became apparent, and within a year of the first deployment, the Army was working hard to find new tactics, and to bridge the gap between the rifle and the warning shot and teargas and batons.

Conclusion

The British Army's approach to counterinsurgency is built on a very strong small-wars heritage. The question is, however, just how relevant is all its experience and its doctrinal approach to contemporary insurgencies? Many argue that there has been such a profound change in the character of insurgency that those theories developed in the face of largely Maoist-inspired revolutions and insurgencies are no longer relevant today.[99] Yet the US military's return in 2006 to a classic population-centered approach in its doctrine, and put into practice most effectively in Iraq, would indicate that the classic influences that shaped it—Galula, Thompson, Kitson, and T.E. Lawrence[100]—were not as irrelevant as some observers may have thought. The British Army, as Bulloch observes, has been somewhat slower to develop its counterinsurgency doctrine than it has been to adapt in the field. For example, it took nearly 20 years to replace *Counter-Revolutionary Operations* with *Counter-Insurgency Operations*, despite ongoing operations in Northern Ireland. Although the fundamentals that underpin British doctrine are well founded and remain valid, the demands of counterinsurgency warfare mean that there can be no resting on the past. What might have been dismissed, not even ten years ago, as an irrelevant form of warfare is now one that defines the character of conflict in the first decade of the twenty-first century, and the problem at its heart essentially remains the same.

As British doctrine makes clear, "insurgency and counter insurgency are essentially about the battle to win and hold popular support, both at home and in the theatre of operations."[101] Britain's military operations in the first decade of the twenty-first century have started to define a new form of interventionist counterinsurgency: one where the key campaign instruments of executive and legislative authority—and where intelligence, over which Britain had previously been able to exercise direct control, or exert significant influence—are now the responsibility of independent sovereign countries. Britain's small-wars theory now finds itself in a new era, and it is having to evolve.

The drawbacks of the evolutionary approach to doctrine include the dangers of taking lessons from one campaign and applying them injudiciously to another. What Jeffries concluded, following Aden, remains prescient:

> Participation, especially by officers, in one or more IS operations in other parts of the world does not mean that they know all about things in a new theatre. A liberal dose of humility is essential, whilst making use of previous experience, to learn from the experience of others.[102]

Since there are clear indications that small wars will be a feature of the strategic environment for some time to come,[103] it is important that those charged with developing doctrine really understand the character of the problem and that they validate doctrine's principles or they discard them. British experience has produced a doctrine built on the fundamentals of minimum force, civil-military cooperation, intelligence, and learning and adaptation. When applied in full, these have met with success: when applied piecemeal, problems have followed. How the Army's doctrine will evolve in the light of Iraq and Afghanistan is not clear. What is certain is that its evolutionary approach has established firm foundations, which history and sound theory clearly indicate it would be unwise to disregard.

The issue for British counterinsurgency doctrine is not the extent to which time-tested principles remain valid. It is to understand that the strategic context in which they are now applied has changed. The themes are multinational alliance or coalition operations, based on a revisionary understanding of sovereignty and legitimacy, and on influence operations and the battle to win and hold popular support at home and in the theater of operations. The challenge for the doctrine writer will be to put these changes, and more, into context. Historical experience, and that gained more recently in the field, has a role to play in framing the principles and approach in a contemporary context. The question is not whether broad principles are relevant, but the extent to which those principles of British doctrine have been followed, resourced, and applied. Presence matters; numbers are required, and plans need resources. Without them, in counterinsurgency, securing the population is an unachievable aspiration.

Notes

1 Julian Paget lists 34 British counterinsurgency campaigns between 1945 and 1970. See Julian Paget, *Counter Insurgency Campaigning*, London: Faber and Faber, 1967, p.180.

2 See the introduction to Hew Strachan (ed.), *Big Wars and Small Wars: The British Army and the Lessons of War in the 20th Century*, London: Routledge, 2006, p. 6.

3 Charles Edward Callwell, *Small Wars: Their Principles and Practice*, Lincoln: University of Nebraska Press, 1896 (1996), p. 21.

4 Thomas R. Mockaitis, *British Counterinsurgency, 1919–1960*, London: Macmillan, 1990; Thomas R. Mockaitis, *British Counter-Insurgency in the Post-Imperial Era*, Manchester: Manchester University Press, 1995; Gavin Bulloch, "Military Doctrine and Counterinsurgency: A British Perspective," *Parameters*, Vol. 26, No. 2 (1996), 4–16; Ian Frederick William Beckett, *Modern Insurgencies and Counter-Insurgencies*, London: Routledge, 2001; and Ashley Jackson, "British Counterinsurgency in History: A Useful Precedent?," *The British Army Review*, No. 139 (2006).

5 Colin S. Gray, "Irregular Warfare: One Nature, Many Characters," *Strategic Studies Quarterly* (Winter 2007), 48.

6 Mockaitis, *British Counterinsurgency, 1919–1960*, p. 146.

7 Hew Strachan, "British Counter-Insurgency from Malaya to Iraq," *RUSI Journal*, Vol. 152, No. 6 (2007), 9.

8 The War Office published a report by that title—*Keeping the Peace (Duties in Support of the Civil Power)*—in 1957 and in 1963. *Keeping the Peace* was the detailed field manual that defined duties in support of the civil power and antiterrorist procedures, and provided detailed information on basic principles of English law, conduct of internal security operations, operational tasks and roles of security forces, air support, intelligence, and psychological and public relations aspects of internal security operations.

9 Brig. Gavin Bulloch (Retd), MBE was the Army's principal doctrine writer at the Directorate of Doctrine and Development at Upavon, Wiltshire, between 1994 and 2008. He was responsible for the Army Doctrine publications series, the Army's field manual, in particular the 1996 and 2001 editions of *Counter-Insurgency Operations*. Bulloch's contribution to British counterinsurgency doctrine from 1992 to 2008 is significant.

10 Charles Gwynn, *Imperial Policing*, London: Macmillan, 1939, p. 6.

11 Maj. Gen. Tony Jeapes records that the Oman campaign "took place under conditions of secrecy which today would probably be impossible to achieve. The Labour Government of the time was trying to disengage from Britain's residual colonial commitments, and to admit that some of its troops were engaged in the biggest campaign in which British troops had been involved since Korea would have been embarrassing." See Tony Jeapes, *SAS Secret War*, London: William Kimber, 1980 (republished HarperCollins, 2000), p. 11.

12 Mockaitis, *British Counterinsurgency, 1919–1960*, pp. 13–14. These were included in the 1996 edition of counterinsurgency doctrine as the "broad fundamentals of doctrine developed and adapted by the British for counter insurgency." Army Field Manual, Vol. V, "Operations Other Than War," Section B. *Counter-Insurgency Operations*, London: Prepared under the direction of the Chief of the General Staff, 1996, p. i.

13 Learning and adaptation, and their institutional implications for armies, are the central theme in John Nagl's comparison of British and American counterinsurgency approaches in Malaya and Vietnam. See John A. Nagl, *Learning to Eat Soup with a Knife: Counterinsurgency Lessons from Malaya and Vietnam*, Chicago: University Chicago Press, 2005.

14 Paget, *Counter Insurgency Campaigning*, pp. 163–4.

15 Army Code 71749, Army Field Manual, Vol. I, "Combined Arms Operations," Part 10. *Counter-Insurgency Operations (Strategic and Operational Guidelines)*, London: Prepared under the direction of the Chief of the General Staff, July 2001, p. B-6-2. Henceforth referred to as *Counter-Insurgency Operations*.

16 Callwell, *Small Wars*; Gwynn, *Imperial Policing*; Robert Thompson, *Defeating Communist Insurgency: The Lessons of Malaya and Vietnam*, New York: Praeger, 1966; Frank Kitson, *Low Intensity Operations: Subversion, Insurgency, Peace-keeping*, London: Faber and Faber, 1971.

17 *Counter-Insurgency Operations* was revised in March 2007 to better reflect the realities of Iraq and Afghanistan. It retained the principles developed in the 1990s and derived from Kitson and Thompson. The list of official doctrine includes *Keeping the Peace (Duties in Support of the Civil*

Power), London: The War Office, 1957 and 1963; "Land Operations," Vol. III, *Counter-Revolutionary Operations*, Part I, "General Principles," London: Prepared under the direction of the Chief of the General Staff, 1969, revised 1977; Army Field Manual, Vol. V, "Operations Other Than War," Section B, *Counter-Insurgency Operations*, Part 2; *The Conduct of Counter-Insurgency Operations*, London: Prepared under the direction of the Chief of the General Staff, 1995; and *Counter-Insurgency Operations*, 2001.

18 *Counter-Insurgency Operations*, p. B-3-1.

19 Gen. Sir Frank Kitson was the most important twentieth-century British *military* thinker in the field, publishing the widely acclaimed *Low Intensity Operations* and *Bunch of Five*, both based on his operational service in Kenya, Malaya, Cyprus, and Northern Ireland. After publishing *Low Intensity Operations*, Kitson's influence spread through the School of Infantry, where he was commandant; the Staff College, again where he was commandant; and the United Kingdom Land Forces, where he was a brigade and divisional commander and, eventually, commander-in-chief. Frank Kitson, *Bunch of Five*, London: Faber and Faber, 1977, p. 283.

20 *Counter-Insurgency Operations*, p. B-3-1. The issue of intellectual fashion was to prove central in the debate surrounding the development concepts and the Doctrine Centre's proposals concerning *Countering Irregular Activity* during 2006–7. Its inability to establish a workable intellectual foundation, and the authors' determination, even if their ideas were sound, to relegate counterinsurgency to being a subset of stability operations, in contrast to the position adopted by the US Army and US Marine Corps, failed to gather the broad support needed.

21 Ibid., p. A-2.

22 Ibid., p. B-2-1.

23 "[T]he approach will differ from country to country [and should take] account of local circumstances and the analysis of the type of insurgency faced." Ibid., p. B-3-3.

24 Gen. Sir Frank Kitson, interview with Paul Melshen, January 8, 1986, quoted in quoted in Paul Melshen, "Mapping out a Counterinsurgency Campaign Plan: Critical Considerations in Counterinsurgency Campaigning," *Small Wars & Insurgencies*, Vol. 18, No. 4 (2007), 667.

25 Joint Warfare Publication 0-01, British Defence Doctrine (2nd edn), Prepared under the direction of the Chiefs of Staff, October 2001, p. 1-1.

26 *Counter-Insurgency Operations*, 1996, p. 1-2.

27 For example, see Ian F.W. Beckett, *Insurgency In Iraq: An Historical Perspective*, Carlisle Barracks, PA: Strategic Studies Institute, 2005, p. 16. Michael Crawshaw, *"Running a Country": The British Colonial Experience and its Relevance to Present-Day Concerns*, Shrivenham: Defence Academy of the United Kingdom, The Shrivenham Papers, No. 3, 2007. Thomas G. Mahnken, "The British Approach to Counter-Insurgency: An American View," *Defense & Security Analysis*, Vol. 23, No. 2 (2007), 227–32.

28 Robert Cassidy, "The British Army and Counterinsurgency," *Military Review*, Vol. 85, No. 3 (2005), 58.

29 Rod Thornton goes further, suggesting that it "informs virtually all of the actions carried out by the British in COIN operations . . . The principle is far more deeply rooted and therefore quintessentially a guiding philosophy for British COIN techniques." Rod Thornton, "Historical Origins of the British Army's Counterinsurgency and Counterterrorist Techniques," in Theodor H. Winkler, Anjah Ebnöther, and Matsb Hansson (eds), *Combating Terrorism and its Implications for the Security Sector*, Stockholm: Swedish National Defence College, 2005, p. 28.

30 *Counter-Insurgency Operations*, p. B-3-14.

31 Srinath Raghaven, "Protecting the Raj: The Army in India and Internal Security, c. 1919–39," *Small Wars & Insurgencies*, Vol. 16, No. 3 (December 2005), 257.

32 Ibid., 258.

33 British Government despatch to the Government of India, cited in Valentine Chirol, *India Old and New*, London: Macmillan, 1921, emphasis added.

34 Hew Strachan, *The Politics of the British Army*, Oxford: Oxford University Press, 1997, p. 169.

35 Thornton, "Historical Origins of the British Army's Counterinsurgency and Counterterrorist Techniques," 43.

36 James S. Corum, "The Myth of Air Control: Reassessing the History," *Aerospace Power Journal* (Winter 2000), 61.

37 Bruce Hoffman, *British Air Power in Peripheral Conflict 1919–1976*, Santa Monica, CA: Rand Corporation, 1989, p. 13.

38 Sir John Bagot Glubb, quoted in Charles J. Dunlap, Jr, "Air-Minded Considerations for Joint Counterinsurgency Doctrine," *Air and Space Power Journal*, Vol. 21, No. 4 (2007), 65.
39 Gwynn, *Imperial Policing*, pp. 222–3, emphasis added.
40 Air Commodore Arthur Harris, Air Officer Commanding in Palestine, quoted in Corum, "The Myth of Air Control: Reassessing the History," 72.
41 Gwynn, *Imperial Policing*, p. 377.
42 Mockaitis, *British Counterinsurgency, 1919–1960*, p. 35.
43 Callwell, *Small Wars*, p. 41.
44 Ibid., pp. 131–4.
45 Ibid., p. 41.
46 Ibid., p. 23.
47 Ibid., p. 33.
48 Palestine 1936 and Waziristan 1937 are included in the 1937 edition. Charles Townsend notes that "most remarkably, Ireland [1916–21] was not included among the case studies [Gwynn chose]. Gwynn cryptically explained that he has 'thought it inadvisable' to draw on Irish experiences, however 'instructive form a military point of view,'" despite the fact that they would reinforce Gwynn's principles. Charles Townsend, "In Aid of the Civil Power: Britain, Ireland and Palestine 1916–48," in Daniel Marston and Carter Malkasian (eds), *Counterinsurgency in Modern Warfare*, Oxford: Osprey Publishing, 2008, p. 27.
49 Gwynn, *Imperial Policing*, p. 7. It is interesting to note that *Notes on Imperial Policing* (London: The War Office, 1934), an official military pamphlet, was also published the same year as Gwynn's book and may have been written by him (see Beckett, *Modern Insurgencies and Counter-Insurgencies*, p. 44). *Notes on Imperial Policing* reflects the pressures of the time, and explains the nuances of minimum force: "firing beyond [the point at which a crowd starts to disperse] with the ultimate object of impressing the population generally and discouraging rebellion in other localities should not be countenanced." Unlike Gwynn, it makes no reference to civil-military coordination: its focus is purely the military contribution, and it joins the tactics for dealing with rebel groups—today's insurgents—and the measures to deal with civil disturbances and riots, population control, and the imposition of martial law. Its principles also have themes doctrine would develop further: the provision of adequate forces and the necessity for offensive action, coordinated intelligence under military control, efficient intercommunication, mobility, and security measures.
50 Gwynn, *Imperial Policing*, p. 5.
51 Ibid., pp. 12–14.
52 Kitson, *Low Intensity Operations*, pp. 58–61.
53 Gwynn, *Imperial Policing*, p. 23.
54 Ian F.W. Beckett, "Robert Thompson and the British Advisory Mission to South Vietnam, 1961–1965," *Small Wars & Insurgencies*, Vol. 8, No. 3 (1997), 44.
55 Thompson, *Defeating Communist Insurgency*, p. 52.
56 Beckett, "Robert Thompson and the British Advisory Mission to South Vietnam, 1961–1965," 43.
57 Gavin Bulloch, "The Development of Doctrine for Counter Insurgency—The British Experience," *British Army Review*, Vol. 3 (December 1995) 23.
58 Bulloch notes that this edition of doctrine ("Land Operations," Vol. III, *Counter-Revolutionary Operations*, Part 1, "General Principles," 1969) had "the heavy scent of the jungle and rural operations in far away colonial territories" and it paid little attention to the Latin American insurgencies, "[not] even the communist/racist events in British Guiana (1964) or the UN sponsored operations in the Congo (Zaire) sparked any lessons for the future." Bulloch, "The Development of Doctrine for Counter Insurgency," 23.
59 Thompson, *Defeating Communist Insurgency*, p. 55.
60 The last principle, implicit in *Defeating Communist Insurgency*, was actually developed in 1994 by Bulloch at the suggestion of John Pimlott, one of the leading academics at the Royal Military Academy, Sandhurst, during the development of the first draft of what would be the Army's new counterinsurgency field manual. The principle first appeared as "Development of Long-Term Government Reforms to Prevent a Resurgence of the Trouble" in Army Staff College Operations Team, *Staff College Notes on Counter-Insurgency*, Camberley: Army Staff College, wpc4/ds, dated July 4, 1994, p. 26. Brig. Gavin Bulloch (Retd), interview with author, London, June 4, 2007.
61 Thompson, *Defeating Communist Insurgency*, pp. 111–14.

62 From a British perspective, David Galula has gone largely unnoticed. His realistic, often bitter view of counterinsurgency, based principally on his experience in Algeria 1956–8, identifies the fundamental importance of securing and protecting the population, gaining its support, and then acquiring information to identify and locate insurgents in order to defeat the insurgency. Galula's laws and principles focus on the centrality of the population. This is the concept that is the foundation of the approach in FM 3-24, and there is an explicit link from that doctrine to the articles and policy papers that support and explain the current operational concept in Iraq. See David Galula, *Pacification in Algeria 1956–1958*, Santa Monica, CA: Rand Corporation, 1963, 2006 edn; and *Counterinsurgency Warfare: Theory and Practice*, Westport, CT: Praeger, 1966, reprinted 2006.

63 The US Army/Marine Corps Field Manual, *Counterinsurgency* (FM 3-24), pp. 5-18–5-25.

64 For example, Peter Mansoor, "How The Surge Worked," *The Washington Post*, August 10, 2008, B07.

65 *Counter-Insurgency Operations*, pp. B-8-3–8-4.

66 Kitson, *Bunch of Five*, p. 281.

67 Kitson, *Low Intensity Operations*, p. 78.

68 Kitson had both developed and used unorthodox methods to develop intelligence, most notably in Kenya during the Mau Mau uprising, where he and a very small team created clandestine so-called countergangs to infiltrate and disrupt rebel gangs. See Frank Kitson, *Gangs and Countergangs*, London: Barrie and Rockliff, 1960.

69 Kitson, *Bunch of Five*, p. 29.

70 Ibid., pp. 290–1.

71 Frank Kitson, *Practical Aspects of Counter-Insurgency* (Kermit Roosevelt Lecture delivered May 1981), Upavon, Wilts.: Tactical Doctrine Retrieval Cell, Annex A to DCinC 8109 dated June 11, 1981, p. 5.

72 Kitson, *Low Intensity Operations*, p. 165, emphasis added.

73 Ibid., p. 166.

74 Kitson, *Practical Aspects of Counter-Insurgency*, p. 14, emphasis added.

75 Kitson, *Low Intensity Operations*, p. 57.

76 Ibid., p. 59.

77 Although there is no evidence that Kitson's model was followed directly. See Jeapes, *SAS Secret War*, pp. 41–2. More generally, John Akehurst, *We Won a War: The Campaign in Oman, 1965–1975*, Salisbury, Wilts.: M. Russell, 1982.

78 Director of Operations Malaya, *The Conduct of Anti-Terrorist Operations in Malaya*, 1952, republished with amendments 1954 and 1958, pp. III-5-6.

79 *Counter-Insurgency Operations*, p. B-3-11.

80 Ibid., p. B-5-3.

81 Daniel Marston, "Lost and Found in the Jungle: The Indian Army and British Army Tactical Doctrines for Burma, 1943–45 and Malaya, 1948–1960," in Hew Strachan (ed.), *Big Wars and Small Wars: The British Army and the Lessons of War in the 20th Century*, London: Routledge, 2006, pp. 84–114.

82 For a detailed examination of training at JWS see Riley Sutherland, *Army Operations in Malaya, 1947–1960*, Santa Monica, CA: Rand Corporation, prepared for the Office of the Assistant Secretary of Defense/International Security Affairs, September 1964, pp. 42–52.

83 Richard Stubbs, "From Search and Destroy to Hearts and Minds: The Evolution of British Strategy in Malaya 1948–1960," in Marston and Malkasian, *Counterinsurgency in Modern Warfare*, p. 125.

84 Director of Operations Malaya, *The Conduct of Anti-Terrorist Operations in Malaya*.

85 Ibid., p. 7.

86 War Office Code 9455, *Keeping the Peace (Duties in Support of the Civil Power)*, London: The War Office, 1957.

87 General Headquarters, East Africa, *A Handbook on Anti-Mau Mau Operations*, Nairobi: The Government Printer, 1954.

88 Ibid., p. 88.

89 Hew Strachan, "British Counter-Insurgency from Malaya to Iraq," *RUSI Journal*, Vol. 152, No. 6 (December 2007), 11.

90 Brig. Gavin Bulloch (Retd), interview with author, London, June 4, 2007.

91 "Land Operations," Vol. 3, *Counter-Revolutionary Operations*, Part 1, "General Principles," London: Prepared under the direction of the Chief of the General Staff, 1969, revised 1977.

92 John Kiszely, "Learning About Counterinsurgency," *RUSI Journal* (December 2006), 18. Rod Thornton goes further, arguing that the Army's failure to capitalize on that experience, and get its initial approach right, resulted in mistakes that in turn embroiled it in an avoidable counterinsurgency campaign. See Rod Thornton, "Getting it Wrong: The Crucial Mistakes Made in the Early Months of the British Army's Deployment to Northern Ireland—August 1969 to March 1972," *Journal of Strategic Studies*, Vol. 31, No. 1 (February 2007), 73–107.

93 For a detailed, contemporary assessment of military operations in Northern Ireland, see Richard Iron, "Britain's Longest War: Northern Ireland 1967–2007," in Marston and Malkasian, *Counterinsurgency in Modern Warfare*, pp. 167–84.

94 R.C.P. Jeffries, "Operations in Aden—Some Infantry Lessons," *The Infantryman*, No. 84 (November 1968), 19.

95 Jonathon Walker notes that "most infantry units arrived for a six-month tour and left together, taking their knowledge of the deserts, mountains or back streets with them: there were hand over periods but these were inevitably short." See Jonathon Walker, *Aden Insurgency: The Savage War in South Arabia 1962–67*, London: The History Press, 2005, p. 165.

96 For a detailed explanation of how British policy to contain Egyptian influence in Aden and South Arabia failed see Spencer Mawby, *British Policy in Aden and the Protectorates 1955–67: Last Outpost of a Middle East Empire*, London: Routledge, 2005.

97 The Front for the Liberation of South Yemen (FLOSY) and the National Liberation Front (NLF), both supported by Egypt, and both had political and terrorist wings.

98 See Peter Hinchcliffe, John T. Ducker, and Maria Holt, *Without Glory in Arabia: The British Retreat from Aden*, London: I.B. Tauris, 2006.

99 John Mackinlay, *Defeating Complex Insurgency: Beyond Iraq and Afghanistan*, London: RUSI, Whitehall Paper No. 64, 2005; David Kilcullen, "Counterinsurgency Redux," *Survival*, Vol. 48, No. 4 (Winter 2006); Steven Metz, *Rethinking Insurgency*, Carlisle Barracks, PA: Strategic Studies Institute, 2007.

100 Particularly T.E. Lawrence, "The 27 Articles of T.E. Lawrence," *The Arab Bulletin*, August 20, 1917.

101 *Counter-Insurgency Operations*, p. B-3-1.

102 Jeffries, "Operations in Aden—Some Infantry Lessons," 19.

103 Steven Metz, *The Future of Insurgency*, Carlisle Barracks, PA: Strategic Studies Institute, 1993, and *Rethinking Insurgency*; Colin S. Gray, *Another Bloody Century: Future Warfare*, London: Weidenfeld and Nicolson, 2005; Thomas X. Hammes, *The Sling and the Stone: On War in the 21st Century*, St Paul, MN: Zenith, 2006; Mackinlay, *Defeating Complex Insurgency*; Rick Brennan et al., *Future Insurgency Threats*, Santa Monica, CA: Rand Corporation, 2005.

4 Germany

Timo Noetzel

Afghanistan has fomented an intense debate among NATO members. What are the right lessons to take away from the International Security Assistance Force (ISAF)? Germany is at the heart of this debate. As one of the largest military partners within NATO and the third-largest contributor to the overall ISAF-operation it has developed and adopted its own distinctive position.

At its heart the debate within NATO is about the nature of the campaign in Afghanistan. The conflict can be seen as a placeholder for the alliance's future orientation. Should the focus of ISAF be on conducting counterinsurgency, counterterrorism, or stability operations in Afghanistan? If the Atlantic Alliance were to wage a counterinsurgency campaign, it would need to concentrate on protecting the Afghan population and contribute toward strengthening basic services for the Afghan people. It consequently would need to define the indigenous population as the operational center of gravity, it would need to intensify efforts toward supporting the Afghan government, and it would need to integrate this non-kinetic focus with the use of force. An alternative view is that NATO should focus on counterterrorist tasks; i.e. it should focus on combating al-Qaeda and other terrorist groups in Afghanistan. Finally, the third perspective is based on a focus on stability operations. This perspective hinges on the understanding that ISAF force posture should be based on a neutral military presence. According to this perspective, ISAF should concentrate on taking steps against those disturbing peace, and military commanders must concentrate on mandate execution.

Germany's approach to the campaign in Afghanistan is rooted in this third perspective: ISAF is seen as a stability operation. It is a view shared by some continental European NATO members such as Spain and Italy, but thoroughly rejected by NATO members such as the United States, Great Britain, the Netherlands, or Canada, where the debate is whether ISAF should concentrate on counterinsurgency or counterterrorism. Those who are advocating a counterinsurgency approach argue that enemy forces need to be isolated from their support base by earning the support of the local population. Advocates of a counterinsurgency approach in Afghanistan are highlighting issues like economic prosperity, the build-up of infrastructure and the need for power-sharing deals with tribal elders as NATO's operational focus; whilst advocates of a counterterrorism approach argue in favor of concentrating on terrorist elements amongst the insurgency. In summary, whilst advocates of counterinsurgency are perceiving a "large footprint" of western forces as necessary, advocates of a counter-terrorism approach argue in favor of a "light footprint."

The German debate about participating in ISAF is shaped by consistent efforts of large portions of the German political establishment and public not to get involved in this intra-alliance debate about counterinsurgency versus counterterrorism, but to maintain the self-understanding of ISAF being a stability operation. In doing so, Germany's approach is dominated by an inward-looking security policy discourse. The roots of this particular German preference for stability operations can be summarized as follows. With the end of the Cold War, a "peace dividend" had emerged: only reduced military forces were now necessary, and the defense budget could be cut down.[1] The Bundeswehr would no longer need to prepare to engage in large-scale, conventional warfare, but would primarily constitute a supportive element for civilian stabilization efforts: the military as an armed reconstruction assistant. Since then Bundeswehr participation in multinational military operations has seemed to confirm this post-Cold War framework for German strategic thinking: Somalia, the Balkans, the Congo operation, and the naval presence off the Lebanese coast—in all these military interventions active participation of German troops in combat could be avoided. One exception was the German participation in NATO air strikes against Serbia in 1999, but even in Kosovo the use of German ground troops was out of the question: German military presence was to serve as a stabilizing factor; i.e. military power had a largely political impact. Combat operations as part of the potential operational spectrum of the German armed forces seemed to have been relegated to history books.

Consequently, today, faced with a grown-up insurgency and an operation that was not only humanitarian, the German political leadership still understands its military involvement in the context of ISAF as a contribution to a stability and reconstruction effort rather than as counterinsurgency or counterterrorism. Such an understanding of the operation in Afghanistan is fueled by conceptual debate within the German defense establishment about the military conflicts Germany needs to prepare for. Again, this is a very inward-looking debate, particularly because post-World War II Germany has not experienced actual conventional military conflict, and in particular has no record of experience with unconventional wars. Within the German defense establishment the predominant view on its participation in Afghanistan is that this kind of theater engagement constitutes an exception or an aberration, but that it has no particular relevance as a reference point for future German conflict engagements. Willingness to learn from this conflict is limited to those who have strategic and operational command responsibility. Instead skepticism dominates within the German political and military establishment, regarding counterinsurgency in particular. Additional skepticism has, as with much about Germany, a historical source. A fear prevails within the defense establishment that an intensive German debate about the nature of counterinsurgency might touch upon the Wehrmacht's historical record of fighting against resistance movements, a legacy that is deeply connected to war crimes committed during World War II. Thus, the historical memory makes things all the more difficult for the Bundeswehr, a post-World War II institution, which in contrast to Germany's allies has indeed gained no operative and institutional experience in combating insurgencies at all.

The chapter proceeds in four steps. First, the political context to Germany's continuously growing engagement in post-Cold War multinational military operations, leading to its participation in ISAF, will be reviewed. Second, the state of German planning and doctrine for challenges such as the conflict in Afghanistan will be analyzed. Third, the strategic dimension to the ISAF operation will be provided; and fourth, there will be a discussion of the operational level of the German Afghanistan engagement. The chapter will conclude by discussing the potential of bottom-up innovation with operations guiding the development of strategy.

Operational experiences since World War II

Only in 1993, in the framework of Operation UNOSOM II (United Nations Operations in Somalia)—the mandate of which rested on Chapter 7 of the UN Charter—German troops were sent to Somalia, and into armed conflict for the first time since World War II. Bundeswehr soldiers were subject to restrictive rules of engagement and served in a purely "supportive" role: to provide an Indian infantry brigade with the necessary external framework for its operations. In 1995, the Bundeswehr operation in Bosnia followed (IFOR, later SFOR, presently Althea/EUFOR). Germany initially participated in Bosnia under an IFOR (Peace Implementation Forces) mandate from January 1996 with 3700 soldiers, and later under an SFOR (Stabilization Forces) mandate with 3000 soldiers. Its purpose was to contribute to the multinational effort to oversee the implementation of the peace treaty signed in Dayton. In 1999, the Bundeswehr then participated under the NATO-mandated Operation Allied Force with 14 Tornado fighter aircraft in the air war against Serbia. The German participation in Operation Allied Force constituted the first aggressive use of force by the Bundeswehr in its history. After the end of hostilities and an agreement between NATO and the republic of Yugoslavia was signed, KFOR (Kosovo Force)—again furnished with a Chapter 7 mandate— entered Kosovo with the German participation of a contingent of 8500 soldiers. The basis of the operation continues to be both a "robust" UN mandate and rules of engagement meant to guarantee the effectiveness of KFOR. Alongside supervision of the signed agreement, they involve above all a separation of the conflicting parties and a safeguarding of the recon- struction work in the stabilization phase.[2]

Thus, the record of the post-Cold War use of German force is clear. Deployments have been focused on stabilization operations largely relying on neutral military presences: troops were being assigned mandates that would allow them to take steps against those disturbing peace. Operational rules were designed explicitly to ensure mandate execution; military operations were to be focused on military support and subsidiary aid. Civil and military instruments were to be coordinated, but not integrated with each other.

The Bundeswehr's current engagement in Afghanistan had been initiated under similar premises. However, a crucial difference between the dynamics of the Kosovo and Afghanistan operations became clear in recent years: a difference between "neutral" stabilization and becoming party to the conflict due to the manifestation of an insurgency against the host government.[3] That is to say, in the framework of ISAF, the neutrality principle's borderlines increasingly have been dissolved. As a consequence of these changes in the operational environment even in the north of Afghanistan, the Bundeswehr is no longer just a force for peace but is fighting on the side of the Afghan government against an insurgency that is continuously gaining presence. ISAF's operational spectrum of tasks goes far beyond those that characterize mere stabilization operations. In the daily operational reality, commanders are continuously confronted with the difficult task of combining combat operations with stabilization and reconstruction efforts into an integrated and joint strategic and operational approach. It is the Bundeswehr's belated experience of what Charles Krulak once famously called the "three block war."[4] This complex operational spectrum is the decisive new devel- opment now facing the German Army in Afghanistan.

However, as mentioned, the overall view within the German defense establishment is that the current engagement in Afghanistan does not represent an indicative model for the future of Bundeswehr deployments. There is much institutional resistance against making resources available for counterinsurgency and reducing conventional warfare capabilities. Urgent requirements for the Afghan operation are identified but cannot be fully met until the next decade. In particular, this includes transport and combat helicopters, light infantry, and security force assistance capabilities. Consequently, official German defense planning acknowleges that the capability for theater engagements of those German army units, which conceptually are assigned for conducting operations against insurgents, realistically can only be enhanced in a "long-term perspective."[5] The build-up of capabilities for the conduct of small wars is not seen as an issue of priority.

In the German political and strategic debate an impression is often conveyed that, in the context of the war in Afghanistan, stabilization and peace enforcement can be separated from offensive combat operations against insurgent groups in a clear-cut way. However, what can actually be observed is a fluid transition from one operational scenario to the other. The qualitative leap is taken with the emergence of one or several well-organized insurgency groups that pursue political ends with military force. In view of such challenges, stabilization efforts, largely relying on a neutral military presence with flanking civilian reconstruction measures, are clearly limited to only one part of the operational spectrum. The German land forces, therefore, have the difficulty of adapting to a situation that has developed all across Afghanistan at least six years after the Bundeswehr began its engagement there.

The Afghanistan test

In Afghanistan NATO is a party to the conflict. Particularly in the German debate, this issue and resulting implications have remained largely unaddressed so far. Northern Afghanistan, where German soldiers operate predominantly, is still marked by relatively high levels of security even in 2009, particularly when compared to the rest of the country. At the same time, the security situation is steadily deteriorating and no longer stable. However, regardless of the development of the security situation on the ground, a defensive operational military deployment in the context of ISAF remains an uncontested dogma of German politics. The Bundeswehr's Afghanistan engagement continues politically to be based on this understanding. Thus, the German defense debate continues to emphasize a German "post-conflict reconstruction" effort in Afghanistan, a terminology that is designed to avoid the impression that German forces are involved in a war-fighting operation.[6] In the German view, the Anglo-Saxon debate about counterinsurgency concepts overstates the military dimension of the Afghanistan operation. The internal German discourse is heavily framed by a political elite that is fixed on the dogma that the Bundeswehr is not and should not be fighting a "war." By necessity, in order to maintain this kind of strategic discourse, the German debate often has to downplay the high level of violence Afghanistan is experiencing. Acknowledging the growing Afghan insurgency would undermine the paradigmatic German insistence on "progress" being made in northern Afghanistan and on the success of German efforts in the north in recent years in particular. It would also require a readiness to use force offensively within the context of the ISAF operation, for which political consensus is lacking. The term "post-conflict" also conveys a particular German understanding that civilian instruments will not be applied within the framework of ongoing military operations, and civilian and military means will remain separated rather than becoming merged in order to form a truly integrated strategy. Due to this particular framing of the operation, the German political narrative of the country's contribution to ISAF being largely a civilian reconstruction effort, with German forces correspondingly only being engaged for the sake of nation building, remains relatively stable. For years politicians have insisted that the German design of NATO's comprehensive approach, *vernetzte Sicherheit*, constitutes an example to be followed by others. To now concede that northern Afghanistan has also been pulled into the Afghanistan-wide downward spiral would be a confirmation that Germany, with its particular civilian post-conflict reconstruction effort, has not been more successful than others.

In the current German political climate this would be highly risky. Opinion surveys have consistently chronicled a steady decline in support for the ISAF operation; it is debatable how

Germans will react if the security situation worsens, and it remains to be seen how German politics would react to a high level of combat fatalities such as those suffered by French paratroopers as the result of a single ambush east of Kabul in 2008. Because of this insecurity about the stability of the national polity, German debate remains nervous and inflexible about the nature of the conflict in Afghanistan. Moreover, the country seems unable to change this political situation. The German Army's engagement in Afghanistan rests on a fragile consensus. Strategic decision makers in Berlin confront an increasingly skeptical domestic audience with regard to the ISAF mission. Furthermore, the government's room for maneuver is limited by the need to maintain parliamentary support for the Afghan operation. German lawmakers are aware of the prevailing German culture of restraint, and thus refrain from endorsing strategic thinking about the nature of the ISAF operation.

The avoidance process at work here has shaped the German debate about the Bundeswehr's operation in Afghanistan. Were the German political class to acknowledge the critical development of the conflict in Afghanistan, and were politicians to discuss the real operational challenges the Army is confronted with, then presumably the debate in Berlin about Germany's role could begin to connect both with developments on the ground and intra-alliance debate in Brussels. It is a debate that is urgently needed, especially since in the past two years insurgents have succeeded in bringing more and more parts of Afghan territory under their control. Over time, these developments will have a profound impact on German operations in northern Afghanistan. Politically, however, there is no preparation being made for what is on the horizon. Instead the German debate continues to revolve around the understanding of *vernetzte Sicherheit*. Politicians and experts in Germany had been convinced that the concept was an innovative contribution to NATO's dispute on how to succeed in Afghanistan. By now, due to the consistent reluctance to acknowledge the downward trend in Afghanistan over the last few years, it is almost impossible to start a debate about this negative conflict spiral and what actually needs to be done in Afghanistan. There is indeed no substantial argument in domestic political debate that the German approach to the ISAF mission is in need of fundamental revision and that the Bundeswehr needs a proper counterinsurgency strategy; let alone a debate about the need for lessons learnt from the Afghanistan operation to be implemented at ministerial or force levels.

The state of strategic planning for small wars

According to German policy documents such as the Defense Policy Guidelines of 2003[7] and the Defense White Paper of 2006,[8] which strongly influence the Bundeswehr's conceptual orientation and resultant force planning, the German armed forces' focus is on international conflict prevention, crisis resolution, and combating international terrorism. The military leadership has reacted to political directives, budget limitations, and operational experiences by developing a new force structure, based on a three-tiered categorization of the Bundeswehr into so-called intervention forces, stabilization forces, and support forces. The intervention forces are supposed to be trained and equipped for high-intensity operations; the stabilization forces are meant to be prepared for long-term operations of lower intensity. Stabilization forces are to be furnished with the same weapon systems as the intervention forces. Within this force structure, the mission of the support forces is to ensure the operational sustainability of the other two force categories. The status of forces is, for the most part, assigned at brigade level and is generally not variable.

According to German military planning, combating insurgents conceptually belongs to the stabilization forces' spectrum of tasks, and here mainly to the Division for Specialised Operations. Within this division, Airborne Brigade 31 is designated for fighting insurgents and, explicitly, for operations against irregular forces. Because of the demands tied to this, it consists almost exclusively of professional soldiers. The division is lightly armored and highly mobile. Thanks to high-quality infantry training, soldiers are in a position to cover a broad spectrum of tasks in operations. In addition, both their equipment and training allow them to support special operations forces. However, in view of the absence of a basic doctrinal conception covering the entire spectrum of tasks in counterinsurgency operations, the core focus of these forces continues to revolve around the use of force against insurgents. But combating insurgencies and the challenges of small wars require a fundamentally more comprehensive spectrum of capabilities for operations; kinetic capabilities alone are insufficient.

The concentration of force structure and doctrinal aspects on kinetic capabilities is a general weakness shaping German military policy; a weakness that stands in odd disharmony with the German political discourse about stabilization operations as discussed above. Despite a professed focus on reconstruction and peace support, the Bundeswehr's stabilization forces are conceived and equipped for a purely kinetic spectrum of tasks. Overall, the transformation of the German armed forces has not been accompanied by a balanced development of non-kinetic capabilities for operational scenarios such as those faced in counterinsurgency. In the context of the Bundeswehr's current operation in Afghanistan the result is an odd pairing of means and ends: a heavy reliance on force protection and large fortified bases with the goal of an "Afghanization" of the overall war effort. However, recent statements by defense officials indicate a slight change in this approach.

Consequently, so far only conceptual fragments for counterinsurgency exist within the German Army. Doctrinal documents of the German land forces underscore the lack of conceptual thinking on issues concerning unconventional operations. The "Heeresdienstvorschrift (HDv) 100/100—Truppenführung von Landstreitkräften,"[9] a which is the fundamental doctrine guiding German land forces, does not offer a comprehensive view on counterinsurgency for the German armed forces. Instead it merely confirms the political position that the core mission of the Army's stabilization forces is to conduct defensive, stability, and reconstruction operations. The document "Einsatzkonzept Operationen gegen Irreguläre Kräfte,"[10] which deals with operations against irregular forces, then claims that it constitutes an equivalent to the Anglo-Saxon counterinsurgency doctrine. This despite a heavy focus primarily on the kinetic part of military operations against irregular forces. That is to say, German concepts focus heavily on those means intended to neutralize enemy forces, whilst "non-kinetic" means—i.e. means to reach effects aimed at creating an operation environment which is inhospitable to enemy forces but conducive to overall operational aims—are paradoxically undervalued.

Thus, German doctrinal thinking differs fundamentally from the comprehensive counterinsurgency doctrines of allies such as the US or Britain. Allies' respective doctrinal documents stress the importance of population security, the training of local forces, the political nature of local operations, and other non-kinetic aspects, and they assume that all force elements engaged in the theater of operations should operate under the framework of a strategic approach guided by counterinsurgency principles. Such an approach stands in sharp contrast to current German Army thinking.

Reluctantly, the land forces staff has taken up the issue of irregular warfare and counterinsurgency and is currently, as of February 2010, working on a basic doctrinal document that has met considerable resistance within the defense establishment.[11] The aim is to initiate

German debate about small wars. But as is often the case, doctrinal innovation does not happen at home on desks in ministries and headquarters.

Afghanistan: strategic experiences

On the ground in Afghanistan the German contingent is increasingly being given tasks going beyond what German army doctrine covers. The gap between doctrine and operational reality is continuously growing. Above all in the areas of military assistance, security-sector reform and governance advice, Army units have been adopting consultative and support functions for Afghan officials. Thus, operational developments on the ground have moved beyond what doctrinal thinking had anticipated.

Widely recognized as the Bundeswehr's most difficult mission ever, in recent years the ISAF operation has increasingly called into doubt the established understanding of the armed forces' focus on stabilization. With ever-greater frequency, the operation has been shaped by attacks on Bundeswehr bases and units in northern Afghanistan. The Bundeswehr (and civilian actors) in northern Afghanistan now see themselves confronted with a well-organized insurgency that uses military force in pursuit of a political goal: the German withdrawal. The conflict situation in northern Afghanistan is increasingly affected by broader developments in the wider theater.

As an indirect result of the tactical successes of NATO in some areas of the country, insurgents have successfully regrouped themselves into widely independent cells, meanwhile carrying out suicide attacks and ambushes on ISAF troops and Afghan security forces. The insurgency makes use mainly of unconventional military tactics and means in order to embroil the technologically vastly superior NATO forces in a tedious war of political attrition and thus render the goal of stabilization impossible. In the German area of responsibility in northern Afghanistan they predominantly use remotely triggered improvised explosive devices (IEDs) against both patrols and convoys and sporadically attack bases with anti-tank missiles and improvised rockets, but have increasingly relied on suicide attacks and ambushes as well.

The historical record makes evident that insurgents are likely to succeed in this kind of "political war of attrition" against western forces. In the contemporary context of ISAF, prevailing against an insurgency such as the one in Afghanistan proves to be even more challenging as some countries engaged there seem to have the primary goal of finding an exit strategy. Debates about such "exit strategies" reinforce the insurgents' commitment to the fight since this means that it merely has to outlast western forces. Indeed, insurgents have usually been more successful than those combating them. The main reason for this is that time is on their side and they often enjoy or enforce the support of parts of the population. In addition the experience of Germany's allies has shown that counterinsurgency campaigns are protracted and are as a rule generally not lost militarily, but rather politically: when support for continuing the operation vanishes.[12]

At the same time, in the past media attention and the reluctance to lose soldiers have often led the German political leadership to prioritize the issue of force protection to an extent that, at times, has bordered on impairing operations on the ground. As mentioned above, the issue of political nervousness is a particular weak point of German participation in the ISAF operation. Broad portions of the German public are against expanding the military engagement in Afghanistan, or even maintaining it. But the historical record of small-war experiences of Germany's allies suggests that the Bundeswehr will have to stay in Afghanistan for some time to come and should expect greater losses. However, for any government such an operational scenario represents a burden rather than an opportunity for creative policy making, since in the short or medium term political, strategic, or operational successes will remain the exception rather than the rule. [13]

The intensively debated demands in German politics for an ISAF exit strategy from Afghanistan result from an impression that operational aims are unclear and that 'victory' will remain elusive. The perception in the German polity is that the Bundeswehr as an element of NATO sees itself confronted with an enemy that seems to have a profound understanding of how to exploit weak points of German strategic culture. The fear is that the "post-heroic" German society cannot muster the patience needed for a long-term operation such as this one.[14] Overall, the German debate about the need for a NATO exit strategy from Afghanistan is the expression of a deep-seated insecurity within German politics concerning the challenges faced in Afghanistan.

Afghanistan: operational experiences

Throughout the first few years of the Afghanistan engagement, military activities of the German ISAF contingent were widely limited to patrols with minimal troop strength, in the vicinity of bases with a focus on intelligence gathering and ensuring the security of garrisons. This pattern of operational activity remained sufficient until summer 2007, with civilian development and reconstruction programs making some progress. The situation in northern Afghanistan until then was considered relatively calm in comparison to that in the southern and eastern provinces. This phase ended in May 2007 with a suicide attack in the city of Kunduz in which three German soldiers were killed, accompanied by announcements on the Internet. Insurgents subsequently infiltrated the north, particularly the northwestern provinces of Faryab and Badghis. With an estimated strength of 300 men, they attacked small villages and police stations in districts throughout both provinces. At the same time they blocked the "ring road," the country's most important transportation link, which is also vital to ISAF logistics and connects Afghanistan's most important cities in a circle. Meanwhile, insurgent groups also infiltrated the area around Kunduz, making use of the so-called "Pashtun pockets," i.e. small villages on the fringes of Kunduz City where ethnic Pashtuns live in high concentration among the predominantly non-Pashtun population of northern Afghanistan. With the insurgency using these villages as bases to hide weapons caches and suicide attackers the security situation in the area has continuously deteriorated, with rocket attacks on Provisional Reconstruction Team (PRT) Kunduz and suicide attacks and ambushes on patrols and convoys continuously increasing.

Harekate Yolo II

The Bundeswehr reacted to the deteriorating security situation with a series of operations, Harekate Yolo II, carried out in the northwestern Afghan provinces of Faryab and Badghis in fall 2007, being by far the most important. By the time of the operation, various criminal groups either cooperating with the Taliban or steered by it had gained control of broad areas of both provinces, repeatedly attacking police posts. Afghan government representatives had been pushed out of the region, a Taliban shadow regime had been created through threats and open violence, and additional infiltration efforts were clearly on the agenda for the north. In the short term, Harekate Yolo II was aimed at bringing the region back under ISAF military control, and at proving to the civilian population that the Afghan government and ISAF could guarantee security. In the long term, the goal was to provide for regional security in an area in which militarily protected reconstruction assistance could be carried out and made visible. In its emphasis, Harekate Yolo II was an operation conceived from the start in terms of classical counterinsurgency goals. It was based on an equally weighted application of military and non-military means, and was conceived as unfolding over several months. The operation was led by the German ISAF regional commander north, Brigadier General Dieter Warnecke, who held the post from August 2007 to January 2008. The operation was carried out with troops from the Afghan Army and Norwegian and US combat units (the US contributed Embedded Training Teams, ETT), along with German support forces. It was quick and effective, allowing the United Nations Assistance Mission in Afghanistan (UNAMA) after the end of the operation to assess the region's security situation positively—in turn enabling both governmental organizations and NGOs to again take up their activities in the region.

What was intended to follow the application of military power in the framework of Harekate Yolo II was a process of reconstruction and development steered by the civilian side that would be long-term but also generate immediate results—a series of "quick-impact projects." But these projects were in fact never begun, the entire operation thus ultimately failing to bear the intended fruit. With the Bundeswehr itself not having significant reconstruction means at its disposal, it was dependent on the voluntary cooperation of civilian organizations; but in the absence of political support, the integration of civilian and military instruments into a shared operational plan remained illusory. For lack of this, the operation's success was dependent on voluntary decision-making processes in civilian organizations whose main goal is not—and never will be—to fight an insurgency. As a result, in the context of Harekate Yolo II the offensive intervention of ISAF troops and Afghan security forces was able to gravely weaken insurgents operating in the region. But although the operation's military dimension was relatively unproblematic, a prompt introduction of the civilian dimension—strictly separated as it was from its military counterpart—remained a patchwork affair. The chain of processes linking "shape, clear, hold, build" was broken in the middle. However, the effective, success-oriented application and integration of both civilian and military means is of crucial importance for the organization of counterinsurgency operations such as those in Afghanistan.

In addition to the difficulty of coordinating civilian and military capabilities, the operation suffered from the overarching problem that while the operation commanders' intention was set out—to defeat the Taliban in the region and then to provide security for the application of civilian reconstruction programs—German political and strategic support for the operation never materialized. Instead, forces were withdrawn from the region following the end of military operations in late 2007, which allowed the insurgents to slowly reassert control over the area. No civilian resources were made available for the operation and tight operational restrictions were imposed. Political reluctance to acknowledge Harekate Yolo II remained so great that the German army never conducted a comprehensive strategic assessment of the lessons to be learned and the operations impact on the region. Crucial conclusions that clearly needed to be drawn were buried instead. The operation was passed over in near silence by the German government, with neither its goals nor successes being explained to the public.[15] Very much to the contrary: due to nervousness about the political reception of large-scale offensive operational activities the aim of Germany's political and military leadership was to diminish the significance of its goals as much as possible. There was an explicit denial that the operation represented a new development in the Bundeswehr's Afghanistan engagement. Not least for this reason, Harekate Yolo II could not provide a starting point for the German debate.

The conduct of Harekate Yolo II made evident the difficulties German elites have with a strategic and operational thought that advocates the integrated application of civilian and military instruments. However, despite strong skepticism against counterinsurgency doctrine since 2007, Army planners have implemented a range of measures at an operational level that shows a remarkable conceptual evolution.

The Kunduz operation

In reaction to the deteriorating situation in Kunduz province, a region the size of 8000 km with 720,000 inhabitants, the German military leadership initiated a range of measures to counter the insurgency. Army Special Operations Forces (Kommando Spezialkräfte) were inserted into the area for special reconnaissance purposes against the insurgency network. Simultaneously, paratrooper units were sent to strengthen combat capabilities of the Kunduz garrison. In addition, a range of structural measures were implemented in order to transform force posture and to regain momentum.

In view of the large space and persistently weak central authority in Kabul, and specifically the limited reach of the PRTs in the provinces, in operational plans for Afghanistan drafted in 2007 German military planners advocated an approach that would put more emphasis on force presence amongst the Afghan population and in the provinces. The first step in this process was meant to be the introduction of provincial advisory teams (PAT) and temporary combat outposts as outposts of PRT Kunduz. The purpose of this measure was to contribute toward providing basic services for the Afghan population in the province and to extend the reach of political and military influence beyond the vicinity of the PRT. On February 23, 2008 the first German advisory team was set up in the province of Takhar, east of Kunduz province. This team was to have a maximum strength of 40, with the military share consisting of 35 soldiers; the combat outposts were to have around 20 soldiers. In comparison to the PRT, with a troop strength at its peak coming close to 800 soldiers, this constituted a significant conceptual development because it meant that military commanders were willing to reduce force protection, and medical and logistical standards of military bases, in order to gain more presence beyond the main bases. In many ways the PATs were meant to provide a mix of combat outposts and PRTs.

Like the PRT, a provincial advisory team is led jointly by a military officer and a repre-sentative of the German Foreign Ministry. Other officials come from the German Ministry of Development and the Ministry of the Interior, which are responsible for development cooperation with the Afghan government and building up the local police forces, respectively. In their basic conception, the advisory teams, similarly to the larger PRTs, are meant to advise provincial governors and intensify local efforts toward strengthening support for the national Afghan government. The combat outpost concept was initiated in order to enable theater commanders to dispatch patrols to districts threatened by the insurgency. The overnight presence of infantry units in these districts was meant to demonstrate to the Afghan people that ISAF forces were there to protect them against nighttime insurgency activities. The introduction of the advisory teams and the temporary outposts constituted a first step away from an approach that puts a near-absolute emphasis on force protection and logistical support for army units, thus making it impossible to deploy smaller units amongst the Afghan population for fear of increased individual risk for deployed soldiers.

A second step toward reorienting German force posture in the context of the Kunduz operation was based on the use of long-term military patrols into the various provinces. In view of Afghanistan's geographical realities and the bad condition of the road network, such patrols also contributed toward an enhanced force impact extending beyond the vicinity of army bases. Patrols not only served the purpose of demonstrating ISAF military presence to the population but also contributed to improved relations with local leaders and better reconnaissance. For the first time military forces were also meant to contribute to development efforts by identifying possible development projects. Information generated by patrols was meant to serve all participating German authorities with sufficient information for making decisions regarding aid projects, for instance in the framework of the provincial development funds. Overall, the introduction of long patrols provided a break with army thinking in at least two aspects. For the first time conventional force patrols were reaching far beyond the vicinity of bases; second, for the first time forces were directly contributing to development efforts.

The provincial development funds as integrated civilian-military funds in fact represent the third step of the reorientation of German force posture in northern Afghanistan since 2007. Provincial development funds are a common fund for onsite projects controlled by various ministries: foreign affairs, defense, interior, and development. The idea is that German representatives and responsible Afghan bodies decide jointly on the use of the funds. One of its paramount purposes is to sharply increase the flexibility and effectiveness of development efforts. At the same time, there is a desire to underscore the basic principle of "Afghan ownership": that in development projects the Afghan side is deeply involved in the process of decision making, planning, and execution. The introduction of provincial development funds provided a serious effort by the German government to better harmonize civilian and military efforts in the context of ISAF.

So-called "key-leader engagements" constitute the fourth aspect of the reorientation of force posture. These are, in effect, structured meetings held by military and civilian representatives at all levels with important regional and local leaders; in this way contacts are cultivated and information is exchanged. Key-leader engagement is crucial for influencing and shaping Afghan opinion—and for informing the populace of pending military operations in sufficient time. To have effective meetings requires detailed planning, and a suitable supportive apparatus that has not yet been established within the structures of the military leadership of the operational contingents. Instead, the commanders' political and cultural consulting presently takes place on the basis of structures formed in an ad hoc manner. However, the concept of key-leader engagements provides for a rethinking of the value of non-kinetic capabilities in the context of the ISAF operation.

A final contribution to efforts to counter the insurgency in the Kunduz area was the introduction of operational mentoring and liaison teams (OMLT) as security force assistance units to build up the Afghan Army. In recent years German forces have significantly increased their efforts to build up the Afghan Army through joint and combined operations and patrols. Force integration training as an instrument to strengthen Afghan capabilities was a completely novel concept for an army that has no experience or capabilities for military assistance efforts. However, within the context of the ISAF operation it has become more and more significant as an operational instrument.

Thus, German thinking on counterinsurgency on the ground is more creative than the debate in Berlin. Advisory teams and combat outposts, key-leader engagement and provincial development funds are innovative instruments developed because of demand on the ground. Willingness in Berlin to use these lessons and institutionalize them is growing, but it is operations that are guiding the development of strategy and not—as it should be—the other way round.

Conclusion

German counterinsurgency doctrine is evolving in Afghanistan. Due to the deteriorating security situation, force elements that have been deployed in the context of ISAF are implementing urgently needed changes on the ground and are pressing for institutional, doctrinal, and operative changes of army thinking as a result. De facto, the deteriorating security situation is generating German counterinsurgency doctrine from the bottom up. Commanders returning from service in Afghanistan are pushing for the institutional army to deal with the new operational realities. As a result of this, gradually, there is recognition that German politics will have to adapt the Bundeswehr to unconventional warfare. Efforts are being made to write doctrine but also to increase institutional capability for counter-insurgency operations. However, obstacles remain to developing effective German counterinsurgency capability. Particularly, the political leadership of the Bundeswehr does not want to concern itself with a far-reaching debate about German counterinsurgency strategy.

It has been the policy of successive German governments to leave the fight against the Taliban and other enemy forces in the Afghan conflict theater predominantly to US forces within the framework of Operation Enduring Freedom (OEF). In 2008 the Bundestag even discontinued the German Army's participation in OEF in Afghanistan, limiting it to ISAF. This mantra of strategic communication by successive German governments, as well as most politicians in the German Parliament, nurtured the public's view that Bundeswehr units were predominantly support elements for civilian development efforts toward rebuilding Afghan society. The overwhelming notion still prevailing in domestic German strategic debate is that fighting wars belongs to Germany's political past. Yet, in the face of the evolving insurgency in Afghanistan such an understanding of the operational spectrum of the German military inhibits Germany's capacity to adapt to the alliance's counterinsurgency efforts in Afghanistan. But Germany's reluctance to confront realities in Afghanistan is having an unintended political side effect on the development of the overall NATO operation: indirectly, the German reluctance to translate operational lessons learned in Afghanistan into a German position in NATO is contributing to the Americanization of the overall war effort in Afghanistan. Germany might inadvertently contribute to a divide in the alliance—a divide at the strategic level into those who fight and those who do not—even though German soldiers on the ground are facing up to combat and a constantly deteriorating security situation. In light of the German position on ISAF, those advocating a counterinsurgency approach in Afghanistan perceive the German political understanding of the ISAF operation as too static and ignorant of developments on the ground in Afghanistan.

Notes

1   Timo Noetzel and Benjamin Schreer, "Ende einer Illusion. Die sicherheitspolitische Debatte in Deutschland macht einen großen Bogen um die Wirklichkeit," *Internationale Politik*, Vol. 63 (January 2008).
2   On Kosovo see Alister Miskimmon, "Falling into Line? Kosovo and the Course of German Foreign Policy," *International Affairs*, Vol. 85, No. 2 (March 2009). On Bosnia see Hanns W. Maull, "Germany in the Yugoslav Crisis," *Survival*, Vol. 37, No. 3 (Winter 1995/1996). For an overview Timo Noetzel and Benjamin Schreer, "All the Way? The Evolution of German Military Power," *International Affairs*, Vol. 84, No. 2 (March 2008).
3   Timo Noetzel and Martin Zapfe, "Aufstandsbekämpfung als Auftrag. Instrumente und Planungsstrukturen für den ISAF-Einsatz," *SWP-Studies*, Vol. 13 (2008), 7–8.
4   See Charles C. Krulak, "The Strategic Corporal: Leadership in the Three Block War," *Marines* (January 1999).

5   German Ministry of Defense, *Bundeswehrplan 2009*, June 2008. http://www.geopowers.com/ Machte/Deutschland/Rustung/Rustung_2008/rustung_2008.html#BwPlan2009DOK, last accessed July 5, 2009.
6   Timo Noetzel and Benjamin Schreer, "Counter-what? Germany and Counter-insurgency in Afghanistan," *RUSI Journal*, Vol. 153, No. 1 (February 2008), 44.
7   German Ministry of Defense, "Defense Policy Guidelines," Berlin, May 2003.
8   German Ministry of Defense, White Paper 2006 on "German Security Policy and the Future of the Bundeswehr," Berlin, August 2006.
9   German Ministry of Defense, "HDv 100/100—Truppenführung von Landstreitkräften," Bonn, November 2007.
10 German Ministry of Defense, "Einsatzkonzept Operationen gegen Irreguläre Kräfte (EinsKonzept OpIK)," Bonn, December 2005.
11 German Ministry of Defense, "KGv COIN—Konzeptionelle Grundvorstellungen zu Wahrnehmung militärischer Aufgaben im Rahmen von Counterinsurgency," May 2009 (preliminary version).
12 Gil Merom, *How Democracies Loose Small Wars: State, Society, and the Failures of France in Algeria, Israel in Lebanon, and the United States in Vietnam*, New York: Cambridge University Press, 2003.
13 Noetzel and Schreer, "Ende einer Illusion," 101.
14 Herfried Münkler, "Der Asymmetrische Krieg. Das Dilemma der Postheroischen Gesellschaft," *Der Spiegel*, 44 (October 27, 2008).
15 Robert Birnbaum and Hans Monath, "Bundeswehr operiert an der Mandatsgrenze," *Der Tagesspiegel*, November 8, 2007.

5   United States

Conrad Crane

The American Army that rolled into Iraq in 2003 had no counterinsurgency doctrine—or so received wisdom has it. But this is not entirely correct. In reaction to defeat in Southeast Asia, Army schools were directed to throw away their counterinsurgency files in the mid-1970s; but by the 1980s interest had returned because of conflicts in Nicaragua and El Salvador. This re-emergence of counterinsurgency doctrine was based upon an approach emphasizing only a small advisory footprint heavily dependent on Special Forces, instead of active or large-scale military intervention. The creation of a separate Special Operations Command in 1987 reinforced the lack of interest in counterinsurgency from American conventional forces. At the time of Operation Iraqi Freedom in 2003, the capstone US Army doctrinal manual, FM 3-0, *Operations*, only devoted one page to counterinsurgency, and the primary emphasis was on providing minimal support so that hosts could solve their own problems. Vietnam was highlighted as an example to avoid, because the high level of American support "undermined Vietnamese government authority and ARVN (Army of Vietnam) credibility."[1]

By the summer of 2004, the ongoing conflicts in Afghanistan and Iraq convinced Army leadership that new counterinsurgency doctrine was needed. Lieutenant Colonel Jan Horvath at the Combined Arms Doctrine Directorate at Fort Leavenworth was given the mission to fill the gap quickly, and in October 2004 he produced Field Manual (Interim) 3-07.22, *Counterinsurgency Operations*. The number indicated that the subject was seen as a subset of stability operations, and the interim designation meant that the publication would have to be replaced within two years. The 2004 manual was tactically oriented and was filled with specific tactics, techniques, and procedures for counterinsurgency.[2]

The scheduled revision of that interim field manual became the catalyst for the creation of FM 3-24, *Counterinsurgency*, in 2006. By the time Lieutenant Colonel Horvath created a new draft of FM 3-07.22 in late 2005, the Combined Arms Center (CAC) at Fort Leavenworth had a new commander, Lieutenant General David Petraeus, fresh from his second tour in Iraq. He had a vision to use Fort Leavenworth as an "engine of change" to make the Army an improved learning organization, better equipped to fight irregular wars as well as to handle any other assigned missions in an uncertain future. He expanded the Army's Lessons Learned programs to bring insights back from the field faster so they could be incorporated into education, training, and doctrine. Petraeus altered scenarios at collective training centers like Fort Irwin, California, to better reflect the complex realities of warfare in Afghanistan and Iraq. He changed the curricula for officer training to emphasize learning and adapting in irregular environments. And he planned to use the new counterinsurgency doctrine as another driver for these changes. He often used the chart depicted below to illustrate his vision.[3]

One of the most persistent proponents of new counterinsurgency doctrine was Lieutenant Colonel John Nagl, then serving as special military assistant to Deputy Secretary of Defense

An Engine of Change

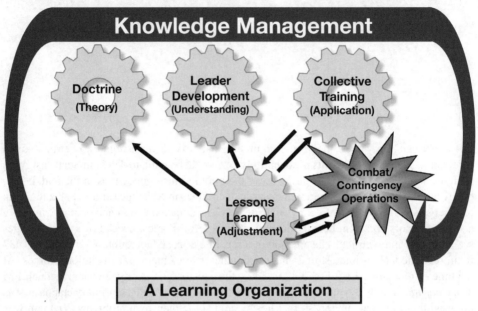

Figure 5.1 David Petraeus' graph to explain the organizational learning cycle

Paul Wolfowitz. After a meeting with Lieutenant General Petraeus in Washington at a Carr Center for Human Rights conference on irregular warfare in early November 2005, Nagl convened a small contingent at a bar that included Lieutenant Colonel Richard Lacquement, who became the author of the interagency chapter of the field manual, and Kyle Teamey, one of the future authors of the intelligence section. They developed an outline for new doctrine on a cocktail napkin.[4] In the meantime, the revision of the interim field manual had already begun, and Lieutenant General Petraeus sent the first draft out to some of his most trusted advisors in academe for comment. They returned poor reviews. Eliot Cohen, professor at the Nitze School of Advanced International Studies (SAIS) at Johns Hopkins University in Washington, urged a concerted effort to rewrite the manual completely. He suggested me as the lead author.[5] In 2002, I had been placed in charge of an Army War College project to develop a plan to rebuild Iraq if the Army was placed in charge of an occupation force after toppling Saddam Hussein. The resulting monograph had received much attention in the press for its prescience, and I had just given a presentation on the project for Eliot Cohen at a conference at SAIS.[6] I was also a West Point classmate of Lieutenant General Petraeus. We had been in the same military history class, and in addition we had overlapped as instructors at the Military Academy in the mid-1980s, he in the social sciences department and myself in history. We had met at the Carr Center conference in early November and talked about the new doctrine he was trying to create. At that time he asked me to review it. He called me on the evening of November 16 to offer me the lead role in rewriting the manual. He was correct that I could not turn down such a "big opportunity to make a lasting contribution,"[7] and General Petraeus is a hard man to say no to.

I also knew John Nagl from teaching at West Point, and I asked for him as the first member of the writing team and my main backup. He provided me with the outline from the napkin and was instrumental in putting together the Army participants for the team. But Lieutenant General Petraeus wanted this to be more than just a US Army product. He envisioned a joint and combined effort with the British and the US Marine Corps (USMC). Unfortunately the overburdened British doctrine writers could not keep up with the ambitious timeline for the project, which was to be completed in a year, though they were consulted often. However, Lieutenant General James Mattis, USMC, in charge of USMC Combat Development Command and responsible for their service doctrine, was in complete agreement with his Army counterpart, believing that new COIN doctrine was necessary and that future wars would require better learning military organizations. Mattis and Petraeus had served together in the Pentagon and Iraq, and had a terrific relationship. The creation of the new Army/Marine Corps COIN manual resulted from the fortuitous linkage of two soldier-scholars, with similar backgrounds and interests forged in the crucible of Iraq. They wanted to change their respective services and were given simultaneous assignments where they could make that happen.

The next week Lieutenant Colonel Horvath flew to the Army War College in Carlisle, Pennsylvania, to brief me on the project. In late November I flew out to Fort Leavenworth to return the visit and to get guidance directly from Lieutenant General Petraeus. The CAC commander was working on an article that would eventually be published in Military Review as "Learning Counterinsurgency: Observations from Soldiering in Iraq."[8] He wanted his insights incorporated into the manual, and all 14 observations eventually worked their way into Chapter 1. We also discussed the outline for the volume and the makeup of the writing team. It was very apparent to me that Lieutenant General Petraeus was going to be an active participant in the creation of the new doctrine, and we soon established a pattern of weekly, and sometimes daily, communications about the manual. Early on, we decided that counterinsurgency was too broad a theme to be subsumed under stability operations, and the new publication was renumbered as 3-24. Lieutenant Colonel Horvath was gracious about the transfer of primary authorship, and would continue to provide yeomen support to the project until he was assigned to the Counterinsurgency Academy in Iraq in mid-2006.

My first task when I returned home to Carlisle was to develop the central principles and tenets that would steer the doctrine. I reread noted counterinsurgency authors Trinquier, Kitson, and Thompson to get a sense of classic COIN theory,[9] while also looking at contemporary writers like Steven Metz and David Kilcullen.[10] The Marines sent me their latest writings on irregular warfare, and Dr Thomas McNaugher of the Rand Corporation generously offered help as well. Besides the writings of Lieutenant General Petraeus, the most influential article on the evolving doctrine would prove to be another from *Military Review*, this one by Major General Peter Chiarelli and Major Patrick R. Michaelis, which described the application of conceptual lines of operation in counterinsurgency.[11] In addition, FM 3-24 would build upon FM 3-0's model that all full spectrum operations consist of offensive, defensive, and stability components that commanders must combine in varying mixes to achieve desired end states. Kalev Sepp's historical analysis of best and worst practices for COIN was also important, and would eventually be summarized in a chart in the new field manual.[12]

John Nagl suggested the team read David Galula's *Counterinsurgency Warfare*, which was particularly enlightening.[13] Galula was probably the most influential "dead theorist" on the writers. The most important insights from his work that affected the new FM were that the "rules" of revolutionary war favored insurgents in an unfair fight, information operations permeated all aspects of counterinsurgency, military forces had to be prepared to do traditionally non-military missions in counterinsurgency, political actions were more important than military ones for lasting success, and it was essential for counterinsurgents to recognize an insurgency existed early and aim at its root causes.

Eventually the writing team agreed upon eight historically based Principles for counter-insurgency:

1   Legitimacy is the main objective.
2   Unity of effort is essential.
3   Political factors are primary.
4   Counterinsurgents must understand the environment.
5   Intelligence drives operations.
6   Insurgents must be isolated from their cause and support.
7   Security under the rule of law is essential.
8   Counterinsurgents should prepare for a long-term commitment.

The influence of Galula, Kitson, and Thompson is noticeable. The last principle came from the Marines. The first was emphasized in Tom McNaugher's contribution as well as in the Chiarelli-Michaelis article.[14]

The focus on legitimacy as the key goal meant that the new doctrine would be population-centric and not enemy-centric. While killing and capturing foes was still important, long-term success would come from gaining and maintaining popular support. But the writers had a lot to learn about what legitimacy meant. Early drafts of the manual relied upon a definition developed by Max Manwaring at the Army War College that was based very much on Western liberal values of political participation. Later revisions recognized that other factors, such as security concerns or religious beliefs, could shape local definitions of legitimacy. Determining those local attitudes is integral to the fourth principle, which would also help produce a radically different approach to military intelligence gathering.

I also proposed, and the writing team seconded, that there were other Imperatives of counterinsurgency that could be divined from observing contemporary conflicts. We eventually settled on five:

1   Manage information and expectations.
2   Use the appropriate level of force.
3   Learn and adapt.
4   Empower the lowest levels.
5   Support the host nation.

I was able to create an acronym of "MULES" with this set of ideas. The second imperative underwent the most revision, as there was debate about whether it should deal with "minimum" or "measured" force. Some American allies have doctrine emphasizing the use of the minimum possible force at all times, but Lieutenant General Petraeus himself took an active role in determining our final wording. The American concept recognizes that there are times when a show of overwhelming force may be useful, even if minimum necessary force is the general rule. These imperatives also highlight the importance of decentralization in a "mosaic war" that differs from town to town and province to province, the building of local institutions to sustain victory, and keeping popular expectations at a realistic level.

To better incorporate Lieutenant General Petraeus' observations, and to emphasize what was different about counterinsurgency from conventional operations, I also proposed a section on Paradoxes. While the writing team wholeheartedly endorsed it, it proved controversial among reviewers of drafts and the published manuscript. It has been described as "zen-like" by both supporters and critics of the manual.[15] The nine are:

1   Sometimes, the more you protect your force, the less secure you may be.
2   Sometimes, the more force is used, the less effective it is.
3   The more successful the counterinsurgency is, the less force can be used and the more risk must be accepted.
4   Sometimes doing nothing is the best reaction.
5   Some of the best weapons for counterinsurgents do not shoot.
6   The host nation doing something tolerably is normally better than us doing it well.
7   If a tactic works this week, it might not work next week; if it works in this province, it might not work in the next.
8   Tactical success guarantees nothing.
9   Many important decisions are not made by generals.

The section was heavily edited by senior officers in the final review, as they added many qualifiers to statements they thought were too dogmatic. For instance, the last paradox initially started with "Most." The intent of the section has always been to stimulate thought, not necessarily to prescribe actions.

The last addition to the list of paradoxes was the third item, which is a condensed version of a lengthy paper given to the writing team by Sarah Sewall, director of the Carr Center for Human Rights. Her involvement was a result of another initiative by Lieutenant General Petraeus, to solicit broad commentary and contributions for the doctrine. Once the Army/ Marine Corps writing team had its first solid draft completed, he convened a unique gathering at Fort Leavenworth to critique the product.[16] He personally approved the guest list which included representatives from the CIA, USAID, and State Department; analysts from important think tanks such as Michelle Flournoy; officers from other services and countries; leading academicians like Eliot Cohen; veterans of past and current conflicts; and media figures such as James Fallows, George Packer, and Linda Robinson. Sewall and her center co-sponsored the event, and she brought in a number of colleagues from the human rights community and NGOs. The conference featured open discussions with no holds barred, and active participation from Sewall and Lieutenant General Petraeus sitting up front. One opening presentation came from British Brigadier Nigel Aylwin-Foster, reiterating the themes of his controversial *Military Review* article about American failures to adapt to the requirements of COIN in Iraq.[17] After each author from the writing team described his or her chapter or appendix, a specially selected commentator, instructed to be particularly critical, would present a critique. Then the floor was opened to comments by all attendees. Everyone was instructed to submit post-conference comments via email, resulting in the writers receiving hundreds of pages of new ideas. All told, the gathering generated significant changes in the field manual.

After the conference, the structure and writing assignments for the manual were finalized, creating a true Army/Marine team effort. Generally, where one service had primary responsibility for a chapter, the other had a secondary reader assigned to review and comment. Lieutenant Colonel Nagl handled the introduction, where he emphasized the importance of learning and adapting. He also developed a reference bibliography to facilitate further study. I maintained primary responsibility for the foundation Chapter 1 on insurgency and counter-insurgency, with considerable input from Lieutenant General Petraeus. Because of the importance of non-military actors in counterinsurgency, Colonel Lacquement's chapter, "Unity of Effort: Integrating Civilian and Military Activities," was placed next.

Despite all the attention paid to Chapter 1, the heart of the manual is really Chapters 3, 4, and 5, which provide the foundation to plan and execute a counterinsurgency campaign. These chapters have also had the most impact on broader institutional doctrine. Chapter 3 incorporates sociocultural themes that have revolutionized the American approach to intelligence in counterinsurgency. It merges the COIN intelligence preparation of the battlefield developed by Kyle Teamey with cultural anthropological insights from Dr Montgomery McFate; these sections were shifted forward from an appendix after the February conference. This new focus has contributed to the development of Human Terrain Teams (HTT) deployed in the field and new courses and institutions at the Army Intelligence Center at Fort Huachuca, Arizona. Dr McFate, an anthropologist, was severely criticized by some who see her as compromising the standards of her profession in creating a "military-anthropology complex."[18]

This detailed analysis of society and culture lays the foundations for the most important contribution to the doctrine from the Marine Corps: Chapter 4, "Designing Counterinsurgency Campaigns and Operations." Marine Colonel Douglas King, with important contributions from Lieutenant General Mattis, wrote that section, a condition set by the Marines if they were to participate in drafting the overall doctrine. The idea that commanders needed to complete a systematic analysis of the problems they faced before developing a campaign plan was new to Army doctrine, as was the assertion that plans had to be continually adjusted in an iterative process as the situation changed. For the enemy-centric operations of the Cold War, the enemy and related defeat mechanisms were fairly standard and relatively easy to identify, but in the complex and murky world of counterinsurgency that is not the case. Campaign design has now become a standard part of all Army operational doctrine.

The necessary campaign activities identified during systematic analysis were to be executed along thematic logical lines of operation described in detail in Chapter 5. (Later doctrine identified them as "lines of effort.") Combat and civil-security operations remain important and serve as the cornerstone for sustained progress. When John Paul Vann described the challenges he faced conducting counterinsurgency in Vietnam, he remarked, "Security may be ten percent of the problem, or it may be ninety percent, but whichever it is, it's the first ten percent or the first ninety percent. Without security, nothing else we do will last."[19] But non-lethal mission sets will also be important. Necessary actions include spurring economic development, nurturing good governance, restoring or establishing essential services, and building host nation capacities in the security sector. When properly executed, the synergistic effect of the logical lines of operation reinforce each other and can shift the population's support from the insurgents to counterinsurgents. While establishing security facilitates re-establishing essential services, the opposite can also be true. Picking up trash removes possible hiding positions for improvised explosive devices (IEDs), and, as people become convinced that supporting COIN can improve their lives, they will tend to produce more intelligence on further attacks. The figure below depicts in graphic form the application of such logical lines of operation.[20]

A series of information activities link and surround all the logical lines of operation. In counterinsurgency, perception is often more important than reality in shaping people's attitudes. Insurgents have the advantage in the information arena, since they are unconstrained in making promises about what they would accomplish if they were in power. The counterinsurgent, meanwhile, must produce actual results, with words matching deeds. Furthermore, counterinsurgents must consider the informational impact of their actions on many audiences. These audiences include international, regional, and local civilian populations. Additionally, friendly military forces must be kept informed, even while an information campaign is directed at the enemy. For Americans especially, maintaining home front support is a key

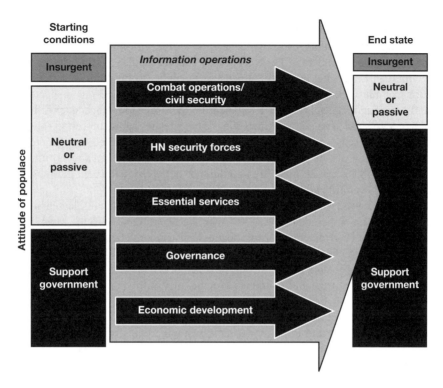

Figure 5.2 Logical lines of operation

factor. Finally, messages to all these audiences must be consistent. In today's globalized information environment, the local populace has access to the Internet or satellite television to monitor the messages being transmitted to the international community and the US public. Any perceived inconsistency reduces credibility and undermines counterinsurgency efforts.

The Marines made significant contributions to Chapter 5. Lieutenant Colonel Lance McDaniel, USMC, built upon a foundation provided by Lieutenant Colonel Horvath to elaborate on moving from campaign design to planning and execution. The chapter "Executing Counterinsurgency Operations" emphasizes a "clear, hold, build" approach to achieve permanent results. Too often in the early phases of the Afghanistan and Iraq campaigns, gains were sacrificed because coalition forces left areas instead of securing them, allowing the enemy to return. While some other alternatives such as "combined action" and "limited support" are mentioned, they receive less detailed treatment. The field manual encourages originality and innovation tailored to fit the unique local situations of the mosaic war that counterinsurgency is, and units in the field have developed other ways to pursue logical lines of operations. In the Diyala Province of Iraq, Colonel David Sutherland pursued a strategy of "establish presence and influence." When surge activities in Baghdad drove insurgent forces into Diyala, Colonel Sutherland found that he did not have sufficient troops to conduct "clear, hold, build." Instead, he established a strong position using offensive strikes, and then used a combination of coercion and incentives to convince local leaders to support counterinsurgency efforts. Though his unit suffered casualties, the strategy worked to keep the enemy on the run.[21] As part of the mandate to create a better learning organization, FM 3-24 will begin a revision soon, and Chapter 5 will require expansion to reflect such alternative approaches.

Chapter 6, "Developing Host Nation Security Forces," highlighted the differences between idealistic and pragmatic views of counterinsurgency. The initial draft was written by Dr James Corum, relying heavily on his research into security sector reform in Germany, Cyprus, and Malaya. Some other members of the writing team, such as Colonel John Martin, who had served with then Lieutenant General Petraeus as a member of the Multi-National Security Transition Command-Iraq (MNSTC-I), criticized the high standards Corum expected. These other authors thought that achieving such standards would take too long and tended to reflect too much of a Western perspective. After trying to rewrite the chapter myself to reconcile the two perspectives, I sent a draft by email to Lieutenant General Petraeus one Saturday night for his review. I knew that with his experience at MNSTC-I he had special interest and expertise in the subject matter. I had his well thought-out revision the next morning, and the chapter changed very little after that.

That experience was typical of the final months producing the manual. Lieutenant General Petraeus made detailed personal reviews of what he determined were the most important chapters, and he and I had many verbal and electronic discussions about what the final wording should be. The version he approved was then sent to the Marines for their concurrence, and to Fort Leavenworth for final editing. One of his last decisions was to include a discussion about the proper ratio of counterinsurgents to population in paragraph 1-67. Not only was that a topic that needed to be added, but he also expected to be asked about it at his upcoming confirmation hearings before he headed to Iraq.

Chapter 7, Leadership and Ethics for Counterinsurgency, also underwent considerable revisions. Colonel Richard Swain (Retd) of the US Military Academy wrote the first draft, with help from other Academy faculty members. It included a "ticking time-bomb" scenario discussing the ethical decision-making process concerning extreme interrogation measures to foil catastrophic terrorism. That section sparked considerable debate at the February conference at Fort Leavenworth. The strong consensus of that group was to eliminate any discussion that seemed to imply acceptance of torture, especially after the revelations from Abu Ghraib prison and the passing of the Detainee Treatment Act, which made the strict rules for interrogation described in FM 2-22.3, Human Intelligence Collector Operations, the legal standard. Later legal reviews reinforced that decision, and the section was removed. The draft chapter also included a long, detailed historical vignette by Lieutenant Colonel Lou DiMarco, US Army (Retd), a faculty member at the US Army Command and General Staff College, about the disastrous impact of French moral excesses in Algeria, a section that had to be considerably shortened for the final version of the manual. The full account appeared in the Army War College journal *Parameters*.[22] That article and many others that appeared in military journals were spun off from the work of the writing team. Because of time constraints, Dr Swain had to stop work on the project after the conference, but noted military theorist Dr Frank Hoffman assumed responsibility for finishing the chapter. Hoffman's particular contributions emphasized the intense pressure on leaders to maintain high standards of behavior amidst the ambiguity and frustration that can characterize COIN. Hoffman also contributed a considerable amount to Chapter 4.

Chapter 8 resulted from the persistent efforts of Major Sean Davis, a student at Fort Leavenworth who found out about our writing project and believed it needed a chapter on logistics. He eventually persuaded the writing team that there were many unique aspects of logistic support of counterinsurgency, and he wrote most of the first version of the chapter that was vetted at the February conference. But he had full-time academic requirements as well, and Lieutenant Colonel Marian Vlasak, combat veteran and historian, was recruited to take over that chapter. It emphasizes how logistics for counterinsurgency differ from conventional operations, and describes such support across the various logical lines of operation. It closes with a primer on contracting, an increasingly important feature of contemporary American military operations.

A recurring point of contention among the writing team and in critiques of the manual concerned its length. Many thought it was too long, but the consensus of the writers was that, because we were trying to fill gaps in many critical and neglected areas, the publication could not be shortened. Some topics did not merit full chapters, but were included as appendices because they deserved special recognition.

Appendix A, "A Guide for Action," resulted from an article John Nagl solicited from Dr David Kilcullen, then working for the Department of State. It was based on Kilcullen's observations as an Australian officer conducting counterinsurgency.[23] Steve Capps, our very capable copy editor at Fort Leavenworth, reformatted the piece to fit American planning paradigms, and it was included in the manual because of the important tactical insights it provided. Capps also played a key role in controlling the writing level of the manual, though it is aimed at college level, unlike most other American field manuals, which are written at high-school level. The writers, and Lieutenant General Petraeus, felt that this more elevated discussion was necessary because of the complexity of the topic, and because the target audience was generally officers at battalion level and higher. From the enthusiastic reception of the new doctrine by junior officers as well, it is clear that the writing level of the manual has not been an issue in the field.

Appendix B was originally intended to be just an annex on the intricacies of social network analysis, written primarily by Lieutenant Colonel Brian Reed from West Point. These new techniques had been used to develop the intelligence to capture Saddam Hussein, and are invaluable for dissecting friendly and enemy social structures. However, the US Army Intelligence Center at Fort Huachuca initially balked at the new intelligence approaches touted in FM 3-24. In September I convened a special meeting in Alexandria, Virginia, between McFate, Teamey, some of the secondary writers on our team, and representatives from Huachuca, to iron out the differences. The result was that the US Army Intelligence Center not only endorsed our procedures, they also provided some other useful analytical tools for counterinsurgency that were added to the appendix.

Appendix C, "Linguistic Support," was initially written by Lieutenant Colonel Horvath and was included with some modifications because of a consensus that the proper handling of interpreters was essential in counterinsurgency. The next appendix, on "Legal Considerations," was handled by officers at the Judge Advocate General's Legal Center and School at Charlottesville, Virginia. They aimed to summarize the most important legal aspects of counterinsurgency, to include relevant sections of the Detainee Treatment Act of 2005.

One of the more controversial sections of the manual has been the Airpower Appendix. Marine authors thought its presence was redundant, since anyone knowledgeable about counterinsurgency or joint operations would know that the role of air units was integrated or understood. But Army authors wanted to highlight and extol the special attributes airpower could bring to the counterinsurgent, especially in non-strike missions. Lieutenant General Petraeus and I also hoped the Airpower Appendix would foster increased Air Force interest in COIN. That section of the manual was produced with input from official USAF doctrine writers, but was not well received by that service's leadership, who felt they had been "relegated to an appendix."[24] Besides sparking a series of articles defending the importance of airpower in counterinsurgency by Major General Charles Dunlap, USAF, another contributor to this book, FM 3-24 inspired the USAF to develop their own doctrine for irregular warfare.[25] Airpower has indeed been a major contributor to the success of recent operations in Iraq, proving again the superiority and necessity of joint military operations. However, the course of the war in Afghanistan has vindicated the warnings in the FM about excessive reliance on airpower and trying to substitute firepower for boots on the ground. A shortage of troops combined with civilian casualties from airstrikes have had catastrophic effects on public opinion in key provinces and throughout the country, while tarnishing the international image of the NATO effort.[26]

Probably no other military field manual has ever caused a stir like the finished FM 3-24. It was downloaded more than 1.5 million times from Army and Marine websites the first month it was available after its publication in December 2006. It received a very positive review from Pulitzer Prize-winning author Samantha Power in *The New York Times*.[27] Because of my work creating the new doctrine I was named one of *Newsweek*'s "people to watch in 2007." The University of Chicago Press republished it with some added introductions by Nagl and Sewall, and it is used as a textbook in college courses. Copies of the manual have been found in Taliban training camps in Pakistan. It inspired the State Department to begin an effort to create an interagency counterinsurgency guide, and has influenced our allies as they wrestle with similar doctrinal problems. Besides the USAF AFDD 2-3 mentioned above, it has led to the writing of Joint Publication 3-24 for interservice American counterinsurgency doctrine, and has helped motivate NATO to begin developing its own counterinsurgency guidelines.

But not everyone has been pleased with the content of FM 3-24. Critics appeared as soon as drafts began to be circulated. Lieutenant General Petraeus' approach was to engage them. Ralph Peters provides a good example of how this was done. In June, a coordinating draft of the manual was sent to the field for comments. It can be said that FM 3-24 had a dozen primary authors, another dozen secondary authors, and 600,000 editors, because all of the Army and Marine Corps got a chance to provide their suggestions. In August the writing team assembled to digest the thousands of comments. Many of them provided insights from Afghanistan and Iraq. While the intent of the writing team was to produce a manual that would apply beyond those conflicts, the incorporation of many of those useful ideas did give the manual more of a contemporary focus. At the same time many senior officers were also reading it. Some were uneasy with the paradoxes section, and that list was toned down with qualifiers. The result of many of these alterations was to give the manual more "teeth," dealing in greater detail with the killing and capturing of implacable ideological extremists. Lieutenant General Petraeus himself created some of the changes. In October 2006, Peters penned a blistering critique of the June draft, claiming it was too soft and was inadequate to deal with religious fanatics.[28] Lieutenant General Petraeus invited Peters to Fort Leavenworth, where he debated John Nagl with Colonel Peter Mansoor, then director of the Counterinsurgency Center there, as recorder and referee. Though many of Peters' complaints had already been dealt with by other ongoing revisions to the draft, as a result of this new input, a few more sentences were altered to project an even harder line. However, I also managed to keep the qualification that counterinsurgents need to carefully analyze opponents to figure out who was really implacable. When the manual was finished in December, Peters wrote another article praising it as "the most improved government publication of the decade."[29] He has since reverted back to a position closer to his earlier stance, which appears to ignore the late changes to the manual and remains very enemy-centric.

The next major criticism came from Edward Luttwak in the pages of *Harper's* magazine. Terming the new doctrine "military malpractice," he actually endorsed a population-centric approach, but with a different focus. For Luttwak, the proper role models for counter-insurgency are the Romans and the Nazis, and success comes from intimidating the people by a willingness to "out-terrorize the insurgents."[30] At a conference in 2007 in Paris, American, British, German, and French doctrine writers unanimously rejected such an approach, based on international law, the realities of the current media environment, and a shared conviction that such an approach is counterproductive.[31] But those who agree with Luttwak would argue in response that Western counterinsurgency efforts are therefore doomed to failure. A uniquely American critique along this line is offered by Jeffrey Record at the Air War College. He posits that US counterinsurgency is almost always going to fail, because the military is not properly structured or motivated to conduct it, and the American people are easily frustrated by limited wars and conflicts where national interests are not obvious. Accordingly, the United States should avoid counterinsurgency unless it is clearly essential for national security.[32]

One of the most thoughtful critics of the doctrine is Stephen Biddle. While he concedes its utility in defeating popular insurgencies, he argues that it is not as suitable for civil wars like the one we have seen in Iraq. In such situations intervening forces have to act more like peacekeepers than counterinsurgents, brokering ceasefire agreements between factions, instead of automatically supporting a government. Holding premature elections or quickly rebuilding security forces might only serve to strengthen one side, or harden sectarian divides.[33] While the current FM 3-24 notes that any insurgency typically "contains at least some elements of civil war,"[34] Biddle's cautions about properly sequencing actions based on social and political realities are important, and will be incorporated in the manual when it is revised.

Some critics of the new doctrine are in uniform. The most prolific has been Colonel Gian Gentile from the History Department at West Point. He commanded a battalion in combat in Iraq during 2006, and has been identified as a leading spokesman of a "conservative school" within the Army by Andrew Bacevich.[35] Gentile argues that the new doctrine gets too much credit for success in Iraq. Other unique circumstances were more important, including the fact that we "bought off" most of the opposition by hiring "concerned local citizens" or "Sons of Iraq." He asserts that an enemy-centric approach might be appropriate in some cases, and fears that the Army is moving too far and too fast in the direction of reorienting to irregular warfare or French models of revolutionary warfare. In the process, there is danger of losing important fighting skills that will remain essential to deal with conventional threats, as well as tough insurgents. He also fears that the Army and policy makers may get overconfident, which could lead to risky foreign policy decisions.[36] His cautions about losing warfighting skills have been echoed by some generals, including the Army Chief of Staff, General George Casey, and must be kept in mind for a future featuring the hybrid threats highlighted by Frank Hoffman. Competent enemies also learn and adapt, and future foes will combine the most lethal technologies and conventional tactics with the problems of war among the people and an adept information campaign.[37] However, it must be noted that American units in Afghanistan and Iraq have already been fighting that kind of war, and there is not a more combat-experienced force anywhere in the world.

Arguments concerning the flaws of a "ground-centric" approach to counterinsurgency point to the difficulties of conducting protracted conflicts requiring large deployments of ground troops.[38] Such arguments are valid, but recent events in Afghanistan have reinforced the fact that bombs from the air cannot substitute for boots on the ground when such deployments are necessary. The alternative instead is to rely on the other elements of national power to conduct the population-centric activities necessary for success, in lieu of the military.

But those civilian capacities lag far behind those of the military, which presents a major difficulty for American policy makers. Even an avid supporter of the new doctrine like Sarah

Sewall has described it as a "moon without a planet," since the interagency capacity and guidance for the US government to properly conduct counterinsurgency are so sadly lacking.[39] The process of developing a national capacity for successful counterinsurgency should ideally start with a coherent national security strategy that sets out policies and objectives for such conflicts. Then the government should develop the capabilities and procedures for each interagency contributor as part of a unified effort. The Department of Defense should then define joint doctrine for COIN, followed by each service's creation of their own. In fact this process is going backward, beginning with the individual services and moving upward. Until the rest of the government catches up in resources and procedures, the American military is destined to bear a heavy burden in any counterinsurgency effort.

General Petraeus understood this reality when he took command of the Multi-National Forces in Iraq (MNF-I). He quickly turned the manual's general guidelines into specific actions. To protect and stay in contact with the people, and support the growth of Iraqi security forces, he moved American military forces off large operating bases in favor of combat outposts and joint security stations in the neighborhoods that needed to be secured. He embedded civilian PRTs with brigade combat teams to facilitate coordination, access, and security for development efforts. This forced association maximized the interagency capacity within his command. His forces were very knowledgeable of tribal dynamics in Iraq and worked with indigenous leaders and organizations. His MNF-I were also relentless in tracking and targeting insurgents in superb joint operations, often aided by local security forces who once had been insurgents themselves.[40]

The influence of the new doctrine was apparent in the formal published guidance Petraeus provided to the forces under his command. The Iraqi people were identified as "the decisive terrain," and they had to be secured and served. This required foot patrols to engage the populace and know each neighborhood. While enemies had to be pursued tenaciously, he noted "we cannot kill our way out of this endeavor." Reconciliation and legitimacy had to be fostered, and expectations managed. He admonished his subordinates to "be first with the truth" in fighting the information war so crucial to success, which included acknowledging mistakes and avoiding trying to "put lipstick on pigs."

Petraeus acknowledged the complexity of modern counterinsurgency: "Counter-terrorist forces alone cannot defeat Al-Qaeda and other extremists; success requires all forces and all means at our disposal—non-kinetic as well as kinetic." Civilian and military efforts had to be synchronized but also decentralized, so assets were pushed down to the levels of those who most needed them. He placed a strong emphasis on preserving and holding gains while finding sustainable solutions that the Iraqis could eventually maintain on their own. His counterinsurgent forces had to always be prepared to exercise initiative and exploit opportunities, though never at the cost of high moral values. And he closed his guidance by emphasizing the key theme of the new doctrine—learn and adapt.[41]

But even the most avid supporters of the new doctrine must admit that it is not a universal solution to conflict. It is not even a blueprint for success in the global war on terror. It is designed to help guide forces in a theater to design and execute a successful counterinsurgency campaign. If al-Qaeda is indeed a global or transnational insurgency as many have described it, including the authors of FM 3-24, then countering such an enemy will require a much broader focus, involving international coordination and cooperation.[42] It will take much more than one field manual for the ground forces of one nation to conduct one mode of irregular warfare to insure global security, or even success in regional counterinsurgency.

Notes

1 Conrad C. Crane, *Avoiding Vietnam: The U.S. Army's Response to Defeat in Southeast Asia*, Carlisle, PA: Strategic Studies Institute, 2002.

2 Headquarters, Department of the Army, Field Manual—Interim 3.07-22, *Counterinsurgency Operations*, Washington, DC: HQDA, 2004.

3 Lt. Gen. David Petraeus, Introductory Remarks to COIN FM Workshop, Fort Leavenworth, KS, February 23, 2006.

4 Cullen Nutt, "Petraeus' Big Tent," *The Star Ledger*, March 2, 2008, Perspective section, p. 1. John Nagl insists that he jotted his notes on the napkin, but others in attendance at that meeting also remember a notebook.

5 Linda Robinson, *Tell Me How This Ends: General David Petraeus and the Search for a Way Out of Iraq*, New York: Public Affairs, 2008, p. 77.

6 Conrad C. Crane and W. Andrew Terrill, *Reconstructing Iraq: Insights, Challenges, and Missions for Military Forces in a Post-Conflict Scenario*, Carlisle, PA: Strategic Studies Institute, 2003.

7 Email from Lt. Gen. Petraeus to author, November 17, 2005.

8 David Petraeus, "Learning Counterinsurgency: Observations from Soldiering in Iraq," *Military Review*, Vol. 86 (January/February 2006), 2–12.

9 Frank Kitson, *Low Intensity Operations: Subversion, Insurgency, and Peacekeeping*, London: Faber and Faber; 1971; Robert Thompson, *Defeating Communist Insurgency*, St Petersburg, FL: Hailer Publishing, 2005 (reprint of 1966 edition); Roger Trinquier, *Modern Warfare: A French View of Counterinsurgency*, New York: Praeger, 1964.

10 Steven Metz and Raymond Millen, *Insurgency and Counterinsurgency in the 21st Century: Reconceptualizing Threat and Response*, Carlisle, PA: Strategic Studies Institute, 2004; David Kilcullen, "Countering Global Insurgency: A Strategy for the War on Terrorism," *Journal of Strategic Studies* (August 2005), 597–617.

11 Peter W. Chiarelli and Patrick Michaelis, "Winning the Peace: The Requirement for Full-Spectrum Operations," *Military Review*, Vol. 85 (July/August 2005), 4–17.

12 Kalev I. Sepp, "Best Practices in Counterinsurgency," *Military Review*, Vol. 85 (May/June 2005), 8–12. The conclusions of this article became Table 1-1 of the new field manual.

13 David Galula, *Counterinsurgency Warfare: Theory and Practice*, London: Praeger, 1964.

14 Email from Tom McNaugher to author, December 4, 2005, with attachment "Core Principles of Counterinsurgency."

15 See, for example, John A. Nagl, Foreword to The US Army/Marine Corps Field Manual, *Counterinsurgency* (FM 3-24), Chicago: University of Chicago Press, 2007, p. xvii.

16 The COIN FM Workshop was held at Fort Leavenworth on February 23 and 24, 2006.

17 Nigel R.F. Aylwin-Foster, "Changing the Army for Counterinsurgency Operations," *Military Review*, Vol. 85 (November/December 2005), 2–15.

18 Robert J. Gonzalez, "Towards Mercenary Anthropology?" *Anthropology Today*, 23 (June 2007), 14–19.

19 Quoted in Neil Sheehan, *A Bright Shining Lie: John Paul Vann and America in Vietnam*, New York: Random House, 1988, p. 67.

20 FM 3-24, Figure 5-1.

21 From the author's personal observations and discussions with Colonel Sutherland in Diyala, November 2007.

22 Lou DiMarco, "Losing the Moral Compass: Torture and Guerre Révolutionnaire in the Algerian War," *Parameters*, Vol. 36 (Summer 2006), 63–76.

23 It was published as "Twenty-Eight Articles: Fundamentals of Company-level Counterinsurgency," *Military Review*, Vol. 86 (May/June 2006), 103–8.

24 Remarks of General Ronald E. Keys, Commander, Air Combat Command, dinner presentation at Air Force Symposium 2007: Counterinsurgency, April 24, 2007, Maxwell AFB, AL. The USAF input provided to the writing team did clash with USMC concepts for the employment of airpower, and their differences were adjudicated by Clint Ancker, director of the Combined Arms Doctrine Directorate at Fort Leavenworth.

25 Headquarters, Department of the Air Force, Air Force Doctrine Document 2-3, Irregular Warfare, Washington, DC: HQUSAF, 2007

26 Dr Craig Charney, "Afghanistan: Public Opinion Trends and Strategic Implications," presentation at USAID-sponsored conference, "Poverty Reduction in Conflict and Failed States: Institutions and

State Legitimacy," Washington, DC, April 2, 2008. Marc Garlasco, *Troops in Contact: Airstrikes and Civilian Deaths in Afghanistan*, New York: Human Rights Watch, 2008.

27 Samantha Power, "Our War on Terror," *The New York Times*, Sunday magazine, July 29, 2007.

28 Ralph Peters, "Politically Correct War," *New York Post*, October 18, 2006.

29 Ralph Peters, "Getting Counterinsurgency Right," *New York Post*, December 20, 2006.

30 Edward Luttwak, "Dead End: Counterinsurgency Warfare as Military Malpractice," *Harper's* magazine, February 2007, 33–42.

31 Workshop on Counterinsurgency and Stability Operations: US, French, British, and German Approaches, held at the Institut français des relations internationals in Paris, June 4, 2007.

32 Jeffrey Record, "The American Way of War: Cultural Barriers to Successful Insurgency," Cato Institute Policy Analysis 577, September 1, 2006.

33 Typical of Stephen Biddle's critiques is "Seeing Baghdad, Thinking Saigon," *Foreign Affairs*, Vol. 85 (March/April 2006), 2–14.

34 FM 3-24, paragraph 1-5.

35 Andrew Bacevich, "The Petraeus Doctrine," *Atlantic Monthly*, October 2008, found at http://www.theatlantic.com/doc/200810/petraeus-doctrine.

36 For examples of Gian Gentile's critiques, see "The Dogmas of War," *Armed Forces Journal International* (November 2007) at http://www.afji.com/2007/11/3155836; and "A (Slightly) Better War: A Narrative and its Defects," *World Affairs* (Summer 2008) at http://www.worldaffairsjournal.org/2008%20-%20Summer/full-Gentile.html.

37 For a succinct discussion of this phenomenon, see Frank Hoffman, *Conflict in the 21st Century: The Rise of Hybrid Wars*, Arlington, VA: The Potomac Institute for Policy Studies, 2007.

38 See Chapter 8 by Charles Dunlap for an expansion of this argument.

39 Sarah Sewall, "A Radical Field Manual," Introduction to FM 3-24, the University of Chicago Press Edition.

40 These observations were obtained during a visit to Iraq at General Petraeus' invitation in November 2007.

41 Headquarters, Multi-National Force-Iraq, "Multi-National Force-Iraq Commander's Counterinsurgency Guidance," June 21, 2008.

42 Kilcullen, "Countering Global Insurgency," David Kilcullen, "Counterinsurgency Redux," *Survival*, Vol. 48 (Winter 2006/2007), 111–30, and David W. Barno, "Challenges in Fighting a Global Insurgency," *Parameters*, Vol. 36 (Summer 2006), 15–29; FM 3-24, paragraphs 1-22 and 1-23.

Part II

Operational aspects

6 Army

Peter Mansoor

Counterinsurgency warfare is fought on the ground, among the people. The operations of ground forces, therefore, are decisive in the successful prosecution of a counterinsurgency strategy. A useful model for counterinsurgency operations developed by the British Army breaks ground force missions into two categories: framework operations and surge operations. Simply put, framework operations are those tasks a counterinsurgent force must accomplish, such as securing population centers and lines of communication, force protection, and sustainment activities. Surge operations are the tasks a force should undertake as conditions and resources permit, such as offensive operations to clear enemy safe havens and targeted raids to kill or capture insurgent operatives.

These categories are best introduced in reverse fashion, since surge activities are essential to *clearing* enemy forces from an area, and framework operations are necessary to *hold* it in the long run. To these categories we can add civic action and humanitarian assistance, both necessary to *build* civil infrastructure, ensure the needs of the people are met, and increase the legitimacy of the governing authority. Finally, ground forces are charged with running detention facilities in a legal and humane manner. This function, although often overlooked, is a fundamental aspect of counterinsurgency operations. Indeed, while detention facilities have too often tarnished the image of counterinsurgent forces, in Iraq since 2007 the successful application of counterinsurgency principles "inside the wire" has led to significant successes in moderating the behavior of the detainee population.

Surge operations

If insurgents wore uniforms and operated openly in the manner of conventional armies, their war would most likely be over quickly. Since they instead wear mufti and hide among civilians, a concerted effort is required to isolate them from the local population. To do this without alienating the people, focused and precise intelligence is required. Otherwise, ground forces are a blunt instrument whose impact is felt by the civilian population in a seemingly brutal and imprecise manner, potentially strengthening, rather than weakening, an insurgency. Indeed, insurgents rely on the widespread and imprecise application of force by armies and police forces to alienate the people and drive them further from support of the government. To be sure, enemy-centric approaches to counterinsurgency, focused on destroying insurgent forces, have on occasion worked in the past—the destruction of Che Guevara's nascent insurgent movement in Bolivia in 1967 being among the prime examples of this method.[1] For more entrenched insurgent movements, however, extensive use of firepower, widespread devastation of civilian habitats, and strict control of populations, along with the collateral damage and civilian deaths that such a strategy entails, are often required to eliminate an insurgent force embedded among a population. Perhaps Tacitus is the best authority on such matters, when he quotes a native chieftain regarding Roman military operations: "To ravage, to slaughter, to usurp under false titles, they call empire; and where they make a desert, they call it peace."[2]

In the absence of precise intelligence and discriminating targeting, a strategy focused on the elimination of insurgent forces is only viable provided a counterinsurgent force is willing to accept massive civilian casualties and to suffer the negative publicity that will invariably surround the measures enacted to carry it out. Russian forces in Chechnya used massive firepower to destroy guerrilla forces and sanctuaries in the second Chechen war, beginning in 1999, with over 25,000 dead, mostly Chechen civilians.[3] The capital city of Grozny earned the dubious distinction as "the most destroyed city in the world" by the United Nations in 2003. The US, European nations, and the United Nations all roundly condemned the conduct of Russian forces in Chechnya, but Russian President Vladimir Putin's ability to withstand this criticism enabled Russian forces to execute operations to destroy armed Chechen resistance, with minimal concern for the civilian population of the region.[4]

Another technique used to destroy insurgent movements is the concentration of civilian populations in camps or villages to inhibit their ability to support insurgent forces and to enable ground forces a free hand to use their combat capabilities in the surrounding areas. During the Boer War the British interned 120,000 Boer families, mostly women and children, in 50 concentration camps; nearly 20,000 died in less than two years of confinement.[5] When faced with an uprising in Kenya in the early 1950s, Britain again concentrated the population to prevent their support for guerrilla forces. In the spring of 1954 the British put Nairobi under military control and arrested 17,000 Africans suspected of supporting the insurgency. Many of those arrested were innocent, but the sheer scale of the operation put many of the passive supporters of the Mau Mau insurgency into detention camps. By the end of 1954 the British forced more than 75,000 Kikuyu tribesmen into detention camps, where treatment was often brutal and inhumane. Another million-plus Kikuyu tribesmen were forced into 854 villages to control their movements and activities. The British colonial government prohibited movement in the Aberdares Range and Mount Kenya, areas used by the Mau Mau guerrillas as bases. Anyone caught in these restricted areas could be shot on sight. Isolated from their sources of supply and recruits and hunted incessantly in their sanctuaries, the Mau Mau guerrillas were dealt a lethal blow; by 1956 the insurgent movement collapsed. Tens of thousands of Kenyans died in the Mau Mau uprising and in the resulting operations to repress it. To prevent backlash among the public back home and in the larger court of world opinion, British colonial authorities covered up the atrocities in the detention camps and the excesses of their counter-guerrilla operations.[6]

The US has its own history of relocating civilian populations to enable the destruction of guerrilla forces. During the Philippine War of 1899–1902, US forces in Luzon concentrated civilian populations in towns, either through enticements such as improved government services and provision of free education or through forced relocations, to enable military forces to hunt and kill guerrilla bands in the surrounding hills and jungles.[7] During the Vietnam War, US and British advisors worked with the South Vietnamese government to establish the strategic hamlet program, the goal of which was to separate the Vietnamese people from the communist guerrillas by forcing their relocation into protected villages. Surrounding areas were then deemed "free fire zones," into which the US and South Vietnamese militaries poured massive amounts of firepower in an attempt to destroy guerrilla forces. Between 1961 and 1963 over 8 million people were relocated into strategic hamlets, but the program's poor administration enabled insurgents from the National Liberation Front to overrun or infiltrate most of the villages. The program also alienated the Vietnamese peasantry by driving them away from their ancestral homes, and into the waiting arms of the communist insurgency.[8]

It is unlikely that western democracies can end an insurgency by destroying guerrilla forces once they are firmly established among the people. Given the pervasive media and information environment of the twenty-first century, and the adherence by western powers to ethical conduct in war, any strategy that entails massive civilian suffering will meet with stiff public resistance. Even with precision guided munitions and high technology intelligence, reconnaissance, and surveillance systems, Western militaries will never be able to target enough of an insurgency's leaders and infrastructure to collapse an organization once it is firmly embedded among the people. Collateral damage and civilian casualties, on the other hand, are magnified through insurgent propaganda and skillful use of the Internet, satellite television, and other media resources to sway popular opinion against the counterinsurgent. So-called "kinetic operations" all too often delegitimize the counterinsurgent cause and drive more people to support the insurgency. Insurgent propaganda must be anticipated and countered with immediate press releases and factual evidence. Commanders must fight the information war relentlessly, be first with the truth, and engage the media continuously to insure the insurgent narrative does not dominate the airwaves and therefore the public's attention. Even with the most skillfully conducted information operations campaign, however, Western governments today will not condone the massive level of violence and collateral damage needed to suppress an insurgency through force once it has grown beyond the embryonic stage.

US military campaigns in Iraq from 2003 to 2006 and in Afghanistan from 2001 to 2008 bear out this assertion. In Iraq the forces of Combined Joint Task Force-7, under the command of Lieutenant General Ricardo Sanchez, focused military operations in 2003–4 on killing or capturing insurgents. Although the positioning of US forces inside Iraqi cities during this period provided the population with a degree of protection, the lack of sufficient military forces in Iraq, combined with the disbanding of the Iraqi army by Ambassador L. Paul Bremer, prevented the execution of a counterinsurgency strategy based on protecting the Iraqi people. Instead, military forces conducted targeted raids and cordon and search operations to destroy insurgents in their strongholds. Often, US forces vacated areas once they were cleared of an overt insurgent presence, only to discover that the enemy returned to these same areas after military forces withdrew. Iraqi citizens who cooperated with coalition forces were then placed at the mercy of the insurgents; terrorists tortured and killed many civilians for their collaboration with the occupation.[9]

Multi-National Force-Iraq (MNF-I), under the command of General George Casey, initially continued this offensive strategy to destroy insurgent forces in Iraq. Beginning in the spring of 2004, MNF-I ordered US forces to withdraw from battalion and company outposts in Iraqi cities and to position on large forward operating bases on the outskirts. The thinking was that US forces were a virus infecting Iraqi society, and the only way to prevent the forces of liberation turning into a hated occupation was to remove them from among the people. The lack of trained and ready Iraqi police and army units doomed this policy to failure. Once US forces withdrew from Iraq's cities, Sunni insurgents and Shi'ite militias took control of a large part of Baghdad and other urban areas. US forces, patrolling neighborhoods in armored vehicles from their bases on the periphery, could not maintain control or protect the population. In the spring of 2004 Sunni insurgents gained control of Fallujah, requiring a massive offensive operation in November to root them out of their urban stronghold.[10]

General Casey needed an alternative strategy to rescue a failing mission. He seized on the transition of security responsibilities to Iraqi forces as his primary goal, neatly summed up by President George W. Bush in a nationally televised speech: "As the Iraqis stand up, we will stand down."[11] But the strength and abilities of the insurgency were growing faster than the numbers and capabilities of the Iraqi security forces. The bombing of the al-Askari Shrine in Samarra by operatives of al-Qaeda-Iraq (AQI) in February 2006 put this strategy to the test, and it was found severely wanting. Iraqi forces, sometimes themselves complicit in ethno-sectarian violence, could not contain the resulting conflict as the Jaish al-Mahdi militia swept through Baghdad and other Iraqi cities, torturing and murdering Sunni inhabitants in retribution for the destruction of the "Golden Dome" mosque. Sunni insurgents, increasingly under the sway of AQI extremists, gained substantial control of al-Anbar province and several neighborhoods in Baghdad, Baqubah, and Mosul. By the end of 2006, the war was nearly lost as sectarian conflict wracked Baghdad and Iraq teetered on the edge of civil war.[12]

The early course of the war in Afghanistan since the US invasion in 2001 has also demonstrated the inability of western forces to destroy an entrenched insurgency through offensive operations. Between 2001 and 2005 US ground forces launched a number of large-unit operations to destroy al-Qaeda and Taliban forces, with mixed results. Despite suffering significant losses to air strikes and ground combat, Taliban forces grew in size and capability in the next several years.[13] Complicating matters, the Pashtun areas of western Pakistan provided safe havens for Taliban forces. Occasional strikes by armed unmanned aerial vehicles killed a number of insurgent and al-Qaeda leaders, but also produced a backlash among the Pakistani public, who widely condemned the violation of their sovereignty. By 2008 the Taliban had gained control of significant swaths of Afghan territory and put in doubt the outcome of the conflict.

Even if a counterinsurgent force desires to prioritize protecting the population, surge operations are necessary to clear areas of overt insurgent presence, weapons caches, and roadside bombs. There is nothing inherently wrong with large-unit cordon and search operations to clear areas, provided they are conducted in a humane manner and there is follow-through to hold the territory after the conclusion of the operation. Any number of examples from the Iraq war prove this point. In April 2004 forces of the Jaish al-Mahdi took control of Karbala, compelling commanders to dispatch units of the 1st Brigade, 1st Armored Division to root them out of the city. In a three-week operation in May 2004, Task Force 1-37 Armor attacked to clear Karbala of militia forces. Combined efforts by air and ground forces killed a large number of Shi'ite militia, captured significant amounts of ammunition, and dislodged the enemy from the city. The key to consolidating this success, however, was the ability of coalition forces, in this case the Polish 1st Brigade Combat Team along with Iraqi police forces, to hold the city at the conclusion of combat operations and thereby to enable reconstruction and the building of civic institutions to proceed.[14] By way of contrast, US forces failed to hold Tal Afar after repeatedly clearing the city early in the war, which enabled insurgent forces to return to terrorize the population and force their acquiescence. By 2005 Sunni guerrillas had turned Tal Afar into a major insurgent stronghold.[15]

Framework operations—protecting the population

In a seminal work on counterinsurgency theory written in 1964, French Army Colonel David Galula posited that the protection of the population is the key to a successful counterinsurgency strategy. Since insurgents cannot win an outright military victory against the conventional forces of a state, they must move the conflict to different ground, one of their own choosing:

The population represents this new ground. If the insurgent manages to dissociate the population from the counterinsurgent, to control it physically, to get its active support, he will win the war because, in the final analysis, the exercise of political power depends on the tacit or explicit agreement of the population or, at worst, on its submissiveness.[16]

The counterinsurgent must contest the insurgent for the support and control of the population to be successful. As discussed above, the counterinsurgent cannot normally force guerrillas into battles where they can be engaged and destroyed. For the counterinsurgent, then, the protection of the population from insurgent violence, intimidation, and proselytizing is essential to defeating an insurgency. This task cannot be accomplished by high-tech weaponry. It must be done the old-fashioned way, with boots on the ground.

The only way to protect a people effectively is to live among them. Leaders must understand native culture and study local history in order to determine what motivates the people. In the end, the people must choose to support the counterinsurgent and the legitimate governing authority. Many armies, configured for conventional, high-intensity combat, have difficulty adjusting to this reality. During the Vietnam War, the US Army for several years persisted in applying a conventional warfighting doctrine to an irregular warfare situation.[17] The resulting strategy of attrition, exemplified by search and destroy operations focused on body counts of dead guerrilla fighters, failed to lessen significantly the strength of the National Liberation Front. While combat against North Vietnamese Army regiments may have necessitated a degree of high intensity combat, the need to secure the South Vietnamese population from Communist guerrillas required a different strategy. The situation only changed after the Tet offensive in 1968 shocked Military Assistance Command, Vietnam (MACV) into altering its methods and its new commander, General Creighton Abrams, embraced a revised strategy focused on protecting the population.[18]

The Israel Defense Forces (IDF) have approached their operations against Palestinian guerrillas with a similar kinetic mindset. During the al-Aqsa Intifada from 2000 to 2005, IDF commanders used their tactically proficient forces to cordon and search urban areas on the West Bank and in the Gaza Strip, while severely limiting Palestinian movement through the use of checkpoints and security barriers. These methods succeeded in tamping down terrorist violence within Israel proper, but at the expense of devastating the Palestinian economy, of incarcerating nearly 10,000 Palestinians, and of driving the Palestinian people further into support of Hamas extremists.[19] Perhaps gaining the support of the Palestinian people is not in the cards, but the failure of Israel to deal with the root causes of Palestinian discontent and to work with local Palestinian authorities to protect the people from extremist intimidation and recruitment has led to temporary neutralization of Palestinian terrorism at the expense of a more critical strategic solution to the long-term problem.

US Army units in Iraq suffered from a similar conceptual shortfall in the first years of the conflict. The lack of a coherent campaign plan left division and brigade combat team commanders to fashion their own solutions to the tactical challenges they faced. Most undertook offensive operations in a vain attempt to destroy the growing insurgency in their areas. There were exceptions, however. In 2005–6 the 3rd Armored Cavalry Regiment (ACR), under the command of Colonel H.R. McMaster, conducted an inspired operation in the city of Tal Afar in northwestern Iraq that later became a model for operations elsewhere in the country. When the 3rd ACR arrived in Tal Afar in the spring of 2005, the city was under the control of foreign insurgents and their Iraqi allies, who used it as a base of operations and a transit point for men and materiel smuggled into the country from neighboring Syria. The insurgents had intimidated the population into submission to their brutal authority. The

Turkoman population, divided along Sunni–Shia lines, was engaged in horrific sectarian violence. For all intents and purposes, Tal Afar had become a dead city.[20]

McMaster employed a strategy of "clear and hold" to restore Tal Afar to coalition control. His troops first surrounded the city with a berm to force traffic through security checkpoints and to isolate the insurgents and terrorists from outside support. Leaders then spent countless hours engaging the people, sorting out the local power structures, and lending a sympathetic ear to grievances while slowly turning the narrative from a Sunni–Shia civil war to one of all Iraqis against the foreign jihadists who had taken control of and terrorized their city. Instead of a massive assault to clear the city, as coalition forces had done the previous November in Fallujah, McMaster employed his forces in small combat outposts scattered throughout Tal Afar to provide the people with security against terrorist depredations. He also worked diligently to recruit both Sunnis and Shi'ites, to provide a sectarian balance within the police force. By the time the 3rd ACR departed Iraq in early 2006, Tal Afar was once again under coalition control.

The 1st Brigade, 1st Armored Division (the Ready First Combat Team), under the command of Colonel Sean MacFarland, replaced McMaster's forces in Tal Afar and continued the campaign to hold the city while restoring government functions and essential services.[21] The desperate situation further south in al-Anbar province, however, forced MNC-I in June 2006 to move most of the brigade combat team to Ramadi, a city designated by AQI as the capital of its future Iraqi caliphate. With the exception of a handful of Marine bases, Sunni insurgents enjoyed almost complete freedom of movement throughout the area. Jihadists had terrorized the population into submission, and their brutal administration of Islamic law left deep-seated scars on the community. Faced with a problem in Ramadi similar to that encountered by McMaster in Tal Afar the previous year, MacFarland employed similar techniques to clear the city and then hold it against terrorists and insurgent forces.

Units of the Ready First Combat Team challenged terrorists and insurgents in their long-held sanctuaries within the city by establishing combat outposts in their midst, staffed by US troops, Iraqi security forces, and civil affairs teams. Frenzied enemy counterattacks to destroy these installations resulted in severe casualties to insurgent forces. Meanwhile, MacFarland and his leaders engaged local tribal sheiks, who were fed up with al-Qaeda violence and their loss of prestige and influence, to solicit their cooperation and to recruit their young men into neighborhood watch units or into the Ramadi police force. Colonel MacFarland and one of his staff officers, Major Niel Smith, reflected on the importance of tribal engagement after the event:

> The tribes represent the people of Iraq, and the populace represents the "key terrain" of the conflict. The force that supports the population by taking the moral high ground has as sure an advantage in COIN as a maneuver commander who occupies dominant terrain in a conventional battle.[22]

As the people shifted their allegiance away from the jihadists, the Ready First Combat Team was able to recruit significant numbers to join the Iraqi security forces. Resurgent Iraqi police and tribal elements raided al-Qaeda safehouses and seized hundreds of weapons caches. Slowly but surely, the advance of combat outposts, combined with support from the growing Sunni tribal rebellion against al-Qaeda, squeezed the enemy out of Ramadi. As security was re-established, neighborhood by neighborhood, the combat team worked to restore the city's infrastructure and to provide essential services to the civilian population.[23]

US operations in Tal Afar and Ramadi provided a model for use elsewhere in Iraq. Population security in these cities, as well as further west in Qaim, delivered concrete results and brought to life the type of operations conceptualized in the new US Army and Marine Corps counterinsurgency doctrine published in December 2006.[24] These successes came not a moment too soon; by the end of 2006 the Iraq War was nearly lost as Iraqi society tore itself apart in a spasm of sectarian bloodletting. Scores of dead bodies appeared on the streets daily, many with hands bound and exhibiting signs of torture. Simply put, political progress toward reconciliation and the building of an Iraqi state that equitably shared power and resources among competing sectarian and ethnic groups was not possible until violence was reduced to a socially acceptable level. Sensing that the time for a change in strategy had come, and pressured by the Democratic victory in Congressional mid-term elections, President Bush seized on the "clear, hold, build" approach to the war and in January 2007 ordered five additional US Army brigade combat teams and two Marine battalions to Iraq.[25] These "surge" forces were empowered to pursue operations focused on population security under the leadership of General David Petraeus, who assumed command in February 2007, and Lieutenant General Raymond Odierno, who deployed to Iraq in command of MNF-I late in 2006.

The new strategy was much more important than the additional forces. While continuing large-unit cordon and search operations to clear areas of an overt insurgent presence and to locate and seize weapons and ammunition caches, Petraeus and Odierno also ordered US units to deploy out of the large forward operating bases where they had been stationed since the spring of 2004 and to establish smaller joint security stations and combat outposts in Iraqi neighborhoods and communities. There they could partner with Iraqi security forces, support local neighborhood watch groups (the "Sons of Iraq"), and provide much-needed security to the Iraqi people to insulate them from terrorist violence and militia intimidation. Rather than conducting vehicular patrols from large bases on the outskirts into Baghdad's neighborhoods and then returning to the safety of the bases afterwards, US forces would station with Iraqi police and army units forward in local communities. From these outposts combat forces would conduct increased foot patrols and thereby benefit from more intimate contact with the people living in their assigned zones.[26]

US commanders used other techniques as well to prosecute counterinsurgency operations during the period of the surge in 2007–8. In conjunction with local Iraqi community leaders, they used cement barriers to wall off neighborhoods and make it difficult for terrorists to get in or militiamen to get out, or vice versa depending on the nature of the area. Market areas were similarly walled off and entry limited to pedestrian traffic in order to prevent vehicle bombs from targeting crowds of shoppers. Iraqi units manned numerous checkpoints that made terrorist and insurgent movement in Iraq's cities more difficult. US units conducted comprehensive censuses to identify exactly who was living in each neighborhood, to catalog their sect and ethnicity, to determine their occupation, and to gather other important identifiers that could help commanders piece together the mosaic of Iraq and determine local power structures. They enrolled Iraqis into biometric databases so that soldiers could quickly determine who belonged and who did not belong in a given area. US forces also used improved surveillance and reconnaissance tools such as armed unmanned aerial vehicles (UAV) and various communications intercept devices to gather information and target insurgent and militia operatives.

The revised counterinsurgency strategy, the improved techniques used by US commanders, and the provision of more forces served as the catalyst to significantly improve security in Iraq. The arrival of US reinforcements signaled renewed resolve and assured Sunni tribal leaders that they would not be abandoned once they turned their guns against AQI, as had happened once before in 2005. The tribal rebellion accelerated after the surge forces arrived and US and Iraqi units moved to fill the void.

People freed from the specter of terrorism and violence are less likely to see the need to pay protection money to violent thugs; accordingly, the improved security provided by US and Iraqi security forces also led to a loosening of the grip by Shi'ite militias on a number of key areas in Iraq. In August 2007 after a gun battle between rival militias in the holy city of Karbala, Muqtada al-Sadr declared a unilateral ceasefire that took his Jaish al-Mahdi militia out of the conflict, at least temporarily.

Coalition leaders also worked to separate reconcilable elements of the insurgency from the hardcore extremists who had to be killed or captured. Amnesty legislation, local ceasefires, and other political bargains reduced the number of fighters opposing the government. Finally, the increase of Iraqi security forces by more than 140,000 troops in 2007 and 2008, along with their improved capabilities, led Prime Minister Nouri al-Maliki to feel emboldened enough in the spring of 2008 to confront the Shi'ite militias in their strongholds in Basra, Amarah, and Sadr City, and to bring the vast majority of southern and central Iraq under Iraqi government control. The change in strategy and additional forces provided by the surge made these significant security improvements possible, and thereby gave Iraqi leaders the opportunity—if not the certainty—to settle the competition for power and resources through more peaceful political means.[27]

It is possible to reconcile an enemy-centric strategy with the requirement to secure the population. Even for a force bent on killing or capturing the enemy, the lessons of the surge suggest that military forces are most effective when special operations forces operate within the envelope of conventional units. Operations by conventional forces to clear and hold areas in order to control and protect civilian populations force insurgents to move and communicate, which then enables them to be targeted and killed or captured. Relentless pursuit of an insurgent force on the run is necessary to finish its destruction or to prevent it from consolidating in a new safe haven. In the final analysis, however, the neutralization or destruction of insurgent forces or terrorist networks demands a holistic solution and the employment of all of a counterinsurgent's assets, not just military force.

Civic action and humanitarian assistance

Security is an essential prerequisite for success in counterinsurgency warfare, but by itself it is rarely sufficient to end a conflict. Victory requires the counterinsurgent to address the root causes of the insurgency. These could be many different things, but often boil down to disputes over power, resources, or territory. Nevertheless, if the population is the decisive terrain over which counterinsurgency wars are fought, then convincing the people that a better life lies ahead is essential to restoring the legitimacy of the governing authority. Often deemed the battle over "hearts and minds," this field of activity is more appropriately labeled a race for the people's trust and confidence. The people must be convinced that support for the legitimate governing authority is preferable to support for the insurgent cause. Civic action and humanitarian assistance, therefore, are essential elements of the counterinsurgent toolkit. Since these activities occur on the ground among the people while violence still rages, it often falls to army organizations to accomplish them.

Recent wars have conjured up all sorts of models for the essential elements of civic action and humanitarian assistance. One acronym that has caught on recently is SWEAT-MS, which stands for sewage, water, electricity, academics, trash, medical, and security. These are all undoubtedly important services, but the role of ground forces in providing them to the people (with the exception of security) is less than clear. Ideally, military operations lead to a secure environment, which then allows civilian agencies to provide essential services to the population. In reality, the dangerous nature of many counterinsurgency environments dictates that military forces be prepared to jumpstart the process.

Armies are not without substantial capabilities in this regard. In the US Army, civil affairs units are staffed with experts on all sorts of technical functions, to include rule of law, economic stability, governance, public health and welfare, infrastructure, and public education. Engineer units have considerable capabilities to construct or reconstruct infrastructure and to assist civilian authorities in city management. Medical units can service the medical, dental, and preventive medicine needs of local communities. Veterinarians can provide services in animal husbandry to rural areas. Psychological operations units are capable of keeping the civilian populace informed of important information. Logistical organizations have significant assets that are useful for a variety of tasks, to include transportation, fuel storage, supply management, maintenance, food service, and water purification. Aviation transport units can airlift personnel and materiel. Staff elements such as military lawyers and chaplains can assist in a variety of ways in dealing with local political and religious authorities. Even combat units have latent capabilities in a variety of areas, from trash collection to school repair.

Perhaps the most important asset that armies have to conduct civic action and humanitarian assistance, however, is money. According to General David Petraeus, money is ammunition every bit as (or even more) useful than bombs and bullets in defeating insurgents.[28] In Iraq and Afghanistan, the Commander's Emergency Response Program (CERP) gave money to US commanders to spend on a variety of economic and reconstruction needs. Since company, battalion, and brigade commanders are closer to the people than authorities higher up the chain of command, they often have a better conception of the people's needs and a better understanding of where money spent will provide the most "bang for the buck." Contracting done at the highest levels of the counterinsurgency command has a useful role to play in long-term economic revitalization, such as in repair of the national power grid for example, but is usually not as timely as required to influence the attitude of the people or as sensitive in meeting their immediate needs. In counterinsurgency warfare, local and tailored is usually better than centralized and general.[29]

When considering civic action and humanitarian assistance, counterinsurgents must be careful to make their actions count. They would do well to remember the first rule of economics: anything free will be overused. In providing a civilian population with essential services and reconstruction assistance, it is critical that military organizations force the people to make an active choice in favor of supporting the legitimate governing authority. Otherwise, any aid rendered will be accepted gladly, and have zero impact on the ultimate outcome of the conflict. Counterinsurgency theorist David Kilcullen sums this issue up nicely by examining the statement made in 1952 by General Sir Gerald Templer, director of operations and high commissioner for Malaya, regarding his strategy to defeat the communist guerrillas in that country: "The answer lies not in pouring more troops into the jungle, but in the hearts and minds of the Malayan People." The issue, Kilcullen argues, is not to make the population like the counterinsurgent:

> What is essential here is making the population choose. The gratitude theory—"be nice to the people, meet their needs and they will feel grateful and stop supporting the insurgents"—does not work. The enemy simply intimidates the population when COIN forces/government are not present resulting in lip-service as the population sees

COIN forces/government as weak and easily manipulated. In time, this leads to hatred of COIN forces/government by the population. On the other hand, the choice theory—enable (persuade, coerce, coopt) the population to make an irrevocable choice to support COIN forces/government usually works better. The population typically desires to "sit on the fence" and not commit to supporting any side in an insurgency/COIN environment. COIN forces/government need to get the population off that fence and keep them there. This requires persuading the population, then protecting them, where they live. While this cannot be done everywhere, it must be done where it politically counts.[30]

The people must see the success of the counterinsurgent as being in their interest and then make a choice to support that future over the one offered by the insurgents. This choice has little to do with gratitude, which cannot survive first contact with terrorism and intimidation, and much to do with self-interest, which more often than not trumps all other motivations of human behavior.

Detention operations

Throughout human history, mistreatment of detainees is a long and time-honored tradition. French Army use of torture against captured Front de Libération Nationale (FLN) terrorists during the Algerian War (1954–62) led to tactical success in the Battle of Algiers at the expense of the loss of French moral credibility and eventually, the war.[31] Military forces usually do not make good jailers, as they habitually view prisoners as a burden rather than as an opportunity. This attitude is regrettable, since detainees are a captive population and represent an opportunity for the counterinsurgent to affect their opponents' attitudes. In the Iraq War from 2003 to 2008, detainee treatment progressed from the criminal (Abu Ghraib, 2003) to the abysmal (catch and release, 2004–6) to the sublime (counterinsurgency inside the wire, 2007–8). The key factor in each of these periods, as is the case throughout most of military history, was the leadership exercised by those in charge of the detention system.

If counterinsurgents view the detention mission as merely an exercise in the warehousing of human bodies, then they should expect commensurate results. In 2003 at the Abu Ghraib prison west of Baghdad, the criminal actions of the military police nightshift severely damaged the credibility and image of the United States in Iraq and throughout the world. US leaders compensated by creating a legally sufficient, but extremely ineffective, detention system that treated detainees as minimum-security prisoners, left them with minimal supervision inside the detention facilities, and then released them without rehabilitation and often without judicial hearings to determine their guilt or innocence. The upshot was that the extremists took control of the detainee population through intimidation and violence, and converted a number of them to the jihadist cause. Periodic mass releases to appease Iraqi political sensitivities merely exacerbated the situation. By the spring of 2007, detainee uprisings were a common occurrence at Camp Bucca in southern Iraq; the most dangerous one occurred in May, with upward of 10,000 prisoners rioting and nearly breaking through the wire. These events jeopardized the ability of MNF-I to continue detentions without resorting to lethal force. The situation was explosive and dangerous.

Task Force 134, under the command of Marine Major General Douglas Stone, realized that it needed to change the procedures used to hold and rehabilitate detainees or face defeat in this crucial facet of coalition operations in Iraq. The task force began by creating thousands of high-security detention cells, into which it placed the most hardcore extremists who were responsible for converting other detainees to the jihadist cause, who held Islamic courts inside the detention camps to enforce discipline, and who led the uprisings against coalition authorities. Over the course of 2007 and 2008, several thousand extremists were segregated from the general detainee population, and thereby prevented from using Camp Bucca to create the next terrorist class to join the jihadist ranks upon release.[32]

Just as importantly, Task Force 134 began to view the general detainee population as a strategic opportunity. The vast majority of the detainees were enrolled in a variety of rehabilitative programs to include literacy classes, trade and craft courses, and work at a brick factory created on site (stamped on each brick in Arabic was the phrase: "Brick by brick we rebuild the nation"). An art gallery allowed detainees to express themselves in a variety of media. Prisoners were encouraged to sing the Iraqi national anthem. Imams teaching a mainstream, moderate version of Islam were allowed to hold regular, voluntary courses for the inmates; the classes were oversubscribed. Families were allowed to visit detainees on site at regular intervals. Perhaps most importantly, US and Iraqi authorities held hearings for each detainee every six months, and allowed detainees to appear at these inquiries to tell their side of the events that led to their imprisonment. The result of all of these programs was the isolation of the hardcore extremists, a large drop in detainee violence, the rehabilitation of low-risk prisoners, and the release back into Iraqi society of thousands of men who had become part of the solution to Iraq's future rather than the bane of Task Force 134's existence. As of mid-2008, the recidivism rate among those released who had gone through these revised programs was less than 1 percent—an enormous achievement for a detention system that was considered among the worst in the world only five years earlier.[33]

Conclusion

Whether used in an enemy-centric or a population-centric strategy, ground forces are vital to the conduct of counterinsurgency warfare. They seek out and destroy insurgent forces, they neutralize enemy sanctuaries and safe havens, they hold ground, they build or reconstruct infrastructure and civil institutions, and they are responsible for the detention of prisoners. Armies, steeped in the tradition and doctrine of conventional warfare, all too often enter counterinsurgency operations without the awareness and knowledge necessary for their effective prosecution. Their ability to catalog and learn from their mistakes then becomes a crucial factor in whether they are able to restructure their forces and revise their warfighting doctrine in time to make a difference in the eventual outcome of the conflict. Since insurgencies are normally long-run affairs, ground forces have time to adapt provided they can sustain popular support for their continued involvement. The question, then, is how many body bags commanders will fill in the interim as they grapple with the changes required to fight successfully, and ultimately to win these kinds of wars.

Notes

1   Henry Butterfield Ryan, *The Fall of Che Guevara: A Story of Soldiers, Spies, and Diplomats*, Oxford: Oxford University Press, 1998.
2   Tacitus, *Agricola*, Chapter 30. Translation available at http://www.gutenberg.org/dirs/etext05/8aggr10.txt.
3   The Jamestown Foundation, "Amnesty International Issues Reports on Disappearances," May 24, 2007, http://www.jamestown.org/programs/ncw/single/?tx_ttnews[tt_news]=4179&tx_ttnews[back Pid]=189&no_cache=1.
4   John Russell, "Chechnya: Russia's 'war on terror' or 'war of terror'?," *Europe-Asia Studies*, Vol. 59, No. 1 (January 2007), 163–8.

86   *Peter Mansoor*

5   Byron Farwell, *The Great Anglo-Boer War*, New York: W.W. Norton, 1976, pp. 392–7.
6   Caroline Elkins, *Imperial Reckoning: The Untold Story of Britain's Gulag in Kenya*, New York: Henry Holt, 2005.
7   Brian McAllister Linn, *The U.S. Army and Counterinsurgency in the Philippine War, 1899–1902*, Chapel Hill: The University of North Carolina Press, 1989, pp. 163–5.
8   Neil Sheehan, *A Bright Shining Lie: John Paul Vann and America in Vietnam*, New York: Random House, 1988, pp. 540–2.
9   Peter R. Mansoor, *Baghdad at Sunrise: A Brigade Commander's War in Iraq*, New Haven, CT: Yale University Press, 2008, pp. 104–9.
10 Bing West, *The Strongest Tribe: War, Politics, and the Endgame in Iraq*, New York: Random House, 2008, pp. 47–61.
11 CNN.com, "Bush: 'As the Iraqis stand up, we will stand down,'" June 28, 2005, http://www.cnn.com/2005/POLITICS/06/28/bush.excerpts/index.html.
12 West, *The Strongest Tribe*, pp. 159–66.
13 Daniel Marston, "Lessons in 21ˢᵗ Century Counterinsurgency: Afghanistan 2001–2007," in Daniel Marston and Carter Malkasian (eds), *Counterinsurgency in Modern Warfare*, Oxford: Osprey, 2008, pp. 231–2.
14 Peter R. Mansoor, "Counterinsurgency in Karbala," in Thomas G. Mahnken and Thomas A. Keaney (eds), *War in Iraq: Planning and Execution*, London: Routledge, 2007, pp. 187–97.
15 George Packer, "Letter from Iraq: The Lesson of Tal Afar," *The New Yorker*, April 10, 2006.
16 David Galula, *Counterinsurgency Warfare: Theory and Practice*, New York: Praeger, 1964, p. 4.
17 Andrew F. Krepinevich, Jr, *The Army and Vietnam*, Baltimore, MD: The Johns Hopkins University Press, 1986.
18 Lewis Sorley, *A Better War: The Unexamined Victories and Final Tragedy of America's Last Years in Vietnam*, Orlando, FL: Harcourt, 1999.
19 Sergio Catignani, "The Israel Defense Forces and the Al-Aqsa Intifada," in Marston and Malkasian, *Counterinsurgency in Modern Warfare*, pp. 203–19.
20 Packer, "Letter from Iraq."
21 The author commanded the Ready First Combat Team in Iraq in 2003–4, and turned command of the organization over to Colonel MacFarland the following year.
22 Niel Smith and Sean MacFarland, "Anbar Awakens: The Tipping Point," *Military Review* (March/April 2008), 52.
23 Ibid., 41–52.
24 The US Army/Marine Corps Field Manual, *Counterinsurgency* (FM 3-24), Chicago: University of Chicago Press, 2007.
25 For an early analysis of the genesis of the surge strategy, see Bob Woodward, *The War Within: A Secret White House History 2006–2008*, New York: Simon & Schuster, 2008.
26 Linda Robinson, *Tell Me How This Ends: General David Petraeus and the Search for a Way Out of Iraq*, New York: Public Affairs, 2008, pp. 119–24.
27 Peter Mansoor, "How the Surge Worked," *The Washington Post*, August 10, 2008.
28 David Petraeus, "Learning Counterinsurgency: Observations from Soldiering in Iraq," *Military Review*, Vol. 86 (January/February 2006), 4–5.
29 Mansoor, *Baghdad at Sunrise*, pp. 135–7.
30 David Kilcullen, Small Wars Center of Excellence Counterinsurgency Seminar 07, Quantico, Virginia, September 26, 2007, http://smallwarsjournal.com/blog/2007/10/hearts-and-minds/.
31 Alistair Horne, *A Savage War of Peace: Algeria, 1954–1962*, New York: Penguin, 1979, pp. 195–207.
32 Major General Douglas Stone, Briefing, *Small Wars Journal*, June 11, 2008, http://smallwarsjournal.com/blog/2008/06/major-general-douglas-stone-br/.
33 Ibid.

7 Marine Corps

Frank Hoffman

The US Marine Corps approach to dealing with insurgencies is framed by its own experiences in the twentieth century. This includes two separate periods of extensive exposure to ambiguous diplomatic support missions before World War II and in the Vietnam War era. This chapter details how that foundation was formed, and how it influences the Corps' adoption of updated doctrine to deal with the complex insurgencies of the twenty-first century.

The Marine Corps' reputation for their mastery of small wars is firmly grounded in the so-called Banana Wars of Central America and the Caribbean. But their initial exposure to stability operations actually started in the Philippines. After Dewey's dramatic 1898 victory at the Battle of Manila Bay, the pacification of the Philippine people did not go well. The Marines were ordered to organize and dispatch a regiment, which was the largest deployed formation up until that time. Under the command of Major Littleton Waller, the Marines helped tame the rebellion led by the Filipino leader Emilio Aguinaldo. Working closely with Army and Navy officers, the Marines helped dampen the rebellion with an arduous campaign fought principally in the jungle and on the fringes of population centers. During this campaign the Marines honed counterinsurgency skills and jungle combat techniques, learning to maintain jungle base camps, train indigenous personnel, employ translators, and adapt to foreign cultures. From the Army, the Marines learned the non-kinetic aspects of a counter-insurgency, especially public works, local governance, and the training of native police forces.[1]

This experience was applied a little more than a decade later when the Marines were ordered into Haiti in 1915 to restore order. The Marines were not strangers to Haiti or its capital Port au Prince, having conducted 19 landings there between 1857 and 1913 to quell disorder and protect the lives and property of American citizens. This time however, the president ordered the Navy to take charge, and more than 2000 Marines were sent in again under the command of the ubiquitous Colonel Waller.

The Marines provided local security, as well as medical care, feeding the elderly and disabled, and disarming the population. Generous amnesty conditions and weapons buyback programs also proved to be valuable. Eventually the Americans exerted pressure to install a favored official as the local face to the US-dominated government, but this produced a backlash among the local population. This uprising was quickly crushed by aggressive assaults by the Marines on rebel strongholds, as well as courteous treatment for prisoners, surrendered *cacos* (as the peasant guerrillas from the North were known), and supporters.

Ultimately the Marines turned to raising the *Gendarmerie d'Haiti*, a cadre of local police led by the famous Marine Lieutenant Colonel Smedley Butler and officered by young Marine non-commissioned officers (NCOs). These aggressive NCOs developed effective small local units, and the *Gendarmerie* was sufficient to keep the peace for a few quiet years until a second *caco* war began in 1919. The *Gendarmerie* was increasingly ineffective at maintaining local order or in dampening the growing power of the *cacos*. The rebel leader Charlmagne Peralte and his 5000 followers persistently attacked the Marines for the latter part of 1919. Peralte was killed by a Marine sergeant, but pictures of his corpse gave the locals the mistaken impression that their leader had been crucified. The Marines knew the impact of village gossip but here they learned the importance of psychology and the power of imagery.

While improving local governance and public infrastructure was the principal thrust of the American campaign, credible military force and local security were also required. The Marines are credited with killing 2250 *cacos* and took 11,000 prisoners over a five-year period, at the cost of 13 Marines.

The Marine experience in Nicaragua followed much the same pattern. The Marines had been stationed there since 1912 when they had landed to put down a revolt. A legation guard remained until President Harding decided in 1924 to withdraw them. But election disputes and local disorder brought them back in 1926, to protect US lives and property but more accurately to bolster the pro-US government of Adofo Diaz. A total of 2000 Marines were dispatched. They bolstered the government and stiffened American diplomatic efforts to arrange a truce between competing factions. The Marines garrisoned more than a dozen towns, and their complement grew to a full brigade of 3300 Marines, including two squadrons of aircraft.

Most of the contesting factions were willing to negotiate but one holdout, Augusto Cesar Sandino, refused to participate. He held out for five years, eluding every snare. As in Haiti, the Marines raised up a local *guardia* as a constabulary force which augmented their number and afforded them better local intelligence.

The Marines continued to apply pressure against the insurgents, pressing deeper into rebel territory and using rivers to penetrate into guerrilla strongholds. The goal was to maintain constant pressure on the rebels and deny them sanctuary. These patrols relentlessly tracked the rebels and slowly wore down their forces, supplies, and safe zones. As in all the Banana War campaigns, these patrols reflected lessons the Marines had absorbed into their doctrine and culture. The value of aggressive small-unit leadership, decentralized operations, disciplined and accurate marksmanship, rigorous training, relentless patrols and pressure, and intimate interaction with local units, were the principal characteristics learned by the Marines in this era.

The Marines published their lessons learned in their *Small Wars Manual*, first printed in 1935.[2] Almost 75 years later, the manual is still an excellent primer on low-intensity conflict and is still required reading in Marine Corps institutions of military education. The Marines gained an early appreciation of the political and socioeconomic aspects of counterinsurgency or guerrilla warfare. Operations were characterized by a detailed understanding and empathy for the local population, small-unit patrolling to maintain pressure and to isolate insurgents, and the training of locally grown constabulary forces.

The Marines dusted off this experiential foundation in Vietnam with their promotion of the Combined Actions Program (CAP). Marines trace CAP back to their own experiences in the "small wars" of Central America, specifically Nicaragua. The CAP proved to be an innovative concept and a cost-effective program for irregular conflict. Several US Army students of the war in Southeast Asia credit the Marines with a unique and valuable initiative.[3]

The CAP placed Marine squads in villages to serve as security and mentoring forces to bolster local militia platoons, known as popular forces or PFs. These PF units were generally poorly trained and outgunned even by the Viet Cong (VC). Each of the Marine squads was originally integrated into a PF platoon to form what was known at first as a "joint action platoon." These units would live, eat, train, and operate together within a village. The Marines would provide training, moral support, and advice on patrols; they would strengthen the defensive positions in and around the village, and provide fire support coordination from US assets if needed. The program grew over time, and included crash courses in Vietnamese culture and political architecture at the local level.

Early results were achieved, and local security improved to the point that government officials and elders began sleeping in their homes again instead of at fortified positions. As the villagers felt more secure from VC coercion they began to provide tactical intelligence. Thus, other Marine units throughout the I Corps zone emulated the technique. Ultimately the CAP effort got official support from senior Marine leaders, especially Lieutenant General Lewis Walt, the commanding general of III Marine Amphibious Force and a veteran of the earlier small-wars era. Yet the program was criticized by Army leaders more oriented toward directly eliminating the insurgents via "search and destroy" missions.

At its apex in 1969 some 2000 Marines were engaged in this effort, allocated to 114 CAP platoons organized into four combined actions groups. By the metrics of the day, it was hugely successful. It was a low-cost program, and many Marines bonded effectively with their local units and with the villagers themselves. As demonstrated in Francis "Bing" West's book *The Village*, the Marines bonded with their villagers and PF teammates in most cases, and organized an effective combined Marine/PF defense that helped set the stage for the population's security and established a foundation for other pacification efforts to take root.[4]

The important point to take away from the CAP is the concept that defeating an insurgency is rarely a function of the external force achieving victory through kinetic means. The CAP did not attempt to defeat the insurgency directly; it sought to isolate the VC guerrillas and deprive them of the support and sanctuary they garnered by intimidating the local villagers. Not surprisingly, the Marines almost reflexively relied upon a modified version of CAP in Iraq at the very beginning of their operations in the post-conflict states of Operation Iraqi Freedom.[5] The Army-Marine Corps effort to develop updated counterinsurgency doctrine also incorporated a brief discussion of this approach.[6]

This indirect approach remains critical to the Corps operational philosophy in all modes of warfare. The essence of maneuver warfare is the creative and bold application of forces to generate and exploit opportunity. "Maneuver" in this context has a wider meaning than the usual use of the word: it is not limited to movement in a spatial sense, but seeks to generate an advantage in several dimensions. As defined in Marine Corps doctrine, "That advantage may be psychological, technological, or temporal as well as spatial."[7]

The noted British historian Basil Liddell Hart is responsible for this "maneuver" orientation. He ultimately found that military and strategic success was rarely the result of climatic battles or the direct clash of symmetrically arrayed and conventionally armed forces. Instead of attrition of forces in direct battles, he found that significant success was usually the result of what he called "*the indirect approach.*" Rather than costly attacks, he stressed taking the line of least resistance and avoiding direct engagements; instead, appearing where the opponent least expects it was thought to psychologically dislocate the enemy. Liddell Hart defined this orientation as the indirect approach, the essence of which is "to seek a strategic situation so advantageous that if it does not of itself produce the decision, its continuation by battle is guaranteed to do so."[8]

While the direct approach is characterized as relying solely on physical force, the indirect approach prizes surprise, maneuver, and adaptability over all. Liddell Hart found that the great captains strived to achieve the dislocation of the enemy's psychological and physical balance as a prelude to victory. Unlike the direct approach, the indirect approach incorporates both physical and psychological elements. The enemy's mental or moral equilibrium must be upset as a requisite to success. This psychological element plays such a key role, the indirect approach can be described as "more an attitude of mind than an arrow on the map."[9]

While traditionally associated with Liddell Hart's contributions to modern armor theory and the development of the German blitzkrieg concepts, this approach is not limited to massed columns of tanks. It does include an appreciation for the peculiar nature of irregular warfare, as Liddell Hart admired T.E. Lawrence and drew upon the *Seven Pillars of Wisdom* when developing his ideas about the indirect approach.[10]

The US Marines subscribe to this approach in their principal doctrinal manual, and refer to it as a warfighting philosophy as much as a doctrine.[11] Their approach builds on Liddell Hart as defined by the operational theory of the late Colonel John Boyd.[12] This maneuver warfare philosophy is well suited for winning against insurgents because it accepts the inevitability of chaos, complexity, and friction and the pre-eminence of the human element in conflict.

Maneuver warfare places a premium on intelligence, flexibility, and adaptability—essential attributes of a successful counterinsurgency force. Just as important, maneuver warfare emphasizes the human creativity and intellectual preparation that are crucial to the cognitive element in counterinsurgency. Maneuver warfare also places greater focus on achieving effects indirectly rather than simply applying mass firepower in order to conduct attrition of the opponent. Thus, the Marine Corps has the intellectual framework that positions it well for an era of small wars or global insurgency. This approach is completely consistent with the distilled wisdom of classical counterinsurgency theory.[13]

This background in the Marine understanding of small wars is the basis for a set of planning considerations or precepts for approaching this peculiar and protracted mode of conflict. These considerations are not a set of principles or "commandments." They require judgment and application based on the situation at hand, but were developed in order to capture the considerable history of these conflicts along with the several critical new elements in today's environment that mandate adaptation of classical counterinsurgency theory.[14]

Culture.   Commanders and planners must understand the complex dynamics of the threat and its cultural and political context, including the wider environment.[15] As stressed in the *Small Wars Manual*, a detailed understanding of human psychology, social customs, and the history of a people is crucial to preclude pitfalls and of primary importance in the development of plans.[16] The manual notes that "The campaign plan and strategy must be adapted to the character of the people encountered."[17] Planners must focus on the local population—the human terrain. This emphasis requires acute cultural intelligence; detailed knowledge of the ethnic, tribal, racial, economic, technical, religious, and linguistic groups in the host nation, as well as the underlying cultural beliefs and narratives that distinguish their value system.[18] Cultural awareness is definitely a force multiplier and friction reducer.[19]

Decentralization.   The nature of the opponent and the character of this mode of conflict place an emphasis on many small decisions being made in a timely manner with numerous contact points between the government and the population occurring simultaneously every day. Many of these contacts can accumulate to support the commander's overall intent if properly communicated and reinforced. The Marine concept of the "strategic corporal" captures the importance of tactical decisions producing strategic effects.

Collaboration. Unity of effort must be established by constantly integrating and completely coordinating with the host nation, coalition partners, the international community, and local officials. This is a significant leadership challenge at all levels. As noted in Marine doctrine, strong leadership is the foundation for unity of effort. The organizing imperative is focusing on what needs to be done, not on who does it.

Intelligence. Most intelligence is derived from the bottom up, from units on the street, but must be integrated with other sources. Existing intelligence networks may need to be adjusted to become more effective. Human intelligence will take on a dominant role, and commanders may elect to form special units specifically tasked with the collection and management of this intelligence. In the context of counterinsurgency, much more information will come from the bottom up. A lot of information will be acted upon immediately, to leverage its value. Much more will have to be collected, painstakingly connected to other sources to generate true intelligence. Quality tactical intelligence is required to enable Marine units to adapt faster and more effectively than the adversary.

Communicate. Communication—horizontally and vertically—is crucial in Lawrence's ever expanding circles. In conventional warfare, destruction is the norm, whereas in small wars, persuasion and influence are more often the objective. This shift in emphasis from destruction to persuasion is key to success in counterinsurgency. Words matter, and must be framed with relevance to the culture being communicated with. Expectations and perceptions must be managed carefully. The enemy's narrative must be countered and our "counterbattery" fires in the information domain should be as precise and timely as traditional kinetic fires.

Population emphasis. The population's security and needs are central. As per the maneuverist approach the Marines seek to "create gaps" between the population and the adversary, and "avoid surfaces" or directly confronting insurgents. The idea is to fight the enemy's strategy, not his forces by direct confrontation.[20] Fighting the insurgency directly only provokes more reactions and undermines the protection of the population.

Discriminant force. There is a classic statement in the venerable *Small Wars Manual*: "instead of striving to generate maximum power with forces available, the goal is to gain decisive results with the least application of force and the consequent minimum loss of life."[21] Excessive force is generally counterproductive and feeds the enemy narrative. The enemy seeks to provoke violent overreactions and is prepared to exploit casualties and collateral damage to its benefit. Force application is required but it must be purposely designed and well executed as part of the overall campaign.

Adaptability. Insurgencies are wars of learning and adapting. As the adversary adapts, success is the ability to quickly negate his initial success or identify in advance what he would be likely to do next, and negate it prior to execution. Insurgencies are a thinking man's game, and commanders are challenged to think about how they should adapt, and how the adversary will adapt as well. This will facilitate the cognitive challenge presented by irregular threats, and permit greater anticipation and initiative. Without initiative, maintaining the pressure on the insurgent becomes problematic. This implies continual assessment and an active effort to ensure that operations and metrics are being accurately captured.[22] Furthermore, adaptability requires being an objective critic of one's own operations.[23] Throughout a counterinsurgency campaign, programs, plans, and operations will either work or fail. It is imperative that operations are continually assessed as to their overall effectiveness to accomplish long-term goals. Some operations may provide initial success, but failure to assess the second- and third-order effects could result in a shortlived gain that could put you two steps forward then one step back. Learning and adaptation are critical to success in counterinsurgency.[24]

There is a strong correlation between the *Small Wars Manual* and the 2006 *Counterinsurgency* manual (FM 3-24). This correlation can be seen by comparing the general precepts of the pre-World War II manual with the formal principles and imperatives of counterinsurgency in FM 3-24. This explicit correlation is depicted in the table opposite. The only difference deals with the duration of operations. The *Small Wars Manual* strives to resolve matters quickly (regardless of the long duration missions executed in the 1920s), while FM 3-24 prepares its audience for the historically more protracted character of counterinsurgency operations.

To be successful at effectively countering irregular threats, the military must first view both the problem and the solution more holistically and completely. This is not an easy task. "Small wars involve a wide range of activities including diplomacy, contacts with the civil population and warfare of the most difficult kind."[25] Countering irregular threats requires an approach that effectively integrates US military operations with other instruments of influence. In many cases this will amount to supporting a host nation (government, populace, and military) in its efforts to effectively resolve the conditions that sustain an insurgent's cause or movement.

The Marines emphasize the holistic approach to countering irregular threats, and the need to work within a comprehensive approach that incorporates the full range of interagency tools and capabilities. This expanded perspective of campaign design reflects a broader appreciation of both the problem that leads to an intervention activity and the requisite solutions. This framework is laid out in a major concept document published at Quantico, which is consistent with FM 3-24.[26]

The construct groups the various efforts, or what might be seen as supporting mission elements, into six "lines of operation." These include the following: *combat operations, training and employment of host nation security forces, essential services, economic development, promotion of governance,* and *information operations.*[27] These lines of operation are not intended to be prescriptive in any way. They require increased coordination with other government agencies and potentially require tactical and operational integration.

The six lines of operation constitute a collection of mission elements that are generally involved in counterinsurgency operations. These lines of operation would be most effective if integrated and synchronized within a situation-specific concept of operation—none exists in isolation, nor should they be planned or executed in isolation of the other lines. "Success" in a singular line of operation may produce a gap relative to the other lines if the effort is not conducted in an integrated manner. The opponent could exploit this "gap" if he senses it. For this reason, Marine commanders closely integrate the various components of their operations, rather than think of the lines of operation as stovepipes. Moreover, Marine leaders are taught to ask themselves, "What will the effect of this action or effort be on the other lines of operation?"

Small Wars Manual	FM 3-24
"The purpose should always be to restore normal government or give the people a better government than they had before . . ." "The application of purely military measures may not, by itself, restore peace and orderly government because the fundamental causes of the condition of unrest may be economic, political or social."	*Legitimacy as the main objective*
"Small wars involve a wide range of activities including diplomacy, contacts with the civil population and warfare of the most difficult kind." "The efforts of the different agencies must be cooperative and coordinated to the attainment of the common end."	*Unity of effort*
"The military strategy of small wars is more directly associated with the political strategy of the campaign than is the case in major operations."	*Political factors are primary*
"The campaign plan and strategy must be adapted to the character of the people encountered."	*Counterinsurgents must understand the environment*
"This necessitates a knowledge of the mental soil in which the ideas that direct its course have to germinate."	*Intelligence drives operations*
"The resistance to an intervention comes not only from those under arms but also from those furnishing material or moral support to the opposition. Sapping the strength of the hostile ranks by the judicious application of psychological principles may be just as effective as battle casualties."	*Insurgents must be isolated from their cause and support*
"Military police functions and judicial authority, to the extent that they have been assumed by our military forces, are gradually returned to the native agencies to which they properly belong."	*Security under the rule of law is essential*
"The military strategic plan should include those means which will accomplish the purpose in view quickly and completely."	*Counterinsurgents should prepare for a long-term commitment*
"In small wars . . . instead of striving to generate the maximum power with forces available, the goal is to gain decisive results with the least application of force and the consequent minimum loss of life."	*Use the appropriate level of force*

Every operation will be particular, and while lessons from previous experiences may apply, there is not a "success template" that can be laid down across the various intervention activities in which the Marine Corps is likely to be engaged. Commanders have to use their education and intensive discourse with their staffs to identify the commonalities as well as the unique discontinuities that distinguish case histories from the problem at hand.[28] These lines of operation are not offered as a preset pattern. Each instance of conflict involving irregular threats will require a unique emphasis on the different lines of operation, and that is where the practice of operational art becomes most important.

Marine Corps forces will be engaged in countering irregular threats during all phases of a given intervention activity, and these lines of operation are relevant to all phases. However, a different emphasis may be placed on the various lines during the different phases.

Of the six lines of operation, the Marine Corps is most comfortable with planning and conducting combat operations. However, the combat operations required to counter irregular threats are often more complex and ambiguous in nature than conventional operations against a foe employing regular forces. These combat operations will pit Marines against an elusive enemy who will seek to avoid direct combat so that he can survive to strike another day.

Marine combat operations in an insurgency focus on securing the population's security and on protecting the government. To maintain freedom of action, operations may be planned to deny the insurgent sanctuary or to destroy weapons and logistics supplies. Operations may also seek to isolate the opponent in the physical sense, from any means of material aid. Irregular threats, be they traditional insurgents or non-state actors, must be cut off from external support as well. Historically, insurgent organizations seek outside assistance in order to survive.

Because of the need to reduce violence and to generate an advantage with a civilian population in counterinsurgency, large operations and sweeps are to be avoided. Rather than focus on using fires to attrite an adversary's forces by physical destruction, the counter-insurgency force must maneuver in the broader sense, creating multidimensional advantages to secure the civilian population, and build up the local government, protecting and enhancing its critical infrastructure and economic resources. The counterinsurgency force may seek a physical positional advantage with military or security forces in order to preserve its freedom of action, so as to move freely throughout the entire battlespace and to maintain close contact with the population.

Marine forces focus on the security of the population and on isolating the insurgents from the population. Policing or constabulary activities may, over time, begin to take precedence. Conversely, large-unit operations should not be the norm. The overwhelming priority should not be focused on "kill/capture" the enemy. Of course, this is not to say that larger operations will not occasionally be necessary. However, over time, most insurgencies evolve into small-unit actions in which large-scale operations with large units are less effective. Large-unit operations, especially if they are predicated on vague intelligence, are generally imprecise and indiscriminate, tend to disturb the population, and are rarely able to locate the insurgents. In the end, large-unit operations can often create more animosity than positive results (and thus continue to fuel the insurgency.)[29]

Another important consideration is the placement of military units as close to the population as possible. Large "secure" bases are good for "force protection," but they run counter to the idea of ensuring the population's security. Physical proximity and shared hardship with the people will help to establish and reinforce the population's perception that their security and needs are important, and will also symbolize a close relationship between counterinsurgents and population. Ultimately, it is the relationship that is most important and anything that separates the intervention force from the population, physically or psychologically, makes forming that relationship more difficult. The intelligence gained from a positive relationship and proximity is usually highly actionable if follow-up is prompt.

In all operations, whether they are combat or simply security operations, the emphasis is on countervalue targets versus counterforce efforts. That is to say, Marine operations do not focus directly to counter the insurgent's force. Instead, their operations are conducted to secure and advance the needs of the population and its legitimate government. They seek to build up value and credibility for the population, and deny the opponent the same. Anything that builds up the narrative that the local population is valued and that their needs are paramount is positive, and anything that targets the ability of the insurgents to generate or support their narrative is a countervalue target.

Force application, when required, is executed with careful discrimination. History shows that a lack of rectitude or an excess of violence leads to prolonged conflict.[30] The grasp of this historical element was central to the resistance of Marine leaders to conduct sweeping operations in Fallujah in March of 2004. They understood that with time, intelligence preparation, and a careful shaping of the battlespace, many lives could be spared and negative consequences of kinetic force could be avoided. That said, the need to conduct offensive operations when absolutely required is inherent to expeditionary operations, which the Marines ably demonstrated in November of that same year in Fallujah.

Another requirement of Marine counterinsurgency operations is engagement with and training of indigenous security forces. Governments of failed or failing states are unable to provide for the basic needs of the people and are unable to provide security within their borders. Consequently, non-state actors and insurgents from neighboring nations can take sanctuary there. To help these nations maintain stability, the US military will interact with the militaries and other security forces of selected nations that wish to be involved. Many of these engagement activities will be aimed principally at assisting these nations with the organization and training of their fighting units and with their police and security forces. [31]

The Marines realize from their own efforts in the small-wars era that there is a temptation to train foreign militaries "in our own image," with American equipment and standards. The Marines resist this urge and instead train the indigenous military in a manner that befits their purpose and situation. Context, culture, and operational requirements drive the training. The Marines have found that what is most effective in fighting an insurgency is a focus on training to obtain "brilliance in the basics" of small-unit operations.[32] When designing the training of foreign militaries and security forces, Marines in Iraq and Afghanistan have considered their specific purpose, and train to the level necessary to accomplish that purpose.

In many of the areas that the US becomes involved with, the existing government (assuming that there is one) often has difficulty providing for the people's needs. Expeditionary forces help re-establish essential services such as food, power, potable water, the handling of waste, and rudimentary medical care. When the Marines began stability operations in their assigned sectors in Iraq in 2003, they found that local governance and essential services became their principal tasks, and they struggled to adapt to the people's immediate requirements.

Part of achieving and maintaining stability in a region or country is the ability of the governing authority to meet people's basic human needs. Marine leaders need to make best use of their assessment teams, which should include personnel with expertise in these areas. Assessment teams should be employed during the initial stages of intervention to determine needs and to work with the rest of the staff to develop a plan to deal with these needs. The needs will change over time (perhaps quite rapidly) and Marine leaders need to be sensitive to these changing needs.

One of the most important aspects of a functioning society is the rule of law. There simply cannot be any lasting stability or order if there are no laws or enforcement of these laws. When Marines become involved in some form of intervention, they need to assess the state of the existing government's legal system. If one does not exist, Marines will need to help the local people develop and implement one. This may seem far afield from traditional warfighting tasks, but when it comes to building (or rebuilding) a nation's capacity to govern itself, it may prove to be one of the most critical areas. A functional legal system must minimally include civil and criminal laws, courts, a judiciary, and a means of incarcerating those people who the indigenous government's judiciary finds in breach of the laws. The judiciary should be incorruptible and viewed as such by the people. Likewise, the police force should be effective and should operate within the rule of law, and should be seen as responsive and protective.

Beyond the rule of law, a governmental bureaucracy must be formed (or re-formed). This bureaucracy or public administration must include ministries established along functional lines to manage the nation's governmental programs. These ministries will include (but not be limited to) interior functions such as power generation and distribution, water, public health, police (including recruiting, equipping, training, paying, and supervising), firefighting, border guards, education (primary and secondary), finance, infrastructure and transportation (roads, railroads, etc.), housing and human services, communications, agriculture, and natural resources. The ability of the local government to deliver positive results is vital to winning the allegiance of the population. The legitimacy of the government is closely linked to credible performance.

Economic development and stability is an underlying principle of American foreign interventions. The idea that governments need to help the whole population improve their lots, specifically their economic well being, plays an important role in US foreign policy. This line of operation must blend seamlessly with the other lines, and in fact may not be possible to act upon until some measure of security and governmental capacity is achieved. The intent here is to purposefully stimulate economic growth—to "mature" an economy. However, in many cases, before this economic growth can even begin to occur there must be adequate security for the population. Further, mass unemployment, if allowed to persist for even a modest amount of time, can provide a concrete element of discontent on which an insurgency can capitalize. In many intervention cases, there must be both a short-term and a long-term economic plan, the short-term plan being to find some productive way to employ large numbers of unemployed males—if only until more enduring employment opportunities can be developed. Of course, the long-term plan will entail measures that allow for self-sufficiency (that is, a strategy not reliant on US direct assistance).

In the early post-conflict phase of Operation Iraqi Freedom, the Marine Corps came face to face with the need to jumpstart the local economy and employment situation. The innovative use of Commander's Emergency Response Program (CERP) funding gave Marine commanders an invaluable opportunity to apply assistance with great discrimination and accuracy. In Iraq, commanders enjoyed some early latitude with cash discovered during raids or in abandoned Iraqi government facilities. But later the CERP funding was more centrally controlled and less responsive to local conditions and near-term requirements. Long-term economic development needs envisioned by the reconstruction and development experts have to be balanced with the need to jumpstart local employment and get potential insurgents focused on a better future. Beginning in 2004, Marines in al-Anbar province in Iraq made economic development their principal form of "maneuver."

Insurgencies frequently involve a "battle" of ideas and ideology. This political struggle, by its very nature, involves two groups contending for the support and control of the civilian population. Too often governments and their security forces are slow to perceive this struggle, and reluctant to embrace instruments of persuasion. But the Marines have long ago learned of the power of a strong narrative and the need to operate consistently with the central message and critical themes of that narrative. They agree with a key element of FM 3-24 that information operations are often the most critical line of operation.[33] The Marines also agree with Lawrence Freedman that everything gained in the physical environment is of little utility until it is exploited in the information domain.[34]

Ideas and grievances are the seeds of insurgencies, and modern information technology has given anyone with access to a computer the ability to spread a message globally at a fraction of what it used to cost, and at the speed of sound. Given that counterinsurgency efforts are ultimately won or lost in the political and psychological dimension, the importance of communications and information dissemination is vital. The velocity of information flows and the power of imagery can now be readily transmitted instantly. This can generate significant support for one's cause throughout the international system or through a network of sympathizers and supporters. It can be a force multiplier to the side that can employ the informational domain to secure and sustain a positional advantage in the moral or psychological dimension. Since popular opinion or support may be the center of gravity, the importance of these technological shifts cannot be overlooked.

This aspect of modern counterinsurgency has risen in salience as future irregular combatants continue to exploit Information Age tools to broaden their appeal and their resource base. "Winning hearts and minds" may have a more global orientation thanks to the ubiquitous and diffuse nature of modern communication techniques. The old *Small Wars Manual* noted the rapidity by which a revolution could develop due to modern communications technologies.[35] Today's "24/7" news cycles and graphic imagery produce even faster response cycles from audiences around the globe and offer powerful new "weapons" to those who can master them.[36]

The cumulative impact of many shaping actions can eventually achieve a "tipping point" in the minds of the civilian population. This describes a point in time where the population accepts and desires the existing government as the legitimate platform for the representation of its views, and authorizes the government to act on its collective behalf for the delivery of services and governance. This is the decisive point in the conflict. In al-Anbar in late 2006, in retrospect, we can see that the tipping point was ultimately gained with the tribal leadership. Al-Qaeda's corrosive tactics and the patient Marine security forces combined to create the conditions needed for that tipping point of the local population to be reached.

Conclusion

The Marine Corps has extensive experience with countering insurgencies and other so-called small wars. Over the years, consistent with Congressional direction, the Marines evolved into an expeditionary "force in readiness" in response to strategic changes in the security environment and turned away from many counterinsurgency principles. In the process, it forgot some of the lessons it learned during its storied past. Fortunately, many lessons captured in the *Small Wars Manual* have helped commanders and the Marine Corps educational system to accelerate the relearning cycle since 2003. The hard-earned experiences of Iraq and Afghanistan have locked in these lessons. The Marines recognize that this kind of conflict might characterize much of the foreseeable future and dominate the Corps' operational focus.[37] Though the Marine Corps will remain a multicapable force, its focus is set to shift more toward what appear to be more frequent complex and irregular conflicts of our age.

Notes

1 This section relies upon Max Boot, *The Savage Wars of Peace: Small Wars and the Rise of American Power*, New York: Perseus Books, 2002; Allan R. Millett, *Semper Fidelis: The History of the United States Marine Corps*, New York: Free Press, 1991; and Jon T. Hoffman, *Once A Legend: "Red Mike" Edson of the Marine Raiders*, Presidio, CA: Novato, 1994.

2 US Marine Corps, *Small Wars Manual*, Washington, DC: Government Printing Office, 1940. For a history of the development of this doctrine see Keith B. Bickel, *Mars Learning: The Marine Corps' Development of Small Wars Doctrine, 1915–1940*, Boulder, CO: Westview Press, 2001.

3 Andrew F. Krepinevich, *The Army in Vietnam*, Baltimore, MD: Johns Hopkins University Press, 1986. John A. Nagl, *Learning to Eat Soup with a Knife: Counterinsurgency Lessons from Malaya and Vietnam*, Chicago: University of Chicago Press, 2005.

4 On the CAP in Vietnam see Francis West, *The Village*, Madison, WI: University of Wisconsin Press, 1985.
5 On the CAP in Iraq see Jason G. Goodale and Jon Webre, "The Combined Action Platoon in Iraq," *Marine Corps Gazette* (April 2005), 35–42; Zachary J. Iscol, "CAP India," *Marine Corps Gazette* (January 2006), 54–60; Phillip C. Skuta, "Introduction to 2/7 CAP Platoon Actions in Iraq," and "Partnering With Iraqi Security Forces," *Marine Corps Gazette* (January 2006), 60.
6 FM 3-24, *Counterinsurgency*, Washington, DC: Department of the Army, 2006, p. 2-3.
7 US Marine Corps Doctrinal Publication 1, *Warfighting*, Washington, DC: GPO, June 20, 1997, p. 72.
8 B.H. Liddell Hart, *Paris: The Decisive Wars of History*, Boston: Little, Brown, 1929.
9 Alex Danchev, *Alchemist of War: The Life of Basil Liddell Hart*, London: Weidenfeld and Nicolson, 2003, p. 159.
10 B.H. Liddell Hart, *Lawrence of Arabia*, New York: De Capo, 1989. On the connections between Lawrence and Liddell Hart, see Azar Gat, *A History of Military Thought, From the Enlightenment to the Cold War*, Oxford: Oxford University Press, 2001, pp. 665–82.
11 US Marine Corps Doctrinal Publication 1, *Warfighting*.
12 For the best exposition of John Boyd's strategy theory see Frans P.B. Osinga, *Science, Strategy and War: The Strategic theory of John Boyd*, New York: Routledge, 2007.
13 Frank Kitson, *Low Intensity Operations*, Harrisburg, PA: Stackpole Books, 1971; David Galula, *Counterinsurgency Warfare: Theory and Practice*, St Petersburg, FL: Hailer, 2005; Robert Thompson, *Defeating Communist Insurgency: The Lessons of Malaya and Vietnam*, New York: Praeger, 1966.
14 F.G. Hoffman, "Neo-classical Counterinsurgency Theory?," *Parameters* (Summer 2007), 71–87.
15 US Marine Corps, *Small Wars Manual*, p. 1-11.
16 Ibid., p. 1-11: "The knowledge of the people at any given moment of history involves an understanding of their environment, and above all, their past."
17 Ibid., p. 1-8.
18 The Marine Corps places significant resources behind this point, having established a formal center on operational culture within its training and education establishment, and creating chairs in culture at the Marine Corps University. See Barak A. Salmoni and Paula Holmes-Eber, *Operational Culture for the Warfighter: Principles and Applications*, Quantico, VA: MCU Press, 2008.
19 David H. Petraeus, "Learning Counterinsurgency: Observations from Soldiering in Iraq," *Military Review*, Vol. 86 (January/February 2006), 8.
20 David J. Kilcullen, "Twenty Eight Articles," *Military Review* (May/June 2006), 107.
21 US Marine Corps, *Small Wars Manual*, p. 1-17.
22 Kilcullen, "Twenty Eight Articles," 106. Kilcullen stresses the need to take stock regularly.
23 Angel Rabasa, Lesley Warner, Peter Chalk, Ivan Khilko, and Paraag Shulka, *Money in the Bank; Lessons from Past Counterinsurgencies*, Santa Monica, CA: Rand Corporation, 2008, p. 69.
24 The principal theme of the work of Army veteran and scholar John A. Nagl (*Learning to Eat Soup with a Knife*, Chicago: University of Chicago Press, 2005) and the underlying critical thread throughout FM 3-24.
25 US Marine Corps, *Small Wars Manual*, p. 1-17.
26 US Marine Corps, *A Tentative Manual for Countering Irregular Threats: An Updated Approach to Counterinsurgency*, Quantico, VA: Marine Corps Combat Development Command, August 7, 2007.
27 Peter Chiarelli and Patrick Michaelis, "Winning the Peace: The Requirement for Full Spectrum Operations," *Military Review* (July/August 2005), 7.
28 Eliot Cohen, "Military Strategy and the Historical Mind," *Orbis* (Fall 2005), 575–88 .
29 Kalev I. Sepp, "Best Practices in Counterinsurgency," *Military Review* (May/June 2005), 10.
30 Anthony James Joes, *Resisting Rebellion: The History And Politics Of Counter-insurgency*, Lexington, KY: University Press of Kentucky, 2004.
31 Julian D. Alford and Edwin O. Rueda, "Winning in Iraq, Time to Change our Operational Paradigm," *Marine Corps Gazette* (June 2006), 29–30.
32 Sepp, "Best Practices in Counterinsurgency," 10.
33 FM 3-24, p. 5-8.
34 "Superiority in the physical environment is of little value unless it can be translated into an advantage in the information environment." Lawrence Freedman, *The Transformation of Strategic Affairs*, London: IISS, Adelphi Paper No. 379, 2006, p. 20.

35 US Marine Corps, *Small Wars Manual*, p. 1-13.
36 Audrey Kurth Cronin, "Cyber Mobilization: The New Levee en Masse," *Parameters* (Summer 2006), 77–87.
37 James Conway, *Marine Corps Vision and Strategy 2025*, Washington, DC: Headquarters Marine Corps, June 2008.

8   Airpower

Charles J. Dunlap, Jr

Basically . . . we're the bullet sponge.

First Lieutenant David Wright, US Army, Afghanistan, 2008

"Bullet sponge?" A flip comment by a junior officer perhaps, but according to the lieutenant's superior, the actual tactic was not much more sophisticated: the young American officer's isolated command was to serve as a "Taliban magnet" to draw attacks away from Afghan villages.[1] Though this may be a time-honored infantry approach to finding and fixing the enemy for attack, it is unfortunate that after more than seven years of counterinsurgency operations, US strategy accords such a melancholy and distinctly primitive role to our ground forces. Where, one might ask, is America's technological prowess? Where is America's airpower?[2]

Actually, even though its potential has yet to be fully exploited, America's airpower plays an increasingly important role in counterinsurgency operations. Although the much-vaunted Field Manual, *Counterinsurgency* (FM 3-24), confined airpower to a five-page annex,[3] in practice the use of airpower has skyrocketed in both Iraq and Afghanistan in recent years. Anthony Cordesman, while acknowledging that press reports of both wars focus "on the ground dimension," asserts that the conflicts are "air wars as well, and wars where airpower has also played a critical role in combat."[4]

Of course, airpower is not—*and can never be*—"the" exclusive solution to counterinsurgency challenges. Rather, it takes a sophisticated application of the capabilities of the entire joint team, as well as those elements of national power beyond the armed forces, to succeed.

Still, the lack of appreciation for the role of airpower as one element of the counterinsurgency solution frustrates many. Air Force Association president Michael Dunn argued in 2008 that the "so-called troop surge" into Iraq has "really been an airpower surge."[5] He maintains that air "sorties are up 85%; air strikes are up 400%; weight of ordnance dropped is up 1000%," and adds, "[s]ome insiders say that 90% of the terrorists being killed are being killed by airpower."[6] Regarding Afghanistan, analyst Lara M. Dadkhah insisted in *Small Wars Journal* in December of 2008 that "[a]irpower's role in counterinsurgency may be relegated to an appendix in the US military's COIN manual, but American air dominance has been and continues to be crucial to sustaining combat operations in Afghanistan."[7]

Why then does the COIN manual put so little stock in airpower? Several rationales are possible, but the most likely is not nefarious. FM 3-24 represents a brilliant distillation of "lessons learned" from past counterinsurgency operations, and especially the half-century following World War II. What was derived from that effort is a paradigm for success that is overwhelmingly ground-force intensive. In fact, FM 3-24's marginalization of airpower does not differ appreciably from other studies of earlier counterinsurgency operations.

A 2006 Rand Corporation report exemplifies the consensus. It found that historically "insurgencies do not present opportunities for the overwhelming application of the air instrument."[8] Accordingly, it reports, "air power has been used in a less-visible supporting role."[9] Most analysts to date seem to agree with this "supporting role" assessment. James S. Corum and Wray R. Johnson wrote in their 2003 book, *Airpower in Small Wars*, that "[t]he support role of airpower . . . is usually the most important and effective mission in guerrilla war."[10]

Unfortunately for the FM 3-24 writers, the technological changes in airpower have been so rapid and so recent that it is almost impossible to have accommodated them in the traditional doctrine drafting process. Even so, the exigencies of the ongoing wars have led to the fielding of a variety of airpower capabilities that have, according to Army General Barry McCaffrey (Retd), "fundamentally changed the nature of warfare." In the fall of 2007, he observed that:

> We have already made a 100-year war-fighting leap-ahead with MQ-1 Predator,[11] MQ-9 Reaper,[12] and Global Hawk.[13] Now we have loiter times in excess of 24 hours, persistent eyes on target, micro-kill with Hellfire and 500-lb JDAM bombs, synthetic aperture radar, and a host of ISR [intelligence, surveillance, and reconnaissance] sensors and communications potential that have fundamentally changed the nature of warfare.[14]

In short, the rise of *precision*—in strike, airdrop, and reconnaissance—along with the *persistence* and *information* revolutions, requires a complete rethinking as to how the US ought to conduct counterinsurgency operations. Accordingly, this chapter contends that the future of counterinsurgency—at least insofar as the US is concerned—must depart from the manpower-intense formula of FM 3-24. While it does *not* assert that American counterinsurgency operations should necessarily be air-centric, it does argue that they should be *technology-centric*.

Counterinsurgency today

The most significant analytic issue of contemporary counterinsurgency operations is the difficulty in ascertaining exactly what is proving effective. Theories abound. In late 2008, America's most widely read newsweekly, *Parade*,[15] reflected popular perceptions about the dramatic decline in violence in Iraq: "Military analysts credited [the decline to the] 'surge' of 30,000 fresh US troops that began in 2007 and the emergence of the Sons of Iraq . . . former insurgents paid by the US to help protect neighborhoods and provide intelligence."[16] Moreover, according to *Defense News*, it was a "softer approach" by soldiers and Marines that had "won allies" in Iraq.[17]

All of this is in keeping with what has become the "public persona" of FM 3-24; that is, that defeating insurgencies centers around deploying masses of ground-force counterinsurgents (20 per 1000 of the population according to FM 3-24), each ideally performing at various times a role the manual describes as a "social worker, a civil engineer, a school teacher, a nurse, [and] a boy scout." Such "soft" approaches, it is widely believed, win for counterinsurgent forces the "hearts and minds" of the local populace.

This view is not especially surprising given what one participant in FM 3-24's drafting process called the "odd fraternity" that was assembled to aid military personnel in developing the doctrine. Described as "representatives of human rights nongovernmental

organizations and international organizations, academic experts, civilian agency representatives, [and] journalists,"[18] they obviously were influential in shaping the final text away
from what had been history's proven (albeit often troubling) solution to insurgencies: hard
power relentlessly and remorselessly applied.[19]

The New Yorker magazine describes the strategy this "odd fraternity" produced as being:

> [W]arfare for northeastern graduate students—complex, blended with politics, designed
> to build countries rather than destroy them, and fashioned to minimize violence. It was
> a doctrine with particular appeal to people who would never own a gun.[20]

Naturally, such a construct of counterinsurgency gives airpower—and particularly its kinetic
dimension—short shrift. It also makes hostility to the relevance of "killing and capturing" an
unchallenged totem of counterinsurgency theory today.

The "inconvenient truth" is that the counterinsurgency success since 2007 is more than
simply the application of a "softer" approach. Indeed, it appears that the role of "hard power"
may be undervalued in the literature. Consider the utility of "capturing." At one stage in 2007,
the first year of FM 3-24's implementation and the year most consider the turning point in
Iraq, "nearly 30,000"[21] Iraqis were imprisoned, a huge escalation over the previous high of
16,000 detainees. This number is all the more significant when one considers that as late as
the fall of 2006, the *total* number of insurgents in Iraq was estimated by the Brookings
Institution at only 20–30,000.[22]

Tragically, killing surged as well. *USA Today* reported in September 2007 that the number
of insurgents slain was already 25 percent ahead of 2006.[23] Unconfirmed reports indicate that
the total number killed may have nearly doubled, or more, over 2006.[24] Importantly, it appears
that it was not just killing insurgents per se that was effective; it was the attrition of particular
individuals that may have been most significant.

The Washington Post enunciated this new interpretation while discussing Bob Woodward's
recent book, *The War Within*.[25] It argues that the surge "was not the primary factor behind
the steep drop in violence there during the past 16 months."[26] Instead, it was new covert
techniques to "target and kill insurgent leaders and key individuals in extremist groups."[27]
Though "killing" is not, and can never be, the whole answer to insurgency—and is certainly
undesirable—it is, nevertheless, apparently a more effective element to overall strategy than
some COIN aficionados are wont to think.

Additionally, emerging evidence indicates that "surging" foreign forces into countries
suffering from an insurgency may be less helpful than popular wisdom assumes; indeed, as
a "lesson" applicable to future counterinsurgency operations, deploying masses of US troops
may be exactly the wrong approach. Expert after expert has come to much the same conclusion
as William R. Polk did in his 2007 history of insurgencies. The "fundamental motivation"
for insurgencies, he says, is "primarily to protect the integrity of the native group from
foreigners."[28]

Zbigniew Brzezinski likewise insists, "most of the anti-U.S. insurgency in Iraq has *not* been
inspired by al-Qaeda" but rather by jihadist groups that are "able to identify themselves with
the fight against a hated foreign occupier."[29] A 2008 Rand Corporation study similarly found
that combating terrorist groups requires a light US military presence or none at all.[30] In fact,
a large American military footprint, it assessed, "is likely to increase terrorist recruitment."[31]

Most importantly, notwithstanding *Defense News'* assertion to the contrary, the data seem
to demonstrate that few "allies" were actually "won." A February 2008 poll of Iraqis shows
that 61 percent believe that the presence of US troops in Iraq made the security situation

worse.[32] Among those who believe the security situation improved, only 4 percent attributed it to US troops; even Muqtada al-Sadr garnered more credit (5 percent).[33] Disturbingly, in spite of the purportedly "softer" approach, 42 percent of Iraqis stated that they still found attacks on US forces "acceptable."[34]

An early 2009 poll of the US public ought to be of even greater consequence to counterinsurgency strategists. Despite the military success in Iraq since 2007, 61 percent of Americans still believe the war was "not worth it."[35] Furthermore, in other polls 63 percent said they still oppose the war,[36] and 58 percent expressed the view that it was "the wrong thing to do."[37] The implications of such attitudes are profound. Dr James Corum, a contributor to FM 3-24, believes that given the US experience in Iraq, it is doubtful that the American body politic would support like efforts elsewhere, "no matter how necessary or justified they might be."[38]

Furthermore, the manpower-intensive methodology of FM 3-24 is extremely costly. The 74,000 additional troops that then undersecretary of defense for policy Ryan Henry said the Army needs for the "irregular type of campaign that we can find ourselves in"[39] will cost the service an astounding $40 billion *annually.*[40] Indeed, the Center for Strategic and Budgetary Assessments found that by late 2008 the cost of deploying just *one* soldier for a year escalated to a mind-numbing bill of $775,000.[41]

Yet in the face of such data, *The Atlantic* magazine reported in its October 2008 issue that the "Iraq-style counterinsurgency is fast becoming the US Army's organizing principle."[42] Can airpower help to offer decision makers alternatives to the manpower-intensive "Iraq-style counterinsurgency" approach?

Airpower and tomorrow's COIN

Airpower allows for the US to maintain a small footprint of ground forces when waging counterinsurgency campaigns. It represents an alternative to the manpower-intensive counterinsurgency style of campaign seen in Iraq. Undeniably, counterinsurgency and other forms of "irregular war"[43] are likely to continue to challenge US interests. According to the National Defense Strategy, "[f]or the foreseeable future, winning the Long War against violent extremist movements will be the central objective of the U.S."[44] For that reason, defense professionals must devise courses of action to address that threat, which could manifest itself in an insurgency anywhere on the globe.

There is no obligation to employ "Iraq-style counterinsurgency" as the "organizing principle" for doing so. In a 2000 article about urban operations, the current Air Force chief of staff expresses what should be a central tenet (if not an "organizing principle") of twenty-first-century American counterinsurgency efforts; that is, exploiting airpower to help "control an adversary without necessarily introducing a large ground-combat force, thus minimizing casualties while achieving the desired effect."[45]

What can modern airpower offer? To explore the answer fully (an effort beyond the scope of this short chapter) it should be understood that while America has but one "Air Force," the air arms of the sister services (and other government agencies) are also vital elements of the nation's overall airpower capability. Joint and complementary uses of the airpower capabilities so defined are "musts" in twenty-first-century counterinsurgency operations. For its part, the Air Force has outlined its capabilities and related operations in Air Force Doctrine Document (AFDD) 2-3, Irregular Warfare.[46] Although distributed in August 2007, it is already under revision in an effort to account for the dramatic technological changes that are rapidly overtaking it (just as such advances have rendered FM 3-24's treatment of airpower obsolete).

Still, AFDD 2-3 effectively identifies a range of Air Force resources and competencies relevant to counterinsurgency. These include intelligence, surveillance, and reconnaissance (ISR) systems, air mobility, agile combat support, precision engagement, and command and control. It also reiterates one of airpower's most important virtues: it avoids the issues associated with a sizeable presence in the host country. It observes that a large US ground force on foreign soil "may exacerbate the local situation while providing adversaries a new target set for attacks and propaganda"; while airpower "can deliver a variety of effects from great distance without increasing force presence in a region or country."[47]

Indeed, the most attractive option for decision makers may well not be "Iraq-style" COIN, but rather a small "footprint" approach that effectively and efficiently leverages technology, to include airpower. Air Force Colonel Phillip S. Meilinger (Retd) insists that in the twenty-first century the US "must find a way to achieve its political goals with the least cost in blood and treasure."[48] To Meilinger, the paradigm ought to be not "Iraq-style" counterinsurgency, but rather the "US-led victories in Bosnia (1995), Kosovo (1999), Afghanistan (2001), and Iraq (2003), achieved using a combination of air and space power, special operations forces, indigenous ground forces, and robust intelligence assets."[49] (One might add to this list the quiet successes in Colombia[50] and the Philippines.)

The impetus for this "small footprint" approach does not come exclusively from aviators, however. General John A. Wickham, the former chief of staff of the Army, argues that "[l]arge military forces alienate local populations, succeed less and cost more."[51] His approach has many of the same elements as Meilinger's, as it focuses on training and equipping indigenous forces, and backing them with US-provided "modern" intelligence, communications, and "aerial support."[52]

Both plans have several common denominators. With respect to intelligence, the ISR capabilities of unmanned aerial systems (UAS) are well known, but perhaps less recognized is what other aircraft like the E-8C[53] can provide today. This airborne battle-management platform can "gather and display detailed battlefield information" and convey it to ground forces.[54] What is particularly interesting is the ability to "backtrack" after an incident occurs. It can literally replay the event and trace the origin of an attack, and provide that data to friendly forces.[55]

The combination of US advisor corps, such as that recommended by John Nagl,[56] and high-tech air assets vastly increases not just the combat power of indigenous forces, but also their belief in themselves. For example, during one of the earliest Iraqi-led operations, the Iraqi army "showed itself to be considerably resilient when backed by coalition airpower."[57]

One of the rationales for downplaying the role "killing and capturing" plays in counter-insurgency's success is the idea that an insurgency has an endless supply of recruits. Perhaps so, but the reality is that there is a finite number of effective leaders and other skilled personnel. Even FM 3-24 agrees that "leadership is critical to any insurgency," so eliminating that "critical" component would diminish an insurgency's effectiveness. Interestingly, one analyst argues that eliminating individuals with required technical skills "will degrade the insurgency's ability to operate more than the removal of its ostensible leadership."[58]

Airpower can play a big role in striking these individuals. Indeed, what is revolutionary about twenty-first-century airpower is its unprecedented ability to do exactly what *The Washington Post* argued was so decisive in suppressing violence in Iraq; that is, the ability to "target and kill insurgent leaders and key individuals in extremist groups." Journalist Mark Benjamin described airpower's current capabilities this way:

> The Air Force recently watched one man in Iraq for more than five weeks, carefully recording his habits—where he lives, works and worships, and whom he meets . . . The

military may decide to have such a man arrested, or to do nothing at all. Or, at any moment they could decide to blow him to smithereens.[59]

Today's capabilities create a proverbial "unblinking eye" staring at insurgents.[60] According to Lieutenant General Gary L. North, commander of US Air Forces Central, the ISR technology is such that: "We literally have pilots now walking ground forces through cornfields and backyards, telling them where insurgents are hiding."[61] Is all this having an effect? The *Los Angeles Times* quoted European experts as saying that the "aerial onslaught" in Afghanistan is depleting al-Qaeda leadership to the point where it is "having genuine problems replacing some of [its] top individuals."[62]

Impacting insurgent psychology

As important as it may be to kill particular insurgents, it is equally—or more—important to affect their psychology. In fact, the chief effect of the precision and persistence advances that General McCaffrey says have "fundamentally changed warfare" may be as much psychological as physical. Where once airpower pioneers sought to use bombing to crush the morale of entire populations,[63] the technological qualities of today's airpower creates opportunities for airmen to impose extreme stress on *specific* individuals and groups.

Inflicting *precise* airpower *persistently* upon adversaries unable to defend against it devastates morale. A former Republican Guard officer told *The Washington Post* in 2003 that the intense air bombardment so unhinged Iraqi troops that their "will to fight was broken outside Baghdad."[64] Afghan leaders told Army General Tommy Franks much the same in 2001. They related that precision fire from AC-130 gunships[65] "destroyed the spirit of the Taliban and the Arabs."[66] The same year a disconsolate Afghan told *The New York Times* that Afghans prayed for "American soldiers to kill" but gloomily conceded "these bombs from the sky we cannot fight."[67]

More recently, a Taliban fighter declared that "[t]anks and armor are not a big deal," but insisted that the "fighters are the killers."[68] He also revealed a personal apprehension: "I can handle everything but the jet fighters."[69] Likewise, *Newsweek* reports that Iraqi insurgents have "learned to fear" even the sound of aerial drones because they "know it's associated with 'my buddy getting killed.'"[70] Interestingly, the fear of modern airpower extends beyond South Asia. Reports of wholesale desertions from Colombia's Revolutionary Armed Force of Colombia (FARC) rebel group cite "the sheer terror of being bombed by Colombian fighter planes" as an important motivator to abandon the fight.[71]

Airpower's capabilities are forcing insurgents to alter their behavior, sometimes with extremely counterproductive results. For example, the *Los Angeles Times* recounts how Taliban militants, fearing that cellphones were responsible for successful targeting by coalition air forces, began blowing up cellphone transmission towers. The effect, according to the *Times*, "could hardly have been a worse public-relations move for the insurgency" as the attacks raised the ire of Afghans who view the system not just as a "vital link" but also as a "symbol of pride."[72]

By early 2009, Afghan insurgents were trying to time their attacks in a way that would allow them to melt away before the feared air assets could arrive.[73] While closing this time gap will always be a challenge, airmen today believe that through the careful management of aviation resources, "there is nowhere in Iraq or Afghanistan that [they] can't bring the effects of airpower to bear within a few minutes."[74]

Again, the rapidity with which airpower can persistently inflict precise combat power is having a psychological impact. Describing the experiences of recent al-Qaeda recruits, the *Los*

Angeles Times said they "learned that life in the shadow of the Predator is nasty, brutish and short."[75] The paper also reported "drone airstrikes have sown suspicion and disarray [among al-Queada] and stoked tension with tribes in northwestern Pakistan." The effect on the recruits was manifest: "Fearful of the drones as well as informants spotting them and targeting hide-outs for missile strikes, the trainees hunkered inside during the day." Clearly, twenty-first-century air capabilities can put adversaries under persistent and extreme stress. Putting insurgent resources under extreme stress is not limited to holding the insurgents themselves at risk. An enduring feature of insurgencies, including contemporary ones, is the importance of external support.[76] Modern American airpower can address this problem in two different ways: first, the new family of UAS platforms can patrol borders and interdict transits as may be required. Second, although insurgencies themselves may present, as Rand report concluded, few opportunities for the "overwhelming application of the air instrument,"[77] nation-states generally present more. Airpower can hold at risk countries supporting insurgencies.

Taking advantage of America's airpower can produce other asymmetric advantages. One of the most powerful weapons—both physically and psychologically—emerging from insurgent arsenals are improvised explosive devices (IEDs).[78] Again, airpower provides two different means of helping to address this problem. One way is through surveillance of roadways, as well as airstrikes against adversaries planting bombs, or even against the IEDs themselves.[79] Air assets are proving to be extremely effective counter-IED weapons,[80] and will become even more so as automated UAS craft are fielded.[81]

The other method is to "outflank" *vertically* insurgents who increasingly aim to choke off supply routes in unforgiving terrain like Afghanistan.[82] Air transport permits thousands of trucks and personnel to avoid the hazards of IED-infested roadways.[83] In Afghanistan, air mobility is especially significant as there are large numbers of bases manned with US troops that are reachable only by air.[84] Improved precision airdrop methodologies (using satellite-guided cargo pallets) have resulted in a huge increase in air-delivered supplies—a doubling in the amount airdropped in 2008 over the previous year.[85]

The civilian casualty conundrum

Unlike the mujahideen who were able to stymie Soviet airpower with US-supplied state of the art Stinger anti-aircraft missiles,[86] insurgents have yet to devise anything that can effectively strike the high-performance aircraft that they fear the most. Consequently, their main "air defense" is effects-based; that is, to manipulate civilian casualty incidents to create a propaganda *effect* that is as successful as any traditional military means. For insurgents, it is a cheap way to offset US and coalition air dominance.[87]

There is no question that, especially in Afghanistan, insurgents have enjoyed much success in creating hostility among the populace for counterinsurgency operations generally, and air operations specifically. They have, as one writer put it, "mastered media manipulation."[88] They will use almost any means to accomplish this end. For example, a US official reports that the Taliban held a wedding party captive as they fired on American forces in an attack "designed to draw airstrikes on civilians and stoke anti-American sentiment."[89]

Some have argued that more "boots on the ground" would reduce civilian casualties from airstrikes.[90] Analyst William Arkin points out, however, that there is no empirical evidence that "airpower is more deadly [to civilians] than equivalent ground engagements."[91] To the contrary, a September 2008 report by Human Rights Watch concluded that civilian casualties "rarely occur during planned airstrikes on suspected Taliban targets" but rather "almost always occurred during the fluid, rapid-response strikes, *often carried out in support of ground troops*."[92] Logically, more troops on the ground—however necessary they may be—will nevertheless likely produce more incidents, not fewer.

In fact, without endorsing airstrikes, Marc Garlasco of Human Rights Watch concedes that they "probably are the most discriminating weapon that exists."[93] Still, perceptions count in twenty-first-century counterinsurgency operations, and communicating the truth to host audiences is crucial. This is why Jaap de Hoop Scheffer, the secretary general of NATO, considers communications a "strategic battleground."[94] He rightly calls upon the international community to "prioritize strategic communications" in a way that highlights NATO efforts at progress, and reminds the world "that the Taliban remain the ruthless killers and abusers of human rights that they have always been."[95]

In that regard, counterinsurgents must frame their messages carefully in order to avoid creating, in effect, a sanctuary for the enemy. When NATO representatives announce, "NATO would not fire on positions if it knew there were civilians nearby," and that "[i]f there is the likelihood of even one civilian casualty, we will not strike, not even if we think Osama bin Laden is down there" unintended consequences are invited. Hence, it is predictable that the enemy, given such announced policies, will "locate themselves amongst the civilian populations"[96] as is widely reported to be the case.

The political viability of air operations in COIN requires proper execution, in fact *and perception*. Affecting the latter is but one part of the larger strategic communication issue about which the NATO secretary speaks, and one to which airpower can contribute. Some examples include "[a]irborne information operations such as jamming communications, broadcasting on public channels through EC-130 aircraft, dropping leaflets, [and] intimidating adversaries through combat air-presence flights."[97] Not only do these techniques counter insurgent propaganda efforts, they do so at zero risk to innocent civilians.

Such approaches may become even more important as insurgents are now using the airways to intimidate and terrorize.[98] Furthermore, given General David Petreaus' observation that "[t]oday, extremist media cells recruit, exhort, train, share expertise, and generate resources in cyberspace," better countercyber methodologies—which is a core competency of the Air Force[99]—could provide opportunities that would fit with a small-footprint approach to COIN.

Conclusion

As stated in the beginning of this chapter, no single component of the US military or, for that matter, armed forces *in toto*, can defeat twenty-first-century insurgencies alone. The other instruments of American and allied power—to include especially diplomatic and economic means—must be brought to bear to achieve lasting success.[100] At best, military force can buy time for a political solution to work.

It may be, as the National Defense Strategy envisions,[101] that battling "violent extremist movements" will be the "central objective" of the American military in the near term.[102] Nonetheless, defense professionals must be prepared to meet the full range of challenges in an uncertain world. Consequently, a growing number of commentators are expressing concern that too much emphasis on counterinsurgency will undermine America's ability to counter what they interpret as truly existential threats posed by nation-states.[103]

Columnist Mark Helprin's views typify the concerns. He argues that the military's recasting of itself in response to difficulties experienced in Iraq has come "at the price of transforming the military into a light and hollow semi-gendarmerie focused on irregular warfare and ill-equipped to deter the development and resurgence of the conventional and strategic forces of China and Russia."[104] The debate extends beyond civilian observers; it is growing within the ranks.[105]

Airpower can be part of the solution to this conundrum, as *flexibility* and *versatility* are its central tenets.[106] Counterinsurgency operations since 9/11 demonstrate the remarkable degree to which aerial platforms designed for high-tech, symmetrical war have become extremely effective weapons in irregular war. For example, combat aircraft—from fighters to heavy bombers—turned out to be astonishingly effective close air support weapons in counter-insurgency situations, much because of the extraordinary precision advanced laser-designated and satellite-guided munitions provide.[107] The integration of this high-tech airpower with ground forces has progressed to the point where Army Brigadier General Mark Milley, the 101st Airborne Division deputy commander, recently declared that "[t]he infantry's best friend is the pilot."[108]

High-end aircraft such as the F-16 employed in a "nontraditional ISR" mode now regularly provide tactical intelligence data to ground forces. Moreover, an improved camera carried by the F-16 produces images taken from 10,000 feet "sharp enough to reveal a coffee cup on the hood of pickup truck."[109] Further, Major General Paul A. Dettmer, the Air Force's assistant deputy chief of staff for ISR, predicts that the service can capitalize on platforms like the F-22 and F-35 because "both have impressive sensor suites that will act as ISR vacuum cleaners, sucking up data about the enemy posture and feeding it to military networks."[110]

As discussed above, other aircraft ranging from the E-8C Joint Stars to transport planes—*all designed for wars against conventional opponents*—have shown themselves to be indispensable to COIN operations.

The point is that most of America's airpower platforms—including the rotary wing combat aircraft of the surface forces—are exactly the same ones that can deter and defeat the high-end nation-states that someday might threaten the US. The flexibility and versatility intrinsic to airpower can minimize the need for counterinsurgency-unique equipment.[111] Furthermore, using the same aircraft across the spectrum of conflict is a force-multiplier in the sense that airmen can employ the same skills to operate and maintain them.

In short, much of the air component can readily adapt to any level of conflict, even if the surface forces choose to use "Iraq-style" counterinsurgency as their "organizing principle." Such adaptability will likely become increasingly valued in an era of constrained defense resources. A caution: most of the UAS platforms that are proving so significant in counter-insurgency today require a nearly completely docile air environment to survive.

Even a relatively primitive air defense system would drastically curtail the effectiveness of the vast majority of UAS platforms. The use of drones by Hezbollah against the Israelis in the 2006 Lebanon War no doubt will accelerate the development of counters that will inevitably filter back to nonstate actors who comprise today's—and tomorrow's—insurgents. Thus, high-tech, survivable, manned platforms able to deliver "nontraditional ISR" may prove essential, especially for waging the "hybrid war" that many experts forecast will predominate in the twenty-first century.[112]

A final reiteration: although it is unpopular to tout technology these days, dismissing it as irrelevant to counterinsurgency is fraught with peril.[113] High technology is, as Colin Gray observes, the "American way of war," and could provide decision makers with options that do not require asking Americans to offer their sons and daughters to serve as "bullet sponges." Today's high-tech airpower, wielded by dedicated and skilled airmen from the entire joint and coalition team, offers unparalleled prospects to help the US achieve, as Colonel Meilinger puts it, America's "political goals with the least cost in blood and treasure."[114]

Notes

1 C.J. Chivers, "GIs in Remote Afghan Post Have Weary Job, Drawing Fire," *The New York Times*, November 9, 2008, 1, available at http://www.nytimes.com/2008/11/10/world/asia/10outpost.html (quoting First Lt. Daniel Wright, US Army). The full quote is:

> Col. John Spiszer, the commanding officer for the larger task force in the region, distilled how the mission often worked. The American presence, he said, is a Taliban magnet, drawing insurgents from more populated areas and enhancing security elsewhere.

> First Lt. Daniel Wright, the executive officer of the American cavalry unit—Apache Troop of the Sixth Battalion, Fourth Cavalry—put things in foxhole terms. "Basically," he said, "we're the bullet sponge."

2 For an airpower approach to finding, fixing, and targeting an adversary in counterinsurgency situations, see Charles J. Dunlap, Jr, "Shortchanging the Joint Fight? An Airman's Assessment of FM 3-24 and the Case for Developing Truly Joint Doctrine," Air University, 2008, available at http://www.au.af.mil/au/awc/awcgate/au/dunlap_ari1.pdf (monograph).

3 Headquarters, Department of the Army, Field Manual 3-24, *Counterinsurgency*, December 15, 2006 (FM 3-24), also designated by Headquarters Marine Corps Development Command, Department of the Navy, as Marine Corps Warfighting Publication No. 3-33.5, 1, *Counterinsurgency*, December 15, 2006, available via Jim Garamone, "Army, Marines Release New Counterinsurgency Manual," *American Forces Information Service*, December 15, 2006, available at http://www.defenselink.mil/news/NewsArticle.aspx?ID=2453 (hyperlink to "Counterinsurgency Manual" at bottom of the press release).

4 Anthony H. Cordesman, "Air Combat Trends in the Afghan and Iraq Wars," Center for Strategic & International Studies, March 11, 2008, available at http://www.csis.org/media/csis/pubs/080 318_afgh-iraqairbrief.pdf.

5 Michael M. Dunn, "The Pile-On Effect," Air Force Association, July 9, 2008, available at http://www.afa.org/EdOp/edop_7-10-08.asp.

6 Ibid.

7 Lara M. Dadkhah, "Close Air Support and Civilian Casualties in Afghanistan," *Small Wars Journal*, December 30, 2008, 2, available at http://smallwarsjournal.com/mag/docs-temp/160-dadkhah.pdf.

8 Alan J. Vick et al., *Air Power in the New Counterinsurgency Era*, Santa Monica, CA: Rand Corporation, 2006, p. 111, available at http://www.rand.org/pubs/monographs/2006/RAND_MG509.pdf.

9 Ibid.

10 James S. Corum and Wray R. Johnson, *Airpower in Small Wars*, Lawrence, KS: University of Kansas Press, 2003, p. 427.

11 Department of the Air Force, MQ-1 Predator Unmanned Aerial Vehicle, fact sheet, September 2008, available at http://www.af.mil/factsheets/factsheet.asp?fsID=122.

12 Department of the Air Force, MQ-9 Reaper Unmanned Aerial Vehicle, fact sheet, September 2008, available at http://www.af.mil/factsheets/factsheet.asp?fsID=6405.

13 "RQ-4A/B Global Hawk High-Altitude, Long-Endurance, Unmanned Reconnaissance Aircraft," SPG Media Limited, 2008, available at http://www.airforce-technology.com/projects/global/.

14 Gen. Barry R. McCaffrey, Memorandum for Col. Mike Meese, United States Military Academy, Subject: After Action Report, October 15, 2007, p. 5, available at http://www.mccaffreyassociates.com/pages/documents/AirForceAAR-101207.pdf.

15 See, "A Brief History Of Parade," Parade.com, July 2008, available at http://www.parade.com/corporate/parade_history.html ("*Parade* Magazine, the most widely read magazine in America with a circulation of 33 million.")

16 "Turning Points on Two Battlefronts in 2008: A World of Change," *Parade*, December 28, 2008, 5. For a more academic analysis, see Linda Robinson, *Tell Me How This Ends*, New York: Public Affairs, 2008, pp. 272–3.

17 "Link Hard, Soft Power," *Defense News*, September 8, 2008, available at http://www.defensenews.com/story.php?i=3712849.

18 Sarah Sewall, "Modernizing U.S. Counterinsurgency Practice: Rethinking Risk and Developing a National Strategy," *Military Review* (September/October 2006), 103, available at http://www.ksg.harvard.edu/cchrp/Sewall%20-%20military%20review%2010_2006.pdf.

19 See for example Ralph Peters, "COIN Lies We Love," *Armed Forces Journal* (April 2009), available at http://www.armedforcesjournal.com/2009/04/3978447 ("[T]he evidence of history is not only that insurgencies almost always have been defeated, but that they have been defeated through military means. History indicates that fighting insurgencies is at least 90 percent a military mission and often 100 percent a matter of arms.")

20 Steve Coll, "The General's Dilemma," *The New Yorker*, September 8, 2008, available at http://www.newyorker.com/reporting/2008/09/08/080908fa_fact_coll.

21 Gordon Lubold, "Do US Prisons Breed Insurgents?" *Christian Science Monitor*, December 10, 2007, available at http://www.csmonitor.com/2007/1220/p01s01-woiq.html.

22 Michael E. O'Hanlon and Jason H. Campbell, "The Iraq Index," *Brookings Institution*, October 1, 2007, available at http://www.brookings.edu/fp/saban/iraq/index.pdf.

23 Jim Michaels, "19,000 Insurgents Killed in Iraq Since '03," *USA Today*, September 26, 2008, available at http://www.usatoday.com/news/world/iraq/2007-09-26-insurgents_N.htm.

24 See for example "List of Insurgent Fatality Reports in Iraq," Wikipedia, April 2, 2008, available at http://en.wikipedia.org/wiki/List_of_insurgents_killed_in_Iraq.

25 Stephen Luxenberg, "U.S. Spied on Iraqi Leaders, Book Says," *The Washington Post*, September 5, 2008, A01, available at http://www.washingtonpost.com/wp-dyn/content/article/2008/09/04/AR2008090403160.html.

26 Ibid.

27 Ibid.

28 William R. Polk, *Violent Politics: A History of Insurgency, Terrorism & Guerrilla War, from the American Revolution to Iraq*, New York: Harper, 2007, pp. xiv–xv.

29 See Zbigniew Brzezinski, *The Washington Post*, March 30, 2008, B03, available at http://www.washingtonpost.com/wp-dyn/content/article/2008/03/27/AR2008032702405_pf.html.

30 Seth G. Jones and Martin Libicki, *How Terrorist Groups End: Lessons for Countering Al Qa'ida*, Santa Monica, CA: RAND, 2008, p. xvi, available at http://www.rand.org/pubs/monographs/2008/RAND_MG741-1.pdf.

31 Ibid.

32 "Security Gains Reverse Iraq's Spiral Though Serious Problems Remain," ABC/BBC/ARD/NHK Poll, March 17, 2008, 32, available at http://www.abcnews.go.com/images/PollingUnit/1060a1Iraq WhereThingsStand.pdf (last accessed January 19, 2009).

33 Ibid., 24.

34 Ibid., 4.

35 ABC News/Washington Post Poll, January 13–16, 2009, as reported in Iraq, PollingReport.com, available at http://www.pollingreport.com/iraq.htm.

36 Ibid., citing CNN/Opinion Research Poll, December 1–2, 2008.

37 Ibid., citing Quinnipiac University Poll, November 6–10, 2008.

38 James S. Corum, *Bad Strategies: How Major Powers Fail in Counterinsurgency*, Minneapolis, MN: Zenith Press, 2008. p. 238.

39 John T. Bennett, "Interview: Ryan Henry, U.S. Principal Deputy Undersecretary of Defense for Policy," *Defense News*, May 7, 2007, available at http://www.oft.osd.mil/library/library_files/article_567_Defense%20News%20Interview%20with%20Ryan%20Henry.pdf.

40 John T. Bennett, "40B Price Tag for Larger Army," *Defense News*, December 15, 2008, available at http://www.defensenews.com/story.php?i=3863617.

41 Steven M. Kosiak, "Cost of the Wars in Iraq and Afghanistan, and Other Military Operations Through 2008 and Beyond," Center for Strategic and Budgetary Assessments, 2008, available at http://www.csbaonline.org/4Publications/PubLibrary/R.20081215.Cost_of_the_Wars_i/R.20081215.Cost_of_the_Wars_i.pdf.

42 Andrew J. Bacevich, "The Petraeus Doctrine," *The Atlantic*, October 2008, available at http://www.theatlantic.com/doc/200810/petraeus-doctrine.

43 William Safire, "On Language: Irregular Warfare," *The New York Times* magazine, available at http://www.nytimes.com/2008/06/08/magazine/08wwln-safire-t.html.

44 Department of Defense, National Defense Strategy, June 2008, available at http://www.defenselink.mil/pubs/2008NationalDefenseStrategy.pdf.

45 Norton A. Schwartz and Robert B. Stephan, "Don't Go Downtown Without Us: The Role of Joint Aerospace Power in Urban Operations," *Aerospace Power Journal* (Spring 2000), 3, available at http://www.airpower.maxwell.af.mil/airchronicles/apj/apj00/spr00/schwartz.pdf.

46 Department of the Air Force, Air Force Doctrine Document (AFDD) 2-3, Irregular Warfare, August 1, 2007, available at http://www.e-publishing.af.mil/shared/media/epubs/AFDD2-3.pdf.

47 Ibid., 15.

48 Phillip S. Meilinger, "Counterinsurgency from Above," *Air Force Magazine*, July 2008, 36, 39, available at http://www.airforce-magazine.com/MagazineArchive/Pages/2008/July%202008/0708COIN.aspx.

49 Ibid., 39.

50 See for example Scott Wilson, "Which Way in Afghanistan? Ask Colombia for Directions," *The Washington Post*, April 5, 2009, B01, available at http://www.washingtonpost.com/wp-dyn/content/article/2009/04/03/AR2009040302135.html.

51 John A. Wickham, "Why a Smaller Footprint is Good," *Arizona Daily Star*, November 9, 2008, available at http://www.azstarnet.com/allheadlines/266151.

52 Ibid.

53 Air Combat Command Public Affairs, E-8C Joint STARS fact sheet, September 2007, available at http://www.af.mil/factsheets/factsheet.asp?fsID=100.

54 See for example, SrA Clinton Atkins, "Airmen in Sky Give Warriors on Ground Situational Awareness," *Air Force News Service*, January 12, 2009, available at http://www.af.news/story.asp?id=123130911.

55 Ibid.

56 John A. Nagl, "Institutionalizing Adaption," Center for a New American Security, June 2007, available at http://www.cnas.org/files/documents/publications/Nagl_AdvisoryCorp_June07.pdf.

57 Michael Knights, "Rocky Road for Basra Operation," *Jane's Defence Weekly*, April 23, 2008, 28.

58 Martin J. Muckian, "Structural Vulnerabilities of Networked Insurgencies: Adapting to the New Adversary," *Parameters* (Winter 2006–7), 14, 19, available at http://www.carlisle.army.mil/usawc/Parameters/06winter/muckian.htm.

59 Mark Benjamin, "Killing 'Bubba' From the Skies," Salon.com, February 15, 2008, available at http://www.salon.com/news/feature/2008/02/15/air_war/.

60 John Barry and Evan Thomas, "Up in the Sky, An Unblinking Eye," *Newsweek*, June 9, 2008, available at http://www.newsweek.com/id/139432.

61 Rebecca Grant, "The All-Seeing Air Force," *Air Force Magazine*, September 2008, available at http://www.airforce-magazine.com/MagazineArchive/Pages/2008/September%202008/0908airforce.aspx.

62 Laura King and Sebastian Rotella, "U.S. Airstrike Killed Key Al Qaeda Figure in Pakistan, Official Says," *Los Angeles Times*, October 31, 2008, available at http://articles.latimes.com/2008/oct/31/world/fg-habib31.

63 See for example Giulio Douhet, *Command of the Air*, Washington, DC: Office of Air Force History, 1983 (1927).

64 William Branigin, "A Brief, Bitter War for Iraq's Military Officers," *The Washington Post*, April 27, 2003, A25, available at http://www.iraqwararchive.org/data/apr27/US/wp11.pdf.

65 Department of the Air Force, AC-130H/U, fact sheet, October 2005, available at http://www.af.mil/factsheets/factsheet.asp?fsID=71.

66 Tommy Franks, *American Soldier*, New York: Regan Books, 2004, p. 312.

67 Barry Bearak, "A Nation Challenged: Death on the Ground," *The New York Times*, October 13, 2001, B01, available at http://query.nytimes.com/gst/fullpage.html?res=990CE7DE133FF930A25753C1A9679C8B63.

68 Rowan Scarborough, Pentagon Notebook, *Washington Times*, June 26, 2008, available at http://www.washtimes.com/news/2008/jun/26/pentagon-notebook-mcpeak-calls-mccain-too-fat/?page=2.

69 Ibid.

70 See Barry and Thomas, "Up in the Sky, An Unblinking Eye."

71 Juan Forero, "Colombia's Rebels Face Possibility of Implosion," *The Washington Post*, March 22, 2008, A01, available at http://www.washingtonpost.com/wp-dyn/content/article/2008/03/21/AR2008032103536_pf.html.

72 See King and Rotella, "U.S. Airstrike Killed Key Al Qaeda Figure in Pakistan, Official Says."

73 Tom Vanden Brook, "Afghan Insurgent Tactics Shift to Dodge Airstrikes," *USA Today*, January 20, 2009, 8, available at http://www.usatoday.com/news/military/2009-01-19-airstrikes_N.htm.

74 Col. Gus Schalkham, "Agility and Flexibility; Key Components of Air Power Teamwork," US

Air Forces Central Public Affairs, October 10, 2008, available at http://www.centaf.af.mil/news/story.asp?id=123118930.

75 Sebastian Rotella, "Al Qaeda Recruits Back in Europe, But Why?," *Los Angeles Times*, May 24, 2009, 1, available at http://www.latimes.com/news/nationworld/world/la-fg-junior-jihadis24-2009may24,0,2193912.story.

76 See for example Alistair Horne, *A Savage War of Peace: Algeria 1954–1952*, New York: NYRB Classics, 2006 (1977), p. 18 (discussing external support as a persisting quality of insurgencies).

77 Vick et al., *Air Power in the New Counterinsurgency Era.*

78 See generally "Congressional Research Service, Improvised Explosive Devices (IEDs) in Iraq: Effects and Countermeasures," February 10, 2006, Library of Congress, available at http://stinet.dtic.mil/oai/oai?&verb=getRecord&metadataPrefix=html&identifier=ADA454399.

79 See for example Sean Kimmons, "Fighting Bombs with Bombs," *Stars and Stripes*, August 13, 2008, available at http://www.stripes.com/article.asp?section=104&article=56715.

80 See for example Noah Shachtman, "Drone, Copter Team Kills 2,400 Bombers in Iraq," Wired.com, January 21, 2008, available at http://blog.wired.com/defense/2008/01/drone-copter-te.html; and "Fighting IEDs in Afstan: US Task Force ODIN," *The Torch*, January 18, 2009, available at http://toyoufromfailinghands.blogspot.com/2009/01/fighting-ieds-in-afstan-task-force-odin.html.

81 See "U.S. Readies Three Anti-IED UAVs for Field," *Defense News*, January 5, 2009, 12.

82 See for example Mark Thompson, "How the Taliban Hopes To Choke U.S. Afghanistan Mission," Time.com, December 9, 2008, available at http://www.time.com/time/world/article/0,8599,1865223,00.html.

83 See for example Jim Michaels, "US Supply Missions Fly over Dangerous Roads," *USA Today*, December 12, 2008, 10A, available at http://www.usatoday.com/printedition/news/20081212/airdrops12_st.art.htm.

84 Michelle Tan, "Army Hopes New Airdrop 'Shute' Delivers," *Army Times*, November 24, 2008, 18.

85 Bruce Rolfsen, "Airdrop Crews Double the Cargo in 2008," *Air Force Times*, January 6, 2009, available at http://www.airforcetimes.com/news/2009/01/airforce_afghan_airdrops_010509w/.

86 See Stephen Tanner, *Afghanistan: A Military History from Alexander the Great to the Fall of the Taliban*, New York: Da Capo, 2002, p. 267.

87 Something of a precedent may have been set during the Gulf War when an attack on the Al Firdos bunker—which was, unbeknownst to coalition forces, being used as a shelter by the families of high Iraqi officials—resulted in political restraints. According to authors Michael R. Gordon and Bernard E. Trainor, the "raid had accomplished what the Iraqi air defenses could not: downtown Baghdad was to be attacked sparingly, if at all." See *The General's War: The Inside Story of the Conflict in the Gulf*, Boston: LittleBrown, 1995, p. 326.

88 Sean D. Naylor, "Insurgents in Afghanistan Have Mastered Media Manipulation," *Armed Forces Journal* (April 2008), available at http://www.armedforcesjournal.com/2008/04/3489740.

89 Jason Stratziuso, "Official: Taliban Tricking the U.S. Into Killing Civilians," *The Arizona Republic*, November 8, 2008, available at http://www.azcentral.com/arizonarepublic/news/articles/2008/11/08/20081108afghanistan1108.html.

90 See for example Jim Michaels, "Airstrikes in Afghanistan Increase 31%," *USA Today*, November 5, 2008, available at http://www.usatoday.com/news/world/2008-11-05-afghanstrikes_N.htm (quoting Army Brig. Gen. Michael Tucker: "If we got more boots on the ground, we would not have to rely as much on" airstrikes).

91 William M. Arkin, "In Defense of Airpower," *The Washington Post* (blog), December 11, 2007, available at http://toyoufromfailinghands.blogspot.com/2007/12/afstan-in-defense-of-air-power.html, as quoted by John T. Correll, in "Verbatim," *Air Force Magazine*, February 2008, available at http://www.airforce-magazine.com/MagazineArchive/Pages/2008/February%202008/0208verb.aspx.

92 "Troops in Contact," Airstrikes and Civilian Deaths in Afghanistan, Human Rights Watch, September 2008, 4, available at http://hrw.org/reports/2008/afghanistan0908/afghanistan0908web.pdf, emphasis added.

93 As quoted by Josh White, "The Man on Both Sides of Air War Debate," *The Washington Post*, February 13, 2008, A05, available at http://www.washingtonpost.com/wp-dyn/content/article/2008/02/12/AR2008021202692.html (last accessed September 23, 2008).

94 Jaap de Hoop Scheffer, "Afghanistan: We Can Do Better," *The Washington Post*, January 18, 2009, B7.

95 Ibid.

96 See "Inside US Hub for Air Strikes," BBC America, November 29, 2008, available at http://news.bbc.co.uk/2/hi/south_asia/7755969.stm.

97 See Schwartz and Stephan, "Don't Go Downtown Without Us: The Role of Joint Aerospace Power in Urban Operations."

98 Richard A. Oppel, Jr, "Radio Spreads Taliban's Terror in Pakistani Region," *The New York Times*, January 25, 2009, A1, available at http://www.nytimes.com/2009/01/25/world/asia/25swat.html.

99 See for example "Secretary of the Air Force Michael W. Wynne, Cyberspace as a Domain in which the Air Force Flies and Fights," Air Force Link—Speeches, November 2, 2006, available at http://www.af.mil/library/speeches/speech.asp?id=283.

100 See for example Remarks by Secretary Rice at Signing Ceremony for US Government Counterinsurgency Guide, US State Department Press Release, January 13, 2009, available at http://smallwarsjournal.com/blog/2009/01/print/signing-ceremony-for-us-govern/.

101 Department of Defense, National Defense Strategy, June 2008, available at http://www.defense link.mil/pubs/2008NationalDefenseStrategy.pdf.

102 Ibid., 7.

103 See for example George Friedman, "The U.S. Air Force and the Next War," *Geopolitical Weekly*, STRATFOR, January 11, 2008, available at http://www.stratfor.com/weekly/geopolitical_ weekly_u_s_air_force_and_next_war; and Caspar Weinberger, Jr, "Gates and the Air Force," *Human Events*, June 24, 2008, available at http://www.humanevents.com/article.php?id=27146.

104 Mark Helprin, "Bush Has Made Us Vulnerable," *The Wall Street Journal*, December 19, 2008, available at http://online.wsj.com/article/SB122965053466920579.html.

105 See for example Gian P. Gentile, "Mired in 'Surge' Dogma," *International Herald Tribune*, December 5, 2008, available at http://www.iht.com/articles/2008/12/04/opinion/edgentile.php; and Peter Katel, "Rise in Counterinsurgency," *CQ Researcher*, September 5, 2008, 697 ff.

106 Department of the Air Force, Air Force Doctrine Document 1, Air Force Basic Doctrine, November 17, 2003, 30, available at http://www.dtic.mil/doctrine/jel/service_pubs/afdd1.pdf.

107 The weapons generally rely upon global positions system (GPS) satellites. See generally, Department of the Air Force, Global Positioning System, fact sheet, March 2007, available at http://www.af.mil/factsheets/factsheet.asp?fsID=119.

108 SSgt Tammie Moore, "Topcover: Airpower Integral to Ground Force's Success," Air Force Recruiting Service, October 2, 2008, available at http://www.rs.af.mil/news/story.asp?id= 123118199.

109 See William Matthews, "Sharper Eye in the Sky: Pod Gives U.S. Forces Instant View of Enemy," *Defense News*, November 10, 2008, 32 (discussing improved theater airborne reconnaissance system (TARS)).

110 John A. Tirpak, "High Stress Numbers Game," *Air Force Magazine*, December 2008, 30, 33, available at http://www.airforce-magazine.com/MagazineArchive/Pages/2008/December%20 2008/1208game.aspx.

111 One example is the costly mine resistant ambush protected (MRAP) vehicle. See for example Associated Press, "GAO Warns of Runaway MRAP Costs," Military.com, July 17, 2008, available at http://www.military.com/news/article/gao-warns-of-runaway-mrap-costs.html ("Congress has appropriated $22 billion to acquire more than 15,000 mine resistant ambush protected vehicles, also known as MRAPs.") Some MRAPs may only be useful in selected COIN situations. See for example Nathan Hodge, "Afghanistan Diary," Danger Room, *Wired*, October 16, 2008, available at http://blog.wired.com/defense/2008/10/afghanistan-d-2.html (discussing complaints by Marines in Afghanistan that MRAPs are too large and too heavy for that environment).

112 According to analyst Frank G. Hoffman: "Hybrid Wars incorporate a range of different modes of warfare, including conventional capabilities, irregular tactics and formations, terrorist acts including indiscriminate violence and coercion, and criminal disorder. Hybrid Wars can be conducted by both states and a variety of nonstate actors." Frank G. Hoffman, "Conflict in the 21st Century: the Rise of Hybrid Wars," Potomac Institute, December 2007, available at http://www.potomac institute.org/images/stories/publications/potomac_hybridwar_0108.pdf.

113 Ronald Haycock and Keith Neilson, *Men, Machines, and War,* Waterloo, ONT: Wilfrid Laurier University Press, 1988, p. xii ("Technology has permitted the division of mankind into ruler and ruled.").

114 Meilinger, "Counterinsurgency from Above."

9   Naval support

Martin N. Murphy

Conflicts are decided on land. Few would dispute Corbett's dictum that great issues are decided by armies and what navies can do in their support.[1] Nonetheless, even if maritime forces decide events only rarely, they can influence them, in some cases profoundly—a quality captured most memorably by Mahan when he wrote about the "far distant, storm-beaten ships" of the British Navy standing between Napoleon and domination of the world.[2] Similarly, students of insurgency and counterinsurgency have concentrated on what happens in jungles and cities but have done so at the expense of the maritime aspect of insurgency, which has often been poorly appreciated, and naval support for counterinsurgency, which has tended to be underplayed or ignored.

Admittedly that oversight is somewhat understandable when it comes to the study of insurgents, few of whom have found maritime operations necessary. Those that have taken to the water have generally restricted their actions to rivers and coastal shallows; the very limited number of groups that have made use of the open sea have done so mainly because they have had no alternative way to obtain supplies. Even so, the majority of insurgents have behaved like criminals, avoiding contact with naval or police forces to preserve their freedom of action. The groups that have been prepared to contest their opponent's use of rivers and shallows have done so in the main from the shore or riverbank. Those that have contested the opponent's use of the open sea have done so close to shore. Like most things, this picture is not immutable. It could change in response to technological developments or political needs, but it nonetheless remains the case that of the few groups that have planned or made preparations to extend their insurgent campaigns into the maritime environment even fewer have actually done so.[3]

Maritime operations in counterinsurgency

The focus of this chapter, however, is on naval support for counterinsurgency; the use of naval force to confront not merely the very small number of insurgent groups that have taken to the water but the contribution navies can make to countering land-based insurgencies. The most fundamental support navies can provide is the most obvious and at the same time the easiest to overlook. Every counterinsurgency campaign conducted by the Western powers since World War II has been undertaken in the certain knowledge that their navies, and behind them the US Navy, had control of the sea lines of communication stretching back to their home ports. Even landlocked campaigns, such as that in Afghanistan, would have been impossible without sea control. The hundreds and thousands of men and later women, who fought on the ground, would never have made contact with the enemy, nor been successfully evacuated afterwards, without naval protection and support—to say nothing of hundreds and thousands of tons of supplies and equipment that needed to be shipped to each theater.

Furthermore, in almost all cases where counterinsurgency campaigns have been waged in littoral areas, the adjoining green water has been "owned" by a friendly navy. Although control of the shallow water and riverine environments has often been less assured, this threat to counterinsurgent forces has rarely been mounted on the water itself. The main naval support activities of blockade, denial, supply, interdiction, amphibious landing, air and gunfire support, and the wider roles of naval diplomacy and deterrence, have only rarely been constrained by the need to engage maritime insurgents directly. That this list of support functions is so long is a reflection of the inherent flexibility and versatility of naval power. However, as with naval power more generally, none of these activities has been decisive independently and each one has been effective only as part of a strategically coherent whole.

This chapter will touch on the strategic and policy implications of the use of naval power in counterinsurgency. It will highlight the lesson that naval involvement depends, as does the effectiveness of all other services and agencies in similar circumstances, on accurate intelligence, intimate understanding of the operational environment, and a willingness to endure and persist. Moreover, these qualities need to be exercised in the context of a clear understanding of the political risks and effects of any action taken, while gaining and retaining the initiative means working in close tactical and operational coordination with all other agencies in theater to achieve strategic objectives and policy goals. The chapter will use brief accounts of several campaigns to illustrate some of the enduring patterns of maritime counterinsurgency and, conversely, the tyranny of the particular when it comes to their implementation.

Varieties of experience

Naval support played a prominent role in western counterinsurgency efforts throughout the twentieth century. When considering the modern applicability of naval power to counterinsurgency it is useful to consider six historical examples: France and the US in Indochina; Britain and France in the Mediterranean; Israel and its neighbors; Sri Lanka; Britain in Southeast Asia; and Portugal in Africa.

France and the US in Indochina

The Indochina conflict demonstrated almost all aspects of possible naval support but two in particular are noteworthy: river-based support for ground force interdiction activity, and blockade—the attempt to cut off insurgents from external sources of arms, equipment, and fighters.

The French attempt to regain control of its Indochinese possessions began in 1945 as it rushed to fill the power vacuum left behind by the defeated Japanese. By the end of the first quarter of 1946, Cochinchina and Annam as far north as the 16th parallel were in French hands, due largely to the efforts of the Navy.[4] Mobility was essential: the French had control of the sea but their control of roads and inland waterways was contested. By 1947 the war had settled into a pattern that would become familiar to American servicemen two decades later: the French controlled the cities, leaving the Vietminh in control of the countryside.[5]

The principal unit of the river force was the *division navale d'assault*, more commonly known by its abbreviation as a *dinassault.* Composed of a variety of landing craft it was versatile and gave the French the ability to mount amphibious operations, not only on the major river systems but also to a limited extent along the coasts (the addition of armor made the boats unstable in anything other than calm conditions). Rivercraft played key roles in three major actions: the repulse of the three major Vietminh offensives launched in the Red

River delta between January and May 1951, during which they were used to transport troops and provide gunfire support; the French counteroffensives in June, for which control of the Day River was essential; and Operation *Lotus* launched in November to gain control of the Black River. On November 14, French paratroopers seized the city of Hoa Binh on the river's west bank 37 miles west of Hanoi. The overland route to the city was severed almost immediately, leaving the river as the only way in or out. The Vietminh, like most insurgents, never developed a countervailing maritime capacity of their own but sought to attack the *dinassault* using swimmers, mines, and ambushes launched from the riverbanks. These methods succeeded in halting the *Lotus* operation that attempted to keep this vital route open. The operation continued until January 12, 1952 when at a place known as Notre Dame Rock five boats were sunk in a murderous hail of fire, effectively rendering the Black River impassable beyond that point. The *dinassaults* were able to mount only one more mission, in which they succeeded in passing the Rock and evacuating the French force in the city.[6]

Although the *dinassault* was a sound operational concept it suffered from a lack of resources, like all aspects of the French effort; something which its American successors did not. Critically, because it lacked air support—helicopters in particular—its effective radius was limited to the rivers alone. Granted, given the weather patterns in northern Vietnam, air support could not always be delivered even if available, but this too was a limitation the US was able to overcome. Finally, although the relationship between the French Army and Navy generally worked well, resource shortages impinged on actual operations, limiting collaboration and restricting training to the extent that ground commanders, unaware of the units' potential, frequently looked to them for supply rather than combat support.[7] Similar conceptual differences between the services affected subsequent US operations.

In 1966 the US commander in Vietnam, General Westmoreland, agreed to the estab- lishment of the Mobile Riverine Force (MRF or TF-117). Comparable in organization to the French *dinassault* units, it was equipped with heavily armored craft that could fire cannons, mortars, heavy machine-guns, and, on some boats, flamethrowers or howitzers, to support the US Army "search and destroy" missions in the Mekong Delta. Few questioned that it was effective in its assigned role or that, particularly during the Tet offensive of 1968, its performance was anything less than heroic. However, organizationally and conceptually it was flawed. Organizationally, at the field operations level, command arrangements were similar to those adopted by the French but at higher command levels the army regarded the MRF as a supplement to the 9th Infantry Division. The Navy, on the other hand, saw it as an independent command free to respond to situations as they developed. The more fundamental fault was conceptual: in the crowded environment of the Mekong Delta where it was easy to hit targets unintentionally, the notion of "search and destroy," to which the US Army was wedded, was not merely inappropriate but counterproductive.[8]

The dominance of the great river systems in the north and south of the country ensured that counterinsurgency operations in Indochina were inconceivable without a river presence. Equally, the importance of waterborne transport to the insurgents for the infiltration of men and *matériel* remained high throughout the Indochina War and followed a common pattern throughout both its phases. While overland supply routes were more secure they were highly inefficient. Consequently the Vietminh, and later the Viet Cong (VC), undertook two types of movement by sea: first, they shipped men and equipment between the various enclaves they controlled along the coast by mingling their junks and fishing craft with the thousands of others engaged in coastal commerce; second, they received shipments from outside the country in larger craft, often trawlers that sailed well outside territorial waters before turning toward the shore.

To prevent these movements both French and US forces established blockades. As in many counterinsurgency campaigns, geography affected the results profoundly. Once the communist forces had triumphed in China in 1949, external supplies were brought across the Gulf of Tonkin from Hainan Island and the French, particularly after they were able to mount air patrols, proved reasonably successful in limiting this route. However, they were much less successful at restricting coastal traffic as they lacked the resources needed to mount patrols along the length of Indochina's long and highly indented coastline. Furthermore, blockade is always influenced by the skill and determination of the insurgents in evasion, and the Vietminh boatmen became adept at using the natural cover of the coast and the outer islands, combined with clever tactics, to avoid French patrols.[9]

US forces experienced similar successes and difficulties. The first insurgent shipment reached the South in October 1962 and others followed. Political reservations prevented what from a military point of view was the most effective interdiction method: the mining of North Vietnamese harbors, Haiphong in particular, through which flowed an estimated 85 percent of the enemy's war supplies. Mines sewn in just a few ports in the early years of the US engagement would have had a disproportionate effect on the North's war effort.[10] When the mining of Haiphong and other ports from the air was finally sanctioned in 1972 (Operation Pocket Money), it demonstrated once again the effectiveness of sea mines, but the effort came too late to influence the war—even though the North Vietnamese logistical system was placed under immense strain, halving the delivered tonnage, as shipments were forced to divert through Chinese ports and were exposed to the Linebacker air raids once they crossed the North Vietnamese border.[11] The inverse, of course, could also have been true, and it was perhaps only because the insurgents wished to continue to use the sea for supply operations, or wanted to ensure that they did not alienate local fishermen and seafarers, that they did not mine the coastal waters themselves—a move which would have posed French and US forces with considerable problems.

Instead of using mines to interdict supply operations at their most vulnerable point, US Military Assistance Command, Vietnam (MACV) established a coastal blockade in March 1965. Entitled Operation Market Time (eventually TF-115), it grew quickly. Although always under naval command, US Coast Guard vessels were involved almost from the outset.[12] It was a layered program. Air patrols identified suspicious craft and reported their locations to Coastal Surveillance Centers, which dispatched vessels from either the inner or outer surface patrol barriers to interdict. The outer barrier operated about 40 miles (74 km) off the coast from the 17th parallel down to the Gulf of Thailand; the inner barrier hugged the South Vietnamese coastline concentrating on high traffic areas such as the Mekong Delta.

Patrolling was hard, tedious work; during the period they operated, between March 1965 and December 1972, Market Time patrols reportedly boarded a vessel every 15–30 seconds and captured around 50 intruders. Apart from a desperate attempt in February 1968 to resupply its forces following the Tet offensive, North Vietnam gave up trying to use coastal supply routes between July 1967 and only resumed after August 1969 when they lost access to Sihanoukville in nominally neutral Cambodia. Even then TF-115, the successor to Market Time, succeeded in preventing all but one of the known attempts to penetrate its coastal screen.[13]

To support Market Time another operation, Game Warden, was established in December 1965. The River Patrol Force (TF-116), which was part of Game Warden, aimed to deny to the VC use of the major delta rivers and the Rung Sat Special Zone south of Saigon, by pushing patrols up to 25 miles inland from the coast. The Force averaged 1200 two-boat patrols per month in 1966, which stopped and searched some 9000 boats out of 50,000 observed. By 1968 it had the capacity to mount patrols on every major river in the delta, and in that year alone interrogated over 600,000 local vessels. The effectiveness of the program was hard to determine. Clearly some shipments were detected; others were probably deterred but how many got through is unknown. However, it succeeded in disrupting VC control of the population, prevented them from collecting taxes, and limited their ability to mount waterborne operations.[14]

The effectiveness of Market Time was also difficult to assess although the judgment made was that it accomplished its primary mission "by deterring the enemy's use of the sea to support the political-military offensive against South Vietnam."[15] As with so much in counterinsurgency, these successes need to be carefully weighted against the disruption to normal shipping and the resentment such interference caused. They also need to be set beside the fact that, for political reasons, the US decided against interdicting shipping using Sihanoukville from where 21,600 tons of military and 5333 tons of non-military supplies were moved overland between December 1966 and April 1969 to resupply VC and North Vietnamese Army units operating in the South.[16]

What both Market Time and Game Warden operations failed to do was to satisfy the need identified in the 1964 report of the Vietnam Delta Infiltration Study Group (known more commonly as the Bucklew Report) which concluded that a "sea quarantine would be futile in the absence of a companion effort to block inland infiltration routes" and recommended the establishment of a force of high-speed small craft along the Cambodian and Laotian borders.[17] In 1968 this omission was rectified with the establishment of SEA LORDS (Southeast Asia Lake, Ocean, River, and Delta Strategy), a concept which drew on elements from all three task forces. Its twofold aim was to make the enemy engage US forces by disrupting its vital supply routes from the Gulf of Thailand to the upper Mekong River and to pacify the transdelta inland waterways.[18]

SEA LORDS perhaps came closest to distilling all the painful lessons that the US had learned about naval support for counterinsurgency. The recognition that effect needed to be realized beyond the riverbank and coastal strip had already been absorbed. It had been achieved primarily by the employment of airpower, one element of which, the Sea Wolves helicopter gunship squadron, was dedicated to the riverine force and integrated into the command structure. SEA LORDS, however, took integration to another level by bringing together both riverine and sea-based elements to achieve a common aim. Nonetheless it too fell far short of its objectives; in many cases because it failed to get the support it needed from the Vietnamese armed forces, a weakness common to many other combined operations during the Vietnam War. Despite this, it complicated the tactical and logistical operating environment for the VC, forcing them to move supplies in smaller and less efficient loads and contributed to returning life on the delta's rivers and canals to something like normal.[19]

Britain and France in the Mediterranean

The French Navy left Indochina in 1954, which was also the year the Algerian uprising began. The techniques of maritime surveillance that had been honed in Southeast Asia were transferred to the Mediterranean. The difference was that while no major shipping lanes passed close to Vietnam, the Gibraltar–Port Said route ran along the Algerian coast in waters that had nurtured smuggling and illicit activity for centuries. The system of coastal surveillance (or *sunar*) the French put in place was based on three principles: intelligence to identify suspect craft, aerial surveillance to track them, and surface vessels to carry out interdictions. The whole process had to be tight and precise, watching for ships that followed unusual patterns or sailed without lights to ensure they did not unload guns and other supplies onto fishing vessels which then ran into small ports or isolated coves.

The blockade, which included the use of landing parties to search coastal caves and other points inaccessible from land, succeeded in deterring the Front de Libération Nationale (FLN) from attempting to deliver supplies to Algeria directly. Instead it forced the FLN to divert vessels to either Morocco or Tunisia, from where insurgents attempts were made to smuggle loads across the closely guarded land border. Consequently, any vessel that was suspected of trying to circumvent the close blockade by taking supplies to either country had to be boarded on the high seas outside French jurisdiction. Interceptions took place up to 200 miles (370 km) from the coast and, in one instance, in the North Sea. Such action could only be taken on the basis of accurate information. The blockade's effectiveness can be judged by the fact that, despite the risks, by the war's end only about a third of the insurgents had weapons. This success naturally came at a cost; the ten interceptions that took place were achieved as the result of 18,000 steaming days by ships and 25,000 flight hours by aircraft.

In addition to the blockade, the French Navy provided air support, marines and marine commandos for ground operations, repaired vehicles, and serviced the electrified border fences. When the ceasefire was declared in 1962, the Navy evacuated the thousands of *colons* who did not want to remain behind in the new republic.[20]

The British campaign to subdue the EOKA (Greek National Organization of Cypriot Fighters) rebellion on the island of Cyprus lasted from 1954 to 1959. Blockade was, once again, a crucial element and although it was never completely secure, EOKA's pre-conflict plan to use the Greek island of Rhodes as a rear area was nullified. The Navy also provided useful mobility around the coast, enabling ground forces to exploit the element of surprise. Moreover, the lesson learnt in Malaya about the importance of interagency cooperation was transferred to Cyprus, where the Navy worked closely with police and customs in the Maritime Headquarters set up in 1955, and quickly moved next to the chief of staff's Operations Room to improve operational efficiency.[21]

Israel and its neighbors

The Palestinian Arab Navy was created just prior to the 1967 Six-Day War, eight years after the Cyprus rebellion ended and five years after France withdrew from Algeria. Little progress was made in its development until after September 1970 (Black September in the annals of Palestinian history), when the Palestine Liberation Organization (PLO) was driven out of Jordan and into refugee camps in Lebanon. Confronted with few opportunities to attack Israel overland, the PLO focused more resources on Israel's exposed, maritime flank with the objective of landing raiding parties and supplies. Although this investment took time to bear fruit, a clandestine ferry service was established between Cyprus and the Lebanese coast and three out of the four major Palestinian attacks mounted against Israel during the 1970s came from the sea, such that by the end of the decade the various Palestinian groups were regarded as possessing collectively the most substantial maritime capacity of any insurgency.

The initial Israeli response to this threat was to establish coastal exclusion zones close to the Lebanese border. The Palestinian reaction was to use mother ships to launch raiding parties further south. Israel counterpunched by staging commando raids on the departure points in Lebanon, usually disrupting Palestinian activity for several months at a time. The 1978 Coastal Road Massacre demonstrated that these raids were no longer sufficient, and Israel opted to invade southern Lebanon with the objective, amongst others, of forcing the Palestinian maritime bases further north. Between 1979 and 1986 no Palestinian raiding party succeeded in penetrating Israel's coastal defenses. Although this achievement coincided with developments in the Israeli Navy (IDF/Navy), which made it much more effective at making interceptions, it cannot be ascribed to the Navy alone. First, after Israel had reinforced its presence in Lebanon from 1982 onward, the PLO and other groups redirected their attacks onto exposed Israeli land-based targets in southern Lebanon. Second, because the Israelis had driven the main Palestinian maritime bases out of Lebanon to Libya, Tunisia, and Algeria, the Palestinian raiding parties were forced to make longer and more exposed voyages to reach their objectives.

However, the improvements in the IDF/Navy's effectiveness now made it a target, especially for the new Islamist-inspired groups, Hezbollah, Hamas, and Palestinian Islamic Jihad, which were beginning to emerge in Lebanon and the Palestinian territories Hezbollah based its operations in northern Lebanese ports well away from Israeli interference. In 1987 the IDF/Navy noted for the first time that small-boat "swarm" attacks, which were a feature of the 1984–8 Iran–Iraq "Tanker War" in the Persian Gulf, were being employed against its vessels. In 1988 it suffered its first suicide boat attack.

In 1993 the Palestinians were granted limited self-rule on the West Bank and Gaza. In contravention of the Oslo accords, arms smuggling into Gaza not only did not stop, but actively increased. The Israelis established what was effectively a blockade, and while many small consignments almost certainly slipped through under cover of the large number of boats that fished off the Gaza coast each night, the IDF/Navy succeeded in making a number of high-profile interceptions, of which the most famous was the *Karine-A* in the Red Sea 300 miles (550 km) off Eilat.

Knowing that in any confrontation with Hezbollah, the IDF/Navy would provide Israel ground forces with gunfire and air defense support, Iran inserted sophisticated anti-ship cruise missiles (ASCMs) and a firing team into the theater prior to the 2006 Israel–Hezbollah war. At least one double-salvo was launched, resulting in serious damage to a corvette, the INS *Hanit*. Evidence suggests that since the turn of the millennium, Iran allowed Hezbollah's maritime cadres to train on small-boat "swarming" attacks with the Iranian Revolutionary Guard Corps Navy (IRGCN) and that after the 2006 war it significantly reinforced Hezbollah's ASCM capability.[22]

Sri Lanka

Like most sophisticated insurgencies, the Liberation Tigers of Tamil Eelam (LTTE) relied on external supply. Because Sri Lanka is an island these supplies had to be brought in by sea, making the group vulnerable to blockade. Many of the group's leaders, born into smuggling families from the coastal town of Valvettithurai, were conscious of this risk. Their leader, Velupillai Prabhakaran, was reputed to have said that, "geographically the security of Tamil Eelam is interlinked with that of its seas. It is only when we are strong on the seas and break the dominance the enemy now has that we will be able to retain the land areas we liberated and drive our enemies from our homeland."[23] The primary thrust of the LTTE's maritime effort was to ensure continuity of supply from the group's base areas overseas—which at various times have reputedly been located in southern India, Burma, Thailand, and Indonesia—and the security of arms consignments from suppliers as far away as Europe. To fulfill these objectives it maintained a clandestine fleet of ocean-going cargo ships together with a force of fast attack and logistic craft capable of offloading these ships at sea about 120 miles (222 km) off Sri Lanka before running their loads to drop-off points along the coast or, alternatively, picking up loads from the Indian state of Tamil Nadu and smuggling them across the Palk Strait to the rebel-held areas on the island. Although the journeys from the offshore supply ships into the beach areas often turned into running battles, for much of the conflict the SLN lacked the equipment, tactical doctrine, and air support to be able to challenge these operations effectively.

Aside from this core mission the LTTE's maritime arm, known as the Sea Tigers, also disrupted the Sri Lankan government's supply lines to its own forces using mines, or attack boats and suicide craft often operating in "swarms"; they infiltrated suicide boats and swimmers into Sri Lankan naval bases; sent commando teams into government-held areas; and even executed large-scale amphibious landings. One such landing, the assault on the Elephant Pass in 2001, led to the capture of the Jaffna Peninsula and the collapse of the government's position across the north of the island.[24] As a consequence the Sea Tigers, which over the course of the war destroyed around a third of the Sri Lankan Navy's (SLN) strength, gained a reputation as the most formidable insurgent maritime force of recent times, one that in terms of effectiveness and capability amounted to a non-state navy. Little wonder, therefore, that when during the ceasefire negotiations in 2003 the LTTE suggested it should be granted de facto jurisdiction over the coastal waters off the land areas under its control and that the Sea Tigers be given semi-official status, not only Sri Lanka but also India were strongly opposed to the legitimization of such a potentially destabilizing presence in their region.[25]

Despite these setbacks, and the sustained use the Sea Tigers made of suicide attacks on the SLN's boats at sea and sailors on land, the SLN succeeded in concentrating its forces in defense of Sri Lankan supply movements, of which the action involving the troop ship *Pearl Cruiser II* in 2006 was a prime example. Its comparative lack of success against Sea Tiger supply runs between its ocean-going fleet and the coast meant that it transferred the focus of these operations to international waters, interdicting these ships beyond the range of the Sea Tiger assault craft. In common with the French experience during the Algerian War, success depended on sound intelligence, to which Sri Lanka rarely had access. However, as the nature of the LTTE's threat became appreciated more widely, unnamed outside powers proved increasingly willing to provide the information necessary. As a direct result the SLN sunk two LTTE ships 200 miles (370 km) off the Sri Lankan coast in 2003; and in 2007 sunk two more at 200 miles (370 km) range, three at 600 miles (1100 km), and the last, the MV *Matsushima,* 920 miles (1700 km) south of Dondra Head in an operation far beyond anything it had attempted before—one that stretched its capability to the limit.[26]

When it came to defeating Sea Tiger coastal craft the SLN found it was more effective to abandon their larger Dvora and Super-Dvora Patrol boats and adopt the small boat "swarming" tactics of their enemy. In early 2008 they established a Rapid Action Boat Squadron (RABS) equipped with much smaller 14-meter "Arrow" boats. Each boat was fitted out with a heavier weapon than its Sea Tiger equivalent such as 23mm cannon, rapid-firing 40mm grenade launchers, or two 0.50-cal machine guns. These were grouped into packs of three or four boats under the direction of a larger 17-meter Arrow or a Dvora. Their activities were organized using simple tactics and simple communications methods such as lights. Because they were of a shallower draft than the Dvora vessels they could pursue the small, fast Sea Tiger boats closer to shore and deploy from Forward Operating Bases (FOBs) much closer to LTTE territory.

Throughout their existence the Sea Tigers' ability to innovate and engineer novel technologies was demonstrated nowhere more clearly than in their pursuit of a submersible capability. The group attempted to build what was described as a submarine and three mini-submarines in Phuket, Thailand but these were discovered in 2003. More craft described as "submersibles" were found in LTTE territory on Sri Lanka after it was recaptured by the Sri Lankan Army early in 2009. Links were also believed to exist between the Sea Tigers and

Colombian Drug Trafficking Organizations (DTOs) that possibly extended to the exchange of designs and technology.[27]

Britain in Southeast Asia

The bulk of British experience was gained, largely contemporaneously with the French and American, in Southeast Asia. There were several common elements between the three campaigns but the balance between them differed. For ten years between 1948 and 1958 Britain fought to suppress the Malayan Communist Party insurgency in peninsula Malaysia (West Malaysia) in a campaign that has come to be seen, because it brought the military and civil elements together in a unified whole, as the epitome of the British approach to counterinsurgency. As so often, however, histories and assessments of the campaign have rarely mentioned the maritime dimension, although it was considerable. What one observer described as the "constant but unspectacular" blockade by a joint and combined force of Royal Navy and Royal Malaysian Navy vessels, and RAF aircraft, stopped over 1000 local craft in 1952 alone and succeeded, it is believed, in preventing any arms or supplies being landed. Naval gunfire support was another regular although somewhat limited feature as the insurgents were able to withdraw into the interior. However, in those cases where it could be applied it proved invaluable. On occasion British warships, including HMS *Amethyst* which in 1949 had been trapped by Chinese Communist forces on the Yangtze and famously escaped after 103 days, sailed upriver to deliver fire support inland. Naval helicopters were introduced into the theater in 1953 and proved their value. Navy ships were used for a whole range of additional tasks such as visiting areas that had witnessed insurgent activity and hosting local officials, activities which as Benbow points out have "useful although unquantifiable benefits in COIN, establishing the presence of the security forces in a routine and positive way."[28]

Between 1962 and 1967 Britain and Indonesia engaged in an undeclared war over the future of the newly formed Malaysian Federation. The British called it the "Confrontation" by adopting and adapting Indonesia's own term, "Konfrontasi." Indonesia wished to break up the Federation and, in the process, take possession of some of its constituent parts on Kalimantan. The conflict took place in a political, diplomatic, and military environment of particular delicacy given the Vietnam War that was being conducted to the north, Indonesia's domestic fragility, and the currency accorded the "domino theory" of Communist expansion which saw Indonesia as highly vulnerable. The effect in theater was that Indonesian air and ground forces could enter Malaysian territory, but British and Commonwealth forces could only make limited, precisely targeted, and, above all, deniable incursions into Indonesia.[29] A similar one-sidedness applied at sea, while another level of complexity was added by the existence of disputed maritime boundaries and the need to conduct operations amidst many small local fishing and trading craft that habitually sailed freely between Indonesian and Federation waters.

British forces were introduced initially in December 1962 to suppress an insurrection in Brunei. Half of the force arrived by sea and was reinforced a week later by the commando carrier (Landing Ship Helicopter, LPH) *Albion*, which had sailed from East Africa. Her flight deck provided Navy, Army, and Air Force helicopters with a crucial, mobile launch platform for tactical operations in a theater where the almost complete absence of all-weather roads made mobility dependent on rotary wing aircraft or rivercraft. The revolt was suppressed in a month, but starting in April 1963 Indonesia began to infiltrate its own forces along the almost 1000-mile (1600 km) land border. Naval support continued as it had for the Brunei revolt but when, in August 1964, Indonesia sought to extend the conflict beyond East Malaysia to peninsula

Malaysia, naval involvement increased; the only way Indonesian forces could be inserted was either by air (and one parachute drop was made but the force was captured within a week using troops transported in helicopters from *Albion*'s sister ship, HMS *Bulwark*) or by sea across the Malacca Strait. To prevent this the Navy established a barrier patrol made up of over 50 vessels, including warships plus Malaysian and Singaporean police craft, arranged in two lines and supplemented by coast-watchers. In addition it deployed an anti-aircraft destroyer and carrier-based airborne early warning (AEW) patrol to compensate for the virtually non-existent Malaysian air defenses.

The presence of the Far East Fleet, which by 1964 included two carriers; an LPH; a cruiser; squadrons of destroyers, frigates, submarines, and coastal minesweepers—as well as additional escorts and support ships—deterred Indonesia from escalating the conflict but would have played a larger and more crucial role had the British decided that escalation was their only option.[30] In all, naval forces fulfilled an extraordinarily wide range of support functions that ranged from deterrence to "hearts and minds" projects, such as medical assistance and school-building, via the more common tasks of patrolling, air and gunfire support, search and rescue, amphibious raids and landings, and resupply.[31]

Portugal in Africa

Portugal recognized that as anticolonial movements arose in its African possessions the geography of its three colonies—Angola (including the Cabinda enclave), Mozambique, and Guiné—meant that it needed to develop a riverine capability. Having no worthwhile experience of its own, it studied that of France and Britain and decided that French organization was most relevant to its situation.[32] The missions of the new African naval force were defined as denying the insurgents use of the colonies' waterways and sea approaches, supporting the Army by providing mobility and gunfire support, supporting the police and customs service, and supporting cross-border operations to deny the insurgents use of sanctuary.[33] In Angola the principal rivers were the Zaire, which for 80 miles (130 km) formed the border with the Congo, and the Cuanza, which, although it formed one of the largest river systems in Africa, was barely navigable for much of its extent. The Zaire River patrol began operations in 1960 and was reinforced in 1961 with the deployment of *fuzileiros* (marines) to relieve the boat crews of the need to serve as naval infantry.[34] Once the infrastructure to sustain operations was in place fully by 1966, the Navy, using a combination of fixed posts and mobile patrols, forced the insurgents to abandon use of the waterway, apart from occasional incursions, and to move their operations 620 miles (1000 km) to the east.[35]

In Mozambique, responsibility for the Rovumba River that formed the northern border with Tanzania was assigned to the Army, which established a series of fixed posts supported by land patrols. This barrier proved to be ineffective. The lack of a river presence which could defer and, if that failed, respond rapidly meant that, in contrast to what the Navy had implemented on the Zaire, the insurgents could disperse into the difficult terrain with relative ease once they were across. In an attempt to prevent the Army being outflanked, the Navy concentrated instead on patrolling Lake Nyassa (now Lake Malawi), a large body of water to the east that was shared with Malawi, and the Indian Ocean coast to a point about 160 miles (260 km) south of the Rovuma estuary, a combination that proved remarkably successful.[36] The security of the lake proved to be particularly demanding as the boats that were needed had to be transported overland from the coast on rough roads. Nevertheless, a force of armed landing craft and *fuzileiros* was assembled that denied the insurgents use of the Portuguese portion and disrupted their operations on the lake littoral. This success was aided by a carefully cultivated relationship with Malawi's leader, Hastings Banda, who severely limited the use of his country's territory as sanctuary. However, for political reasons he chose not to suppress all insurgent activity, forcing the Portuguese to employ highly secretive paramilitaries to disrupt those who remained.[37] Taken as a whole, these operations forced the insurgents to relocate to new bases in Zambia in order to attack Mozambique south of the Zambezi River, but the Portuguese domestic collapse occurred before the Navy was able to redirect its efforts to counter this move.[38]

Perhaps the most challenging theater, however, was the West African territory of Guiné (now Guinea-Bissau), which is hot and wet with annual rainfall of 118 inches (3 m) on the coast, declining to 49 inches (1.25 m) inland. It is an environment where metal rusts and just about everything else rots. The rivers are edged with mangroves that hide clandestine movement. The west is tidal, which creates impenetrable swamps at high water. When the tide is in, and the rains have inundated other low-lying areas, only about two-thirds of the territory is habitable. Despite the fact that the Navy was the most active service and naval support was the key to every operation, the Navy was made subordinate to the Army. From the start of the conflict in 1963 the Army command elected to divide Guiné into defensive zones and subdue them in a manner modeled on French practice in Algeria, instead of exploiting the country's unique but inhospitable geography by taking control of the coastal and inland waterways—an omission which the insurgents exploited. Because they were able to use the neighboring country of Guinea (previously a French colony) as sanctuary throughout the war, in 1970 the decision was taken to mount a raid on the capital, Conakry, with naval support. The objectives were to release prisoners, cripple the insurgents' command structure, and temper the Guinean government's ability to support further insurgent operations.[39] Although militarily successful, the Guinean government was able to pillory Portugal at the United Nations, undermine the support it received from the United States and other Western nations, and give the Soviet Union an added pretext to support the insurgency.[40]

Patterns of naval engagement

Is there a distinctive *naval* role in counterinsurgency? Arguably yes, but only in the sense there is a distinctive naval role in all expeditionary operations: to deliver the land force; to secure the battlespace and sea lines of communication against hostile naval action that could affect the land force's freedom of action; to provide secure offshore bases for command and control, surveillance, signal intercept, air and fire support assets; to provide in-theater mobility, enabling the land force to exploit surprise by moving men and supplies rapidly or sustain positions in the face of hostile action; and to withdraw the force when its mission is complete.

The quintessential naval support operation at sea has been blockade. In each and every case blockades have consumed seemingly disproportionate quantities of men and equipment for apparently little reward, but mostly have returned that investment. They have restricted insurgents' movements and degraded their effectiveness by forcing them to pay a high price in terms of delay, and uncertainty, and direct scarce resources to circumvent their presence. Where they have clearly been successful, as in Algeria, Malaya, and Indonesia, they have made vital contributions to the coercive effort. Even successful blockades, however, cannot be isolated from political pressure: British blockading action during the "Confrontation" was always mounted with extreme circumspection to avoid giving Indonesia any pretext to escalate the conflict. Although the Israeli isolation of Gaza has never been effective using naval power alone, the very public breaking of the embargo by peace protestors in 2008 demonstrated that while maritime blockades generally operate out of the public eye, they are not immune to symbolic manipulation and, in the end, are only as effective as political circumstances allow.[41]

Blockades that seek to isolate or restrict access to the battlespace will most likely continue to be relevant, but if future insurgencies expand to include multiple locations around the world as al-Qaeda operations have done, the naval role is set to grow accordingly. Interdictions of foreign flagged vessels on the high seas demand precise intelligence, and either the permission or acquiescence of the international community. Sri Lanka might have been able to escape censure when it sank ships in the vastness of the Indian Ocean, but similar action by a major power is unlikely to be tolerated. However, the benefits of positioning naval forces in critical locations with the mandate to mount interdictions has been displayed by the longevity of both the NATO-backed Operation Active Endeavour (OAE) in the eastern Mediterranean and the UN-sanctioned Combined Task Force 150 (CTF-150) in the Arabian Sea.

It is the debate about the naval role on coastal and inland waterways, however, that gives rise to the most substantial disagreement. There are many in the world's navies, in the US Navy in particular, who believe that the rapid development and proliferation of sophisticated anti-access weapons means that the risk to naval surface ships operating close to shore will increase so substantially, that future naval operations may need to be conducted almost exclusively from the deep ocean.[42] They point to the proliferation of quiet diesel submarines and long-range ASCMs, which Iran at least appears prepared to use to support insurgent groups as displayed by the attack on the INS *Hanit* from Hezbollah-controlled territory. These newer threats come on top of the challenges presented by older but cheaper weapons such as mines and small missile craft operating in "swarm" formations. Given limitations on resources, the concern is that money spent on the large numbers of small ships that are needed for blockades and the small, shallow-draft vessels required for coastal and riverine operations would be wasted. US forces came to dominate the Mekong and the waterways around Saigon, but at the expense of deploying one vessel for every 6.46 miles. Cann shows that the Portuguese in Africa maintained a similar ratio but that the French in Indochina could only maintain one vessel every 70 miles and would have needed another 800 vessels to achieve a similar level of effectiveness.[43] In those theaters where geography and insurgent tactics demand the maintenance of a supplementary coastal blockade, the investment would be commensurately higher. Yet experience of actual conflicts demonstrates time and again that the demand for such vessels is always substantial.

The debate is a legitimate one and hinges entirely on the interpretation of the long-term threat. However, if as seems entirely likely, insurgent activity—and even insurgent activity undertaken by proxies on behalf of nation-states—continues to be an effective way in which to confront the US and its allies, then resources will need to be reallocated within the overall naval budget to provide for specialized forces to support ground operations and survive in environments within range of insurgent or state-supported anti-access weaponry, including mines, boat "swarms" and even relatively sophisticated ASCMs. Moreover it is likely that they will need to survive for extended periods because one of the lessons of successful counterinsurgency is persistence.[44] Insurgencies can take a long time to die. Once ground forces are committed naval forces will need to support them. They cannot become the weak link. As Admiral Andrew Cunningham famously said when rejecting the suggestion that he should abandon the British Army on Crete in 1941 because otherwise he would lose too many ships: "It takes three years to build a ship and 300 years to build a tradition."

Fighting on rivers has, moreover, traditionally been a naval activity and the US experience in Vietnam and the Portuguese experience in Africa would appear to confirm that this still holds true. Generally speaking, ground forces see inland waterways as obstacles and fail to exploit them on their own terms. That said, naval engagement with riverine warfare has tended to be reluctant and episodic. The oceanic nature of the Cold War at sea, and the doctrine of "ship to objective maneuver" of the subsequent expeditionary era of the 1990s and 2000s that emphasized the need to avoid beach landings and littoral engagement, has left navies poorly prepared to engage in small-scale coastal combat.

What navies need to learn, therefore, are the counterinsurgency lessons that ground forces have learnt so painfully over the past 50 years: persistence above all, the primacy of the political, interagency cooperation, joint and combined interoperability, flexibility and adaptability. These qualities need to be combined with the recognition that civil affairs and staying close to the people, are important because it is their information which is vital to the intelligence battle, they who will give the counterinsurgent force legitimacy on the water as much as on the land, and their support which will ultimately discourage and defeat the insurgents. David Kilcullen has made the point that the hardest task in COIN is working out what is actually going on.[45] Recent US experience with Joint Task Force 515 in the Philippines assisting Filipino armed forces on the ground in the hunt for Abu Sayyaf Group (ASG) fighters has demonstrated that naval ships can provide important ISR support using data and images captured using unmanned aerial vehicles (UAVs). But while technical means are an invaluable supplement they are not a substitute for face-to-face contact. Finally, navies need to relearn the old lesson that rivers flow down to the sea. Inland waterways and the ocean constitute a continuum, open to exploitation by friend and foe alike. Naval attempts to separate one from the other and to stand offshore only leave openings that insurgents can exploit.

Notes

1 Julian S. Corbett, *Some Principles of Maritime Strategy*, Annapolis, MD: Naval Institute Press, 1988 (1911), p. 16.
2 Alfred Thayer Mahan, *The Influence of Sea Power upon the French Revolution and Empire, 1793–1812* (4th edn), London: Samson, Low, 1892, p. 118.
3 Martin N. Murphy, "The Blue, Green and Brown: Insurgency and Counter-insurgency on the Water," *Contemporary Security Policy*, Vol. 28, No. 1 (April 2007), 63–4.
4 Charles W. Koburger, Jr, *The French Navy in Indochina: Riverine and Coastal Forces, 1945–54*, Westport, CT and London: Praeger, 1991, pp. 7–11.
5 R.L. Schreadley, *From the Rivers to the Sea: The US Navy in Vietnam*, Annapolis, MD: Naval Institute Press, 1992, pp. 17, 19.
6 Ibid., pp. 20–1. Koburger, *The French Navy in Indochina*, pp. 43–9. Thomas J. Cutler, *Brown Water, Black Berets*, Annapolis, MD: Naval Institute Press, 1988, pp. 44–5.
7 Victor Croziat, *The Brown Water Navy: The River and Coastal War in Indo-China and Vietnam, 1948–1972*, Poole: Blandford Press, 1984, pp. 60, 65.
8 Ibid., p. 132. Schreadley, *From the Rivers to the Sea*, pp. 102–9.
9 Schreadley, *From the Rivers to the Sea*, p. 22. Spencer C. Tucker, "Naval Blockades during the Vietnam War," in Bruce A. Elleman and S.C.M. Paine (eds), *Naval Blockade and Seapower: Strategies and Counter-strategies, 1805–2005*, London and New York: Routledge, pp. 168–79.
10 Tucker, "Naval Blockades during the Vietnam War," p. 170. Schreadley, *From the Rivers to the Sea*, pp. 22, 83, 86. Koburger, *The French Navy in Indochina*, pp. 39–40, 46–7.
11 Tucker, "Naval Blockades during the Vietnam War," pp. 173–7.
12 Schreadley, *CDR*, p. 86. Alex Larzelere, *The Coast Guard at War: Vietnam, 1965–1975*, Annapolis, MD: Naval Institute Press, 1997, pp. 2–8. Jonathan S. Wiarda, "The US Coast Guard in Vietnam: Achieving Success in a Difficult War," *Naval War College Review* (Spring 1998), 30–46.
13 Edward J. Marolda, *By Sea, Air and Land*, Washington, DC: US Department of the Navy, Naval Historical Center, 1994, pp. 151, 315.
14 Tucker, "Naval Blockades during the Vietnam War," pp. 171–3, 177.
15 Marolda, *By Sea, Air and Land*, p. 161.
16 Tucker, "Naval Blockades during the Vietnam War," p. 177.
17 Schreadley, *CDR*, pp. 57–8.
18 Ibid., pp. 149–50.

19 Ibid., pp. 160–1.
20 Bernard Estival, "The French Navy and the Algerian War," *Journal of Strategic Studies*, Vol. 25, No. 2 (June 2002), 79–94.
21 Tim Benbow, "Maritime Forces and Counter Insurgency," *Contemporary Security Policy*, Vol. 28, No. 1 (April 2007), 86.
22 Martin N. Murphy, *Small Boats, Weak States, Dirty Money: Piracy and Maritime Terrorism in the Modern World*, New York and London: Columbia University Press/Hurst, 2009, pp. 287–305.
23 R. Hariharan, "Sri Lanka: How Strong Are The Tigers?" South East Asia Analysis Group, *Note No. 297*, February 28, 2006, available at http://www.saag.org/%5Cnotes3%5Cnote297.html, last accessed February 29, 2006.
24 "The Fall of Elephant Pass," *The Sunday Times* (Colombo), April 22, 2001, available at http://www.sundaytimes.uk/010422/spec.html, accessed August 2, 2008.
25 Murphy, *Small Boats, Weak States, Dirty Money*, pp. 310–21.
26 Ibid., p. 354.
27 Ibid., pp. 252–3; Tim Fish, "Sri Lankan Troops Uncover LTTE Submersibles," *Jane's Navy International*, February 17, 2009.
28 Benbow, "Maritime Forces and Counter Insurgency," 85.
29 Christopher Tuck, "Borneo 1963–66: Counterinsurgency Operations and War Termination," *Small Wars and Insurgencies*, Vol. 15, No. 3 (Winter 2004), 97–101.
30 Ibid., 102–3.
31 Benbow, "Maritime Forces and Counter Insurgency," 87–90. Gisbourne (pseudonym), "Naval Operations in Malacca and Singapore Straits, 1964–66," *Naval Review*, Vol. 60, No. 1 (January 1967), 43–6.
32 John P. Cann, *Brown Waters of Africa: Portuguese Riverine Warfare, 1961–1974*, St Petersburg, FL: Hailer Publishing, 2007, pp. 51–2.
33 Ibid., pp. 97–8.
34 Ibid., pp. 90, 101.
35 Ibid., pp. 110–11.
36 Ibid., pp. 159–60.
37 Ibid., pp. 168, 177.
38 Ibid., pp. 184–5.
39 Ibid., pp. 123–7, 138.
40 Ibid., pp. 209–32.
41 Katie Cooksey, "Peace Protest Boats Arrive in Gaza," *Guardian*, August 23, 2008. At http://www.guardian.co.uk/world/2008/aug/23/israelandthepalestinians. Rory McCarthy, "Middle East: Israel Declares Gaza Protest Boats Will Not Reach Their Destination," *Guardian*, August 23, 2008, available at http://www.guardian.co.uk/world/2008/aug/23/israelandthepalestinians.middleeast, last accessed September 8, 2008.
42 Michael G. Vickers and Robert C. Martinage, *The Revolution in War*, Washington, DC: Center for Strategic and Budgetary Assessments, 2004, pp. 171–6.
43 Cann, *Brown Waters of Africa*, p. 39.
44 Martin N. Murphy, "Blue Berets," *Armed Forces Journal* (April 2007), 20–4.
45 David Kilcullen, "Counterinsurgency in Iraq: Theory and Practice, 2007," Presentation, Quantico, Virginia, September 26, 2007, slide 48, available at http://smallwarsjournal.com/documents/kilcullencoinbrief26sep07.ppt.

10　Special forces

Kalev I. Sepp

When the civil wars in Iraq and Afghanistan subside, the lawful governments around the world will still face a jarring age marked by global extremist activity. Now more experienced and more realistic, they will carefully weigh their options. As defense ministers and generals consider how their forces might be again committed to counter those insurgencies, they must wonder if they can bear the burdens of such tasks. If—as in Iraq—counterinsurgency means a campaign that will cost $2 trillion, engage 150,000 troops, see the deaths of some 5000 of those soldiers, and last for at least six years with an indeterminate end, then only the United States can do it, and probably only once in a generation.[1]

But what if an armed insurgency in an allied country could be suppressed at a cost to the intervening powers of about $1 billion a year in military and economic aid, a commitment of less than 100 troops at any given time, while suffering less than two dozen fatalities over 12 years?—simultaneously democratizing the besieged country, building governmental capacity to enforce rule of law, and establishing elected civilian control over a reformed military that protects rather than oppresses their citizenry? This was the remarkable accomplishment of the US intervention in the Salvadoran Civil War, 1979–91, and the key military component in this successful campaign was special forces.[2]

This successful counterinsurgency notwithstanding, the question remains: under what conditions would countries commit themselves to engage in such operations in foreign lands to support rule of law in the world? It is in the national interest of all law-abiding countries to be able to fight insurgencies. If nations are indeed dedicated to the international rule of law and global stability, their governments and armed forces must be able to conduct or support counterinsurgency, counterterrorism, and stability operations.[3] Special forces are particularly well suited to engage in these missions.

The involvement of large conventional forces in counterinsurgency operations today in Iraq and Afghanistan does not obviate the original decision to create special forces. That choice was based on the experiences of specialized Allied teams aiding guerrillas fighting against German and Japanese occupation troops across Europe and Asia during World War II. Allied leaders came to learn that carefully selected personnel, who were older, more experienced, more resilient, physically tougher, and more independent than the greater body of soldiers and officers, were discovered to be the most successful at training, advising, and often leading indigenous peoples in irregular warfare. This is still true.

What has changed is the scale and scope of the terrorist threat to global stability now confronting the international community. This often amorphous threat drives the question: what factors will affect the shape, capacity, and modes of operation of armed forces in future wars, like counterinsurgencies? This is not a choice of "one warform over the other"; that is, of counterinsurgency over conventional warfare.[4] The North Atlantic Treaty Organization

(NATO) nations, for example, cannot ignore the rise of China, the resurgence of Russia, or smaller states armed with weapons of mass destruction. NATO was originally formed to be able to fight a continental-scale conventional or nuclear war. For almost half a century, it was organized, manned, equipped, trained, and, in particular, educated to that singular end.[5] NATO's special forces, however, can be useful across the broader spectrum of possible conflicts.

US secretary of defense Robert Gates expressed his view of the international security situation in a speech shortly after his appointment:

> The real challenges we have seen emerge since the end of the Cold War—from Somalia to the Balkans, Iraq, Afghanistan, and elsewhere—make clear we in defense need to change our priorities to be better able to deal with the prevalence of what is called "asymmetric warfare." . . . [I]t is hard to conceive of any country challenging the United States directly in conventional military terms—at least for some years to come. Indeed, history shows us that smaller*, irregular* forces—insurgents, guerrillas, terrorists—have for centuries found ways to harass and frustrate larger, regular armies and sow chaos. We can expect that asymmetric warfare will be the mainstay of the contemporary battlefield for some time. These conflicts will be fundamentally political in nature, and require the application of all elements of national power. Success will be less a matter of imposing one's will and more a function of shaping behavior—of friends, adversaries, and most importantly, the people in between.[6]

Despite Secretary Gates' views on the importance of counterinsurgency, a debate raged inside the US defense establishment, described by *The Wall Street Journal* as "This-War-itis vs. Next-War-itis."[7] Gates has publicly stated that "next-war" proponents are shortchanging current needs in Iraq and Afghanistan for advanced weapons that may never be needed.

Opponents of Gates say the defense secretary is taking a shortsighted position, and will leave the United States and its allies unprepared for future threats. Gates is aware of this, and with the support of the newly elected president, Barack Obama, is seeking a reasonable balance between these two types of warfare.[8] In this case, "balance" means the proposed apportionment of 80 percent of the defense budget for conventional forces, and 20 percent for irregular warfare operations—up from approximately 10 percent.[9]

In any regard, it is more likely that any given country would engage in foreign military operations if small numbers of special forces can be committed, rather than large numbers of conventional troops. Why a small-numbers, special-forces approach to counterinsurgency? Commitment of a nation's youth—19-year-old soldiers—is understood to be necessary for wars of national survival, and similar vital national interests, but not necessarily for lesser conflicts. Special forces, on the other hand, are better trained and more experienced professionals: older, long-serving volunteers, who clearly understand the risks of their chosen line of work. Putting them at risk for less-than-vital national interests is acceptable. Success is more likely precisely because of who they are—elite special forces, who are more survivable, better able to train foreign armies, and to teach and enforce respect for human rights.

With small numbers, intervening forces can be engaged and influential, but not irretrievably committed. Aid and advisors can be readily withdrawn if conditions require it. Long-term engagement, necessary in counterinsurgency, is possible because a handful of advisors are inexpensive and sustainable year after year. Also, with small numbers the supported nation shouldn't feel the advisors are running their units, or their war. "Ownership" of the effort cannot be either handed over to or assumed by the intervening forces. Greater reliance upon and accountability of the host nation is a necessity of the situation. Thus, in counterinsurgency wars, "less may be more."[10]

Future prospects

In considering future counterinsurgency operations, it is useful to understand how the United States envisions warfare over the next two decades. This understanding can inform allied armed forces on how they can integrate themselves, in a complementary fashion, into military campaigns with the United States, and particularly regarding the emerging concept of irregular warfare. One distinct aspect of current counterinsurgency operations is that very few countries attempt counterinsurgency unilaterally. The United Nations should be involved, at least for the political viability gained, and other international organizations and alliances will likely participate in such conflicts as they arise. The United States may well be an ally of any nation in a counterinsurgency effort, as nations' interests and strategic goals, especially as regards international stability, are closely aligned. In this, special forces play a key role.

Much of this concept is in response to the threat of irregular warfare.[11] Now, and for decades to come, the United Nations, and particularly the United States and all its international partners, must contend with a number of serious challenges: terrorism with a global reach; rogue regimes that provide support to terrorists and seek to acquire weapons of mass destruction; threats emerging in and emanating from fragile states and poorly governed areas; and new manifestations of ethnic, tribal, and sectarian conflict.

Many of these threats come from countries with which neither the United States nor any of its allies are at war. The responses they demand extend well beyond the traditional domain of any single government agency or department.

Irregular warfare includes a variety of operations and activities to prevent and respond to these particular challenges. These missions include, but are not limited to, counterterrorism, unconventional warfare, foreign internal defense, counterinsurgency, and stability operations. In the context of irregular warfare, these missions involve establishing—or re-establishing—order in a fragile nation or a collapsed state.

Irregular warfare operations may occur independently of, or in combination with, traditional warfare campaigns. Many of the capabilities required to execute them are resident in some parts of the US armed forces, but not with sufficient capacity to meet expected demand. Thus, allies are critical. In some cases, the United States and allied militaries need to develop new capabilities to address these emerging challenges.

Irregular warfare strategy

Irregular threats require an irregular warfare strategy. The old strategic paradigm held by the United States was to be able to win two conventional wars, or traditional wars, simultaneously, or near-simultaneously.[12] The new strategic paradigm being considered is that the United States is now in a protracted irregular war. The 2006 US Department of Defense Quadrennial Defense Review document (QDR) recognized and described irregular war, and also directed that the US armed forces must still be ready to conduct conventional campaigns.

But irregular war is still war; it is a major commitment. So, in addition to traditional or conventional warfare, the new strategy envisions three campaigns in the context of irregular wars. These are support to a large-scale counterinsurgency, support to large-scale unconventional warfare, and steady-state warfare.

The first campaign is support to a large-scale counterinsurgency. In large-scale irregular warfare like this, integration of special forces with conventional forces is essential. This special and conventional force combination in Iraq and Afghanistan, after six years of combat, is working well for the US forces there. The conventional forces employed in these campaigns—these surges—may not always be American or other foreign forces because, ultimately, local forces must defeat insurgencies.

The second campaign is a surge to support unconventional warfare. Unconventional warfare is conducted against a hostile state, an occupying army, or a transnational terrorist group. In a large-scale counterinsurgency, special forces usually support the conventional forces as they do in Iraq. That is the current practice. However, in unconventional warfare, conventional forces will almost always support special forces. Unconventional warfare requires partners and surrogates. It necessitates low-visibility operations, with some direct action and clandestine operations capabilities. An unconventional warfare campaign can drive some special forces capability requirements. An example is infiltration and exfiltration into and from denied areas.

It is likely the United States and its allies will face—and should plan to face—a formidable set of potential enemies. These likely opponents will have very strict border and internal controls, and will be enabled with biometrics, anti-access technologies, and first-class, full-spectrum anti-aircraft systems. Special forces will need particular skills to survive in these denied areas. They will also have to maintain contingency languages, based on projections for their most likely employment. These might be as widely spoken as Chinese, or as rare as a specific clan dialect.

The third campaign, steady-state warfare, is how the United States wants to win the long-term war against transnational terrorists. The steady-state effort will require a global network of special forces in greater numbers than ever before. They will work with national intelligence agencies imbedded in the partner or allied forces that will support the United States in this effort. The operational core of this counterterrorist effort will be special and conventional forces, as well as intelligence services, plus partners and allies. The US military will seek to achieve the right mix of forward-stationed and rotational forces.

This will require both indirect and clandestine capabilities, which the United States will accomplish primarily via a combination of intelligence work and "by, with, and through" approaches with allies.[13] Intelligence drives the "find, fix, finish, exploit, analyze" cycle against the terrorists, and more personnel are needed to do intelligence-related work.[14] The implication of all this is the requirement to build a global counterterrorist network.[15]

What sort of contingencies might occur, where it would be suitable for special forces to engage? One possible scenario might be a crisis following the internal collapse of the existing autocratic government in a semi-industrialized country. A compounding difficulty could be the impoverishment and primitive condition of large parts the country, calling for humanitarian assistance on the scale of major disaster relief. Any deployment would have to occur with appropriate legal accords, and possibly under the direction of the United Nations.

In this scenario, special forces troops—this includes civic action and psychological operations units—could deploy quickly in order to: secure military arsenals, and nuclear facilities if they exist; maintain order and establish stability; obtain the cooperation of the remnant military units of the collapsed state;[16] prevent looting;[17] de-mine minefields; protect the national economic infrastructure, resources, and cultural and historic sites; provide humanitarian assistance to the population; stop any exodus of refugees; re-establish communications, power, and water supplies; and eliminate fanatics who intend to wage guerrilla warfare to bring back the old dictatorship.[18]

Rapid action by professional units is the key. It is best to stop an insurgency before it starts. Special forces units can conduct almost all of these missions, but equipment must be procured and activities instituted to enable them.

Countering terrorism vs insurgency

Direct action missions, also called raids and strikes, are a necessary part of any larger campaign to suppress terrorism, crime, and insurgency, but cannot be the sole or even principal effort. Many special operations units were originally formed specifically to conduct counterterror missions—that is, direct action. When deployed to Iraq and Afghanistan, it is only reasonable to expect them to do what they have been trained for.

In Afghanistan, special operations units have been conducting direct action missions since 2002, but the Taliban insurgency has continued to grow. A senior US military officer in Afghanistan reported in March 2009, "I thought we could decapitate the insurgency. I was wrong. We've gone through twenty-two [high value targets] in this province, but [the insurgents] nominate someone new to take over the leadership very fast. The duration of our success is not more than three to four weeks before the insurgents have a new leader, and often that person is younger and more brutal. Even if someone killed [the head of the Pakistani Taliban], someone else will simply take over." [19] Commando raids and strikes must be conducted in the context of, and subordinate to, a complete counterinsurgency campaign. The summary directive of "clear, hold, build" must dominate military planning, with the emphasis on building a host nation's government structure and raising its security forces.

Technology

Technology will significantly support these three campaigns. Intelligence, surveillance, and reconnaissance (ISR) technologies and platforms are the top priority for the counterterrorism fight, and will be necessary in all three campaigns. ISR platforms, notably armed Predator and Reaper unmanned aircraft carrying precision-guided munitions, have powerfully enabled special operations and unconventional warfare, such as during the 2001 expedition to Afghanistan to overthrow the Taliban regime.[20] The US Department of Defense had initially underinvested in ISR platforms. A concerted building program is underway to meet the pressing demand from field commanders. The US must also replace losses—almost a third of the unmanned aerial fleet has been lost over time, mostly due to crashes.

Because of these shortages, the Defense Department must centrally manage its assets, platform by platform and mission by mission. Eventually, the allied forces will need a variety of ISR platforms. Models similar to current versions will operate in permissive environments. Advanced platforms must be "penetrating models," capable of surviving in high-threat air defense environments, to conduct special missions and to support special forces in denied areas.[21]

The demand for aerial ISR platforms in current counterinsurgency operations around the world is enormous, and often unsatisfied. Many allied countries do not have specialized ISR aircraft like the US Navy's P-3 Orion, or a fleet of unmanned aerial vehicles. However, all that is required to conduct effective airborne ISR is a secure radio, a sensor system, and an aircraft to carry them. Countries without purpose-built ISR aircraft can attain a near-term capability sufficient for some irregular warfare applications by mounting an advanced targeting pod to a fighter or patrol aircraft.[22] With some additional training, an allied pilot— who already speaks English, the international aviation language—could provide some ISR support for special forces ground units.

Other manned aircraft can be valuable, as well. Bombers, able to carry large loads of precision-guided munitions, can be very useful in both conventional and irregular conflict. Gunships have definitively proven their worth in Vietnam, El Salvador, Colombia, Iraq, and Afghanistan. However, four-engine gunships carrying multiple guns and cannon are expensive, hard to maintain, and are limited in number. It could be better to have a larger number of twin-engine fixed-wing gunships, mounting a single gun and carrying small-diameter guided bombs.[23] Additionally, small single-engine turboprop attack aircraft are well-suited for precision close air support.

Air-ground integration is critical in special operations.[24] In Iraq and Afghanistan, NATO and coalition special forces air-ground integration works well because US special operations forces work directly with international special forces ground teams, acting as liaison to US special aviation aircraft. Expanding this liaison capability would be limited only by the availability of US special forces personnel who could be attached to allied units. English-speaking allied special forces, trained in tactical air control, would be a viable augmentation to coordinating the air-ground effort.

An expansion of joint aviation training and exercises would improve special forces employment options. The Coalition Special Operations Forces Subject Matter Expert Exchange Program, based at Hurlburt Field in Florida, allows allied special forces personnel to train with US special aviation platforms, such as the MC-130 Talon and the AC-130 Specter. This program could include more personnel, and emphasize tactical skills such as convoy escort, infiltration and exfiltration, strike, and intra-theater mobility operations.

In the same way, US special operations air planners should also be educated on allied air capabilities and procedures by attending training and exercises abroad, in those partner countries. This would make US planners aware what allied special forces, both ground and air, can and cannot do before engaging in actual operations.

Aerial refueling is a high-priority training requirement for US pilots and crews, but due to the demand for refueling aircraft in theaters of war overseas, stateside aircrews only gain limited proficiency in this skill. Even KC-135s and KC-10s, the mainstay tankers for the US Air Force, are not available in sufficient numbers in-theater for all the requests to support special forces fixed-wing aircraft.

To alleviate this training shortfall, allied aerial refuelers could participate in the refueling exercises in the United States. US receiver aircraft crews train in accordance with the procedures in NATO standard refueling publication ATP-56. This would also give the visiting aircrews experience in refueling fixed-wing special operations aircraft, in addition to fighters and bombers. The mutual confidence and increased capability gained from such combined training would also be valuable in integrating allied refueling aircraft into special operations worldwide.

To take advantage of the increased capacity and capability in aerial refueling that would accrue from this training, all aerial refueling aircraft in the theater of operations should be combined under a single command. This would allow the US refuelers to concentrate on supporting special aviation helicopters, which is almost a solely American requirement. In the same way, all allied air mobility aircraft should be combined into a single fleet when deployed. Most allied air forces have smaller turboprop cargo aircraft, well suited for tactical intra-theater missions, like C-160s and G222s. This could relieve the US Air Force from having to use long-range strategic inter-theater lifters, particularly its C-130s and C-17s, in tactical missions, like moving small special forces units inside the area of operations. Also, US special operations aviation aircraft could perform more of the missions for which they are uniquely equipped, particularly nighttime helicopter aerial refueling.

The nature of a particular conflict—the size of the area of operations, of the population, of the enemy forces, of the number of allied special forces available—may require conventional forces to augment special forces. National immediate reaction forces, like the NATO Response Force, may not necessarily be the appropriate unit for this effort. These kinds of units are primarily intended to provide humanitarian assistance in a disaster, stabilize sub-war situations, and conduct direct action missions. They are usually not organized or trained for counterinsurgency operations in the way that many special forces units are. The very requirements necessary to produce elite units ensure there will never be enough special operations forces to meet the worldwide demand.

A possible solution for this shortfall in the quality and quantity of personnel to engage in counterinsurgencies is to create what the US military calls "SOF-like" forces from the body of conventional troops available in land armies.[25] ("SOF-like" means units or personnel with capabilities "like special operations forces.") There are several ways to achieve this additional capability. It is unrealistic to attempt to make a 19-year-old infantryman into a "SOF-like" soldier. In the near term, the fastest way to create "SOF-like" forces is to put conventional units under the command of special forces officers and sergeants. At a small-unit level, this has produced excellent results in the US joint military transition teams formed from individual volunteers to train Iraqi and Afghani security forces. The commanders of the advisory program at Fort Riley, Kansas where these teams are organized and trained, have stated that the teams led by US Army special forces officers were the most cohesive, effective, and confident. Another method to create "SOF-like" forces is to use special forces headquarters to direct operations using conventional forces.

In the long term, the best solution is to focus on making an officer corps more "SOF-like." This breed of officer would be: more politically aware, through graduate civil schooling; fluent in the language of an at-risk country or region; and able to think beyond the "manager of violence" self-image—to be not just a warrior, but a warrior-diplomat.[26]

For example, instead of habitually assigning officers to internal headquarters and staffs, the defense ministries and departments should post more officers to embassies, other government agencies, and overseas exchanges.

As part of this enhancement, US and allied officer corps should educate and develop special forces and counterinsurgency strategic planners. The various armed forces could begin by grooming select special forces officers to perform in strategist roles, to shape irregular warfare and counterinsurgency strategies for their respective countries. Their management should include assignments to conventional force commands as members of primary staffs, and duty as leaders in special and conventional units. Conversely, conventional force officers could be exposed to special units and operations early in their careers. As an example, US Army Special Forces officers are required to attend conventional forces "captains' courses" after they are chosen for Special Forces. This conventional training is essential for these Special Forces officers; corresponding schooling in special operations for some number of conventional officers must likewise be beneficial.

Languages

One of the distinguishing characteristics of deployable special forces soldiers is their ability to speak different languages. Among the armed forces on each continent, there are a variety of languages spoken in every country, and the rank and file of the militaries are often familiar with these. For overseas and "out-of-area" deployment, however, many other languages are necessary in order to be able to engage with the local population, security forces, government officials, and even with the enemy. Language skills make any soldier more "SOF-like."

Much of any success that might accrue to troops deployed "out of area" to fight an insurgency will depend on their skill at personal communication with the indigenous peoples—that is, at speaking the local language. In military interventions when these skills have been good, the counterinsurgent has held a marked advantage over his enemies.

Hiring interpreters is a "quick fix," but not an optimal solution. Local interpreters often have uncertain backgrounds and loyalties. Some may be from different local ethnic groups, and may be attacked by their rivals. In any regard, the ability of an officer or sergeant to speak directly with members of the local population is essential to quickly establish rapport and intelligence sources, rather than having to speak through a hired native of uncertain linguistic skill and allegiance.[27]

The large number of at-risk regions and countries that might require military intervention presents a great number of indigenous languages and dialects. Officers and long-term soldiers in special operations units should become multilingual, particularly in these contingency languages. Their specific linguistic capabilities should derive from the counterinsurgency assessments and subsequent nation by nation requirements that result.

Some taskings for language proficiency may be readily aligned to regions where allied nations have longstanding relationships. Others will involve schooling in arcane tribal languages. Even if only a single person in a military expedition is able to converse in the native dialect, it may be enough to make the best kind of difference. The axiom is true enough: "Learning a language is the way to learn a culture."[28]

Training and advising

Training and advising foreign armies is a central special forces skill. The emerging thrust of the new strategy in the Afghanistan counterinsurgency will be a much increased dedication of personnel to the mission of training and advising Afghan security forces. Similarly, in the Iraq counterinsurgency in 2009, the new administration has announced plans to withdraw US combat forces, but to leave a large residual force of advisors and trainers. The US forces are finally taking the advice of their own Special Forces commanders from the Vietnam War. They fought alongside Montagnard, Nung, and Khmer tribesmen, as well as South Vietnamese, and took the chief lesson of the Vietnam War to be "teach them to fight for their own country—don't do it for them."

Intelligence

When Lieutenant General Sir Gerald Templer arrived in British Malaya in 1951 to take over as the combined civil-military leader of the fight against the communist insurgency there, his dramatic first words to his staff were "This is an intelligence war."[29] The British leaders in the three years of the Emergency up to that point had not seized on this critical understanding. Much the same could be said for the US-led effort in Iraq for the first three years of the occupation, as ground force commanders wrestled with enemies whose objectives, methods, culture, languages, and motivations they did not understand.

One American unit was positioned to overcome these shortfalls much more quickly than the other US forces: the US Special Operations Command. But even this unit discovered the need for more and better intelligence to more precisely and rapidly find the enemy, particularly insurgent, terrorist, and criminal leaders who came to be labeled "high-value targets," operating not just inside Iraq, but throughout the Middle East and, in fact, around the world.

Their solution to this difficult targeting task was the intelligence fusion cell, in direct support of the primary special operations combat unit, in Iraq itself. The membership includes all US government agencies and departments with intelligence capabilities. In any given cell, there are capable representatives from the Defense and Central Intelligence agencies, the Federal Bureau of Investigation, the departments of the Treasury, Homeland Security, and Justice, the National Geospatial Intelligence and National Security agencies, the National Counter-terrorism Center, the US Central and European commands, unmanned surveillance aircraft units, and from the special units in combat themselves, among others.[30]

The chief of any given intelligence fusion cell is not an intelligence officer. Instead, he is a former special unit commander, usually a senior major or new lieutenant colonel marked for promotion and higher command, who has intimate knowledge of exactly what the special units need to conduct their operations. The individual military members of a cell are usually company-grade officers, such as experienced lieutenants and mid-grade sergeants. The civilian members are of comparable rank, already with one or two tours of duty in the overseas conflict zones.

The member's rank is less important than personality—of necessity aggressive and engaging, with a keen, quick mind. Most importantly they need two things: the confidence of their superior that allows the member to speak for them, and direct access to their superior, when necessary, at any time of the day or night. The intelligence fusion cells, although led by special forces officers and often closely associated with special units, work for anyone in the theater of operations. They will prepare and hand off target packets to any unit commander who makes a suitable request.

Trust is the most important element in "fusing" intelligence—each component of the intelligence community must freely offer up its share of information. To accomplish this, the location of a fusion cell is well forward in the zone of action, in the immediate vicinity of the unit operations. It has been discovered that this has the effect of building trust among the members. Certain intelligence agencies with the reputation for always wanting information but never sharing their own become highly cooperative in these circumstances. It is human nature to bond with one's comrades in arms. This sharing of intelligence must extend to all allies. As difficult as it seems, there must be no "keeping secrets" from allies in combat.

So, from a stumbling start in 2003 in Iraq, the US military has developed a highly useful and efficient solution to one of its major intelligence challenges, in the form of the intelligence fusion cell. In counterinsurgency, fusion is necessary because there is more than one enemy, and there is more than one war, as government and allied forces contend with criminals, terrorists, insurgents, and foreign interventionists. The intelligence fusion cell is also a metaphor for how all departments and agencies of a government must work together to achieve success.

Future issues

Several issues related to the global employment of special forces are emerging, and deserve close attention. First, senior military leaders should consider establishing standing multi-national headquarters to plan and direct combined special operations in a given region. For example, NATO has the Special Operations Forces Coordination Center at Mons, Belgium that conducts courses to train NATO officers to serve on special forces task group staffs. The Center, which will soon be renamed a NATO "headquarters," also has a separate state-of-the art communications system providing direct connectivity with the national special forces headquarters of every country in NATO (it is technologically more advanced, in fact, than much of the existing NATO signal equipment). Similarly, the United Nations Command in Korea has the Combined Unconventional Warfare Task Force Headquarters to plan and coordinate special forces operations in the event of a crisis or war on the Korean peninsula.

Second, a common threat perception might be useful. It would aid all the governments and their defense establishments in their various alliances and partnerships if they could reach an agreement about who and what constitute "threats" to them and their allies, collectively and individually.

Third, military planners should establish how information operations will support special forces; or, following the example of several terrorist entities, how special forces might support information operations. Several nations have sophisticated psychological operations capabilities and experienced units with similar doctrinal approaches, which ought to allow integration into allied operations overseas.

Fourth is logistics. US commanders in the overseas conflict zones report that some allied special units are over-reliant on US logistical support. This detracts from the contribution an allied unit might otherwise offer. Logistics is not a "niche" capability, a responsibility to be borne by just a few countries. Some degree of self-sufficiency is a necessary capability for all special forces to permit the maximum possible flexibility in employment. This is most important to the national governments in deciding to commit their special forces in either allied or unilateral operations overseas.

Fifth on the to-do list could be intelligence. US Special Forces experience in Iraq and Afghanistan has revealed the need for increased human intelligence capacity and capabilities in overseas contingency operations, particularly counterinsurgency.[31] Dennis C. Blair, the new US administration's director of national intelligence, openly said that after eight years the United States still lacks intelligence about the power structures inside Afghanistan and other basic information necessary for a counterinsurgency campaign.[32]

Sixth, terminology continues to be confusing. The national-level political and military leadership must sort out and agree on definitions of key terms, especially counterinsurgency, counterterrorism, counterproliferation, counternarcotics, and foreign internal defense operations. This is not an academic exercise; it is necessary to ensure unity of effort. They should not be distracted by new terms and "buzzwords" for long-established and familiar activities.[33]

Finally, scenario planning may be improved. To explore these issues fully and usefully, special forces commanders and staffs, and their civilian superiors, should conduct a continuing series of "futures games"—not just exercises, which are for training, but to look 10 and 20 years into the future in order to define likely problems and situations; to determine requirements; and to test processes, organizations, and possible solutions. These seminar-style games must engage all the relevant players—political and governmental leaders, allies, international organizations, etc. The objective is not to predict the future, but to help design special forces units with the flexibility and resilience to deal with an unpredictable future.[34]

Summary

As simple as this guiding principle seems, the United States, and hence its allies and partners, should *support* a counterinsurgency campaign in a given country, rather than conduct or lead it.[35] The doctrinal foundation for this perspective is in the official American definition of a foreign internal defense campaign, or FID: "Participation by civilian and military agencies of a government in any of the action programs taken *by another government* or other designated organization to free and protect its society from subversion, lawlessness, and insurgency."[36]

Allied governments must reconcile the moral and practical standard of avoiding undue belligerence, with the obligation of the NATO states to assist in suppressing crime and violence that threatens developing nations, particularly nascent democracies. Defense scholars Timo Noetzel and Benjamin Schreer note that Germany, with one of the largest economies in the world and a large, sophisticated, and professional defense establishment, has chosen to cast its engagement in Afghanistan not as a counterinsurgency mission, but as a "stability and reconstruction operation." By way of explaining their deviation from the NATO-designated mission, German officials offer that ". . . unlike many of its allies, the Federal Republic never engaged in a 'small war.' Germany lacks historical memory of such conflicts which could inform current debate."[37]

This lack of a small-wars expeditionary tradition since 1918 is arguably to the Germans' benefit. They will, for want of such martial conditioning, be much less likely to over-commit troops, resources, and political capital to a developing crisis, avoiding the American tendency some have criticized as: "if it's worth doing, it's worth overdoing." Nonetheless, the German government and people believe in the value of a peaceful and stable world order, from which they and other nations will benefit. This stability must be enforced, and that will occasionally require more force than can be brought to bear by law enforcement agencies. Careful and limited intervention by military forces is achievable, and can make the best kind of difference in many crisis situations. To imagine that these military forces can simply provide logistical support or base security and thereby avoid battle, and thus casualties, is not realistic. The military strategist and author David Kilcullen notes, "The distinction between combat and non-combat forces in a counterinsurgency environment is largely theoretical."[38]

In contemplating the design and employment of special forces to conduct counter-insurgency operations, it is vital that the allies in such efforts do not become myopic and over-focus on this particular brand of conflict, possibly creating vulnerabilities to other threats. Rand Corporation senior analyst, former defense deputy assistant secretary and Iraq veteran Celeste Ward cautions, "The question is not whether counterinsurgency works, but where, when, and to what ends it is wise to commit US power and resources."[39] This warning extends to all governments, as well—not to see all limited wars as counterinsurgencies, and not to remake all their armed forces, including their special operations units, thereby over-optimizing them to combat insurgencies. Special forces are in the best political and military position to provide the sufficient answer, the better option, and the weapon of choice to respond to the conflicts of the new century.

Notes

1 Terry Kelly of Rand Corporation made this prescient observation at the NATO Defense College in Rome, Italy, June 5, 2009. Chris Schnaubelt of the NATO Defense College led the conference where such issues were raised and discussed, and inspired the ideas presented in this paper.
2 For brevity and readability, the term "special forces" will be used throughout this paper to refer collectively to all nations' and services' elite combat and counterterrorist units, rather than the longer-term "special operations forces" or its US military acronym "SOF," unless specifically cited as US Army Special Forces or distinct units.
3 For example, the Netherlands Ministry of Defense lists "promoting the international rule of law and international stability" as one of the three "main tasks" of the Dutch Armed Forces.
4 Speech by author to NATO Parliamentary Assembly and US Congressional Representatives Pentagon Conference, January 28, 2008.

5 As of 2009, at the NATO Defense College where senior military and civilian officials attend a graduate-level course in alliance operations, there are no counterinsurgency courses in the curriculum. According to Dr Benjamin Schreer of the Aspen Institute, Germany, the German armed forces officer schools do not teach this type of warfare at all. Interview with author, June 4, 2009.

6 Robert M. Gates, US secretary of defense, speech at AUSA Convention, Washington, DC, October 10, 2006.

7 August Cole and Yochi J. Dreazen, "Boots on the Ground or Weapons in the Sky?," *The Wall Street Journal*, October 30, 2008, p. A14.

8 Robert M. Gates, "A Balanced Strategy: Reprogramming the Pentagon for a New Age," *Foreign Affairs* (January/February 2009).

9 Eric T. Olson, "A Balanced Approach to Irregular Warfare," *Journal of International Security Studies* (Spring 2009), 1.

10 See also Hy Rothstein, "Less is More: The Problematic Future of Irregular Warfare in an Era of Collapsing States," *Third World Quarterly*, Vol. 28, No. 2 (2007).

11 From a speech by the author to the National Defense Industrial Association, Washington, DC, February 14, 2008.

12 Colin Clark, "Two War Strategy Dead: Cartwright," *Inside the Pentagon*, July 15, 2009.

13 Linda Robinson, "Inside the 'New' Special Operations," *Proceedings*, July 2009, 33.

14 Lt. Cmdr. Chris Fussell, US Navy, interview with author, April 27, 2009. Lt. Cmdr. Fussell has lengthy combat service in naval and joint special operations units and staffs in Iraq and Afghanistan.

15 John Arquilla and David Ronfeldt, *Networks and Netwars: The Future of Terror, Crime and Militancy*, Santa Monica, CA: Rand Corporation, 2001.

16 Chris Schnaubelt of the NATO Defense College suggested this important task, considering the problematic results of disbanding the Iraqi Army in 2003. Letter to author, August 2, 2009.

17 At the United Nations Command Special Operations Forces in Korea Conference, June 16–18, 2009, the employment of special forces in a collapsed state to prevent looting was considered an imperative, in order to prevent looting on the scale of what occurred in Baghdad, Iraq in 2003, in the absence of security forces immediately following the fall of the Saddam regime.

18 Brig. Gen. Russ Howard, US Army (Retd), developed this detailed list of possible necessary actions, as a recommended response option to a collapse of the North Korean regime. Interview with author, Seoul, Korea, June 17, 2009.

19 Max Boot, Fred Kagan, and Kim Kagan, "Yes, We Can," *The Weekly Standard*, March 23, 2009. Even with the killing of the referenced Pakistani Taliban chief Baitullah Mehsud on August 5, 2009 by a US drone-launched missile, "experts said his death would not end the violent Taliban insurgency . . .," Pir Zubair Shad, Sabrina Tavernise, and Mark Mazetti, "Taliban Leader in Pakistan is Reportedly Killed," *The New York Times*, August 8, 2009.

20 Christopher Drew, "Drones Are Weapons of Choice in Fighting Qaeda," *The New York Times*, March 17, 2009.

21 Speech by the author to Johns Hopkins University Applied Physics Laboratory, March 11, 2008.

22 The LITENING and SNIPER advanced targeting pods are currently available from the US defense industry.

23 Maj. Kevin Huebert, US Air Force, interview with author, August 11, 2009. Maj. Huebert, a veteran AC-130 gunship pilot, notes that smaller, lighter aircraft might not be able consistently to provide the highly accurate cannon-fire presently delivered from the heavier, more stable four-engine AC-130.

24 Maj. David Jesurun, US Air Force, email to author, May 20, 2009. Maj. Jesurun's extensive experience as a US Air Force special operations pilot in combat in Iraq and Afghanistan provided the basis for this series of insights and recommendations for improvement.

25 For an assessment of "SOF-like" qualities in military personnel, see Bennet Sacolick, "SOF vs. SOF-Like," *Special Warfare* (July/August 2009), 9–10.

26 The "manager of violence" definition of a military officer has been promulgated in the American officer corps through widespread study of the late Samuel Huntington's landmark work on military sociology, *The Soldier and the State*, Cambridge, MA: Belknap Press of Harvard University Press, 1957.

27 Maj. Joseph McGraw, US Army, interview with author, May 28, 2009. His observations are based on his repeated tours of duty in combat in Iraq, and correspond with other combat leaders' experiences in conflict zones across time and around the world.

28 Recalled by Lt. Col. Adrian Bogert, US Army, note to author, June 16, 2009. Lt. Col. Bogert has served in Afghanistan and Iraq for over three years.

29   Richard Clutterbuck, *The Long Long War*. New York: Praeger, 1965. John Cloake, *Templer: Tiger of Malaya*, London: Harrap, 1985.

30   Fussell, interview with author, April 27, 2009.

31   Brig. Gen. Hector Pagan, US Army, observed that in his long experience in Special Forces, even though technical and signals intelligence receive the most funding, the preponderance of useful information comes from "humint" sources—human intelligence. Brig. Gen. Pagan presently leads US Special Operations Command-South. Interview with author, Goiania, Brazil, June 22, 2009.

32   Col. David Maxwell, US Army, letter to author, May 9, 2009. Col. Maxwell serves as the chief of staff of the US Army Special Operations Command.

33   For example, military officers at doctrinal conferences often note that terms like "hybrid wars" and "complex operations" are redundant, as all wars are "hybrid," and all military operations, particularly special operations, are "complex." Nonetheless, these may still be useful in helping non-specialists unfamiliar with military activities to grasp their intricacies.

34   Col. Alexander Alderson, British Army, proposed this objective at the NATO Defense College in Rome, Italy, June 4, 2009.

35   Maxwell, letter to author, May 9, 2009.

36   Joint Pub. 3-05, *Doctrine for Joint Special Operations*, December 17, 2003, emphasis added.

37   NATO Defense College, Counterinsurgency Workshop background paper, May 2009.

38   Carlos Lozada, "A Conversation with David Kilcullen," *The Washington Post*, March 22, 2009, B2.

39   Celeste Ward, "Countering the Military's Latest Fad," *The Washington Post*, May 17, 2009.

11 Intelligence

David Kilcullen

> To spend time in Iraq is to acquire a visceral understanding of the flexibility of information and the power of place over knowledge. What is true in Ramadi is not necessarily true in Iskandariyah. What is true in Baghdad is almost never true in Basra. In Iraq, information is tribal like the people who live there. It keeps its own company. Things only seem absolutely true in Washington. The closer you get to the killing, the harder it is to know anything for sure . . .
>
> David J. Morris, 2007[1]

On August 16, 2006, Colonel Pete Devlin submitted a negative assessment of the situation in Anbar province, Iraq. Devlin was a seasoned professional and his team was one of the most competent in theater. He had spent months at Multi-National Force (MNF) West Forward Headquarters in Ramadi, and had "a reputation of being one of the Marine Corps' best intelligence officers, with a tendency to be careful and straightforward," according to colleagues interviewed by *The Washington Post* journalist Thomas Ricks.[2]

Devlin's assessment was damning. He judged that:

> The prospects for securing Anbar province are dim and that there is almost nothing the U.S. military can do to improve the political and social situation there . . . there are no functioning Iraqi government institutions in Anbar, leaving a vacuum that has been filled by the insurgent group al-Qaeda in Iraq [AQI], which has become the province's most significant political force. . . . The report . . . describes Anbar as beyond repair; . . . it concludes that the United States has lost in Anbar.[3]

Not everyone shared this view; some thought Devlin was too optimistic.[4] Others believed Anbar was as good as it would get; it was just inherently nasty, violent, and unstable. Nobody saw the assessment as overly negative: few who worked in Ramadi considered the town anything but a hell of sectarian carnage. The writer and former Marine, David Morris, who patrolled with infantry units in the city in mid-2006, described it as the "graduate school of the insurgency. Marines and soldiers stationed in the city spoke of the place with a sort of detached awe at the baroque madness that had taken root there."[5]

Devlin's assessment was thus the same as, or more optimistic than, almost every other coalition analysis at the time. So, if it turned out to diverge dramatically from reality—and it did—then the explanation cannot be poor performance by Devlin or his analysts: there must be a systemic cause. Devlin was and remains a star player, and Marine intelligence analysts in Anbar repeatedly proved themselves highly competent, both in 2006 and afterward.[6] The truth seems to be more interesting: that intelligence work in counterinsurgency may have its own special dynamics, and that some of the methods of Western, expeditionary intelligence services may be poorly suited to insurgencies in other people's countries.

The Iraqi assessment

In May 2007 Terry Mitchell, an energetic New Zealander serving as civilian advisor to the Iraqi Ministry of Defense (IMOD), called me to a meeting with Iraqi planners at the IMOD building in Baghdad. The planners had asked to brief me on their assessment of the situation. Sitting with the Iraqis, reading their brief by the dim light of a sandbagged window—the electricity had just been cut by a huge car bomb—I stuck at the second page, an assessment of Anbar written by Iraqi military intelligence (M-2) in the same month that Devlin made his gloomy judgment. The Iraqi take on the situation—low-tech, based on tactical reporting from Iraqi army and police units, interaction with the community, and a maintained network of human sources—could not have been more different from ours. IMOD assessed that Anbar was reaching a tipping point, and was about to undergo a radical *improvement*. Key tribes were about to "flip," turning against AQI to side with the coalition (though not necessarily the Iraqi government). There would be a tribal revolt against AQI, and enemy cells would then probably move to Diyala.[7]

Iraqi judgments were thus diametrically opposed to the coalition's assessment. And of course, the Iraqis were right and we were wrong. Since M-2 had written their paper, Anbar had indeed "flipped": the tribes *had* backed the coalition, AQI *had* moved to Diyala, and security in Anbar had radically improved. Far from being lost, Anbar was being won in the very months that our intelligence team was predicting disaster.

My first reaction was to ask the Iraqis why they had not shared their assessment with Multi-National Force-Iraq (MNF-I) headquarters, a few blocks away in the Green Zone. "But we did share it," they said. "The MNF-I planners took one look at our assessment, said 'Nonsense, Anbar's not going to flip' and threw the brief in the trash."[8]

How did this happen, four years into the war and several months after the tribal revolt—which Iraqis called *as-Sahawa al-Anbar*, "the Anbar awakening"—that had already begun to displace AQI from Anbar? Answering this question demands an understanding of how intelligence in insurgencies differs from intelligence in conventional conflicts, and of how intelligence generated by intervening external powers differs from host-nation intelligence.

This chapter builds on an excellent and expanding literature on the subject, which includes the comprehensive chapter in *Counterinsurgency* (FM 3-24),[9] as well as insightful articles by Kyle Teamey and Jonathan Sweet,[10] Brian Jackson,[11] Walter Steinmeyer,[12] Jennifer Sims and Burton Gerber's *Transforming U.S. Intelligence*,[13] and the 1960s classic *Human Factors Considerations of Undergrounds in Insurgencies*.[14] It also draws on the comprehensive study of intelligence failures in Iraq and Afghanistan produced by Rand Corporation analysts in March 2009, and on the forthcoming PhD dissertation by Erin Simpson of Harvard University. Although many of my examples are drawn from current conflicts, I base my observations on a broader study of insurgencies going back to the eighteenth century, in the hope of discovering principles applicable beyond the confines of today's wars.[15]

I will argue that intelligence officers in insurgencies are less like intelligence officers in conventional war than they are like field researchers, engaged in something akin to ethnography. Like ethnographers they attempt, through fieldwork and participant observation, supported by careful evaluation of information from key informants and access to a wide variety of qualitative and quantitative data, to describe the totality of the physical and social environment, allowing events to be understood. But this is the ethnography of hell: it is carried out in appallingly violent circumstances in which people and societies suffer incredible brutality and unbearable pressure, where informants are under intense threat, information is often impossible (or impossibly risky) to acquire or verify, the object of study is changing rapidly, and intelligence officers themselves work under starkly difficult and dangerous circumstances.

Intelligence in insurgencies thus differs markedly from intelligence in "conventional" (i.e. force on force, state on state) warfare.

Intelligence in counterinsurgency

The first key difference is *focus*. In conventional war the focus of intelligence collection and analysis is, rightly, the enemy. This is because the most dangerous element in the environment—the actor most capable of interfering with the mission or harming friendly forces—is the enemy force. For Allied planners in Italy in May 1944, for example, the politics and personalities of civilians in the village of Monte Cassino mattered far less than the strength, activity, location, intentions, and morale of *1. Fallschirmjäger Division*, which was holding the fortified monastery. The civilian population had no impact on the operation, whereas the German parachute division inflicted three bloody Allied defeats before the fourth and final attack carried the objective.[16] Likewise, during the "march-up" to Baghdad during the conventional phase of the Iraq War, in March–April 2003, the location and activities of Republican Guard and Special Republican Guard divisions between Kuwait and Baghdad City mattered far more than the internal politics, community dynamics, and perceptions of ordinary Iraqi civilians in the towns along the route.[17] Once the insurgency began, however, these became precisely the aspects that mattered most.

In insurgencies, enemy-focused intelligence is both more problematic and less important than population-focused intelligence. For a start, understanding which players are "enemy" is complex, and contingent on the situation. For example, in the Zaidon, west of Baghdad, in March 2007, an enemy "order of battle" (ORBAT) would have included the 1920 Revolution Brigade (*Kata'ib Thawrat al-Ishreen*); by June some, but not all, elements of the 1920s network, and some tribes previously aligned with it, were fighting on our side against AQI.[18] At the same time, members of the same group continued to target the coalition, and the whole organization continued to treat our ally, the Shia-dominated government of Iraq, as an enemy.[19] Similarly, during 2004–8 our "allies" the Pakistani Army conducted large-scale operations in the Federally Administered Tribal Areas (FATA) on the Afghan frontier, but simultaneously turned a blind eye to Taliban recruitment, infiltration and training, and to safe havens in the FATA and Baluchistan. They fired on coalition forces in hot pursuit of Taliban on the Afghan side of the frontier, allowed Taliban mortar crews to set up firing positions in full view of Pakistani Frontier Corps posts, and permitted Taliban infiltrators to move back into the FATA through gaps in the Pakistani frontier defenses. Pakistani intelligence simultaneously continued to maintain close links with the Afghan Taliban and Pakistani terrorist groups.[20] Likewise, in East Timor in October 1999, I was engaged in a running firefight with Indonesian police and military and their insurgent ("militia") allies near Motaain on the East–West Timor border, but an Indonesian Army liaison team, including a two-star general, was simultaneously monitoring the firefight from our own force headquarters in Dili, as the operation was technically being conducted at the Indonesian government's request—albeit under duress.

Of course, conventional war is complex too: groups switch sides, civilians are present on the battlefield, and so on. But the complexity of insurgency environments seems to be dramatically greater even than in conventional warfare.

Counterinsurgency operations, then, invoke a higher than "normal" degree of ambiguity: the traditional concepts of friend and enemy are blurred, with organizations and groups switching sides rapidly, or even operating simultaneously as *both* friend and enemy. This is especially true of population groups that hedge against uncertainty by supporting whichever armed actor is strongest in their area at any moment, or (as in some tribes with which I have interacted in Afghanistan) where families ensure they have one son fighting with the government forces and another son with the Taliban—an age-old coping strategy for populations under pressure in the complex and unpredictable environment of insurgency.

Thus, to borrow a term from anthropology, populations in insurgency negotiate a complex process of continuously morphing contingent identity, where each person's or group's status (friend, enemy, neutral, ally or opponent, bystander, sympathizer) changes moment by moment, depending on the nature of the groups with which it is interacting. For example, in 2007 an insurgent from Jurf al-Sakhr, a town 35 miles (56 km) southwest of Baghdad, might self-identify as Janabi when dealing with members of other Sunni Arab tribes, as Sunni when interacting with Arab Shias, or as Arab when confronting Kurds or Iranians. He might identify as someone from Babil province when dealing with an Anbari, as a fighter of the 1920 Revolution Brigade when confronting AQI, as a Sunni insurgent when fighting Shia militia, as a member of the Iraqi "honorable resistance" (*al-muqawamah al-sharifa*) when confronting the coalition, or simply as an Iraqi while watching the Iraqi national soccer team triumph over Saudi Arabia in the 2007 Asian Cup final.[21]

Thus, identity in insurgency is highly fluid. Moreover, in counterinsurgency the enemy is *not* the actor most able to interfere with the mission: as classical counterinsurgency theory suggests, and as practical experience has demonstrated repeatedly, insurgents can be rendered mission-irrelevant provided the population is effectively secured, governed, and won over. This makes the population the center of gravity in an insurgency, which in turn makes the population the central focus for intelligence collection and analysis, an issue we will return to in a moment.

A second difference is *observer effect*. In conventional war it is at least theoretically possible for intelligence agencies to collect information about a target without thereby changing it. By contrast, intelligence in counterinsurgency and counterterrorism is mainly generated by security forces' own operations: acting on the environment, they generate a reaction that produces information, which drives the next cycle of operations, which generates new information, and so on. This action-reaction cycle invokes a strong observer effect, where the observer's presence and actions alter the target. Although such an effect exists in most tactical intelligence problems, conventional or otherwise, the effect seems to be much more marked in counterinsurgency environments.

This effect may also be exacerbated because in counterinsurgency the security forces tend to acquire information about the enemy through one of three main event types: insurgent attacks, insurgent defections or surrenders, and the killing or capture of enemy leaders. Each of these events changes the insurgent network: if an insurgent leader defects or is captured, the network's structure is thereby altered, and the group is almost certain to change procedures and techniques because it now has to assume that these are compromised. Likewise, in a suicide attack, the attacking cell and its weapons are destroyed, so even if analysts can fully understand the techniques used there is no analytical certainty that the same techniques will be replicated in other attacks.[22] This means that, although it is possible to know what the insurgent network *was* (before the event that generated a particular piece of information), it is almost impossible to know what it *is*. Like economic data, data on insurgent activity represent a series of lagging indicators, with clear patterns only emerging after the fact.

A third difference is that of *extrapolation*. A key source of information on the enemy in counterinsurgency is the debriefing of defectors and detainees, with conclusions extrapolated from defector/detainee questionnaires. Likewise, planners may extrapolate from survey or reconnaissance data to make judgments about attitudes or activities of population groups. But this process of extrapolation is analytically problematic. It assumes that detainees are a representative sample of insurgents, which may not be the case—they may represent less motivated, less competent, or simply less lucky insurgent fighters, but it may be impossible for analysts to tell which is the case. Surrendered personnel and defectors, of course, by definition are less motivated than fighters still at large, though they may be useful in negotiating the surrender of their former comrades, a technique often used by Commonwealth forces in the Malayan Emergency.[23] Former communist terrorists (CTs) were instrumental in negotiating the surrender or capture of their former comrades on several notable occasions in Malaya—and similar instances have occurred in almost every instance of insurgent warfare, including in Iraq and Afghanistan.

The problem of extrapolation is particularly difficult in interrogations of captured failed suicide bombers, whose psychology and motivation may not be comparable with that of their "successful" counterparts. Extrapolating from detainee interviews also presumes that insurgents possess the knowledge to speak accurately about their network (even though many insurgent organizations develop cell structures precisely to prevent this), and that they tell the truth under interrogation, another problematic assumption. Applying a reliability/accuracy grading (such as the Admiralty System[24]) to detainee information only partially resolves this problem. It may increase the reliability of conclusions from a specific detainee interview, but when results are aggregated to cover a broader subset of an insurgent movement the level of accuracy naturally falls to the mean, invoking by definition a lower level of analytical confidence.

A fourth factor is the *domestic/intervention* dichotomy. There is a fundamental difference between countering an insurgency in one's own country and intervening in someone else's— a distinction largely ignored in classical theory and current doctrine alike. The theorist David Galula, for example, throughout his seminal 1964 work *Counterinsurgency Warfare,* posits only two sides—the insurgent and the counterinsurgent—and neglects the markedly different strategic calculus, political stake, and options open to the host-nation government (which will be around when the conflict is over) as distinct from the external intervener (who must plan for eventual withdrawal, and must consider domestic public opinion in the home country as well as local perceptions in-theater).[25] Likewise, FM 3-24 discusses host-nation dynamics but arguably does not make enough of the distinction between domestic and intervention variants of counterinsurgency, and although the interagency *U.S. Government Counterinsurgency Guide* (2009) does identify and explain this distinction, it was signed in the dying hours of the Bush administration and it is unclear whether the current US administration even knows of its existence.[26]

Erin Simpson of Harvard University, in her forthcoming doctoral dissertation, explores this domestic/intervention dichotomy in several campaigns over the past 50 years, and demonstrates convincingly that domestic counterinsurgencies differ widely from intervention counterinsurgencies—especially in an intervening actor's ability to generate popular support, and to acquire and interpret information about the environment.[27] This, in turn, makes the intelligence problem in expeditionary counterinsurgency fundamentally different from domestic counterinsurgency. This is intuitively obvious to practitioners but often neglected by counterinsurgency theorists, and it partly explains why host-nation security forces can often generate markedly different intelligence results than those of external interveners, as in the Anbar example quoted earlier.

Thus, counterinsurgency intelligence differs significantly from intelligence in conventional war, and domestic counterinsurgency intelligence clearly also differs from expeditionary intelligence.

Institutional pathologies of expeditionary intelligence services

Indeed, intervention forces in counterinsurgency (that is, forces operating in an expeditionary environment outside their own country and fielding what we might call "expeditionary intelligence services") seem to exhibit six basic institutional pathologies: a preference for quantitative methodological rigor over qualitative local knowledge; a tendency to focus on threats to the intervening force rather than threats to local populations; a tendency to misinterpret culturally-coded signals within the broader intelligence "chatter"; a Eurocentric conception of state-building which prompts them to focus on top-down institutional rather than bottom-up societal indicators; a preference for input metrics rather than outcome metrics; and a vulnerability to loss of situational awareness through tour-length and rotation issues.

The first pathology is an institutional preference for methodological rigor. It is common to most Western intelligence services, but exacerbated in expeditionary environments where commanders on the ground have to justify their actions and judgments to decision makers who may be thousands of miles away and thoroughly out of touch, with little "fingertip feel" for the environment—making quantifiable data a key commodity in the tricky process of handling distant superiors' interventions, and convincing home governments to support on-scene commanders' judgments. Intelligence staffs are therefore pushed to find quantifiable, verifiable, and replicable indicators to support assessments, as ammunition in the discussion with higher headquarters. This is especially so in cultures like that of Western (especially US) intelligence communities, which already place significant weight on numerical data, even if numbers are often used to express largely qualitative judgments.

As an example, in 2007, the Iraqi intelligence analysts told me coalition planners rejected their judgment on Anbar because the Iraqis could not demonstrate quantitative indicators based on "significant activities" (SIGACTs) trends to support their belief that the situation was about to change. Rather than quantitative data, Iraqi intelligence officers were basing their judgments on personal contact with networks of human sources, family members, and community leaders—both in the general population and in insurgent groups—in Anbar, Diyala, and Baghdad. These qualitative data, acquired through informal, open-ended interaction with key sources, were more akin to opinion-polling and key leader engagements (activities also conducted by the coalition, to be sure, but by non-intelligence organizations and as such typically treated as less authoritative than intelligence data). Indigenous information was unacceptably vague and lacking in rigor for some coalition planners, who (according both to my personal participant observations in 2006 and 2007, and to my Iraqi informants) based their judgments on SIGACTs, signals intelligence targeting insurgent networks, trends in incident reporting, and variations in military accessibility (the ability of coalition forces to operate in a given area without being attacked).

This highlights the second key institutional pathology: expeditionary intelligence services tend to focus on "threat intelligence"—information about risks and threats to the intervening force's people and equipment—rather than "mission intelligence"—information about the broader environment, and how it affects the force's ability to achieve its mission. Not coincidentally, force protection risk often arises from insurgent actions while mission risk tends to arise from the actions of local populations, typically through breakdowns in relationships among groups within local society or between the intervening force and the community.

For example, in Afghanistan during 2006 and 2008 I took part in several operations/ intelligence briefings and roundtable discussions with coalition intelligence staffs at battalion, brigade, regional command, and force level, along with many discussions with staff of the provincial reconstruction teams (PRTs) in several provinces in eastern and southern Afghanistan. During these discussions, intelligence staffs of combat units typically focused on enemy ORBAT, activity patterns, and network analysis, while analysis of the "human terrain"—including tribal structures, relationships between key community leaders, and local-level politics—tended to be left to commanders themselves, operations staff, civil affairs personnel, and civilian PRT officers (including political officers from the State Department and officials from the US Agency for International Development (USAID)). Discussions with State Department PRT officers like Dan Green, who served on the Uruzgan PRT in 2005–6, and Karen Chandler, who served in Farah PRT in 2007–8, confirm that the main focus for military intelligence was often on threats to the force, while the focus for civilian officials, commanders and civil affairs staffs was on understanding the population and the local political environment.[28] This tendency became more marked after the fielding of human terrain teams (HTTs) in 2007–8, an event that tended to demarcate tribal and demographic intelligence as a separate analytical discipline from threat intelligence.[29] Meanwhile, my most useful discussions about intelligence as it related to the mission environment (as distinct from the force protection problem) were with PRT members, local civilian officials, and officers of NDS, the Afghan intelligence service.[30]

This tendency to focus on force protection can confuse expeditionary intelligence services into thinking that a campaign is going well, simply because violence against the expeditionary force happens to be low. In Iraq in 2003–4 British forces in the Basra area fell into this trap, believing that since violence against British forces was relatively low, the campaign was progressing better than in other parts of the country where violence was higher. In fact, insurgent organizations (including the Badr organization, Muqtada al-Sadr's Jaysh al-Mahdi and other Iranian-aligned Shia groups) were avoiding conflict with the British at this time, using the relative quiet to build their strength, intimidate and mobilize the population, and fight each other—none of which showed up in attack numbers against the expeditionary force (since this was Iraqi on Iraqi violence), but which contributed to a dramatic loss of control and escalation of violence in 2005–7, once insurgent groups had consolidated their dominance over the population.[31] In the British case, this tendency was exacerbated—as in many recent cases in other armies—because the deployed force included large numbers of troops with substantial experience of peace operations (where the objective is a quiet environment), but very few with actual experience of counterinsurgency (where the objective is a population loyal to the government). Making the transition from a peace enforcement mindset to a counterinsurgency mindset was critical.

The third pathology is that, even within "pure" enemy-focused analysis, expeditionary intelligence organizations often struggle to interpret the significance of events or trends that may mean something specific to local populations, but may be culturally opaque to members of the intervention force. While serving as an intelligence officer with the United Nations force in Cyprus in 1997, for example, I misinterpreted a car bombing near Eleftheria Square, Nicosia, as a likely terrorist attack, whereas local police and community leaders immediately perceived it as organized crime activity—one Chechen mafia boss wiping out another— because of telltale operational signifiers in the techniques used, with which they were familiar and I was not.[32] This, incidentally, was not something they could explain in quantifiable terms—rather it was a matter of fingertip feel or "blink" knowledge acquired over decades in that environment.

Likewise, an earlier generation of intelligence officers in the Netherlands Expeditionary Force Intelligence Service (NEFIS), operating against Indonesian insurgents in West Java in the late 1940s, interpreted the guerrillas' ability to field only one weapon per five fighters as a sign of weakness: the insurgents were poorly armed, indicating to NEFIS that they were likely to decline in strength. Meanwhile, the local population perceived the same observable indicator as a sign of strength: the insurgents were likely to grow stronger, since they had such a powerful recruiting base that they could motivate five times as many fighters as they had weapons, and such a powerful ideology that they could even mobilize fighters to take the field without firearms, using only "sharpened bamboo" (*bambu runcing*) as weaponry. These varying interpretations had much to do with cultural differences: European analysts judged military potential on the basis of material factors, while Indonesians judged military potential based on *semangat*, fighting spirit. This suggests that although counting events or identifying trends may be an objective, culturally neutral act of rational calculation, assigning meaning to such indicators inevitably includes a subjective and cultural component.[33] And since it is the local population's perception of insurgents (rather than the intervening power's perception) that causes the population to support or reject a guerrilla movement, finding a means to access this culturally specific set of perceptions is critically important, yet difficult for an expeditionary counterinsurgent.

A fourth pathology is the tendency to judge success based on progress in creating top-down, state-based institutions, while reposing less value and significance in bottom-up societal indicators. This pathology may not be confined to intelligence services. Rather, it seems to reflect wider Eurocentric attitudes to the process of state formation. Recent research suggests that the international community, including the vast international aid and development bureaucracy and the "peace industry" associated with international organizations such as the United Nations and the International Monetary Fund, tends to have a strong preference for top-down state formation ("nation-building") based on the creation of national-level, "modern," Western-style institutions of the central state.[34] Intervening forces in counterinsurgency environments seem to absorb this broader tendency, with analysts tending to give greater weight to events at the national level, or to elite-level political maneuvering, than to events at the grassroots, civil society level. Thus, while military intelligence agencies tend to focus on threat intelligence, civilian agencies tend to focus on elite-level political intelligence—whereas what most affects the mission may often be grassroots political intelligence, an oft-neglected focus of analysis. This can tend to skew intelligence collection and assessment.

Three examples illustrate this point. In Somalia since 1992 the international community has engaged in a series of failed attempts at top-down nation building in "partnership" with local elites. Simultaneously, just to the north in the former British colony of Somaliland, local clan peace deals in 1992 led to district-level agreements in 1993, the development of regional charters for local governance, and then the formation of provincial and eventually "national" government. This bottom-up process resulted in a greater degree of peace, order, economic recovery, and rule of law in Somaliland (and to some extent in Puntland) than in southern Somalia, despite an almost total lack of international assistance and recognition, and indeed active opposition at times.[35] Since this successful process in Somaliland occurred in the same timeframe as the failed process in Somalia—in the aftermath of the same conflict, in the same international political climate, and among clans of the same ethnicity and similar social, political, and economic structure—the Somali case almost represents a laboratory experiment, with experimental and control groups producing starkly different levels of societal stability (the dependent variable) depending on changes in the independent variable of top-down versus bottom-up peace processes.

As a second example, in Iraq during the Surge in 2007, coalition forces began with the intent to create security for Iraqis, which would then lead to a national-level peace deal, a "grand bargain" at the elite level that would resolve the sectarian conflict that was tearing the country apart. This top-down state-centric approach can be seen in the intelligence assessment at the start of this chapter, which concluded that Anbar was lost because "there are no functioning Iraqi government [i.e. central state] institutions in Anbar, leaving a vacuum . . ." Instead, in the *sahawa* (the awakening)*,* the opposite occurred: a series of local tribal agreements and grassroots reconciliation processes created peace and security at the local level (with our security presence acting as a critical enabler), resulting in an improvement in security overall. Again, this peace-building process was bottom up and civil-society led, not top down and national government based—and this is possibly one reason why it took coalition forces a considerable time to notice and exploit it.

Finally, in Afghanistan the international community concentrated, after the December 2001 Bonn Agreement, on building police, law courts, ministries, and parliament at the national level, and international aid programs bogged down in bureaucracy and inefficiency. Meanwhile, the Taliban came in at the grassroots level and took over the socially important functions of security, mediation, dispute resolution, and community policing, and they brought the world's most convenient and attractive cash crop—the poppy—to the Afghan farmer, a form of welfare and economic development as politically addictive as the drug itself, almost like a Taliban version of the coalition's equally addictive Commander's Emergency Response Program (CERP) funding. The Taliban thus sidestepped the international community's top-down approach to out-govern the Karzai government at the local level. While the international community built a supreme court, wrote a legal code, and trained judges, police, and prosecutors in Kabul, for example, the Taliban established local law courts and began resolving disputes, negotiating settlements, and enforcing a harsh but consistent form of law and order at the local level.[36] The international community's focus on the central institutions of the nation-state not only made it ineffective in facing this Taliban governance challenge, but actually meant that it took a long time for the intervening force to even notice or admit that it was happening.[37] By contrast, the most successful development and governance programs in Afghanistan to date—those associated with the National Solidarity Program—have been precisely those that embodied mechanisms for bottom-up civil society consultation and ownership from the outset.[38]

In an academic sense, this pathology may partly arise because some organizations within the international community lack an officially recognized theory of opposed nation building, or of bottom-up state formation. In intelligence terms, this focus on top-down processes tends to distract collectors and analysts from more important, though less evident, grassroots situational indicators.

The fifth institutional pathology is a preference for measuring effectiveness through inputs (the amount of money or level of effort expended by counterinsurgent forces or the local government on a particular issue) rather than outcomes (the impact of those efforts on local people's perceptions). Input metrics are usually quantitative (a further example of the preference for quantitative data) and may include indicators such as the number of schools built, wells dug, indigenous security forces trained, clinics established, and so on. These inputs are relatively easy to track but, in an opposed development environment where the enemy burns schools, poisons wells, and assassinates indigenous officials, they represent only one side of the equation. The outcomes of these programs—in the eyes of local populations—are what matter, because it is perceived outcomes that drive popular opinion about the coalition, the local government, and the enemy, and it is popular opinion that determines whether people choose to support the enemy or the government. Thus, the number of schools built matters less than the proportion of communities who believe local children have improved access to education, the number of wells dug matters less than the percentage of villages who believe they have improved access to clean water, the number of police trained matters less than the local perception of rule of law and security, the number of clinics built or children inoculated matters less than the local perception of public health, and so on. These outcomes are generally qualitative rather than quantitative, making them harder to measure, track, and report, but they matter more than inputs.

And again, what matters is how a population *feels* about a given issue rather than the objective, quantifiable reality, meaning that analysts must track perceived rather than actual outcomes. For example, when commanding a company on counterinsurgency operations in East Timor in 1999–2000, I interacted regularly with local tribal, village, and district elders. In one meeting with the *conselho* (the local community council) of Balibo district, Timorese leaders complained to me that the Australian troops were not protecting them, and so they did not feel safe to work their fields and plant crops, because they felt the insurgents might attack them at any time. In reality, my unit had patrols in every district, observation posts and patrol bases on every jungle hill, and ambushes and listening posts operating every night: the enemy had been unable to mount a single successful attack on the population in this area for more than two months. Thus, objectively, the people were safe. But we were operating covertly, trying to maintain low visibility and a light footprint, avoiding any heavy-handed interaction with the locals—an approach that was intended to minimize any popular backlash against our presence. Based on my meeting with the elders, it was clear that this well-intentioned approach had backfired, because the population could not see that they were being protected and thus did not *feel* safe. After this meeting, we therefore changed our operating pattern to create a visible, protective presence in the fields and villages, aiming to make the people feel as safe as they actually were—an effort that significantly improved popular confidence, and with it economic and agricultural activity, in only a few weeks.[39]

The difficulty with outcome metrics is that they can only be tracked by collecting information about how various initiatives and events are affecting the local population, and what local public perceptions exist in relation to both the enemy and the counterinsurgent force. In practice, gathering this data relies on public opinion polling, interviews, open-ended interaction, and ongoing engagement with local key community leaders, as well as the tracking of surrogate indicators for popular opinion. Each of these approaches has its problems in a counterinsurgency environment. Public opinion polling must be organized carefully using local researchers, with due attention to ensuring the confidentiality of respondents and generating comparative data sets that can control for sources of perceptual bias in highly divided communities. Surrogate indicators—such as the cost of transportation (an indicator of public confidence in road security), the variety and availability of non-local agricultural products in shops and markets (an indicator of public confidence in the economic, security, and food supply systems, and an indicator that people feel safe enough to farm rather than fight), or the progress of work on local non-government construction projects (an indicator of business and political confidence and labor security)—are very important but can be difficult to develop and are often open to widely different interpretation, both individually and in relation to each other. Key leader engagements are an important means of generating the open-ended, informal relationships with local populations that are essential to understanding public perceptions, but they are fraught with cultural and tactical difficulty, and vulnerable to the phenomenon of elite capture, where local establishment groups coopt, exploit, and gain control over the activities of well-meaning outsiders in order to further their own interests.

Contact between counterinsurgents and members of local communities, which inevitably also includes some witting or unwitting contact with the insurgents themselves, is also often laden with physical risk, as well as with the risk of unintended political and personal consequences. Even authorized contacts may leave an individual vulnerable to intimidation or punishment. For example, in 1998, as the operations officer of a peacekeeping force during Papua New Guinea's separatist conflict on the island of Bougainville, it was part of my job to maintain links with all sides including the insurgent movement, the Bougainville Revolutionary Army (BRA). My BRA contact, *A*, was a young man who visited my house in Arawa late in the evening on most nights, sitting on my veranda to discuss the latest developments and the insurgents' attitude to the peace process, and passing messages as an informal emissary of the guerrilla leadership. *A* regularly asked me for small personal gifts, ultimately asking for a pair of jungle boots with worn-out soles, which I had decided to throw away after repeated falls on a recent jungle patrol in the mountains. I gave him the boots, though they were the wrong size. (Many Bougainvilleans—Melanesians with an ethnic makeup closer to that of Solomon Islanders than to mainland Papua New Guineans, whom they derisively call "redskins"—never wear shoes in their whole lives, and have feet so broad that Western boots are virtually unwearable for them.) *A* wanted the boots as a tangible sign of friendship and favor, however, and as trade goods ("cargo") rather than as a wearable necessity—indeed, he had already been importuning a colleague, the force intelligence officer, for a pair of his boots for some time. My small act of friendship backfired, however: that night *A* was beaten so badly that he could hardly stand. He took weeks to recover, and was replaced by another guerrilla emissary; I rarely saw him again and our relationship was broken forever. The insurgent leadership had taken offense at the favor I had shown *A*: he was (literally) too big for his boots, and they had acted to send both of us a message.[40]

The sixth pathology is a loss of situational awareness through tour-length and rotation issues. Unlike analysts and collectors belonging to an indigenous intelligence service (or, in an earlier era, colonial police and security forces) who spend their whole working lives focused on one target set, expeditionary intelligence services are vulnerable to a repeated loss of situational awareness as analysts and collectors rotate in and out of the conflict. Analysts may become very familiar with a given target during their tour, but then rotate out and leave the theater, being replaced by new analysts unfamiliar with the environment. At the institutional level, intelligence organizations and headquarters periodically lose situational awareness and understanding as these seasoned analysts rotate out, and while individual analysts may develop a reasonable understanding of the situation during their tour, they lack the extended contact with the problem that is needed to track and diagnose trend-lines.

All these tendencies have been evident at times in our experience in Afghanistan. For example, during 2008 a significant difference of opinion emerged among intelligence agencies as to the true progress of the war, with organizations based in country taking a more positive view than agencies based in home countries. In part, this may have reflected pressure on both sets of analysts to generate assessments that supported policy, but it seems more likely that much of the difference of opinion stemmed from different interpretations of trends over time. Some Washington-based analysts, who had been tracking events in Afghanistan since 2000 and had served multiple tours in-theater, tended to take a dimmer view than analysts in Kabul—many of whom were reservists serving their one and only six-month or nine-month tour in Afghanistan. In a short tour, with little opportunity to leave their fortified base area, these analysts had great difficulty in developing detailed familiarity with the environment. Those from coalition partners with shorter tours tended to have greater difficulty than those with longer tours, or who were on their second or subsequent tour. Even those who were able to understand the 2008 environment in depth had difficulty comparing it to earlier years—hence, in part, the difference of opinion.[41]

The same pathology affects human intelligence collection, with experienced case officers rotating out and assets being passed on to incoming, less experienced case officers, sometimes compromising—or, at least, temporarily weakening—the relationship between case officer and agent, and resulting in a loss of situational awareness. In other forms of intelligence (especially imagery intelligence and close-access signals intelligence) lack of operational familiarity with the environment can also compromise collectors' efforts in the early stages of their tours.

Overcoming the pathologies

These six pathologies can be seen, to a greater or lesser degree, in the behavior of all expeditionary intelligence services engaged in guerrilla warfare or insurgency. Some organizations do much better in overcoming them than do others, and an informal survey of counterinsurgency campaigns since World War II suggests that these better-performing organizations tend to have some or all of the following characteristics:

Including local inputs in analysis.   Effective expeditionary intelligence services tend to include local analysts, or inputs from engagement with local communities, as key elements in their assessments. They draw on local perspectives and give these perspectives significant weight in making judgments about the environment. Commanders seek input from local counterparts, and the force makes a real effort to create a close and genuine partnership with local security forces, government, and communities. This approach, of course, creates problems of its own, which are discussed in the next section, but on balance it seems that the dangers of ignoring local inputs far outweigh the dangers of over-reliance on them.

Forward-deployed analysts.   Placing analysts as far forward as possible seems to improve the quality and depth of intelligence in insurgency environments, because at the local sub-unit level the analyst's ability to perceive and assess local motivations and to unpack the complexity of local events, personalities, and localities is exponentially greater. Analysts at higher headquarters tend to receive a sanitized, decontextualized version of events, and in a highly ambiguous and complex environment like that of counterinsurgency, context is key. Thus, lack of the necessary contextual information that allows analysts to interpret events (rather than just count them) can lead to incorrect conclusions. Better-performing organizations thus seem on balance to place more emphasis on forward-deployed analysts.

Caution in relying on quantitative incident data.   Effective expeditionary intelligence services tend to maintain a healthy skepticism about quantitative incident-based data, especially SIGACTs. In particular, SIGACTs often lose a substantial amount of their usefulness as data once they are fed into standardized databases—in Iraq in 2007, for example, I frequently took copies of the latest SIGACT reporting forward with me when visiting units on combat-advising duties. At least once in every unit, and occasionally for every single SIGACT report, the individuals who had reported a given incident did not recognize it when they saw it in its decontextualized form in the SIGACT database. They often disagreed with the way that higher headquarters analysts had interpreted "their" incidents, and often commented that many units failed to report a substantial proportion of the incidents that occurred in their areas, because they did not fit well into the established categories defined in the SIGACT reporting system.

Tour lengths. Intelligence officers who serve longer tour lengths in a given environment tend to develop a greater feel for it, and to be more capable of nuanced understanding. However, such officers also tend to burn out as a result of combat stress, physical or psychological injuries, or increasing cynicism about the mission or local society. They may also be captured by sectional interests—a local friend, a favored group within local society, or a perception about a given community group—and may lose objectivity. Thus, in addition to longer tours, some effective organizations have established overlapping or paired assignments, where two analysts or collectors alternate, one serving in theater and the other "on the desk" back home, allowing individuals to rest between field assignments but still maintain familiarity with the environment. Repeat tours in the same district, or with the same ethnic group, can also build familiarity—though this can also lead to overconfidence, where intelligence officers believe they know an area or a group better than they really do, based on outdated information from previous tours. Despite these complexities, expeditionary intelligence services that focus on longer tours or successfully overlap or pair their analysts and operators seem, in general terms, to be more likely to understand their environment.

Integration of tactical reporting with intelligence collection. At any given moment, an expeditionary force has thousands upon thousands of pairs of eyes and ears out on the ground—patrols, convoys, PRTs, medical and civil affairs teams, advisory teams with indigenous police and military forces, diplomats, aid workers, and so on. Only a small proportion of these people are formally employed as intelligence personnel, and yet their information is vital to understanding the environment and making informed decisions about it. Integrating this tactical reporting from non-intelligence units with streams of formal intelligence reporting from sources and methods controlled by intelligence organizations is therefore a key activity. Expeditionary intelligence services that put in place effective systems for debriefing tactical personnel, capturing their insights and perceptions of the environment and integrating tactical reporting with other sources of information are likely to perform better in a counterinsurgency.

Grassroots political intelligence. As noted, military intelligence often focuses on threats, civil intelligence focuses on elite-level politics, whereas grassroots political intelligence can be critical in understanding popular perceptions. The principal mechanisms for grassroots political reporting are PRTs and local military commanders. For example, Dan Green, a State Department officer in a PRT in Uruzgan province, Afghanistan, in 2006 pioneered a highly effective approach to grassroots political intelligence collection, which proved highly valuable to commanders and analysts.[42] Similarly dedicated individuals—usually local battalion and company commanders like Joe L'Etoile in the Zaidon district and Palmer Philips in Sadr al-Yusufiya[43]—produced equally good results in Iraq. Effective expeditionary forces seem to be those that, among other things, focus on acquiring and interpreting grassroots political intelligence as a matter of priority.

Robust police intelligence systems. Police intelligence is extremely important in counterinsurgency, for three main reasons. First, of all security forces, police tend to have the most intimate, continuous, and prolonged interaction with local communities, often giving them a greater understanding of community perceptions and dynamics than military forces can achieve. Second, police intelligence data track crime, violence, and intimidation between and among groups in local communities—an extremely important indicator of the real security, political, and economic situation—whereas military data (SIGACTs or other incident reporting) tend to over-emphasize violent incidents that involve coalition forces, rather than local on local events. Third, police forces tend to be largely indigenous, and thus tend to better understand the significance of events in the eyes of the local population (as in the Cyprus example given above). Thus, expeditionary forces that emphasize the creation of robust police intelligence systems, focus on the training and development of police, and develop systems to integrate police intelligence with military and political intelligence seem on balance to be more effective.[44]

Integrated structures and fusion centers.   As we have seen, integration of reporting—from military, police, local government, development, administrative, and economic sources—is a key requirement in counterinsurgency intelligence. As we have also seen, deploying analysts as far forward as possible tends to result in greater richness and context-based insight in intelligence, leading to better analysis. One way to achieve both these outcomes is to integrate civil-military structures from the highest to the lowest level, allowing for coordination, reporting, and flow of information among agencies and up or down the chain of command. Intelligence fusion centers at each level of operational control (as in Iraq and Afghanistan) are one way to do this, as are territorial structures such as the State and District War Executive committees formed by the British in Malaya.[45] This sort of structure is easier for indigenous governments to establish than for external interveners, however. Perhaps the best-developed system I have observed is the Center for Coordination of Integrated Action, established by the Colombian government to coordinate action at every level of the counterinsurgency campaign against the FARC, and focusing on 11 priority areas across the country.[46] Though expeditionary forces may find it extremely difficult to establish such a structure, efforts to do so are likely to bring benefits in intelligence terms.

Effective measures to track local opinion.   Last but not least, effective expeditionary intelligence services develop means to track, interpret, and understand local public opinion, including changes in local opinion over time. Indeed, because of the high degree of error and uncertainty inherent in conducting opinion polling in war zones, changes in polling data over time may actually be more significant than the actual results of any one poll, assuming that the margin of error in polling remains relatively consistent over time. Tracking local opinion may occur through survey and interview research, outreach to local opinion leaders, engagement with key players in the local community, and the tracking of rumors, conspiracy theories, and other discussions in local media, markets, and residential areas. It may also include monitoring of *khotba* (sermon) content in local mosques or of homilies in local church services, to track public debate and the views of local leaders. Monitoring local public opinion is an art, and it takes significantly different forms in different types of society, or even different regions or sub-groups in one society. But effective expeditionary forces tend to place significant importance on tracking and understanding popular perceptions, and develop locally tailored mechanisms to do so.

These, then, are some approaches an expeditionary force may adopt to overcome the pathologies identified earlier. It is possible to do all these things and still lose, as Erin Simpson has showed in her forthcoming doctoral dissertation[47]—expeditionary counterinsurgency seems, indeed, to be significantly more difficult than domestic counterinsurgency under almost all circumstances. Yet it is also clear that expeditionary intelligence services neglect these pathologies at their peril.

The methodology of conflict ethnography

As we have seen, intelligence in counterinsurgency differs significantly from intelligence in conventional conflict. In particular, expeditionary counterinsurgency is extremely difficult, and invokes its own special set of institutional pathologies. Overcoming these requires analysts and other intelligence personnel to focus on qualitative, nuanced judgments about public perception, based on a wide variety of open-ended interactions with local populations, and an attempt to integrate all sources of data so as to develop a detailed understanding of the conflict environment, rather than—as in conventional war—primarily focusing on understanding the capabilities, actions, and intentions of armed enemies.[48]

Therefore, to some extent, effective counterinsurgents in expeditionary environments seem to be engaged in something akin to ethnographic research, a methodology that we might define, under the rubric "conflict ethnography," as an attempt to study a conflict in its own ("emic") terms, and to internalize and interpret the physical, human, informational, and ideological setting in which it takes place. Borrowing a phrase from literary criticism, conflict ethnography attempts a "close reading"[49] of the environment, treating it like a text: an attempt to understand in detail the terrain, the key actors in the conflict, the people, their social and cultural institutions, the way they act and think. It attempts what the anthropologist Clifford Geertz called a "thick description,"[50] understanding a war holistically, in its own terms and through the eyes of its actual participants, in their words and in their language.

As we have noted above, the field methods applied in support of this effort include participant observation, face to face interviews, open-ended interaction with key informants, proficiency in local languages, long-term presence on the spot, integration of written sources with personal testimony, and developing well-founded relationships of trust with key informants—along with the fundamental ethical responsibility to protect those informants and advocate for their safety and well being. The aim is to see beyond surface differences between societies and environments, beyond a "military orientalism" that sees insurgents, local communities or traditional forms of warfare through exotic "Eastern" cultural stereotypes, to the deeper social and cultural drivers of conflict, drivers that local participants would understand on their own terms.

This type of approach to understanding a conflict is not, and should not be, unique to intelligence personnel. Indeed, academic researchers, diplomats, aid and development officials, humanitarian NGOs, and almost anyone engaged in an effort to understand and "read" a conflict may seek to apply a similar approach. In more detail, this methodology could be summarized in the following ten points:

1 Conduct research and analysis, as far as possible, using primary sources in the local language.
2 Get as close as possible (in time and space) to the actual events, ideally by being present when they unfold but, at the very least, by seeking first-hand descriptions from eyewitnesses, ideally members of the local community.
3 Use documentary sources (including operational and intelligence reports, captured documents, quantitative data, maps and surveys, media content analysis, and the work of other researchers) to create an initial primary analysis of the environment.
4 Use this primary analysis to identify a more limited number of "communities" (local areas, population groups, villages, or functional categories) for further detailed analysis at the case-study level.
5 Conduct first-hand, on the spot field studies (working through indigenous structures and applying an extended residential fieldwork approach wherever possible) of these secondary communities.
6 Work from unstructured, face to face, open-ended interviews (rather than impersonal questionnaires and surveys) during fieldwork, but integrate this subjective qualitative perspective with quantitative data from the primary analysis.

7   Revisit, in an iterative fashion, the results of earlier fieldwork and analysis using follow-up interviews and contextual studies, developing a continuously updated picture of the environment.
8   Understand and accept the presence of personal and research bias, but act to compensate for it by using the greatest possible variety of human and documentary sources and by explicitly identifying and examining the sources of bias.
9   Treat analogies (with other conflicts, societies, or regions) with extreme skepticism: seek to understand the conflict in its own terms rather than by analogy with some other war.
10 Wherever possible, and always when dealing with local non-combatant civilian populations, accept the fundamental ethical responsibility to protect the identity, and work to further the well being, of any key sources and informants, seek their informed consent to research and publication, and advocate for policies that enhance their welfare.

This methodology is not a panacea. Indeed, it has some very significant limitations. For one thing, getting the intensely detailed first-hand data needed for this approach in an active combat environment is not for the faint of heart: since it requires analysts to get outside the wire on a near-continuous basis, it can be extremely dangerous and indeed sometimes proves fatal. For another, data corruption—especially in the use of officially reported combat statistics such as body counts and SIGACTs, as already noted—can frustrate rigorous analysis, leading to an overemphasis on professional judgment and "blink knowledge"—an instinctive feel for the environment based on long experience—that may have been acquired in radically different conflicts, years before.

There is also a selection bias: for example, as senior counterinsurgency advisor in Iraq, I focused my greatest time and attention on coalition units in the toughest areas, units requiring the most hands-on field assistance but not necessarily providing a representative sample of events across the country. In Afghanistan, I spent much of my time with American special operations forces and provincial reconstruction teams, and had little opportunity to talk to local tribal leaders, except for those willing to work with (or at least talk to) the coalition.

The risk, stress, and effort inherent in warzone fieldwork also clouds judgment and skews emphasis: analysts tend to place more weight on data they collect with difficulty and danger than on insights gathered in the comfort of a headquarters or operations room. This approach's deep regional or district focus, in common with other case-study based approaches, is also not necessarily transferable. And the fact that local-dialect language skills are unattainable for many members of diplomatic services and expeditionary forces tends to privilege the views of male, urbanized, educated, and often English-speaking respondents. Last and most important, emotional factors—sympathy for local informants and leaders, intense concern for the welfare of the civil population, distaste for some political factions, and, over time, intense hatred for an extremely savage enemy—undoubtedly clouded my judgment at times in both Iraq and Afghanistan, and this seems to be a common experience for researchers in these environments.

But within these limitations, it seems clear that this methodology is the best we currently have for getting into the true microdetails of warzone social behavior, and thus for understanding a forbiddingly complex, dynamic, difficult, and dangerous environment. Since, as we have seen, intelligence in counterinsurgency bears a strong resemblance to ethnographic fieldwork (albeit with some extremely significant differences), a fieldwork, evidence-based approach to local popular intelligence makes sense in insurgency environments.

Conclusion

If the foregoing analysis is accurate, intelligence in counterinsurgency has its own special dynamics and requires its own methodological, organizational, and analytical approaches. Since the Western allies are currently engaged in two major expeditionary counterinsurgencies, with many other unstable situations worldwide that may require a counterinsurgency or stability operations response at some point in the future, the study of intelligence in counterinsurgency would seem to be a valuable and potentially war-winning endeavor in its own right.

Luckily there is a growing body of research and analysis on this topic, some of which is cited in this chapter. It is likely that this research will, over time, produce new and innovative approaches to understanding and responding effectively to insurgency. The development of new technology—for intelligence, surveillance, and reconnaissance (ISR); new platforms and organizations; and advancements in robotics, nanotechnology, artificial intelligence, and other enhancements in information processing, collection, and dissemination—will also transform and perhaps invalidate some of the insights in this chapter.

Yet it also seems highly likely that intelligence in counterinsurgency will continue to depend on a population-focused, detailed understanding of all aspects of the environment; one that incorporates local inputs and uses a wide variety of information sources to monitor and track public perceptions, as well as to understand and destroy insurgent networks. As William Tecumseh Sherman remarked after a civil war that included a major component of insurgency and guerrilla operations, "War is Hell"—and intelligence officers in insurgency environments will continue to act, in some ways, like field researchers engaged in the ethnography of hell.

Notes

1 David J. Morris, "The Big Suck: Notes from the Jarhead Underground," *The Virginia Quarterly Review* (Winter 2007).
2 Quoted in Thomas E. Ricks, "Situation Called Dire in West Iraq: Anbar Is Lost Politically, Marine Analyst Says," *The Washington Post*, September 11, 2006, 1.
3 Ibid.
4 Ibid.
5 Morris, "The Big Suck."
6 Author's personal first-hand observation during the 2007 "Surge" operations in Iraq.
7 David Kilcullen, Fieldnotes, Iraq 2007 (2).
8 Conversation with Iraqi intelligence analysts, Baghdad, May 2007, Fieldnotes, Iraq 2007 (1).
9 The US Army/Marine Corps Field Manual, *Counterinsurgency* (FM 3-24), issued December 2006, available online at http://www.usgcoin.org/library/doctrine/COIN-FM3-24.pdf.
10 Kyle Teamey and Jonathan Sweet, "Organizing Intelligence for Counterinsurgency," *Military Review* (September/October 2006), 24–9, available online at http://www.au.af.mil/au/awc/awcgate/milreview/teamey-sweet.pdf.
11 Brian A. Jackson, *Counterinsurgency Intelligence in a "Long War": The British Experience in Northern Ireland*, Santa Monica, CA: Rand Corporation, 2007, available online at http://www.rand.org/pubs/reprints/2007/RAND_RP1247.pdf.
12 Walter Steinmeyer, "The Intelligence Role in Counterinsurgency" *Studies in Intelligence*, Vol. 9, No. 4, 57 ff., available online at https://www.cia.gov/library/center-for-the-study-of-intelligence/kent-csi/vol9no4/html/v09i4a06p_0001.htm.
13 Jennifer E. Sims and Burton Gerber, *Transforming U.S. Intelligence*, Washington, DC: Georgetown University Press, 2005.
14 Department of the Army, Pamphlet No. 550-14, *Human Factors Considerations of Undergrounds in Insurgencies*, Headquarters, Department of the Army, September 1966.
15 David J. Kilcullen, "QDR Irregular Warfare Study, June 2006," unclassified study in the author's possession.

16 For a German account of this battle, see Frido von Senger und Etterlin, *Neither Fear nor Hope: The Wartime Career of General Frido von Senger und Etterlin, Defender of Cassino*, New York: Presidio Press, 1989 (E.P. Dutton, 1964). For an allied account of the same period, see Fred Majdalany, *Cassino: Portrait of a Battle*, London: Longmans, Green & Co., 1957.

17 Remarks by Maj. Gen. James "Spider" Marks, US Army (Retd), at the Johns Hopkins University School of Advanced International Studies, Washington DC, July 22, 2009.

18 Author's interview with Marine Lt. Com. Joe L'Etoile (Retd), Potomac, MD, April 2008.

19 Author's personal field observations, March–July 2007, Iraq.

20 Author's discussions with intelligence personnel in Khost, Kunar, and Kandahar provinces in May–June and October–November 2006; interviews in Kabul with NDS personnel and in Islamabad with Pakistan Army personnel; and personal observation in the FATA, Peshawar, Khost, and Kunar provinces, May–November 2006.

21 Author's first-hand participant observation in North Babil and Baghdad provinces, Iraq, March–July 2007.

22 Author's participant observation and discussion with Indonesian and Australian police crime-scene investigators and bomb-squad analysts during the follow-up to the second Jemaah Islamiyah bombing of nightclubs in Bali, Indonesia, October–November 2005.

23 Indeed, British Commonwealth forces fielded a whole organization, the Special Operations Volunteer Force (SOVF), composed entirely of defected or surrendered Communist Terrorists (CTs—the British term for the insurgents) and commanded by specially trained officers of the Malayan Police. See Hugh Popham, *The Jungle Beat: Fighting Terrorists in Malaya 1952–1961*, London: Weidenfeld and Nicolson, 1990.

24 A system of grading (for reliability of source and accuracy of information) developed by the British Admiralty in the early twentieth century and now the standard method of source grading by military intelligence services in NATO.

25 David M. Galula, *Counterinsurgency Warfare: Theory and Practice*, Newport, CT: Praeger, 1964.

26 Available online at www.state.gov/t/pm/ppa/pmppt.

27 Erin M. Simpson, "Politics, Popular Support and the Paucity of Victory in Third-party Counterinsurgency Campaigns," forthcoming doctoral dissertation, Harvard University, Cambridge, MA, 2009.

28 Daniel Green, personal communication with the author, Kabul and Washington DC, May–July 2006; Karen Chandler, interview, Kabul, March 13, 2008.

29 Discussion with PRT staff and human terrain analyst, Asadabad PRT, Kunar province, March 2008.

30 Fieldnotes, Afghanistan 2006 (1), Afghanistan 2006 (2), Afghanistan 2008 (1).

31 Discussions with British officers at the Directorate General of Development and Doctrine (DGD&D), Upavon, UK, June 2004; Baghdad, March–July 2007; Defence Academy, Shrivenham, UK, March 2008; and Rheindalen, Germany, November 2008.

32 Discussions with UN CIVPOL, Cyprus Police and community leaders, Nicosia, Cyprus, June 1997.

33 See the detailed discussion of insurgency and counterinsurgency in West Java, contained in Chapter 2 of my doctoral dissertation, "Political Consequences of Military Operations in Indonesia 1945–99," University of New South Wales, 2001. See also the copies of declassified Netherlands Forces Intelligence Service (NEFIS) intelligence assessments of West Java included as appendices to the dissertation.

34 Ioan M. Lewis, *Understanding Somalia and Somaliland: Culture, History, Society*, London: Hurst & Co., 2008, p. 91.

35 Ibid.

36 See David J. Kilcullen, *The Accidental Guerrilla*, New York: Oxford University Press, 2009, Chapter 2, for more detail on Taliban court systems and the governance challenge.

37 Discussions with International Security Assistance Force (ISAF) and United Nations Assistance Mission in Afghanistan (UNAMA) officials, Kabul, March–April 2008.

38 Discussions with Ashraf Ghani and Clare Lockhart, Washington DC, February and June 2009.

39 Kilcullen, Fieldnotes, East Timor 1999, field notebook No. 2.

40 Author's participant observation fieldnotes, in Operation Bel Isi X-3 War Diary, Bougainville, July–December 1998.

41 Discussions with analysts at the State Department Bureau of Intelligence and Research, the Defense Intelligence Agency and the Central Intelligence Agency, March–November 2008, and with analysts at the Joint Intelligence Operations Center-Afghanistan and the Kandahar Intelligence Fusion Center, March and July 2008.

42 See Daniel A. Green, "The Political Officer as Counterinsurgent," *Small Wars Journal*, Vol. 9 (September 2008), 1.

43 See Kilcullen, *The Accidental Guerrilla*, Chapter 3.

44 See William Rosenau, *Low-Cost Trigger-Pullers: The Politics of Policing in the Context of Contemporary State-building and Counterinsurgency*, Santa Monica, CA: Rand Corporation, 2009, for a detailed discussion of issues of policing effectiveness in counterinsurgency.

45 For a description of this system see Robert W. Komer, *The Malayan Emergency in Retrospect: Organization of a Successful Counterinsurgency Effort*, Santa Monica, CA: Rand Corporation, 1972.

46 Author's first-hand observation, visit to Colombia, March 2009. See also US Agency For International Development, Office of Transition Initiatives *Colombia Field Report* series, available online at http://www.usaid.gov/our_work/cross-cutting_programs/transition_initiatives/country/colombia2/rpt0907.html.

47 Simpson, "Politics, Popular Support and the Paucity of Victory in Third-party Counterinsurgency Campaigns."

48 This section is adapted from the Note on Sources and Methodology in Kilcullen, *The Accidental Guerrilla*, 2009.

49 In using this term I refer less to the "decontextualized" style of the American New Critics, who popularized the term "close reading," and more to the approach of analyzing a given text in depth, and in its social, political, biographical, and economic context that infuses much of the best of Biblical textual criticism and was first (and perhaps best) expressed by F.R. Leavis in *New Bearings in English Poetry: A Study of the Contemporary Situation*, London: Chatto & Windus, 1932. Conflict ethnography, then, treats a conflict as a living "text" which requires close reading and contextual analysis in its own terms, as well as evaluation in the "etic" perspective of the external observer.

50 Clifford Geertz, "Thick Description: Toward an Interpretive Theory of Culture," in *The Interpretation of Cultures: Selected Essays*, New York: Basic Books, 1973.

12 Local security forces

John Nagl

[F]rom the standpoint of America's national security, the most important assignment in your military career may not necessarily be commanding U.S. soldiers, but advising or mentoring the troops of other nationals as they battle the forces of terror and the instability within their own borders.

Secretary of Defense Robert Gates, speaking to future
Army officers at West Point on April 21, 2008[1]

If, as The US Army/Marine Corps Field Manual, *Counterinsurgency* (FM 3-24) states, counterinsurgency is "the graduate level of war," then advisors to indigenous forces are professors of counterinsurgency. Foreign forces cannot defeat an insurgency; the best they can hope for is to create the conditions and provide the enablers to allow local forces to win—for in the end it is the local forces that have to re-establish security, authority, and legitimacy, and to maintain these conditions. After describing the many complicated, interrelated, and simultaneous tasks that must be conducted to defeat an insurgency, FM 3-24 notes, "Key to all these tasks is developing an effective host nation security force."[2]

Historically, Western armies have struggled with the task of training, advising, and assisting host nation security forces to defeat an insurgency. This is part and parcel of their broader problem confronting insurgencies; conventional military forces are designed for conventional combat, and have historically floundered attempting to adapt to the demands of irregular warfare when their opponents have failed to obligingly fight them in the manner the conventional armies were most prepared for. However, perhaps in no area of counter-insurgency have Western armies been less able to adapt than in the area of training and advising indigenous forces—and in no area has that lack of adaptability been more costly. This chapter will focus on the advisory experience of the American Army, arguably the twentieth century's most successful land power in conventional war, from Vietnam through the current wars in Iraq and Afghanistan. This analysis will demonstrate that advisory efforts are an extremely valuable force multiplier, allowing intervening forces to leverage relatively small numbers of their own forces to dramatically increase the counterinsurgency effectiveness of indigenous forces while simultaneously enhancing the legitimacy of the host nation government. However, despite the demonstrated importance of well-trained, highly qualified and motivated advisors in defeating insurgencies, the American army has historically struggled to provide them in sufficient quality and quantity for large-scale counterinsurgency efforts, and has rarely rewarded advisors commensurate with the impact they have on the course of counterinsurgency campaigns.

This historical survey will attempt to tease out lasting principles of success for this most difficult—and most important—part of counterinsurgency warfare, before deriving lessons learned to help future intervening powers more efficiently and effectively to apply strategic leverage to the defeat of an insurgency through effective, responsive indigenous forces.

Counterinsurgency in theory and practice

An insurgency is an illegal attempt to overthrow a legitimate government or to change its policies through the use of military force. Counterinsurgency, then, consists of the military, diplomatic, economic, and informational efforts of the afflicted government, and of its allies, to deny the insurgents their aim. Counterinsurgency requires the correction of the underlying causes of that insurgency, supporting good governance and providing an opportunity for economic and political development. David Galula, the French counterinsurgency theorist, suggests that counterinsurgency is only 20 percent military and 80 percent diplomatic, political, and economic. In a well-coordinated counterinsurgency campaign, security, governance, development, and information operations can be mutually reinforcing.

Because insurgents do not have the military and financial resources of the state behind them, they generally conduct asymmetric warfare, avoiding the strengths while attacking the weaknesses of the government. They rarely adopt uniforms or attack in plain sight, knowing that to do so would expose them to destruction from conventional military forces; instead, they wage war from among the people, using ambushes camouflaged by the public to wage their attacks. They are, to use Mao's phrase, "fish swimming among the sea of the people."

Defeating an insurgency requires providing enough security to the population so that they are able to take the risk to support the counterinsurgent. The odds are stacked against the counterinsurgency force—it has to be strong everywhere, all the time, while the insurgents have only to succeed in a relatively few places, relatively seldom, to convince the general population that they could all be at risk. Thus insurgents use the techniques of terrorism to coerce support for their cause, even if often unwilling, from the population.

The counterinsurgents are faced with a dilemma: how to provide security everywhere, all the time, with a limited force? Police forces are able to provide security in a domestic environment only through deterrence; they cannot guard everywhere, but respond to emergencies confident in the knowledge that witnesses will indict, and prosecutors punish, perpetrators. In an environment in which bystanders are afraid to bear witness, the system breaks down—the very objective of insurgents, who wish to demonstrate that they are more powerful than the government. For this reason, FM 3-24 suggests that the counterinsurgency force may require 20 personnel for every 1000 in the population—a force ratio that would demand more than 500,000 security force personnel to pacify Iraq, and a greater number in Afghanistan. Given an American Army of about that size in total, this appears an insurmountable challenge.

It would be insurmountable if not for local forces, which have many potential advantages in any counterinsurgency campaign. They know the terrain, both physical and human, and generally speak the language. They understand the social networks that comprise the society and how they are interrelated. In a war in which finding the enemy is harder than killing the enemy, they have the potential to be enormously powerful counterinsurgents. But they also often have disadvantages, including poor training, a high level of illiteracy, low wages, a tendency to engage in indiscriminate use of force, and few of the "combat multipliers" (air and artillery support, medical evacuation and treatment, sophisticated staff techniques and planning tools, and, of course, vast funds) that make Western armies so successful in conventional war.

Squaring the circle is the job of advisors, who in the best circumstances bring combat multipliers and an unblinking eye with which to watch over their local-force brethren.

However, this is an uneasy marriage, often beset by cultural and linguistic misconnections—which are inevitable—and by institutional neglect and indifference, which are not. In Vietnam, the United States put a significant effort into the advisory mission too late, after the American people had lost faith in the war. The Vietnam experience offers many lessons for the ongoing campaigns in Iraq and Afghanistan, where the Army has slowly and somewhat grudgingly come to realize the importance of the advisory effort.

The American advisory effort in Vietnam[3]

"In the years following the Vietnam War, the Army relegated unconventional war to the margins of training, doctrine, and budget priorities," Secretary of Defense Robert Gates said in October 2007. This "left the service unprepared to deal with the operations that followed: Somalia, Haiti, the Balkans, and more recently Afghanistan and Iraq—the consequences and costs of which we are still struggling with today." The secretary's remarks pinpoint a problematic historical legacy. Direct US military involvement in Vietnam began with advisors: on August 1, 1950 the Army created a four-man Military Assistance Advisory Group (MAAG) to the French Army. By the fall of Dien Bien Phu on May 7, 1954, the MAAG had increased to 342 advisors. The MAAG focused on creating a conventional military for South Vietnam. Rather than a counter-guerrilla force dedicated to providing local security, the American advisors sought to build a force that mirror-imaged the American Army, trained to fight an airmobile and mechanized war under the cover of lavish amounts of (US) firepower. In late 1959, a presidential committee to study the advisory effort questioned the MAAG's basic premise: that fighting insurgents was a "lesser included capability" of fighting a conventional war. Instead, the Committee reported that:

> Tailoring a military force to the task of countering external aggression—i.e., countering another military force—entails some sacrifice of capabilities to counter internal aggression. The latter requires widespread deployment, rather than concentration. It requires small, mobile, lightly equipped units of the ranger or commando type. It requires different weapons, command systems, communications, logistics. . .[4]

Understanding this perspective, the Central Intelligence Agency (CIA) began the Civilian Irregular Defense Group (CIDG) program in November 1961. Villagers were armed, organized, and given medical and agricultural assistance under the supervision of US Army Special Forces soldiers. However, the Army saw the experiment as a misuse of the offensive capability of the Special Forces, and CIDG were transferred from CIA to Military Assistance Command, Vietnam (MACV) control in July 1963. The transfer, known as Operation SWITCHBACK, changed the nature of the program from a defensive orientation on population security to a more aggressive, offensive stance. General William Westmoreland, who had been assigned to command MACV in the summer of 1964, redefined the mission of Special Forces soldiers in Vietnam in late 1964 to border surveillance and control, operations against infiltration routes, and operations against Viet Cong (VC) war zones and base areas. The *US Army Special Forces 1961–1971* describes the process as the "conventionalization" of the CIDG.[5]

In "I Corps," the northernmost part of South Vietnam, the US Marine Corps (USMC) also initially focused on advisory efforts to Vietnamese forces. In contrast to Westmoreland's "search and destroy" strategy in the rest of Vietnam, Major General Lew Walt, commander of the III Marine Amphibious Force (MAF) from mid-1965 onward, created a coordinating council of the regional civilian agency heads in sector, Army of Vietnam (ARVN) and US military commanders, and a Vietnamese government representative. He also integrated Marine rifle squads into Vietnamese Regional Forces platoons. These "Combined Action Platoons" lived in the villages of I Corps and focused on pacification, while regular Marine battalions divided their time between platoon-sized patrols and civic programs.[6] General Westmoreland disagreed with this advisor-based counterinsurgency strategy, arguing that "I believed the Marines should have been trying to find the enemy's main forces and bring them to battle, thereby putting them on the run and reducing the threat they posed to the population."[7]

Army Chief of Staff Harold K. Johnson's decision to commission a high-level study in mid-1965 provided what was perhaps the last best chance for the Army to learn that its counterinsurgency procedures were flawed; to accept that fact at a high level within the organization, and to implement organizational and doctrinal change as a result. The Program for the Pacification and Long-Term Development of South Vietnam (PROVN) study, under the leadership of General Creighton Abrams, was tasked with "developing new courses of action to be taken in South Vietnam by the United States and its allies, which will, in conjunction with current actions, modified as necessary, lead in due time to successful accomplishment of U.S. aims and objectives."[8] The results were striking: the key to success in Vietnam was the creation of security forces "associated and intermingled with the people on a long-term basis," such as the CIDG under CIA control, or the USMC's Combined Action Platoons.

While both the political and military leadership of the United States paid lipservice to the importance of combined political-military efforts to advise the local government how to defeat the rural insurgency in Vietnam, little effort was actually expended in this arena before 1967. There was no organization in the US government that was structured, trained, and equipped to perform this mission, and little incentive for existing institutions to adapt to meet the need for one. The personal and very vigorous intervention of "Blowtorch" Bob Komer was instrumental in creating perhaps the most remarkable example of American institutional innovation during the Vietnam War. Komer was able to pull together all of the American civilian and military pacification programs into Civil Operations and Revolutionary Development Support (CORDS) on May 1, 1967.

CORDS was a dramatic change from "business as usual," incorporating personnel from the CIA, USIA, AID, the State Department, the White House, and all the military services. In addition to Komer, who worked directly for COMUSMACV (as the top person in charge of the US military in Vietnam was known), each of the four American Corps Commanders had a deputy for pacification; the "cutting edge" of CORDS, however, was unified civil-military advisory teams in all 250 districts and 44 provinces. CORDS was purpose built for the demands of counterinsurgency warfare in Vietnam, integrating civilian and military personnel at all levels to promote a combined political-military approach to problem recognition and solution.[9]

Westmoreland was replaced by General Creighton Abrams on July 1, 1968. As the United States recognized that it would have to withdraw from Vietnam, President Nixon made the primary mission of American troops to enable the South Vietnamese forces to assume the full responsibility for the security of South Vietnam. The Nixon administration's policy of turning over fighting responsibilities to the South Vietnamese while the United States continued to supply material and financial assistance, including air support for the ARVN, was formally announced in Guam in July 1969 and dubbed "Vietnamization" by secretary of defense Melvin Laird. Under Vietnamization, Saigon rapidly increased the size of its regular and paramilitary forces. The ARVN was given improved equipment and better training.[10]

Unfortunately, while the ARVN became well armed and well equipped, deficiencies remained in officer and non-commissioned officer leadership.[11] The quality of the ARVN's leadership was not helped by the fact that the American advisory effort was being scaled down even as the need for US advisors increased. Ultimately, South Vietnam was unable to defend itself without American advisors and the combat multipliers they bring to the battlefield.

The advisory effort in Vietnam has been widely criticized as "The Other War." Military analysts Peter Dawkins and Andrew Krepinevich have described the often poor quality of Army advisors in Vietnam and the slapdash nature of their predeployment training.[12] Lieutenant Commander Dennis "Buz" Bruzina, twice an advisor in Vietnam, confirms their assessment of the low priority the Army gave to the advisor mission:

> In terms of promotions, in terms of assignments, they would be considered at a second level—the quality would be second tier quality as opposed to people in divisions. On the other hand, the advisors had a better understanding of the people, of what was required to win.[13]

The American advisory effort in Vietnam can be summed up in the bitter words of an army officer serving in our last great counterinsurgency effort:

> Our military institution seems to be prevented by its own doctrinal rigidity from understanding the nature of this war and from making the necessary modifications to apply its power more intelligently, more economically, and above all, more relevantly.[14]

From Vietnam to Afghanistan and Iraq

In the aftermath of Vietnam, the mission of training and advising indigenous security forces was generally assigned to Special Forces soldiers. They had perhaps their greatest success at the Foreign Internal Defense (FID) mission in El Salvador in the 1980s, when Congress placed limitations on the number of American advisors that could be deployed to support the government in its fight against insurgents. However, counterinsurgency and advisory lessons from El Salvador and elsewhere were not absorbed by the conventional Army in the wake of Vietnam, which simply decided that it would not perform these missions in the future and instead prepared for conventional warfare, even after the dissolution of the Soviet Union removed the primary cause for an exclusive focus on that kind of war.

This institutional neglect left the Army and the Marine Corps unprepared for counter-insurgency campaigns in Iraq and Afghanistan. Perhaps in no area has the institutional neglect been more damaging than in the advisory area, where the services have made many of the same mistakes while implementing combat advisory efforts in Afghanistan and Iraq as they made in Vietnam.[15] With demand for advisors to the Iraqi and Afghan security forces far exceeding the ability of the Special Forces to supply sufficient A-Teams to meet demand, the Army began to create "Transition Teams" modeled on A-Teams. FM 3-24 recognized the need for change: "The scope and scale of training programs today and the scale of programs likely to be required in the future has grown exponentially. While FID has been traditionally the primary responsibility of the special operating forces (SOF), training foreign forces is now a core competency of regular and reserve units of all Services."[16]

What were initially called Military Transition Teams, or MTTs, were selected from individual National Guard, Army Reserve, and Active Duty personnel on an *ad hoc* basis; for the first several years of the Long War their training was conducted on several different

Army posts and varied widely in quality. Doctrine for general-purpose forces assigned to the advisor mission was lacking for several years, although it was finally published in 2009.[17] The teams' size and composition were inconsistent, with most Afghan teams in training consisting of 16-soldier teams with no medic, and these were often broken into smaller units when they arrived in Afghanistan; while Iraq teams contained 11 soldiers including a medic. Internal and external studies repeatedly concluded that the teams were too small for the tasks that they had been assigned; many teams consequently were augmented in theater by additional security forces, again on an *ad hoc* basis.

In 2006, the Army centralized training for transition teams at Fort Riley, Kansas—initially giving the training mission to two heavy brigade combat teams, and later consolidating responsibility with the 1st Brigade of the 1st Infantry Division. This unit created a 60-day training program that included both advisory and combat survival skills.[18] Unfortunately, initially very few of the cadre members had been advisors themselves. One of the four battalions conducting the training had just three former advisors among its 96 soldiers in January 2007, although that number had increased to 13 by June 2008. In addition, the training battalions' rank structure hindered optimal training, as junior sergeants were often assigned to mentor teams composed of senior sergeants and officers.

This institutional neglect occurred despite the fact that the Army itself agreed that the need for well-trained, professional combat advisors was unlikely to diminish in the foreseeable future. Numerous national-level leaders, from the President on down, highlighted the importance of the advisor teams; General George Casey, the Army's Chief of Staff, stated on a 2007 visit to the Fort Riley Training Mission: "We will not succeed in our mission in Iraq and Afghanistan without the Iraqi and Afghan security forces being able to secure themselves. So these missions for the transition teams are absolutely essential for our long-term success."[19] Well after the vast majority of conventional US brigade combat teams have departed Iraq and Afghanistan, American advisors will still be required to assist Iraqi and Afghan security forces.[20]

US Army Major Matthew Moore, who served in the Fort Riley Training Mission for a year training future advisors, and then volunteered to serve himself as a military transition team leader, echoed Lieutenant Colonel Bruzina's comments from Vietnam about the quality and experience level of the soldiers being assigned as advisors:

> The guys you have coming to MTT teams are the guys brigades are letting escape; they're not the most experienced leaders. The reason you're having so many MTT teams implode is because the MTT team leaders aren't senior enough to lead Captains. They haven't been to ILE [intermediate-level education] yet. It's not easy taking five Captains and five Sergeants First Class into combat. Maneuver advisors are not career course graduates and haven't commanded yet. We need to send guys who are already branch qualified at their current rank to be advisors. It sucks for the Iraqi unit otherwise, because that guy's never done that before.[21]

Moore suggested that the poor training standard of many of the advisors adversely affected the rate of progress of the Iraqi Army, and hence the timeline for American withdrawal from Iraq:

> What we're looking at now is a generational change to create a self-sustaining Iraqi Army. The Iraqi officers that we're targeting now are lieutenants and captains; when they're majors and lieutenant colonels, they'll be able to maintain a professional, self-sufficient

force that can provide for itself without outside help, that can run its own systems without advisors. With the current advisors, we'll need another eight years.[22]

Moore served in Iraq, which absorbed the lion's share of the national effort; by comparison, the war in Afghanistan was "under-resourced," in the words of the American commander there in 2007 and 2008. In no area was the lack of priority more apparent or more damaging than in the advisory effort to the Afghan National Army (ANA) and Afghan National Police (ANP). According to reports from the Government Accountability Office, the ANA advisory effort was manned below 50 percent of required advisors in April 2008. The situation with the ANP was even worse, with fewer than one in four police units having some form of advisor support—even as US strategy recognizes that the police remain the key interface between the Afghan people and their government.[23] The majority of the advisors serving in Afghanistan, as well as the brigade headquarters overseeing their tactical employment, were National Guard soldiers.

The shortage of forces on the ground necessitated breaking up teams designed and trained to serve in 16-soldier units into smaller *ad hoc* organizations; sometimes just two or three soldiers were assigned to mentor an ANA or ANP battalion. US Navy and Air Force personnel filled positions that in Iraq were filled by the US Army and Marine Corps.[24] Afghanistan's "other war" status and the unwieldy coalition conducting counterinsurgency operations in the theater exacerbated the challenges above and beyond the personnel shortages.[25] National caveats prevented the utilization of many NATO teams in combat, even as these teams were requested in the first place by NATO to address the shortfall in US advisors.[26] Meanwhile, US teams operated far from American logistical and intelligence support, and inadequate support limited their utility in advising Afghan forces, as the primary focus of some teams became their own ability to provision themselves and provide for their own security.[27] In a country with few roads, where a mule train or a helicopter can be the only way to supply a distant police outpost, the Combined Security Transition Command-Afghanistan, the headquarters overall responsible for the advisor mission, possessed not a single dedicated helicopter or airplane during a November 2008 visit.

Even the training for Afghanistan-bound teams suffered from that theater's second-class billing. While USMC advisor teams on their way to Afghanistan trained for mountain warfare in Hawthorne, Nevada to prepare for Afghanistan's difficult terrain, in 2008 there was not a single hour of mountain warfare training in the curriculum for Afghanistan-bound advisors from the US Army, Navy, and Air Force.[28] Tactical training designed specifically to meet the needs of advisors deploying to Iraq was given to Afghanistan-bound advisors despite its limited utility. Advisors deployed to Afghanistan's Pashtun areas received Dari training, although Dari is not spoken in those areas. Written orders bringing US Army personnel to train for the Afghan advisor mission asked them to access an online Arabic language program, despite Arabic not being one of Afghanistan's languages.[29] As one widely read, sarcastic letter from an advisor described the situation, "You will now be sent to the plains of Fort Riley to train as teams for deployment to the mountains of Afghanistan. We will accomplish this by training you to function in Iraq."[30]

The way ahead

Of the six logical lines of operations for a counterinsurgency enumerated in FM 3-24—combat operations, developing host nation security forces, providing essential services to the population, establishing good governance, assisting economic development, and conducting information operations—only "Developing Host Nation Security Forces" has its own chapter in the manual. This is a result of both the extreme importance of developing host nation security forces in a counterinsurgency campaign and the lack of doctrine for and understanding of this mission in the Army and Marine Corps at the time the manual was published. Developing and advising host nation forces is both a campaign in itself and a component of the broader counterinsurgency campaign plan; its success determines at what point the main effort of the intervening power can shift from conducting counterinsurgency itself to assisting the host nation forces in doing so. The exit strategy in any counterinsurgency campaign is a government able to stand largely on its own, with its security forces able to defeat internal threats.

FM 3-24's chapter on "Developing Host Nation Security Forces" makes clear the scope and scale of the work required to create effective and efficient soldiers and police in the demanding circumstances that characterize counterinsurgency campaigns. Reading Table 6-5 from that chapter provides insight into the degree of difficulty required to select, organize, train, and employ combat advisors in a counterinsurgency campaign:

- Try to learn enough of the language for simple conversation.
- Be patient. Be subtle. In guiding host nation counterparts, explain the benefits of an action and convince them to accept the idea as their own. Respect the rank and positions of host nation counterparts.
- Be diplomatic in correcting host nation forces. Praise each success and work to instill pride in the unit.
- Understand that an advisor is not the unit commander but an enabler. The host nation commander makes decisions and commands the unit. Advisors help with this task.
- Keep host nation counterparts informed; try not to hide agendas.
- Work to continually train and improve the unit, even in the combat zone. Help the commander develop unit standing operating procedures.
- Be prepared to act as a liaison to multinational assets, especially air support and logistics. Maintain liaison with civil affairs and humanitarian teams in the area of operations.
- Be ready to advise on the maintenance of equipment and supplies.
- Have a thorough knowledge of light infantry tactics and unit security procedures.
- Use "confidence" missions to validate training.
- Stay integrated with the unit. Eat their food. Do not become isolated from them.
- Be aware of the operations in the immediate area to prevent fratricide.
- Insist on host nation adherence to the recognized human rights standards concerning treatment of civilians, detainees, and captured insurgents. Report any violations to the chain of command.
- Be objective in reports on host nation unit and leader proficiency. Report gross corruption or incompetence.
- Train host nation units to standard and fight alongside them. Consider host nation limitations and adjust. Flexibility is key. It is impossible to plan completely for everything in this type of operation. Therefore, constantly look forward to the next issue and be ready to develop solutions to problems that cannot be answered with a doctrinal solution.
- Remember that most actions have long-term strategic implications.
- Maintain a proper military bearing and professional manner.

This is hard stuff. Although the US Army has made continual improvements in the advisory effort in Iraq and Afghanistan after a slow start, current practice on the ground makes it difficult to argue that it has learned all of the lessons of an ultimately unsuccessful advisory effort in Vietnam. A recent decision by General George Casey, the chief of staff of the Army, to increase career incentives for those who serve on advisory teams, is a step in the right direction. Majors who lead transition teams will now be granted "key and developmental" credit; lieutenant colonels and colonels who lead teams will be centrally selected, as battalion and brigade commanders are currently, and will be given similar credit in recognition of the importance and difficulty of their missions. According to Casey,

> the tasks associated with transition teams will be a major part of full-spectrum engage-
> ment in theaters of interest now and for the foreseeable future. I want to ensure that the
> officers that lead these teams are recognized and given the credit they deserve.[31]

Although the execution of the advisor mission has improved over the past several years, and General Casey's decision will help further in both training and execution, because of the importance of the mission there is still more to be done. This author has suggested the creation of permanent Army force structure to perform the advisor mission more efficiently and effectively;[32] or, failing that, the selection of a senior Army officer with responsibility to improve performance in all areas of the advisory mission.[33]

At least in part in recognition of some of the shortcomings of its previous approach to the problem, in 2009 the Army decided to change the way it sourced advisors for both Iraq and Afghanistan. It modified standard brigade combat teams, providing additional field grade officers and specialized training to create "advisory and assistance brigades" (ABBs). These brigades have the advantage of being built upon the base of a fully formed unit, providing additional unity of command; their performance is likely to far exceed that of the previous *ad hoc* advisory teams as a result. Four AABs are currently scheduled to deploy to Iraq[34] and another to Afghanistan; their development and training marks an important step in the evolution of the Army's ability to train and advise host nation security forces. Also in 2009, the Army finally produced a doctrinal manual for general-purpose forces assigned to conduct the Foreign Internal Defense mission; Field Manual 3-07.1, *Security Force Assistance*, was published in May 2009.[35]

The number of advisors required in Iraq and Afghanistan, not to mention other important security-cooperation efforts that comprise the Global War on Terrorism, will continue to outstrip the capacity of the Special Forces to meet the demand for security forces assistance; it will thus remain necessary for conventional-purpose forces to be organized, trained, equipped, and employed as advisors for as long as the United States remains engaged in an advisory role in the Long War. As retired Lieutenant General James Dubik has noted,

> The conventional forces of the United States Army will have an enduring requirement
> to build the security forces and security ministries of other countries. This requirement
> is consequently not an aberration, unique to Iraq and Afghanistan. Planning, training,
> doctrine, and acquisition must take account of this mission and support it.[36]

Recent improvements in the effort to properly train, field, and reward advisors will have a significant impact on American national security during the wars we are now fighting and for many years to come—if the country learns the lessons of Vietnam, Iraq, and Afghanistan, and properly resources the effort to raise and train indigenous forces. In recognition of this fact, Combined Arms Center commander Lieutenant General William Caldwell gave an important speech to the 2009 Infantry Conference titled "Security Force Assistance: A Change in Mindset" that included the exhortation:

We must internalize the significance of the words,—By, With, and Through. They mean doing everything in YOUR power to make the Security Force Assistance more capable . . . more self-sufficient. As GEN McChrystal said in his guidance, "their success is our success."[37]

Their success is our success—and the most important single factor in the success of indigenous forces is the quality, training, and employment of American combat advisors. Indeed, as Andrew Krepinevich has argued, "Their success will determine whether we win this war, and at what cost, and how soon."[38]

Notes

1 Cited in Jason Sherman, "New National Defense Strategy Emphasizes More Iraq-Like Missions," *Inside The Pentagon*, May 22, 2008, 1.
2 Department of the Army, Field Manual 3-24, *Counterinsurgency*, p. 6-1. Publicly available as The US Army/Marine Corps Field Manual, *Counterinsurgency,* Chicago: University of Chicago Press, 2007.
3 This section draws upon John A. Nagl, *Learning to Eat Soup with a Knife: Counterinsurgency Lessons from Malaya and Vietnam*, Chicago: University of Chicago Press, 2005, Chapters 6 and 7.
4 *The Pentagon Papers: The Defense Department History of United States Decisionmaking on Vietnam* (Senator Gravel Edition: 4 vols), Boston: Beacon Press, 1971, p. 435.
5 Francis J. Kelly, *US Army Special Forces 1961–1971*, Washington, DC: GPO, 1973, p. 48.
6 Neil Sheehan, *A Bright Shining Lie: John Paul Vann and America in Vietnam*, New York: Random House, 1988, p. 636. The best account of a Combined Action Platoon is Bing West, *The Village*, New York: Pocket Books, 2003.
7 William Westmoreland, *A Soldier Reports*, New York: Da Capo, 1989, p. 165.
8 *The Pentagon Papers*, Vol. II, p. 501.
9 Robert Komer, *Bureaucracy Does Its Thing*, Oxford: Westview, 1986, p. 115.
10 Lam Quang Tri, "The View from the Other Side of the Story: Reflections of a South Vietnamese Soldier," in Andrew Wiest (ed.), *Rolling Thunder in a Gentle Land: The Vietnam War Revisited*, Oxford: Osprey, 2006, p. 120.
11 Mark Moyar, "Villager Attitudes During the Final Decade of the Vietnam War," Vietnam Center Symposium Paper, 1996.
12 Andrew Krepinevich, *The Army and Vietnam*, Baltimore, MD: Johns Hopkins University Press, 1986. Peter Dawkins, "The U.S. Army and the "Other War" in Vietnam," doctoral dissertation, Princeton University, 1979. Dawkins served as an advisor in Vietnam during one of his two tours there.
13 Lt. Col. Dennis "Buz" Bruzina (Retd), interviewed at Fort Riley, Kansas, May 16, 2008. Lt. Col. Bruzina served as an advisor to ARVN forces in Phu Loi 1966–7 and at Dak To 1971–2.
14 Cited in Douglas Blaufarb, *The Counterinsurgency Era*, New York: The Free Press, 1977, p. 269.
15 Greg Jaffe, "Problems Afflict U.S. Army Program To Advise Iraqis," *The Wall Street Journal*, October 18, 2006. Scott Cuomo, "It's Time to Make ETTs our Main Effort in Afghanistan and Iraq," *Marine Corps Gazette* (June 2006), 63–7.
16 FM 3-24, p. 6-3.
17 Department of the Army, Field Manual 3.07.1, *Security Force Assistance*, May 2009.
18 The Training Model can be downloaded at http://www.riley.army.mil/view/article.asp?id=775-2006-04-10-35086-69.
19 Dustin Roberts, "Army Chief of Staff Visits Fort Riley," *Fort Riley Post*, 20 (May 17, 2007), 1.
20 One of the primary recommendations of the Iraq Study Group Report. See James A. Baker III, Lee H. Hamilton, et al., *The Iraq Study Group Report*, New York: Vintage Books, 2006, pp. 48–51. See also Andrew Krepinevich, "Send in the Advisers," *The New York Times*, July 11, 2006.
21 Maj. Matthew Moore, 1349 MTT, advisor to 1st Tank Regiment, 34th Armored Brigade at Taji, interviewed at Fort Riley, Kansas, June 29, 2008.
22 Ibid.

23 United States Plan for Sustaining the Afghanistan National Security Forces: Report to Congress in accordance with the 2008 National Defense Authorization Act (Section 1231, Public Law 110-181), June 2008, 22.
24 Personal experience of the author, who trained soldiers, sailors, and airmen for the Afghan mission at Fort Riley, Kansas in 2007 and 2008 and was often unable to tell them where they would be assigned once they arrived in country. See also Seth G. Jones, *In the Graveyard of Empires: America's War in Afghanistan*, New York: W.W. Norton, 2009, pp. 326–7.
25 Thomas Shanker, "Gates Pushing Plan for Afghan Army," *The New York Times*, August 7, 2008.
26 United States Plan for Sustaining the Afghanistan National Security Forces, 33.
27 Daniel Helmer, "Twelve Urgent Steps for the Advisor Mission in Afghanistan," *Military Review* (July/August 2008), 75–9.
28 Corp. Michael S. Cifuentes, "MCAGCC Commanding General Drops in on Mountain Viper," official US Marine Corps website, February 9, 2008.
29 Michael M. Phillips, "In Counterinsurgency Class, Soldiers Think Like Taliban," *The Wall Street Journal,* November 30, 2007.
30 "Congratulations! You've Been Selected for an ETT," Abu Muqawama blog, February 19, 2008.
31 Gen. Casey cited in Yochi Dreazen, "Army To Promote Training As Career Path," *The Wall Street Journal*, 19 June 2008, 3.
32 John A. Nagl, *Institutionalizing Adaptation: It's Time for a Permanent Army Advisor Corps*, Washington, DC: Center for a New American Security, June 2007.
33 John A. Nagl, "Institutionalizing Adaptation: It's Time for an Army Advisor Command," *Military Review* (September/October 2008), 21–6.
34 Donna Miles, "New U.S. Advisory, Assistance Brigades to Deploy to Iraq During Next Troop Rotation," American Forces Press Service, July 15, 2009, available at http://www.mnf-iraq.com/index.php?option=com_content&task=view&id=27267&Itemid=225.
35 Field Manual 3-07.1, *Security Force Assistance*.
36 James M. Dubik, "Building Security Forces and Ministerial Capacity: Iraq as a Primer," Washington, DC: Institute for the Study of War, August 2009, p. 2.
37 Lt. Gen. William Caldwell IV, "Security Force Assistance: A Change in Mindset", September 23, 2009, available at http://smallwarsjournal.com/documents/caldwellspeech.pdf.
38 Andrew Krepinevich, "Send in the Advisers."

Part III

Challenges

13 Governance

Nadia Schadlow

During the summer of 2007, some two dozen men wearing Iraqi police uniforms stormed a bank branch in the Ameriyah neighborhood of Baghdad. Their takeover of the bank was part of a concerted strategy by Iraqi insurgents to reduce services to the Sunni population in the area and to undermine confidence in the Iraqi government. It quickly became apparent to United States Army officers that the reopening of the bank was a critical step toward restoring basic governance services in Iraq and central to convincing Sunnis that they had a political and economic future in Iraq. The Army lieutenant colonel in charge of operations in the area observed that "armed politics" rather than all-out war characterized the challenges he faced, and that his job was to convince the locals "to have more faith in the government than [in] the extremists."[1]

That officer had absorbed one of the lessons of the American experience of four years in Iraq: the restoration of confidence in a nation's government had to be one of the central features of a counterinsurgency (COIN) campaign. The US Army/Marine Corps Field Manual, *Counterinsurgency* (FM 3-24), a product of those who had gained this experience, explains that insurgents specifically seek to displace government authorities and that the "primary objective of a counterinsurgent operation is to foster development of effective governance by a legitimate government."[2]

Bernard Fall, the French-born counterinsurgency expert who spent years in the jungles of Vietnam, observed that insurgencies and counterinsurgencies were essentially competitions over governance. He explained that a government that was losing to an insurgency was "not being outfought; it [was] being out-administered."[3] Conventional war traditionally focuses upon the destruction of an enemy's military forces. A counterinsurgency campaign is focused on restoring the legitimacy of the government. Insurgents have the relatively easy task of sowing disorder—through violence—and seek to break "ties between the people and the governments."[4] An effective counterinsurgency campaign, however, must create order. It must tackle the tougher job of restoring basic government services and administrative structures at the local and national levels. Insurgents use all available tools—political, informational, military, and economic—to overthrow an existing authority. They may use subversion and violence to challenge or seize political control of a region. Counterinsurgents, in turn, must employ all instruments of national power to sustain the emerging government and reduce the likelihood of another crisis emerging.[5]

Governance operations are those activities that counterinsurgents must undertake to re-establish basic local and national government services in order to rebuild a population's confidence in its government. Insurgents and counterinsurgents compete over the need to restore governance functions and services. This type of competition emerged with intensity in America's recent engagements in Iraq and Afghanistan and continues to shape both campaigns. And, some of the toughest challenges in these wars have centered on the need to develop a strategy and operational plan to restore security and basic services to the populace. For a variety of reasons rooted in American political and military history, US military and civilian leaders did not plan adequately for the reconstruction and governance phases of the wars in Iraq and Afghanistan.[6] While defense and civilian experts have made significant progress in thinking through these issues, challenges remain in developing the operational capabilities to implement effective governance operations.

The purpose of this chapter is to describe the relationship between governance and counter-insurgency operations; to provide historical examples of the centrality of governance operations in counterinsurgency campaigns; and to examine some of the contemporary strategic and operational challenges related to this competition for governance (and legiti-macy). At the strategic level, success in reestablishing basic governance requires a serious and resourced commitment to achieve desired political and economic objectives. External actors—including political leaders and their constituencies—must accept that governance requirements are often long term and come with metrics of success that are difficult to determine. Indeed, a key challenge of irregular warfare is how to measure progress. As one analyst has noted, "the political pressure for marking progress is unrelenting," thus making strategic patience essential.[7]

At the operational level of a counterinsurgency campaign the restoration of governance services requires a careful integration and balance among local and external civilian and military actors as well as between short- and longer-term considerations. Expertise regarding the economic, political, and security contexts of the country in question—particularly at the local level—is critical. While insurgents can displace authority with relative ease—through the use of violence, fear, and intimidation—the challenges of rebuilding authority and restoring stability require the right mix of internal and external resources, as well as skilled personnel to begin and implement restoration. This is the challenge of governance operations in counterinsurgency.

Carl von Clausewitz, the Prussian general and theorist of war, observed that "the first, the supreme, the most far-reaching act of judgment that the statesman and commander have to make is to establish . . . the kind of war on which they are embarking . . . This is the first of all strategic questions and the most comprehensive."[8] Understanding the kind of intervention a country has embarked upon is critical. Theories of war have attempted to paint a picture of the character and nature of wars, so that military and civilian leaders can prepare better for its challenges. A central differentiation in the theory of warfare has been that between large-scale, force-on-force warfare—so called conventional war—and "irregular warfare." The dominant strain in the West's thinking about war has been, for the most part, focused on conventional war. In conventional war, governance challenges have been considered, but those concerns focused mainly on actions after major conflict operations or after the war itself. Concerns about the population and government during conventional war centered on policing and provision of basic services in the short term—until the conflict had ended. Furthermore, in the United States military, little training, doctrine, or planning related to governance operations existed, and few military histories explored these challenges. Doctrine and thinking about irregular warfare, however, gave greater prominence to the importance of governance.

Despite the fact that Clausewitz's most famous observation—that "war is an extension of politics by other means"—illuminated the highly political nature of war, his strategic thinking about how to achieve the desired political end state in war was not fully absorbed into American military doctrine and operations.[9]

In contrast to the focus on an opponent's armies, theories of insurgency and counter-insurgency—the irregular warfare that is the focus of this chapter—focused on the population and government as central "fronts" in war. One of the earliest theorists of irregular wars was a young British major, Charles Callwell. His book, *Small Wars—Their Principles and Practice*, was published in 1896. It was one of the first to codify the strategy and tactics associated with small wars. Callwell explained that he did not seek to argue with "the system of regular warfare today." He pointed out that small wars included "all campaigns other than those where both the opposing sides consist of regular troops."[10]

Subsequent theorists of counterinsurgency emerged in the aftermath of World War II. Two important thinkers in this "classical school" of insurgency were the British expert Robert Thompson and the French officer David Galula.[11] Both of their works describe the centrality of political legitimacy and governance in counterinsurgency. Galula's *Counterinsurgency Warfare: Theory and Practice*, published in 1964, described four prerequisites for a successful insurgency: (1) an attractive cause, (2) a weakness in the counterinsurgency camp, (3) a not-too-hostile geographic environment, and (4) outside support in the middle and later stages of an insurgency.[12] His "attractive cause" referred, in essence, to the important link between the political objective of the insurgent and the resonance of this cause among the people. The "cause" needed to be sufficiently compelling to garner enough supporters to propel insurgents to victory. Galula appreciated the centrality of governance to counterinsurgency and described four "organic" instruments that were necessary to control the government infrastructure: (1) the political structure, (2) the administrative bureaucracy, (3) the police, and (4) the armed forces.[13] As will be discussed later, these instruments remain the core elements of governance tasks in a counterinsurgency campaign.

Robert Thompson was an architect of the British counterinsurgency success in Malaya and later served with the British Advisory Mission to South Vietnam. In 1966 he published *Defeating Communist Insurgency*.[14] He focused on five basic principles of counterinsurgency: (1) the government must have a clear political aim: to establish and maintain a free, independent, and united country which is politically and economically stable and viable, (2) the government must function in accordance with law, (3) the government must have an overall plan, (4) the government must give priority to defeating the political subversion, not the guerillas, and (5) in the guerilla phase of the insurgency the government must secure its base areas first.[15] All of these objectives focus on the importance of creating effective governing structures at the local and national levels.[16]

In the Vietnam War, America's failure to take Clausewitz's dictum to heart, and to recognize the kind of war that it was fighting, led to defeat there, followed by a reluctance even to consider how to improve American approaches to counterinsurgency. Many would argue that America began to focus on the governance challenges of Vietnam too late. By the late 1960s, President Johnson was determined to change the course of the war, and began to emphasize pacification, or "the other war," as he called it. This approach sought to remove insurgent support in the countryside, by reaching out to the local population and addressing their security and other basic needs. It represented an important shift away from General Westmoreland's strategic emphasis on search and destroy, toward a strategy that sought to devote more resources and time to training South Vietnamese forces and to addressing the problems of political legitimacy and governance.

President Johnson appointed Robert Komer, a White House official, to develop a plan that would fully integrate the disjointed and disconnected civilian and military efforts taking place around the country. The Civil Operations and Revolutionary Development Support (CORDS) was initiated in 1967 and was a highly integrated civilian and military structure (teams) deployed around the country and designed to provide basic services to the populace. CORDS was also a means of assisting the South Vietnamese government to extend its reach into hamlets and villages, by bolstering its ability to deliver basic services. CORDS was thus an important means of restoring the legitimacy of that government. Some 7000 Vietnamese worked side by side with 6000 American military officers and 1200 or so civilians and placed the previously disparate pacification programs—run by the United States Agency for International Development (USAID), the State Department, the CIA, and the Department of Agriculture—under one civilian manager. That civilian was then appointed as the deputy commander of Military Assistance Command, Vietnam (MACV).[17]

Competing theories about why America lost in Vietnam continue to animate foreign policy debates today.[18] Whatever one's views on the war, it is fair to say that Vietnam created a rift not only among the American public, but within military circles too, and resulted in the relegation of thinking about irregular or counterinsurgency warfare to a "side-bar" of war, with only a small, focused special operations community considering the political dimensions of this kind of war. The military historian Brian Linn points out that those who interpret wars can have a great impact on how lessons are absorbed by military institutions.[19] In the post-Vietnam years, the dominant interpretation was that Vietnam was *sui generis* and similar interventions would be avoided at all costs.

This division in thinking about war had important implications for US military force structure, doctrine, training, and education—indeed, on the "production" of American strategic leaders. The strategic and operational thinking about how to bring together civil and military experts with local actors to affect political change on the ground during war failed to develop fully—a failure that would have profound implications for the wars in Afghanistan and Iraq.

The lessons of successful counterinsurgency are clear to anyone reviewing the historical record. Competition over governance is evident in virtually all counterinsurgency campaigns. Some examples include America's early involvement in the Philippines during the Spanish–American War, its intervention in Vietnam, Britain's campaign in Malaya, and America's involvement in El Salvador. All involved the need to restore political stability and basic governance services, as well as the strengthening of the legitimacy of the indigenous government in the eyes of the population.

In the Philippines, Filipino general Don Emilio Aguinaldo was determined to take advantage of Cuba's newly acquired independence from Spain to lead his own revolutionary movement for independence. At the same time, bolstered by successes in Cuba, more Americans began to clamor for annexation of the Philippines, a view underscored by the popular sentiment that Filipinos could not govern themselves. The Treaty of Paris, signed between the United States and Spain, granted control of the Philippines to the United States, caught the Filipino leader Aguinaldo by surprise, and officially ignited the Philippine Insurrection. The ensuing war was bloody and brutal. It began to shift in America's favor only after President William McKinley appointed William Howard Taft as civil administrator of the islands in 1900.

Taft worked closely with General Adna Chaffee to apply more humane tactics to the conflict and to win indigenous support in order to deny insurgents operating bases. Taft and Chaffee instituted programs to sell land cheaply to Filipinos and they established a wide-ranging civil affairs program, which continued for many years. Taft imported 1000 American teachers to the islands and established a Philippine constabulary to bolster the civil government and provide security for citizens. A report from the period noted this shift in expectations. Filipinos, it said, would cooperate with the Americans in the administration of general affairs. The hope was that they would undertake, under American guidance, the administration of provincial and municipal affairs. By 1902 the major insurrection had ended.

The Malayan insurgency grew from the surrender and departure of Japanese forces in 1945, when a weak Malayan government came under attack from the Malayan National Liberation Army (MNLA), an armed wing of the Communist Party (MCP). From 1948 to 1960, Commonwealth armed forces (the British and Malayan government) and the communist MNLA fought a war for independence. The MNLA employed a strategy of widespread attacks on civil officials and the managers of rubber plantations and tin mines in an effort to disrupt Malaya's economy. The insurgents' goal was an independent Malaya.[20]

The British responded with the Malayan Emergency, a highly integrated civil-military campaign to counter the insurgency by restoring governance and political legitimacy on the islands. Robert Thompson, then serving as the permanent secretary of defense for Malaya, explained what would later become his first axiom of counterinsurgency: that the goal of the Malayan Emergency was to help the government "establish a free, independent, and united country which is politically and economically stable and viable."[21] The Briggs plan, initiated by Lieutenant General Sir Harold Briggs, sought to reorganize the government to defeat the insurgency by instituting measures to protect the population and separate the guerrillas from the people. The government focused on patrols, ambushes, improving intelligence, and population and food control. As a part of this plan, Chinese squatters were resettled into new villages, making it harder for guerrillas to infiltrate and easier for the British to protect the population from attacks.

In addition to the highly integrated civil-military aspects of the Briggs plan, key to its success was that it involved working very closely with Malayan administrators. Thus this was not a "situation in which British administrators were dictating to indigenous counterparts."[22] Another key element behind the success of efforts to implement governance operations was the deliberate shift to a unity of command model. Early in the Emergency effort, no one had been put fully in charge, contributing to implementation problems. In 1952 Sir Gerald Templer assumed leadership over the Emergency efforts. He centralized intelligence around the country, stepped up psychological warfare efforts to counter insurgent messages and laid the groundwork for Malaya's future independence. This was particularly important as part of the effort to retain political legitimacy and limit the insurgency's appeal, since it helped to convince the people that Malaya was on the road to early independence.[23] Britain granted Malaya its independence in 1957.

In El Salvador of the 1980s and early 1990s the battlefield was primarily in the governance sphere, with two groups—insurgents and the government of El Salvador (which was backed by the United States)—seeking legitimacy with the people.[24] Corruption and human rights abuses in El Salvador had increased under its authoritarian military regimes, leading to a growing leftist opposition movement in the country. These groups eventually coalesced into the Farabundo Marti National Liberation Front (FMNL), a coalition of five guerrilla groups. A civil war essentially erupted, with death squads, political killings, assassinations, and human rights abuses intensifying.

Following the program set forth in a US government white paper published in February 1981, the Reagan administration deployed military advisors to the country. The advisors focused on the strategic goal of governance, with the intention of working with the El Salvadorian government to achieve "social justice and stability." Fearful of the creeping escalation that had occurred in Vietnam, Congress forced the White House to abide by a limit of 55 advisors. These United States advisors deployed three mobile training teams (MTTs) to provide infantry, artillery, and military intelligence instruction to the Salvadorian government forces.

The US advisors sought to improve security in the countryside by training peasants and working with them to create local self-defense units. These units kept insurgent forces at bay, provided security, and improved the legitimacy of the government.[25] This indirect approach— the effort to transform the Salvadorian Armed Forces into a more professional force—helped, in turn, to improve its human rights record. The United States was able to strengthen existing governance institutions and regain its legitimacy in the eyes of the majority of the people. In 1992 the government of El Salvador and the FMLN signed a United Nations brokered peace agreement in 1992 following 12 years of armed conflict. The FMLN is now one of the two major political parties in a peaceful El Salvador.

The 2003 invasion of Iraq brought the problem of governance in war to the forefront of American foreign and defense policy, but the delay in recognizing the nature of that conflict generated a number of missed opportunities and exacerbated serious strategic problems. By the summer of 2003 increasing violence threatened to jeopardize operational successes early in the war, as sectarian fighting erupted following the fall of Saddam Hussein's Ba'athist government. Looting and the absence of governmental authorities further emboldened extremists and foreign fighters. In order to address the governance problems, the United States initially established a 200-person Office of Humanitarian and Reconstruction Assistance (OHRA) to provide humanitarian support, reconstruct Iraqi civil infrastructure and institutions, and prepare for the eventual creation of an interim government. That structure quickly proved to be too weak and lacked sufficient plans and resources to establish any effective political authority. It was replaced in May 2003 by the Coalition Provisional Authority, headed by Ambassador Paul Bremer. This entity too was beset by problems from the start, exacerbated by poor coordination with US military command structures on the ground. In addition, although the civilian-led CPA ostensibly oversaw reconstruction efforts in Iraq, it controlled virtually no resources to accomplish its mandate. Moreover, its relationship with local Iraqi leaders was fraught with tension. The invasion had dissolved virtually all formal local governance structures in Iraq,[26] and no serious strategy existed to draw Iraqi leaders into the political process. Processes that did develop emerged in an *ad hoc* and piecemeal manner. Negotiations took place through the fall of 2003 and the winter of 2004 over an approach which would transition more power to Iraqis, establish the conditions to develop a constitution, and undertake the steps required for free and fair elections to take place.

Against the backdrop of these political efforts, the US military scrambled, with little formal guidance, or applicable doctrine, to adapt to the situation. Disparate initiatives undertaken throughout the country sought to target terrorist cells, restore basic services, and create jobs for Iraqis, but a coherent strategy to direct these efforts was lacking. Only after an extended period of trial and error did a strategy finally emerge, placing governance operations as the special focus. In November 2006, on the eve of his return to Iraq as the commander of the Multi-national Force-Iraq (MNF-I), General Raymond Odierno defined US objectives as "an Iraqi government that is legitimate in the eyes of the Iraqi population, an Iraq that is able to protect itself and not be a safe haven for terror."[27]

Afghanistan, competing with the Iraq War for American resources and attention from 2003 onward, also presented significant governance challenges. Following the invasion of Afghanistan in 2001, the United States successfully dislodged al-Qaeda. However, the US was soon faced with the equally tough challenge of developing a political strategy to restore stability there, as politics shifted and realigned following the collapse of the Taliban-led government. By early 2003, with major combat operations ended, it was clear that greater attention had to be paid to the restoration of political order and finding the appropriate balance between the Afghan central government and the provinces. Coalition partners focused on the holding of a nationwide *loya jirga* (grand council) to help draft a new constitution, and eventually to set the stage for presidential and parliamentary elections. Despite efforts to develop broad support for a national government—partly by helping the new government in Kabul to extend its reach into the provinces and provide the populace with basic services— insurgents began to threaten security in the south and east of the country. Under the leadership of Lieutenant General David Barno, who worked closely with the US Embassy in Kabul, the United States shifted toward a new counterinsurgency strategy, emphasizing the importance of governance.[28] While still maintaining pressure on the enemy, this strategy emphasized people as the "center of gravity" with a focus on enabling reconstruction and good governance, especially by extending the reach of the central government. As the then Afghan Ambassador to the United States observed, "Afghanistan is a strong nation, but a weak state."[29]

In both conflicts—in Afghanistan and Iraq—it became clear that the Army and Marines who continued to bear the brunt of the fighting and casualties generated by insurgent attacks needed to change course. The demands of the wars led to the development and refinement of doctrines related to counterinsurgency. Each war had its individual aspects, and each served, to some degree, as the environment for testing the legitimacy, and updating the theories, doctrine, and practice of counterinsurgency warfare.

In 2006, General David Petraeus, who had just returned from a tour in Iraq as the general in charge of training Iraqi security forces, reignited efforts at home to address the problem of how to quell the growing insurgency in Iraq. As the commander of the Doctrine Division of the Combined Arms Center (CAC) at Fort Leavenworth, Kansas, he assumed responsibility for doctrinal development in the United States Army and began to push for the development of a new doctrine to address the challenge of counterinsurgency—doctrine which had not been revisited in over two decades. Under his leadership, a draft of FM 3-24 was completed in a mere two months.

While this ferment and debate was taking place in military circles, the Iraq and Afghanistan conflicts also spurred some of the most significant changes in thinking about conflict and reconstruction at the State Department since the Vietnam War. Despite the increasing calls among policy makers for the use of "all instruments of national power," it had become clear that civilian capacity for governance tasks was severely lacking in Iraq and Afghanistan. From 2004 to 2009, initiatives were undertaken to improve the civilian capacity to participate in stabilization and reconstruction operations.

In early 2004, an office of the coordinator for reconstruction and stabilization was created in the State Department. Its mission was to "lead, coordinate and institutionalize" a US government civilian capacity to prevent or prepare for post-conflict situations and to help stabilize and reconstruct societies in transition from conflict so that they can "reach a sustainable path toward peace, democracy and a market economy."[30] A later presidential directive affirmed that the Secretary of State would have responsibility to coordinate US government efforts to plan, prepare, and conduct stabilization and reconstruction operations.[31] The President then signed a Reconstruction and Stabilization Civilian Management Act, which provided the necessary authorities to create a civilian corps that could respond to crises abroad and perform governance-related tasks as needed in conflict situations.[32] To put the resources behind this civilian initiative in perspective, the Civilian Stabilization Initiative in 2009 requested some $250 million to strengthen civilian capacity to manage and implement reconstruction and stabilization-related tasks (which included funding for the active, standby, and reserve Civilian Response Corps across eight different agencies).[33]

While these steps were important, they did not address significant obstacles to the creation of a civilian expeditionary corps that could be deployed into conflict situations. Still to be addressed were the subjects of the status of civilians in a combat zone, command relations between military and civilian personnel, comparable pay, and much else, including the tremendous disparity in size (numbers of personnel) between Department of Defense personnel and those of any other agency represented.

Despite improvements in the development of doctrine related to counterinsurgency, the actual conduct of activities to restore basic government services to a population and increase the legitimacy of the local and national government hinges upon the effective coordination of myriad complex activities among internal and external, as well as military and civilian, actors. Good doctrine does not guarantee the execution of governance-related tasks. Not only is a strategic-level commitment necessary to help shape and coordinate a range of operations across a theater and country, but sound operational approaches are required as well.

At the strategic level governance tasks require the patience of political leaders—both inside the host government and externally. A counterinsurgency campaign calls for "firm political will and substantial patience by the government, its people, and the countries providing support."[34] Moreover, governance tasks require that sufficient *non*-military resources are committed to the intervention. As noted in FM 3-24, maintaining security in an unstable environment requires vast resources, while a small number of highly motivated insurgents with simple weapons and good operations security can undermine security over a large area. To achieve the required commitment of resources, government leaders need to overcome the traditional division whereby military professionals concentrate on winning battles, while policy makers focus on diplomatic issues.[35] This has contributed to the creation of two separate spheres of responsibility, one for diplomacy and one for combat.[36] In counterinsurgency campaigns the political and economic requirements of reconstructing a legitimate government are paramount, suggesting that these types of traditional divisions must be overcome.

In addition to patience, at the strategic level a political plan among local and external actors on desired outcomes is required in order to avoid what otherwise could devolve into a series of disconnected, *ad hoc* activities. One of Bernard Fall's observations before his death in 1967 was that even when the United States thought about insurgents, it did so by focusing primarily on tactics, as opposed to identifying the requirements of a broader plan to achieve desired political outcomes. Decades later in Iraq, an Army special forces major echoed Fall's observation, observing that the Army had got extremely good at counterinsurgency tactics, understanding how to "gather intelligence and go on a raid" but that it still needed to "understand and to focus on all those other things that will bring an end to violence in Iraq. You can go on a thousand raids and still not help the situation."[37]

Governance tasks are critical elements of any strategic plan in counterinsurgency and are directly linked to the achievement of political objectives in a theater. Although strategic planning is necessary to determine broader economic and political objectives, it is at operational level that civilian and military actors must work together to plan and implement specific governance tasks. The wars in Iraq and Afghanistan initially lacked operational planning or structures to implement governance related tasks. The noted military theorist Colin Gray observed that "how to counter an insurgency is no great mystery. The difficulties lie in translating and adapting theory for effective practice."[38]

Prevailing in the competition over governance requires the successful employment of operational capabilities on the ground. Insurgents and counterinsurgents compete over the use of civil instruments—from the building of schools, to the distribution of food, to control over banks—which are central to reconstituting a desired political system. As insurgents grow stronger they will seek to consolidate their gains by working along several lines of operation. These include establishing an effective civil administration; establishing an effective military organization; providing social and economic development; mobilizing the population to support the insurgent organization; and protecting the population from hostile acts.[39] An American private who had been deployed in western Baghdad described the problem this way: "The insurgents, they see what we're doing and we see what they're doing. Then we get ahead, then they figure out what we've done and they get ahead. It's like a game of cat and mouse. It's just a really, really smart mouse."[40]

Knowledge of specific local conditions is a key requirement for developing and implementing a response to insurgents, but it is possible to generalize and develop a set of governance tasks common to counterinsurgency campaigns. These common tasks can provide a framework for planning the restoration of governance functions. There are several approaches to thinking about the tasks required for the restoration of basic governance functions. The four instruments identified by Galula for exerting control over a population (as described earlier) can be useful for planning tasks necessary for the restoration of governance. He described the need to create: (1) the political structure, (2) the administrative bureaucracy, (3) the police, and (4) the armed forces.[41]

Another framework has been set forth by the State Department in its Reconstruction and Stabilization Essential Tasks.[42] This list identifies three phases. In the initial response phase, the objective is to determine the type of governance structure that is necessary. The second transformation period requires the promotion of legitimate political institutions and participatory processes. The third phase, of fostering sustainability, involves the consolidation of these institutions and participatory processes. The Army's Field Manual, *Stability and Reconstruction Operations*, also identified key governance tasks that are likely to fall to military forces in the initial states of an intervention. These include establishing conditions for a ceasefire; restoring basic policing functions; initiating reform of the judiciary and basic rule of law functions; and restoring basic services, sometimes referred to as SWEAT-MSO (sewage, water, electricity, academics, trash, medical, safety, and other considerations). As the manual notes, "all of these lines of effort are also critical to establishing a safe, secure environment."[43]

In all of these formulations, efforts should help to create an indigenous government that it is considered legitimate by the populace. Ideally, there is a high level of regime acceptance by major social institutions.[44] Specific tasks might include the planning and running of elections or constitutional conventions, or other mechanisms that allow the selection of leaders "at a frequency and in a manner considered just and fair by a substantial majority of the populace and the creation of procedures to allow a high level of popular participation in or support for political processes."[45]

In the later periods of an intervention, as stability is improved, a plan and means for transferring control from external actors (i.e. those assisting or directing the counterinsurgency campaign) to the indigenous government is required. Any formula for this transfer of power should be transparent. It might involve, initially, a transfer from military to political authority and then from control by external actors to control by indigenous leaders.[46]

Parallel to and directly related to the conduct of governance activities, is the rebuilding of local and national police and armed forces—a requirement generally referred to as "security sector reform" (this challenge is addressed in detail in Chapter 12 of this volume). Reform in this area is critical because progress in restoring the legitimacy of a government and in actually achieving progress on governance tasks requires the establishment of basic security.

All of these steps, in combination, are required to "foster the development of effective governance by a legitimate government,"[47] with the goal of governance tasks being the re-establishment of positive linkages between the state and its citizens.[48]

In addition to identifying the specific, functional set of activities that comprise governance in counterinsurgency, the *process* of how governance tasks are accomplished is important. First, and indeed, critical, are the input and involvement of local actors along the full "chain" of an activity. Each counterinsurgency campaign requires specific knowledge of local structures, traditions, and history, as well as of local leaders and personalities. Local actors must be involved in prioritizing requirements, in developing an implementation plan for a particular activity, and ideally in conducting the implementation of a task (for instance, in Malaya, one in three administrators was Malayan, not British). Local involvement helps to generate trust and legitimacy.[49] As one USAID expert observed after spending months on a reconstruction team in Jalalabad, Afghanistan, the goal was "not to buy the community. It [was] to give the community faith in their government so they will take the initiative to deny sanctuary to and provide information about the people trying to destroy the government."[50]

The conduct of governance tasks also requires openness and transparency, which in turn requires adequate communication to inform the populace of progress and successes. One US Army general with extensive experience in restoring governance in Iraq explained that effective communication was essential for "winning on the critical battleground of perception." He explained that military and civilian actors "must be able to explain their intentions, to counter enemy disinformation and propaganda, and to speak up for—and hence bolster the legitimacy of—the government and its security forces. Wherever possible, communications should trace the population's grievance back to the enemy and should expose the enemy's brutality and indifference to the welfare of the population."[51]

Models of civil-military cooperation to implement governance tasks have evolved. As noted earlier, the CORDS model developed during the Vietnam War. In Afghanistan, provincial reconstruction teams (PRTs) were fielded, while in Iraq, versions of these teams, called embedded PRTs (EPRTs) were deployed.[52] Galula had observed that "tasks and responsibilities cannot be neatly divided between the civilian and the soldier, for their operations overlap too much with each other."[53] The PRTs were an operational solution to the problem of how to improve the coordination of diplomatic, economic, reconstruction, and counter-insurgency efforts among various US agencies, to include USAID, the State and Treasury departments, and the military.[54]

PRTs and EPRTs are mixed civil-military teams, numbering anywhere from 20 to 300. Most are staffed heavily with American military personnel, largely due to limited civilian capacity. PRTs work on developing and executing budgets, business development plans, agriculture projects, and public health initiatives, and support the delivery of basic social services. In Iraq, the objective was to strengthen the provincial governments by focusing on five thematic areas: the rule of law, infrastructure for the provision of essential services, economic development, governance, and public diplomacy.[55]

In Afghanistan the PRTs' goal was to increase the host nation's capacity to govern, by building government capacity, and to enhance its economic viability. The PRTs sought to strengthen local governments' ability to deliver public services such as security and health care. PRTs were viewed as a temporary construct, designed to occupy "the vacuum caused by a weak government presence and are hence deterring agents of instability."[56] PRT activities sought to reduce the population's grievances over the central government's inability to satisfy its basic needs, "since anger among the people created opportunities for insurgents."[57]

While historical evidence and recent experience demonstrate the central role of governance activities in a counterinsurgency campaign, effective coordination of effort still remains a work in progress. Effectiveness requires a detailed understanding of the politics of a country and the operational capabilities to implement programs ranging from the restoration of clean drinking water supplies to organizing for elections or town council meetings. For these tasks, mixed military and civilian teams were created in Iraq and Afghanistan in recognition of the need to integrate civil and military skill sets to accomplish governance tasks.

Nonetheless, in many respects the PRT model did not go far enough. The tensions that emerged as civil and military actors in Iraq and Afghanistan tried to implement governance tasks illustrate many of the broader, ongoing challenges associated with governance in counterinsurgency. First, there are tensions over the appropriate balance between military and civilian actors in governance in counterinsurgency. Fundamentally, governance tasks involve the military in highly political tasks. In counterinsurgency political activities are a critical part of the competition between insurgents and counterinsurgents, and thus often take place alongside fighting. In an early phase of a counterinsurgency operation, the challenge is to plan, prioritize, and implement governance activities in a theater "under fire."[58] Members of the military, at all levels, will often be required to "exercise judgment and act without the benefit of immediate civilian oversight and control."[59] Such actions are necessary, because the accomplishment of key governance goals can impact the duration of the kinetic fight.

As Galula pointed out, it would be "senseless" to confine "soldiers to purely military functions while urgent and vital tasks have to be done and nobody else is available to undertake them." He argued that the "soldier must then be prepared to become a propagandist, a social worker, a civil engineer, a schoolteacher, a nurse, a boy scout." At the same time, Galula recognized that the goal was to replace the military, because "it is better to entrust civilian tasks to civilians." This issue persists today.[60]

The level of local involvement will depend partly on the nature of the intervention and the indigenous situation. If a host nation government exists—such as in Afghanistan—military forces may find it easier to work through local authorities. However, in situations of state failure, the military will likely be required to take the lead in initiating and completing essential tasks.[61]

In an operational environment in which the host nation government is not functioning effectively, the military may be the only stabilizing presence. The Army's field manual on stability operations notes that the "the force must be prepared to perform all the tasks essential to establishing and maintaining security and order while providing for the essential needs of the populace." At the same time, military efforts can help other civilian organizations gain access to the area, which in turn can reduce the burden on military forces.[62]

The lack of civilian resources also affects the balance between civilian and military actors in governance operations. In Iraq, for example, the State Department encountered enormous challenges in locating and deploying qualified professionals to staff PRTs long enough to make impact.[63] One PRT participant observed that a key challenge is that the people changed so often. He noted that "the longest anybody stayed there was a year, and a lot of people, especially civilians, did not last that long, and I can remember going in to talk to some Iraqis, who would start with one of their stories and say, 'I just told this to somebody else two months ago.' 'Yes, well, they are gone now.' That was always an issue."[64] To deploy additional foreign services officers to Iraq, the State Department had to initiate "directed deployments" to fill anticipated shortfalls in Iraq. Directed assignments had not been ordered since the Vietnam War.[65]

A second broader tension in governance tasks is the need to coordinate among civil, military, and multinational actors. The PRT models were loosely integrated. They did not have the same streamlined command authorities that existed under CORDS in Vietnam. Agency actors tended, often, to function within their individual agency mindset. One team leader in Iraq described the situation: "USAID was doing the great things that USAID does, the State Department people were primarily trying to operate the Regional Embassy Office, and then the military people were kind of operating on their own out there . . . things seemed kind of disjointed."[66] A USAID officer on an EPRT in Iraq observed that the "reality was, we were embedded with the military and with the brigade and the brigade was providing all of our life support, our movement, everything, in practice, we would be fooling ourselves if we thought we did not report to the brigade commander, also. We depended on the brigade for everything. We got practically zero support from ITAO [Iraq Transition Assistance Office] and NCT [National Coordinating Team] and the State Department."[67]

In bringing about effective coordination of actions, military and civilian organizations must cope with a fundamental difference in how they operate. Military operations are conducted under a unity of command model, in which the chain of command prevails—decisions are taken by the commanding officer, and executed. FM 3-24 (a military document, not a directive to non-Department of Defense agencies) notes that the "command and control of all U.S. Government organizations engaged in a counterinsurgency mission should be exercised by a single leader through a formal command and control system."[68] Nonetheless, in practice, this is not the case. Civil agencies on the ground in counterinsurgency (to include the PRTs) operate on a unity of effort model. The "mosaic nature" of governance and other counter-insurgency operations means that lead responsibility shifts among military, civilian, and host nation authorities.[69] Yet achieving unity of effort—getting all actors to work together—may, in practice, require unity of command. In essence, in Iraq and Afghanistan today, "half" of a counterinsurgency operation operates under a unity of command mode, while the other half (governance-related) operates within a unity of effort framework.

A third fundamental tension related to governance in counterinsurgency is the need to achieve a balance between short-term needs and longer-term development objectives. Governance in counterinsurgency is essentially focused on the shorter term ("clear, hold, build") but must leave a stable foundation for the longer-term building. In Iraq and Afghanistan this balance was not always an easy one to strike. In Iraq, there was continually tension in the early years of the war, between the civilian-led Coalition Provincial Authority (CPA) and its efforts to jumpstart large-scale infrastructure. The CPA believed that large-scale programs would create jobs quickly; others disputed this. USAID officials countered that development was "not building things"; that it required "not engineering," but "institution building."[70]

FM 3-24 includes a medical analogy to describe the challenge of building upon progress. First, it notes the need to "stop the bleeding." Following that, "inpatient care—recovery" takes place; and finally, "outpatient care—movement to self-sufficiency." Ideally, at this later stage, the host nation has established the systems needed to provide effective and stable government that sustains the rule of law.

Efforts to establish a longer-term foundation for progress require strategic patience, as discussed above—and the resources to continue involvement in a country after fighting has ceased. The Inspector General's report on Iraq observed that USAID's "institutional culture embraced a concept of development that went beyond merely rebuilding what war destroyed" and that "physical rehabilitation of damaged infrastructure would be one step in a larger democratic transition." Yet "White House officials were skeptical," since this was "exactly the kind of nation building the Administration had wanted to avoid."[71]

Operational-level plans must be connected to longer-term strategic requirements, because the overall longer-term goal is to "help develop indigenous capacity for securing essential services, a viable market economy, rule of law, democratic institutions, and a robust civil society."[72] For instance, in the economic sphere, actors on the ground will need to identify obstacles to growth and then, ideally, bring in the expertise needed to remove these obstacles. As they are removed, and as the situation stabilizes, more of these activities can shift to purely civilian actors. Furthermore, local efforts must be recognized by and connected to the host government. For example, an effort to build schools at the local level will founder if the education ministry fails to hire teachers, provide educational materials, or allocate funds to sustain the school.[73] One PRT member in Iraq described how short-term requirements to create medical clinics, for example, often were not coordinated with the ministry of health, leaving an area "littered with empty buildings."[74] The same applies to improving the rule of law, since local initiatives—undertaken by US and local actors—must be tied to national-level initiatives too.

In the end, however, even with the good will and cooperation of all the agencies involved in a counterinsurgency campaign, one must recognize that a competition is underway for control of governance. In that campaign, a key objective in COIN is to provide enough security from insurgents so that basic governance services can be strengthened and restored, ultimately improving the legitimacy of political order in virtually all local and national government actors in the eyes of a population—and ultimately, providing a way out for counterinsurgent forces. Further, since COIN operations are among the most complex of military campaigns, they require an extraordinary level of civil-military integration at both the strategic and operational levels. Simply put, politics and political considerations infuse these campaigns from start to finish. Competitions in other spheres, such as strategic communications and intelligence (as discussed in other chapters in this volume), also directly impact and are central to the establishment of basic governance in a COIN operation.

The wars in Afghanistan and Iraq forced the US military, as well as civilian actors, all "under fire," to reassess and renew thinking about how to conduct COIN. As a result, the Army, Marines, and other defense entities, as well as the State Department, took significant steps toward developing comprehensive doctrine and introducing strategic planning mechanisms to address COIN challenges. Despite these meaningful steps at the strategic level, at the operational level—the level where the parts come together on the ground to get things done—significant challenges remain to improving US capabilities to conduct governance operations in COIN.

The United States must still improve the ability of civil and military actors to work together to accomplish objectives in a COIN operation. To accomplish this, bureaucratic prerogatives and stovepipes will need to be put aside to advance US goals. There needs to be a serious effort, when necessary, to establish unity of command, to overcome difficulties that can often lead to myriad *ad hoc* activities rather than one meaningful program. Moreover, civilian leaders in America—from the Congressional and executive branches— must recognize and fight for the non-military funding requirements that are essential to COIN. Without funding for the appropriate agriculture programs, for instance, or the rebuilding of schools, much of the initial funding for bullets is simply not likely to have strategic effects. Third, the military needs to continue to adapt and identify areas of tradeoffs in its professional development demands, so that specialists on the Middle East, on Asia, and on Africa can develop in their ranks, and so that COIN skillsets are valued on a par with so-called conventional skills. Finally, the State Department must consider even deeper changes in its culture and operating modes in order to deploy an effective corps of civilian COIN operators that can work hand in hand with their military counterparts.

Certainly, COIN operations—like any war or significant foreign policy challenge— are replete with external challenges that are difficult for the United States to control. Yet many of the kinds of improvements identified here and elsewhere in this volume are under US control, and can be made—with the right mix of political will and leadership in Washington.

Notes

1 "Unsafe Deposit: In Iraq, an Army Officer Battles to Open a Bank; Military Shifts Fight to Local Politics." *The Wall Street Journal*, March 29, 2007, A1.
2 FM 3-24, pp. 1-34 and 1-113. See also http://usacac.army.mil/cac/repository/materials/coin-fm3-24.pdf.
3 Bernard Fall, "The Theory and Practice of Counterinsurgency," *Naval War College Review* (April 1965), cited by David Kilcullen, "Counterinsurgency Redux," *Survival*, Vol. 48, No. 4 (December 2006), 111–30.
4 FM 3-24, p. 1-71.
5 Ibid., p. 1-3.
6 Nadia Schadlow, "War and the Art of Governance," *Parameters* (Autumn 2003), 85–9.
7 Patrick Cronin, "Irregular Warfare, New Challenges for Civil-Military Relations," *Strategic Forum*, No. 234, Institute for National Strategic Studies, October 2008, available at http://www.ndu.edu/inss/Strforum/SF234/SF234.pdf.
8 Carl von Clausewitz, *On War*, ed. and trans. by Michael Howard and Peter Paret, Princeton, NJ: Princeton University Press, 1976, p. 89.
9 The "Army concept" focused on the object of warfare as the destruction of enemy forces and would later explain the United States' failure to adapt to circumstances in Vietnam. See Antulio J. Echevarria II, *Toward an American Way of War*, Carlisle, PA: Strategic Studies Institute, United States Army, 2004; and Andrew Krepinevich, *The Army and Vietnam*, Baltimore, MD: The Johns Hopkins University Press, 1988, pp. 5–6.
10 Cited by Robert B. Asprey, *War in the Shadows: The Guerrilla in History*, Vol. I, Lincoln, NE: iUniverse Inc., 2002, p. 137.
11 David Galula, *Pacification in Algeria, 1956–1958*, Santa Monica, CA: Rand Corporation, 2006 (1963), with a foreword by Bruce Hoffman. David Galula, *Counterinsurgency Warfare: Theory and Practice*, New York: Praeger, 1964. Robert Thompson, *Defeating Communist Insurgency: The Lessons of Malaya and Vietnam*, New York: Praeger, 1966.
12 Galula, *Counterinsurgency Warfare*, p. 42.
13 Ibid., p. 27.
14 Thompson, *Defeating Communist Insurgency*, pp. 50–60.
15 Ibid.
16 John Nagl makes this observation in *Learning to Eat Soup with a Knife: Counterinsurgency Lessons from Malaya and Vietnam*, Chicago: University of Chicago Press, 2005, p. 29.
17 Dale Andrade and Lt Col. James Willbanks, "CORDS/Phoenix: Counterinsurgency Lessons from Vietnam for the Future," *Military Review* (March/April 2006). For a detailed discussion of CORDS see also Robert W. Komer, *Bureaucracy at War: US Performance in the Vietnam Conflict*, Boulder, CO: Westview Press 1986.
18 See Krepinevich, *The Army and Vietnam*; also Harry Summers, *On Strategy: A Critical Analysis of the Vietnam War*, Novato, CA: Presidio Press, 1995; Rufus Phillips, *Why Vietnam Matters: An Eyewitness Account of Lessons Not Learned*, Newport, RI: Naval Institute Press, 2008.
19 Brian M. Linn, *The Army's Way of War*, Cambridge, MA: Harvard University Press, 2007, pp. 3–5.
20 Walter C. Ladwig. III, "Managing Counterinsurgency: Lessons from Malaya," *Military Review* (May 2007), 58.
21 Joel Hamby, "Civil Military Operations: Joint Doctrine and the Malayan Emergency," *Joint Forces Quarterly* (Autumn 2002), 55.
22 Ibid., 56.

23 Robert Komer, *The Malayan Emergency in Retrospect: Organization of a Successful Counterinsurgency Effort*, Santa Monica: CA: Rand Corporation, 1972, p. 64.

24 For good discussions of the insurgency and governance challenges there, see Todd Greentree, *Crossroads of Intervention: Insurgency and Counterinsurgency Lessons from Central America*, New York: Praeger, 2008.

25 Alfred A. Valenzuela and Victor M. Rosello, "Expanding Roles and Missions in the War on Drugs and Terrorism: El Salvador Colombia," *Military Review* (March/April 2004), 29.

26 Office of the Special Inspector General for Iraq Reconstruction, *Hard Lessons: The Iraq Reconstruction Experience*, Washington, DC: US Independent Agencies and Commissions, 2009, p. 116.

27 Thom Shanker, "The Struggle for Iraq: General Discusses Goals of His Return to Iraq," *The New York Times*, November 20, 2006.

28 David W. Barno, "Fighting 'The Other War': Counterinsurgency Strategy in Afghanistan, 2003–2005," *Military Review* (September/October 2007), 32–44.

29 Ibid, 40.

30 http://www.state.gov/s/crs/c12936.htm.

31 The office sought to codify its efforts in National Security Presidential Directive (NSPD)-44, Management of Interagency Efforts Concerning Reconstruction and Stabilization, December 7, 2005.

32 The Response Readiness Corp is composed of two components: one active, and one standby. In addition, it created a Civilian Reserve Corps which would be comprised of federal/state/local government employees or private sector individuals who could be deployed quickly (in 45–60 days) if needed.

33 The entire corps is envisioned to consist of about 250 active members (who would be deployed within 2–3 days), a standby component of 2000 additional members, and a 2000-member reserve. See Office of the Coordinator for Reconstruction and Stabilization at http://www.crs.state.gov/index.cfm?fuseaction=public.display&shortcut=4QRB.

34 FM 3-24, p. 1-10.

35 Echevarria, *Toward an American Way of War*, p. vi.

36 Ibid.

37 John Koopman, "Military transformed—better gear, new goals," *San Francisco Chronicle,* September 7, 2006 .

38 Colin S. Gray, *War, Peace and International relations*, London and New York: Routledge, 2007, p. 248.

39 FM 3-24, p. 1-34.

40 Alissa Rubin and Edward Wong, "Patterns of War Shift in Iraq Amid U.S. Buildup," *The New York Times,* April 9, 2007. http://www.nytimes.com/2007/04/09/world/middleeast/09surge.html.

41 Galula, *Counterinsurgency Warfare*, p. 27.

42 Office of the Coordinator for Reconstruction and Stabilization, United States Department of State, *Post-Conflict Reconstruction, Essential Tasks,* April 2005, available at http://www.crs.state.gov/index.cfm?fuseaction=public.display&shortcut=J7R3.

43 The Army's stability operations manual explains that *reconstruction* is the process of rebuilding degraded, damaged, or destroyed political, socioeconomic, and physical infrastructure in order to lay a foundation for long-term development. *Stabilization* is the process by which underlying tensions that might lead to resurgence in violence and a breakdown in law and order are managed and reduced, while efforts are made to support preconditions for successful long-term development. (Field Manual 3-07, *Stability and Reconstruction Operations*, Headquarters, Department of the Army, December 2007. Chapter 3, "Essential Stability Tasks," discusses these requirements. The manual can be found online at https://pksoi.army.mil/Docs/DoDD%203000.05%20SSTR.pdf.)

44 FM 3-24, p. 1-117.

45 Ibid.

46 Larry Diamond, "Building Democracy After Conflict: Lessons from Iraq," *Journal of Democracy*, Vol. 16 (January 2005), 17.

47 FM 3-24, p. 1-113.

48 Derick W. Brinkerhoff, Ronald W. Johnson, and Richard Hill, "Guide to Rebuilding Governance in Stability Operations: A Role for the Military?" Peacekeeping and Stability Operations Institute, June 2009, p. 38. See: http://www.StrategicStudiesInstitute.army.mil/.

49 Diamond, "Building Democracy After Conflict," p. 15.
50 Michelle Parker, "Programming Development Funds to Support a Counterinsurgency: A Case Study of Nangarhar, Afghanistan in 2006," Washington, DC: National Defense University, 2007.
51 Brig. Gen. H.R. McMaster, "Centralization vs. Decentralization: Preparing For and Practicing Mission Command in Counterinsurgency Operations," unpublished paper, p. 20. in Thomas Donnelly, *Lessons for the Long War*, forthcoming volume from American Enterprise Institute Press.
52 There is something of a debate about the differences among these teams, with some arguing that PRTs were focused on governance and extending the reach of the government in Kabul, while the EPRTs in Iraq were focused more directly assisting US military forces with governance missions. The challenges faced by both and the activities that they undertook were very similar.
53 Galula, *Counterinsurgency Warfare*, p. 87.
54 See GAO fact sheet, http://www.gao.gov/new.items/d0986r.pdf.
55 See Department of Defense news briefing with Amb. Carney from Iraq, March 9, 2007, available at http://www.defenselink.mil/transcripts/transcript.aspx?transcriptid=3903.
56 International Security Assistance Force, *Provincial Reconstruction Team Handbook*, 3rd edn, February 3, 2007.
57 Ibid.
58 David C. Gompert, Terrence K. Kelly, Brooke Stearns Lawson, Michelle Parker, and Kimberly Colloton, *Reconstruction Under Fire: Unifying Civil and Military Counterinsurgency*, Washington, DC: Rand Corporation, 2009.
59 FM 3-24, p. 2-11.
60 Galula, *Counterinsurgency Warfare*, p. 88.
61 FM 3-07, p. 3-7.
62 Ibid., pp. 1-73 and 3-2.
63 Rusty Barber and Sam Parker, *Evaluating Iraq's Provincial Reconstruction Teams While Drawdown Looms: A USIP Trip Report*, December 2008, by http://www.usip.org/files/resources/USIP_1208_6_0.pdf.
64 United States Institute of Peace, Association for Diplomatic Studies and Training, Iraq PRT Experience Project, Interview No. 36, interviewed by W. Haven North, initial interview date July 15, 2008, available at http://www.usip.org/files/file/resources/collections/histories/iraq_prt/36.pdf.
65 Karen DeYoung, "Envoys Resist Forced Iraq Duty: Top State Department Officials Face Angry Questions," *The Washington Post*, November 1, 2007.
66 United States Institute of Peace, Association for Diplomatic Studies and Training, Iraq PRT Experience Project, Interview No. 16, interviewed by Barbara Nielsen, initial interview date March 27, 2008, available at http://www.usip.org/files/file/resources/collections/histories/iraq_prt/16.pdf.
67 United States Institute of Peace, Association for Diplomatic Studies and Training, Iraq PRT Experience Project, Interview No. 38, interviewed by Sam Westgate, initial interview date June 18, 2008, available at http://www.usip.org/files/file/resources/collections/histories/iraq_prt/38.pdf.
68 FM 3-24, p. 2-9.
69 Ibid., p. 2-13.
70 Special Inspector General for Iraq Reconstruction (SIGIR) Report, *Hard Lessons*, p. 100.
71 Ibid., pp. 20–1.
72 Defense Department Directive 3000.05 , Stability Operations, reissued as an Instruction, September 16, 2009. See http://www.dtic.mil/whs/directives/corres/pdf/300005p.pdf.
73 McMaster, "Centralization vs. Decentralization."
74 United States Institute of Peace, Association for Diplomatic Studies and Training, Iraq PRT Experience Project, Interview No. 57, interviewed by Mehdi Ali, initial interview date August 15, 2008, available at http://www.usip.org/files/file/resources/collections/histories/iraq_prt/57.pdf.

14 Culture

Montgomery McFate

In 1942, the director of the Research and Analysis Branch of the Office of Strategic Services (OSS) received a memo entitled *The Conference with the Social Anthropologists and Resulting Operations, Jan. 10, 1942*, which laid out the sociocultural knowledge requirements of the OSS: "In order to understand the psychological condition of the people we need a systematic description of their social structure and dynamics and of the ideologies of different classes and social groups."[1] The requirements identified by the Office of Strategic Services were never fully addressed.

In 1967, the Defense Science Board, a body that advises the Secretary of Defense, called for exactly the same type of sociocultural knowledge:

> it must be explicitly recognized that the missions of the DOD cannot be successfully performed in the absence of information on (a) socio-cultural patterns in various areas including beliefs, values, motivations, etc.; (b) the social organization of troops including political, religious and economic; (c) the effect of change and innovation upon socio-cultural patterns and socio-cultural organization of groups; (d) study and evaluation of action programs initiated by U.S. or foreign agencies in underdeveloped countries.[2]

The Defense Science Board's recommendations were never fully addressed.

Almost 40 years later, sociocultural knowledge has yet again been identified as a critical element of irregular warfare. For example, in 2005, General James Mattis of the US Marine Corps observed that "navigating cultural and human terrain is just as important as navigating geographic terrain."[3] General David Petraeus noted that "knowledge of the so-called 'cultural terrain' was as important in many cases as knowledge of the physical terrain in contemporary operations. We had to deal with these new challenges because it turns out they are key elements when you plan and conduct military operations."[4] In a Multi-National Force-Iraq (MNF-I) commander's counterinsurgency guidance, General Ray Odierno noted:

> the environment in which we operate is complex and demands that we employ every weapon in our arsenal, both kinetic and non-kinetic. To fully utilize all approaches, we must understand the local cultural and history . . . We must understand how the society functions so we can enable Iraqis to build a stable, self-reliant nation.[5]

A recognition that culture matters for irregular warfare has also been explicitly incorporated into official documents. Following the classified 2005 Quadrennial Defense Review Irregular Warfare Roadmap, in 2006 the Department of Defense issued Defense Department Directive 3000.05, "Military Support for Stability, Security, Transition, and Reconstruction (SSTR)

Operations." The document mandates that the commanders of the Geographic Combatant Commands include information "on key ethnic, cultural, religious, tribal, economic and political relationships . . ." as a component of their intelligence campaign planning.[6] The requirement for sociocultural knowledge has also been incorporated into US military doctrine: in 2006, The US Army/Marine Corps Field Manual, *Counterinsurgency* (FM 3-24), noted that "successful conduct of COIN operations depends on thoroughly understanding the society and culture within which they are being conducted."[7]

This renewed interest in sociocultural knowledge within the national security establishment stems directly from the challenges posed by the conflicts in Iraq and Afghanistan. In fact, it has become accepted wisdom inside the beltway of Washington DC that US counter-insurgency efforts have suffered due to a lack of cultural knowledge at strategic, operational, and tactical levels. For example, according to US representative Ike Skelton, "in simple terms, if we had better understood the Iraqi culture and mindset, our war plans would have been even better than they were, the plan for the post-war period and all of its challenges would have been far better, and we might have been better prepared for the 'long slog.'"[8] Many members of the military have also reached the same conclusion. As Colonel Ahmed Hashim, formerly cultural advisor for 3rd Armored Cavalry Regiment, observed, "there has been a definite lack of . . . cultural understanding both at the local level right up to the national level . . . had we understood that, much of the problems that began in spring and summer of 2003 could have been avoided."[9]

Negative, unintended consequences stemming from cultural misperception are, of course, nothing new in the history of warfare. Lord Chelmsford, for example, lost over 1000 British troops to Zulu warriors at Isandlwana in 1879 because he vastly underestimated the military capability of the Zulus, believing that an unorganized tribal group could never defeat the British Army.[10] Napoleon, as George W. Smith points out in "Avoiding a Napoleonic Ulcer: Bridging the Gap of Cultural Intelligence (or, Have We Focused on the Wrong Transformation?)," failed to analyze the Spanish people—including the relationship of the Navarrese to the central government, the powerful influence exerted by the Catholic Church, and the economic importance of banditry and smuggling—resulting in a disaster for the French Army. As Smith notes, Napoleon's Spanish expedition bears a remarkable similarity to early American misunderstandings of Iraqi society: "much as the French viewed the Spaniards two centuries earlier, US planners were left to peer through an almost exclusively Western lens in their hopeful analysis of how segments of this 25-million-person country might respond to coalition stabilization and support efforts."[11]

Despite various acknowledgments that culture matters, and enthusiastic calls for more of it,[12] there are relatively few evaluations of why cultural knowledge is so relevant in a counterinsurgency. (There are even fewer attempts to address what sort of sociocultural knowledge might be necessary to counterinsurgency operations.[13]) Therefore, this chapter attempts to answer a simple yet fundamental question: why is understanding sociocultural dynamics critical for a counterinsurgency?

New center of gravity

The center of gravity in any counterinsurgency is the civilian population, and the primary goal is to shift the population from passive or active support of the insurgents to support of the legitimate host nation government. From the perspective of the civilian population, neither party has an absolute advantage: civilians will support the side that best meets their interests for security, political order, economic development, essential services, and so forth. To meet those interests, counterinsurgent forces must understand the politics, society, and economics of the local population—in other words, their culture.

Unlike conventional major combat operations, counterinsurgency must be conducted among, and hopefully with the support of, an indigenous civilian population. In order to train a police force, establish a local banking system, develop intelligence sources, or create provisional councils, US personnel must work with local civilians. Working effectively with local civilians to fight an insurgency, establish a legitimate government, and rebuild a country requires knowledge of how the society is organized, who has power, what their values and beliefs are, and how they interpret their own history. As US Marine Corps General Anthony Zinni, the former commander of US Central Command (CENTCOM) and special envoy for the United States to Israel and the Palestinian Authority, has noted:

> What I need to understand is how these societies function. What makes them tick? Who makes the decisions? What is it about their society that's so remarkably different in their values, in the way they think, compared to my values and the way I think in my western, white-man mentality? . . . My decision-making, my military way of METT and T [mission, enemy, terrain, troops and time available], my way of building my synchron-ization matrix, my top-down planning, and my battlefield geometry—all is [sic] worth absolutely zip in this environment . . . What you need to know isn't what our intel apparatus is geared to collect for you, and to analyze, and to present to you.[14]

The type of knowledge that General Zinni refers to is not general, high-level abstraction about the society, but rather must be highly detailed and granular. This is, unfortunately, exactly the kind of knowledge the US military lacks. The vast majority of the defense science budget supports the development of technology, weapons, equipment, and materiel, rather than qualitative social sciences. Of the *total federal* social science research budget of $1.2 billion (which includes basic and applied research) from 2002 through 2004, the Department of Defense spent only 1 percent.[15] Surprisingly, the Department of Defense spent less money on social sciences than all other federal agencies except the Smithsonian, whose budget is obviously considerably smaller.

However, when the Department of Defense does invest money in the social sciences, those funds support building tools or buying more analysts, rather than conducting basic social science research.[16] Most of these tools are developed without the benefit of social science data about the societies they purport to model or simulate, and analysts work with a paucity of data. Without the data, the tools and the analysis have little relevance. As Owen Cate, the assistant director of the Security Studies Program at MIT, noted, "I think it's one of these cases when all the methodology, all the fancy software and all the other stuff—if it's garbage in, it's going to be garbage out, so the question boils down to how much do we know about these groups . . . if we don't know much about these groups, then I don't think these models will have much utility."[17]

The ability to conduct irregular warfare is dependent on basic ethnographic information—the necessary granularity will be absent without social science research on the ground, leaving military personnel with only vague generalities and a list of dos and don'ts. Dr Tom Marks, a professor at the National Defense University who put himself through graduate school by writing for *Soldier of Fortune* magazine, has long encouraged his students to live in the country they study.

> That is the first rule of the analytical game: you can't correctly assess a situation about which you have only second-hand knowledge . . . Who knew better how the Arab revolt

was going, Lawrence or the bureaucrats in Cairo? We might equally cite Lansdale and Bohannan in the Huk Rebellion or John Paul Vann in Vietnam. The point is the same: you have to get out on the street and talk to folks, see what's up.[18]

When US government personnel have access to this type of information, counterinsurgency operations are more likely to be successful. In Iraq's al-Anbar province between January and August 2005, for example, the 3rd Battalion 4th Marines conducted seven offensive operations to disrupt insurgent cells, detained more than 400 suspected insurgents, uncovered a large cache of weapons and explosives, and lost no Marines in combat. In part, the Marines owed their success to their knowledge of the local society. According to Lieutenant Colonel Andrew Kennedy, commanding officer of 3rd Battalion, 4th Marines, Regimental Combat Team-8,

> Basically the operation worked because we knew who the tribal power brokers were and we took advantage of the situation. We knew how they were organized, so instead of making a terrible *faux pas*, we parlayed it into a relationship with the Azawi sheik, and that translated to relations with the sub-sheiks, and this feeling of goodwill extended throughout the area of influence.[19]

Less force

During the Vietnam War, General Westmoreland was asked at a press conference for his views on the answer to insurgency, to which he replied: "Firepower."[20] While the identification and neutralization of targets using lethal force is one of the core functions of any military (and it could be argued that this is the *sine qua non* of any military, historic or contemporary), this approach is often ineffective by itself in a counterinsurgency. Although the most expedient path to the conclusion of hostilities during a major combat operation is the neutralization of targets in the battlespace, the object beyond war in a counterinsurgency is the restoration of civil order and the re-establishment of legitimate and fair governance. Tools other than lethal force (such as economic development, provision of medical services, restoration of legal processes, support to civil society groups, etc.) are often more likely to shift the population from supporting the insurgency to supporting the legitimate host nation government. As Major General Peter W. Chiarelli, the former commanding general of the US Army's 1st Cavalry Division and head of Task Force Baghdad, observed:

> A direct correlation existed between the level of local infrastructure status, unemployment figures, and attacks on US soldiers. The findings were an epiphany to the task force—this was about force protection. These were breeding grounds for anti-Iraqi forces. The choice was to continue to attrit [use attrition] through direct action or shape the populace to deny sanctuary to the insurgents by giving the populace positive options through clear improvement in quality of life.[21]

Counterinsurgency, unlike other forms of warfare, requires more than just effective targeting of the adversary. While FM 3-24 advocates this approach, it is by no means accepted wisdom within the national security community. In the words of an Air Force general, "While the manual is a vast improvement over its predecessors, it would be a huge mistake to take it as proof—as some in the press, academia and independent policy organizations have—that victory over insurgents is achievable by anything other than traditional military force."[22] Edward Luttwak faulted the US military for its "principled and inevitable refusal to out-terrorize the insurgents," which he describes as "the necessary and sufficient condition of a tranquil occupation."[23] Similarly, Ralph Peters wrote in *Armchair General* that, "killing has been the *only* effective tool against insurgencies—especially those rooted in religious or ethnic passion."[24]

A caveat is necessary here: to argue that lethal force *by itself* is ineffective in a counter-insurgency is not to argue that lethal force is unnecessary or should *never* be used. Lethal force clearly does have utility for the attainment of political ends, as so many successful and bloody revolutions have demonstrated. Lethal force also serves a vital role in counter-insurgency: where armed groups seek to impose their will by force, targets must be identified and neutralized. Certainly, the success of the Joint Special Operations Command (JSOC) in the identification and neutralization of key members of al-Qaeda in Iraq, Sunni insurgent groups, and Shia militias, and the so-called "special group" have contributed to the improved security situation in Iraq since the spring of 2007.[25] When lethal force is employed, however (as JSOC's operations have demonstrated), it must be carried out precisely and propor-tionately. Victory over insurgents cannot be achieved purely by traditional military force, but neither is victory possible without lethal force.

Sociocultural knowledge can reduce the need for kinetic force during a counterinsurgency. To provide a concrete example, at the beginning of the Iraq War, the 2nd Battalion, 327th Infantry Regiment, of the 101st Airborne Division entered Najaf, the third holiest city in Islam, after Mecca and Medina. The road to Najaf had been difficult: the battalion had been fighting the Fedayeen (who dressed in civilian garb, used civilians as shields, and took women and children hostage to force men to fight) for many days. Earlier that week, a suicide bomber posing as a taxi driver had killed himself and four US soldiers at a checkpoint outside Najaf. Arriving 30 minutes before the call to prayer, the battalion encountered a crowd of hundreds of infuriated Shi'as blocking the Imam Ali mosque. Although the battalion had entered Najaf at the invitation of Grand Ayatollah Ali Hussein Sistani, the local residents believed that they had come to capture Sistani and attack the Holy Shrine of Ali. People in the crowd began throwing rocks, and dozens of Fedayeen barricaded themselves inside the mosque, from where they would be able to shoot at both the US soldiers and Iraqi civilians.

Instead of entering the mosque, or attempting to control the crowd, the battalion com-mander, Lieutenant Colonel Chris Hughes, ordered his soldiers to point their weapons at the ground and put them on safe. Then he ordered his soldiers to "take a knee!" and to smile at the crowd. While loudspeakers explained that the Americans were there to remove Saddam Hussein from power, Lieutenant Colonel Hughes stood between the crowd and his troops with his arms outstretched. Recognizing that the US forces were not a threat, hundreds of people carrying white flags came across the barrier and went into the mosque to pray. The following day, Grand Ayatollah Sistani issued a decree asking the citizens of Najaf to welcome the US military and give them free movement through the town on the way to Baghdad. As a result, many citizens of Najaf provided intelligence to the battalion about the location of improvised explosive devices (IEDs) in the city.

Reflecting on the events at Najaf, Lieutenant Colonel Chris Hughes credited his interpreter with explaining to him how the local community perceived the battalion's intentions, noting, "it was cultural knowledge that won the battle, not combined arms firepower."[26] The story of what Lieutenant Colonel Hughes did at Najaf illustrates the importance for military personnel of understanding the local society. Had Lieutenant Colonel Hughes not defused the situation, hundreds of Iraqis and scores of soldiers might have died, destabilizing the city of Najaf.

Knowledge reduces casualties

The likelihood of success in a counterinsurgency is inversely proportional to the number of casualties, military and civilian. Casualties, especially those resulting from the use of imprecise and disproportionate lethal force, may strengthen the insurgency by creating martyrs, increase recruiting, strip the government of any remaining political legitimacy, and provide evidence to civilians of the brutality of state forces, resulting in an escalation of the conflict. In 1986, General John Galvin, then commander in chief of the US Southern Command, which was engaged in counterinsurgency in El Salvador, noted that

> The ... burden on the military institution is large. Not only must it subdue an armed adversary while attempting to provide security to the civilian population, it must also avoid furthering the insurgents' cause. If, for example, the military's actions in killing 50 guerrillas cause 200 previously uncommitted citizens to join the insurgent cause, the use of force will have been counterproductive.[27]

For a military organized, trained, equipped, and culturally predisposed to seek a kinetic solution, the natural response to an escalating insurgency is to simply identify and neutralize more targets. The more targets neutralized, the less likely a negotiated political settlement becomes. This "downward spiral"[28] may be particularly deadly in societies that are tribally organized, where members have a duty to avenge the deaths of fellow tribesmen. Such a structure of reciprocal attacks may result in a cyclical escalation of violence,[29] especially when the reprisal is seen as disproportionate to the original crime. Coalition forces refer to this as "bloodline" attacks. According to a US Army captain in Samarra: "It's the Arabic rule of five. If you do something to someone, then five of his bloodlines will try to attack you."[30] As Major Ike Wilson, an operations planner with the 101st Airborne Division, observed:

> Reassessing some of the previous anti-Coalition attacks revealed a few instances where a highly-ineffective attack on US forces followed either a major operation or an operation-based instance of unintended collateral damage. More than a handful of these former attacks, then judged as lethal attacks against our forces, were able to be reassessed as merely symbolic retribution (honor-bound) attacks by tribal members—kin of the offended, injured or killed person. By tribal honor, the relative was required to strike in reprisal. Some of the attacks that we originally saw as "poor marksmanship" were likely intentional misses by attackers pro-progress and pro-US, but honor-bound to avenge a perceived wrong that US forces at the time did not know how to appropriately resolve.[31]

Given this dynamic (in addition to the inherent moral reasons), both civilian and military casualties should be kept to the minimum possible during a counterinsurgency.

One method of reducing casualties during a counterinsurgency is to increase the level of sociocultural knowledge among military forces. The Human Terrain System (HTS), an experimental US Army program, was designed and implemented in order to do just this. Since 2007, HTS has deployed mixed military and civilian teams to serve on brigade, division, and corps staffs in Iraq and Afghanistan. The objective of the program is to provide supported military commands with a more granular understanding of the local population in their area of operations, and the dedicated expertise to integrate that understanding into their military decision-making process, in order to enable the US military to work in partnership with the local population to achieve common goals of physical security, economic development, and political stability.

Preliminary reports indicate that Human Terrain Teams (HTT) do indeed assist the military in reducing both military and civilian casualties. In April 2008, Colonel Martin P. Schweitzer, commander of the 4th Brigade Combat Team of the 82nd Airborne Division, testified before the House Armed Services Committee about his experiences while having an HTT assigned to his brigade over the course of 15 months. According to Colonel Schweitzer:

> By better understanding the human terrain, we reduced the number of kinetic operations that otherwise would have occurred. Not only did we reduce the risk to our soldiers, but we reduced the risk significantly to the communities that we operated within . . . Without the HTT filter on courses of action and the alternative maneuver tools they identified to create the exact same effect, we would have lost double the lives. Using HTT capabilities, we reduced kinetic operations by 60–70%.[32]

A reduction in kinetic operations means that soldiers' lives were not lost, local civilians were not killed, property was not destroyed, and infrastructure was not damaged. A decrease in casualties also enabled the brigade to create positive relationships with local Afghan communities, and to focus on non-kinetic lines of operation, such as economic development and political reconciliation. In the words of Colonel Schweitzer, "When we took over in early 2007, only 19 of 86 formal and informal districts supported the government. Today, we assess 72 of those same Districts support their government. I absolutely attribute some of that change to the HTT." [33]

Human Terrain Teams have also demonstrated their utility in reducing casualties in Iraq. To provide a specific example, in October 2007, two members of an HTT provided support to a maneuver company conducting an operation in a small rural village, known to be an area in which al-Qaeda operated. During the operation, an elderly Muslim man was detained for possession of a riflescope and alleged "Jihadist propaganda." The local villagers were very upset by the man's arrest. Upon the return to the patrol base, one of the HTT members reviewed the alleged "Jihadist propaganda" and discovered that in fact the material included only basic Islamic textbooks, brochures containing sayings from the Prophet, and an elementary Arabic grammar workbook. The riflescope was of the type found on a medium-quality BB gun, commonly used to shoot birds that eat the honeybees kept by villagers in this area. After hearing recommendations from the HTT, the company commander decided to release the elderly man. The HTT coached the company commander on how to remedy the insult by offering a public apology in front of witnesses from his village. As one of the HTT members noted, "we watched them detain the wrong guy for the wrong reasons, we dealt with that and helped the unit to do what they could to repair the damage in the right cultural context, and as a result we're not fighting anyone there. We prevented a disaster."[34] As the company commander explained, "The manner in which we released him was more important than just releasing him . . . we don't want to create insurgents for 10 or 20 years down the road."[35]

On the day following the release of the elderly man, a sheikh of the Dulaymi tribe came to the patrol base and asked to speak to the commander. The sheikh explained that the release of the elderly villager (who happened to be his uncle) was greatly appreciated by the local citizens and that this show of respect had prompted him to seek coalition assistance in securing his village from al-Qaeda. The sheikh indicated that he was ready to begin covert mounted patrols with his 135–50 men, many of whom were professional officers who had served in the Iraqi Army before the war. To avoid being fired on by American helicopters, the sheikh requested air-to-ground coordination for the protection of his men. At the conclusion of the meeting, as a gesture of good will, the sheik told the commander and the HTT the specific location of a deep-buried IED in front of the mosque. As one HTT member noted, "he wanted to open a dialogue; from that we got two IEDs, a cache of mortar tubes, anti-aircraft guns, and lots of other stuff. In particular, the deep-buried IEDs are what catastrophically kills a vehicle like a Stryker."[36] In the words of the company commander: "The combination of cultural sensitivity and the assistance of HTT on the mission to [the village] was the reason for our success."[37]

One of the lessons learned from the human terrain experiment is that information about the local population is necessary but not sufficient: a commander must have dedicated, expert staff members to assist him in understanding the operational relevance of sociocultural knowledge and in finding ways to apply that sociocultural knowledge to his course of action development. Fifteen hundred analysts sitting at Central Command headquarters, no matter how brilliant and competent, will not address the needs of the warfighters on the ground in Iraq and Afghanistan.

Military organization mirrors social organization

In an underappreciated article called "Military Effectiveness: Why Society Matters," Steven Peter Rosen makes the argument that, when evaluating military effectiveness, the culture of the nation matters far less than the social structure. Arguing against both neorealism and the strategic culture paradigm, Rosen writes that military organizations are shaped by internal conditions of their society of origin and that "social structures can carry over into the society's military organizations."[38]

As with state military organizations, the organizational structure of any insurgency will reflect the indigenous social organization of the host nation. Because tribes are a significant component of the social structure of Iraq, for example, they affect how the insurgency is organized and how it operates. Because Iraq has a strong tribal element within its social fabric, the insurgency's leadership structure and dynamics are bound to follow the decentralized tribal model of social organization. As one analyst at the US Army's National Ground Intelligence Center noted, understanding enemy command and control is challenging:

> We see *shura* councils from Iraq and *shuras* and *jirgas* from Pakistan operating similarly in terms of C2 [command and control] and planning before battles: leaders get together, consult, and try to reach consensus on decisions. Neighborhoods are divided up into defensive sectors and networks or cells assigned to them. When the fight begins command is very decentralized, units are autonomous or semi-autonomous. There may not be an overall leader of the council. The whole process is egalitarian. Everyone is trying to maximize honor, and most other tribal values and customs stem from that primary honor value.[39]

The absence of a stable order of battle, the absence of hierarchy, and the networked nature of the cells pose distinct challenges to the US military's conception of military rationality. As Colonel Derek Harvey, US Army, (Retd) has noted,

> Regarding leadership, there is no unified leadership of the insurgency. We, as Americans, are looking for a hierarchy; we want to see a line in a wire diagram. What we're fighting against, however, is very Arab in context ... They're collaborating, and they're

cooperating across multiple networks. They know each other—the networks are built upon past relationships. They're leveraging these things—family and tribe.[40]

Understanding the organizational structure of an insurgent group allows counterinsurgent forces to neutralize it more effectively.

All counterinsurgency is political

Russell Weigley advanced the thesis in *The American Way of War: A History of U.S. Military Strategy and Policy*, that American strategic culture is centered on achieving a decisive military victory over an adversary, whether through attrition or annihilation. This "myth of decisive victory"[41] inhibits clear thinking about the role and function of military forces during a counterinsurgency, and also about the nature of counterinsurgency itself. The expectation that the Taliban are going to sign formal articles of surrender, much as the Japanese did on the decks of the USS Missouri in 1945, can only lead to disappointment. The expectation that a tactical defeat of regular Iraqi forces amounts to an end of hostilities (as President George W. Bush apparently assumed during his speech on the USS *Abraham Lincoln* on May 1, 2003) was at best wishful thinking.

"Victory" in a counterinsurgency cannot be obtained purely through destruction of insurgent forces. In truth, counterinsurgency is a political activity that does not have a purely military solution. Reflecting on his experiences conducting counterinsurgency operations in Northern Ireland, Brigadier General Frank Kitson wrote that:

> The first thing that must be apparent when contemplating the sort of action which a government facing insurgency should take, is that there can be no such thing as a purely military solution because insurgency is not primarily a military activity. At the same time there is no such thing as a wholly political solution either.[42]

US military doctrine also recognizes the political nature of a counterinsurgency: the US Marine Corps *Small Wars Manual* of 1940 notes succinctly: "The application of purely military measures may not, by itself restore peace and orderly government because the fundamental causes of the condition of unrest may be economic, political or social."[43] More recently FM 3-24 notes: "Political power is the central issue in insurgencies and counterinsurgencies; each side aims to get the people to accept its governance or authority as legitimate."[44]

If one accepts the premise that counterinsurgency is fundamentally political in nature, it follows that addressing the competing political agendas of multiple parties to the conflict is a critical first step. At a minimum these parties include: insurgent groups, the host nation government, the civilian population, regional actors, civil society groups, and the counterinsurgent forces. How these political agendas are expressed in thought and action, and how political entities in a society conflict, crosscut, and collaborate with other elements of the social structure, is not just a matter of Jeffersonian politics, but is also a matter of the political culture of local groups. Understanding these dynamics is critical for counterinsurgency operations. In the words of T.X. Hammes:

> the very first step in dealing with the political aspects of the war is to develop a genuine understanding of the political environment where the war is being fought. This requires a deep understanding of the culture, history, and current political structure of the area.[45]

A failure to understand the local political system and local political culture may result in counterinsurgent forces inadvertently escalating the conflict or becoming an unwitting proxy of a particular political group. To provide a specific example, during Operation Restore Hope, Ambassador Robert Oakley, the joint force commander, had a strong grasp of Somali culture, which helped him to remain neutral during inter- and intra-clan disputes.[46] The subsequent UN peace enforcement mission, UNOSOM II, "failed to take certain factors of Somali culture into consideration, contributing to the operation's failure."[47] In particular, little attention was paid to the social structure or political organization of Somalia.[48] According to a senior Department of Defense intelligence officer who worked with the Joint Chiefs of Staff planners, not one person asked him about the Somali political structure.[49] The resultant misunderstandings were devastating for UNOSOM's mission. When the UN forces attempted to "marginalize" General Mohammad Farrah Aideed, whom they perceived as a dangerous, ambitious warlord, the United Nations inadvertently strengthened the position of his key rival. As Tamara Duffey noted in "Cultural Issues in Contemporary Peacekeeping," UN actions unintentionally bolstered General Aideed's power and authority, thereby upsetting the traditional balance of the Somali kinship system.[50] In order to restore his clan's power, Aideed was obliged to fight the UN force, and in the process, the peacekeepers were treated as just another clan. Somali clans fight according to their own customary laws of war, which have little to do with Western conceptions of *jus ad bellum* or *jus in bello*. As General Anthony Zinni has noted, "When you go fight them then, why is it that the women and kids are out in the street committing atrocities on American bodies? Because you went to war with the clan. You declared war on the clan . . . Your enemy is the Habr Gedir. And when you go to war with the clan, the whole clan fights. And you can't understand that in a western context or a western view of the world."[51]

Sociocultural knowledge reduces ethnocentrism

Ethnocentrism can be described as an intellectual fallacy in which one's own group is seen as the center of the universe, with other groups judged in relation and found lacking. Ethnocentrism is also a synonym for being "culture-bound," or lacking the ability to see the world from eyes of different culture or nation.[52] Put simply, ethnocentrism implies a failure to empathize with the viewpoints or experiences of other social groups.

Neither military organizations nor individual soldiers are immune from ethnocentrism. Many soldiers who deploy to foreign countries have little prior knowledge regarding political or social conditions, except for reports glimpsed on television and scanned in the newspapers, and their views often reflect the stereotypes found in popular culture. For example, one soldier serving in the British Army in Northern Ireland baldly noted, "All these [Catholic] estates are horrid, but largely because so many of the inhabitants have no standards and live in them like animals . . . these inhabitants could turn Eaton Square in Belgravia into a slum."[53] The danger faced on a daily basis by military personnel, whose friends and colleagues are killed or wounded by enemies that they cannot identify and do not understand, can exacerbate the tendency toward ethnocentrism. As one Marine officer serving in Iraq noted:

> my Marines were almost wholly uninterested in interacting with the local population.
> Our primary mission was the security of Camp Fallujah. We relieved soldiers from . . .
> Division and their assessment was that every local was participating or complicit with

the enemy. This view was quickly adopted by my unit and framed everything—all of our actions and reactions.[54]

Ethnocentrism may, in some cases, be an adaptive psychosocial response to the imperatives of war. In 1979, Ken Booth wrote in his seminal book *Strategy and Ethnocentrism*, that "ethnocentrism contributes to the 'vilification of the human' which makes killing easier."[55] Certainly, in a conflict such as World War I, where repeated, systematic, intimate killing was expected from soldiers, the vilification of the human offered the possibility of moral distancing through the objectification and dehumanization of the enemy.

Counterinsurgency, however, presents other challenges. In order to convince a population to reject the political, economic, and social solutions offered by insurgent groups and to embrace those offered by the government, the military must be able to accurately perceive the world from the population's perspective. The effective counterinsurgent must be able to understand the insurgents motivation. Thus, unlike the vilification of the enemy needed in large conventional fights such as World War I, waging counterinsurgency warfare requires the breaking down of ethnocentrism among the military force and the development of true cross-cultural understanding.

False assumptions

Understanding the local society in which counterinsurgency operations are conducted is critical for dispelling false assumptions, which can easily result in less than effective policymaking and strategic design. Prior to the Iraq War, for example, it was commonly assumed that the Iraqi military and police, stripped of their top leaders, would bear primary responsibility for re-establishing order. Planners assumed that most of the security force units would remain intact and would be available for duty soon after the end of conventional operations.[56] As then National Security Advisor Condoleezza Rice said, "The concept was that we would defeat the army, but the institutions would hold, everything from ministries to police forces."[57] The assumption that Iraq was a technocratic bureaucracy with functioning, stable governance institutions led senior policy makers toward the conceptual model of a *coup d'état*, in which the head of state could be summarily removed, leaving the rest of the security apparatus more or less intact. This assumption about the social organization of Iraq, however, proved to be false: "etatist tribalism" (in the words of Faleh Jabar) during the late Ba'ath era had weakened the Iraq's bureaucratic, political, military, and social institutions to the degree that the "center could not hold."[58]

Another assumption within the US policymaking community about the society of Iraq that led to a negative strategic outcome was the false notion that power was firmly concentrated in the central government in Baghdad. As Condoleezza Rice noted in 2007, reflecting on the mistakes of the Iraq War, it was not "self-evident" to her that controlling Iraq would require engaging with local, provincial, and tribal authorities: "Arab states can be very centralized. This is actually a fairly new model of local and provincial responsibility."[59] Most scholars of Iraq, however, have observed that the tense disconnection between the center and the periphery dates back to the Ottoman era.[60] Similarly, US military personnel operating on the ground quickly determined that Iraqis are highly suspicious of central government. As one Marine major noted, "Iraqis think of the central government as the enemy. This is not Washington, DC. These towns have no connection with Baghdad."[61] Unfortunately, the Coalition Provisional Authority seems to have misunderstood this and imposed the US model of central government control, which sabotaged attempts at political and economic reconstruction.[62]

In the early part of the twentieth century, anthropologists, following the work of Franz Boas, began by asking: what does this look like from another culture's point of view? Failure to ask this question may result in policies formulated on the basis of unconscious assumptions derived from the policy maker's own culture, which are not necessarily shared by others. For example, during the British colonial administration of Fiji, the indigenous prestige economy (in which a chief's prestige and power was linked to his generosity in distributing food and goods) was replaced with a small peasant production, monetization, and thrifty habits modeled on British cultural norms. The result was near-destruction of Fiji's social structure.[63] As Clyde Kluckhohn, an anthropologist who worked for the Office of Strategic Services, noted in 1949: "Ignorance of the way of life in other countries breeds an indifference and callousness among nations, a misinterpretation and misunderstanding which becomes ever more threatening as the world shrinks."[64]

Conclusion

"The insurgencies in Iraq and Afghanistan," as General David Petraeus once wrote, "were not, in truth, the wars for which we were best prepared in 2001 . . ."[65] The type of war for which the US military was best prepared was conventional war, "of a particularly swift and violent style."[66] Counterinsurgency operations in Iraq and Afghanistan required the US military to restructure, rethink, and redesign many elements of itself, including equipment, contracting regulations, rules of engagement, command and control, supply-chain logistics, equipment, brigade structure, training, and doctrine, to name a few elements. The US military's current interest in sociocultural knowledge is just one of these adaptations, driven by the operational conditions in the battlespace.

To what degree should the US military invest resources, time, and manpower in institutionalizing the adaptations made to the institution as a result of the experiences of Iraq and Afghanistan? Military thinkers such as John Nagl argue that the Army should institutionalize the lessons of Iraq, to enable them to succeed "at building societies that can stand on their own." This would require a change in training, education, acquisition, and organizational culture, to develop "the intellectual tools necessary to foster host nation political and economic development." Other equally thoughtful military officers such as Andrew Bacevich have argued that the Army's current focus on reinventing itself for stability operations will lead to the institution becoming "a constabulary," reducing its capacity for conventional warfighting.[67]

Absolute positions, favoring either preparation for conventional war or irregular warfare, are counterproductive. The US military clearly needs to develop and maintain a capability for both. As the war in Iraq demonstrates, the ability to engage in intensive linear warfare cannot be discounted, but neither can the ability to engage in counterinsurgency and stability operations in the aftermath of conventional war. Continuing to invest in highly priced, technocentric, pet rock projects that result in limited capabilities for the warfighter merely create the preconditions for the same problems faced by the US in Iraq: the military prepared for a linear tank battle against the Soviets in the Fulda Gap but found themselves facing the much more unmanageable challenge of counterinsurgency in a society that was not adequately understood at the requisite level of granularity.

What should be done? First, the US military should institutionalize a large portion of the programs, doctrine, and training developed during the conflicts in Iraq and Afghanistan. In particular, the lesson learned from the HTS experiment—that operational military commanders require dedicated, expert staff focused on incorporating operationally relevant sociocultural information into course-of-action development—should not be forgotten.

Second, the US government should develop a large-scale, systematic research program within its science and technology portfolio to support qualitative social science in non-Western societies where future military operations are likely to occur. Specifically, the US government should initiate a program that would sponsor highly directed research by social scientists to collect phase zero, open-source baseline information on: social structure (ethnic groups, tribes, elite networks, institutions, organizations, and the relationships between them), culture (roles/statuses, social norms and sanctions, beliefs, values, and belief systems), cultural forms (myths, narratives, rituals, symbols), power and authority systems, etc. This information would provide a sociocultural knowledge base to facilitate future stability operations, which depend on the ability of US personnel to operate within a foreign society. This information would also provide the requisite knowledge for the geographic combatant commands to shape, dissuade, engage, and deter much more effectively. Such a research program would also alleviate the burden placed on soldiers in the future, who were often forced to collect this type of information in Iraq and Afghanistan, without the benefit of social science training or tools.

Failing to institutionalize the adaptations generated by the wars in Iraq and Afghanistan presents a real hazard: if the military's gains made in the realm of irregular warfare are thrown out with the bathwater (as they were at the end of World War II and Vietnam) they will have to be rebuilt yet again when the specter of irregular warfare presents itself as an inescapable imperative. Building capabilities during a war is difficult, time-consuming, expensive, costs the lives of civilians and soldiers alike, and imposes a huge strain on the bureaucracy. Given that the US government has known since 1942 that "a systematic description of . . . social structure and dynamics and of the ideologies of different classes and social groups" is necessary for the conduct of irregular warfare, and having rediscovered this again in 1965 and 2005, it would be negligent to ignore the lesson that this history presents.

Notes

1 The Conference with the Social Anthropologists and Resulting Operations, January 10, 1942, available at: http://www.icdc.com/~paulwolf/oss/ossrna.htm#academics.
2 Defense Science Board panel report, Summer 1967, quoted in Seymour J. Deitchman, *The Best-Laid Schemes: A Tale of Social Science Research and Bureaucracy*, Cambridge, MA: The MIT Press, 1976, pp. 415–16.
3 Gen. James Mattis quoted in Max Boot, "Navigating the Human Terrain," *Los Angeles Times*, December 7, 2005.
4 Editors, "Interview With US General David Petraeus," *Der Spiegel*, December 18, 2006, available at http://www.spiegel.de/international/spiegel/0,1518,455199,00.html.
5 Gen. Ray Odierno, Multi-National Force-Iraq Commander's Counterinsurgency Guidance, September 16, 2008.
6 Department of Defense Directive 3000.05, Military Support for Stability, Security, Transition, and Reconstruction (SSTR) Operations, November 2005.
7 The US Army/Marine Corps Field Manual, *Counterinsurgency* (FM 3-24), Chicago: University of Chicago Press, 2007, p. 1-22.
8 Sandra I. Erwin, "US Military Training Fails to Grasp Foreign Cultures, Says Rep. Skelton," *National Defense Magazine*, June 2004, available at www.nationaldefensemagazine.org/issues/2004/Jun/US_Military.htm.
9 Steve Inskeep, "US's Cultural Ignorance Fuels Iraq Insurgency," National Public Radio, April 28, 2006.
10 Paul Williams, *Little Bighorn and Isandlwana: Kindred Fights, Kindred Follies*, London: Phantascope Books, 2007.
11 George W. Smith, "Avoiding a Napoleonic Ulcer: Bridging the Gap of Cultural Intelligence (or, Have We Focused on the Wrong Transformation?)," in *Chairman of the Joint Chiefs of Staff Strategy Essay Competition Essays 2004*, Washington, DC: National Defense University Press, 2004, pp. 21–38.

12 James Baker, "Winning Hearts with Cultural Awareness," *Soldiers*, Vol. 58, No. 7 (July 2003). Barak Salmoni, "Beyond Hearts and Minds, Culture Matters," *Naval Proceedings* (November 2004). Montgomery McFate, "The Military Utility of Understanding Adversary Culture," *Joint Forces Quarterly*, Vol. 38 (2005). Benjamin C. Freakley, "Cultural Awareness and Combat Power," *Infantry*, Vol. 94, No. 2 (March/April 2005). David H. Petraeus, "Learning Counterinsurgency: Observations From Soldiering in Iraq," *Military Review*, Vol. 86, No. 4 (January/February 2006).

13 Jeffrey B. White, "Some Thoughts on Irregular Warfare," *Studies in Intelligence*, Vol. 39, No. 5 (1996). John W. Jandora, "Military Cultural Awareness: From Anthropology to Application," Landpower Essay No. 06-3, Institute of Land Warfare, November 2006. Joseph D. Celeski, "Operationalizing COIN," JSOU Report 05-2, Hurlburt Field, FL: Joint Special Operations University, September 2005. James A. Gordon, "Cultural Assessments and Campaign Planning," Fort Leavenworth, Kansas: School of Advanced Military Studies, United States Army Command and General Staff College, May 2004. David H. Petraeus, "Learning Counterinsurgency: Observations From Soldiering in Iraq," 8.

14 Anthony C. Zinni, "Non-Traditional Military Missions: Their Nature, and the Need for Cultural Awareness and Flexible Thinking," in Joe Strange (ed.), *Capital "W" War: A Case for Strategic Principles of War*, Quantico, VA: Marine Corps University, 1998, p. 267.

15 National Science Foundation, Division of Science Resources Statistics, Federal Funds for Research and Development: Fiscal Years 2002, 2003, and 2004, NSF 05-307, Arlington, VA, 2005. Available at: http://www.nsf.gov/statistics/nsf05307/htmstart.htm 2004. See also, Kei Koizumi, "An Update on R&D in the 2006 Federal Budget," AAAS R&D Budget and Policy Program, October 27, 2005, available at: http://www.aaas.org/spp/rd/prnaaea1005.pdf.

16 Within the Department of Defense, there is also considerable institutional resistance to funding basic, qualitative social science since it is often not considered adequately "scientific." In 2006, I asked a colleague with years of federal science and technology experience why the director of a particular agency was so hostile to the social sciences. The answer was, "he's basically an idea/gizmo guy, and he invests in neat ideas/gizmos, and these materialize in techy/system programs." In other words, if you can't build a machine, it's not science. Email 2005, notes in possession of the author.

17 Karen Roebuck, "CMU Project Targets Terrorism," *Pittsburgh Tribune Review*, June 19, 2004, available from http://www.pittsburghlive.com/x/search/s_199550.html.

18 Thomas A. Marks, "Evaluating Insurgent/Counterinsurgent Performance," *Small Wars and Insurgencies*, Vol. 11, No. 3 (Winter 2000), 21–46.

19 Interview, Lt. Col. Andrew Kennedy, 2006. Taken to an extreme, the quest for local knowledge may entail the assimilation of state military forces into the society experiencing an insurgency. When Brig. Gen. Jack Pershing returned to the Philippines as military governor of the Moro Province between 1909 and 1913, he applied the lessons he had learned as a junior officer during the Philippine insurrection. Pershing recognized that military force alone could not suppress the Moro rebellion, and that an understanding of Moro customs and habits was essential. Appreciative of Pershing's attempt to assimilate into their society, the Moro allowed Pershing inside the "Forbidden Kingdom" and made him a Moro Datu, an honor not granted to any other white man. Sam C. Sarkesian, *America's Forgotten Wars: The Counterrevolutionary Past and Lessons for the Future*, Westport, CT: Greenwood Press, 1984, p. 244, pp. 178–80. Similarly, in Vietnam some Special Forces units who worked with Montagnard tribes assimilated into local societies, participating in tribal ceremonies and establishing deep bonds. Department of the Army, *Vietnam Studies: US Army Special Forces, 1961–1971*, CMH Publication 90-23, Washington, DC: Center for Military History, 1989 (1973), p. 79. The deep relationship between Special Forces advisors and the highland tribes meant that Green Berets were often in a position to mediate between the Montagnards and South Vietnamese officials who were suspicious of the highlanders. Department of the Army, *American Military History: The US Army In Vietnam*, CMH Publication 30-1, Washington, DC: Center for Military History, p. 629.

20 Andrew F. Krepinevich, *The Army and Vietnam*, Baltimore, MD: Johns Hopkins University Press, 1986, p. 197.

21 Peter W. Chiarelli and Patrick R. Michaelis, "Winning the Peace: The Requirement for Full-Spectrum Operations," *Military Review* (July/August 2005).

22 Charles J. Dunlap Jr, "We Still Need the Big Guns," *The New York Times*, January 9, 2008.

23 Edward Luttwak, "Dead End: Counterinsurgency Warfare as Military Malpractice," *Harper's Magazine*, February 2007. Available at: http://www.harpers.org/archive/2007/02/0081384. See the response by David Kilcullen at http://smallwarsjournal.com/blog/2007/04/edward-luttwaks-counterinsurge-1.

24 Ralph Peters, "Myths of Counterinsurgency: How Pop Delusions Prevent Effective Operations," *Armchair General* (September 2007), 10.

25 Bob Woodward, "Why Did Violence Plummet? It Wasn't Just the Surge," *The Washington Post*, September 8, 2008, A09, available at: http://www.washingtonpost.com/wp-dyn/content/article/2008/09/07/AR2008090701847_pf.html. See Max Boot, "More on Woodward," *Commentary Magazine*, September 8, 2008, available at: www.commentarymagazine.com/blogs/index.php/category/contentions?author_name=boot.

26 Interview, 2008. Notes in possession of the author.

27 John R. Galvin, "Uncomfortable Wars: Toward a New Paradigm," *Parameters*, Vol. 16, No. 4 (Winter 1986), 6.

28 Thanks to Col. Steve Fondacaro, US Army (Retd) for this observation.

29 Paul Dresch, *Tribes, Government and History in Yemen*, Oxford: Clarendon Press, 1989. Christopher Boehm, *Blood Revenge: The Anthropology of Feuding in Montenegro and Other Societies*, Lawrence: University of Kansas Press, 1984. Roger V. Gould, "Collective Violence and Group Solidarity: Evidence from a Feuding Society," *American Sociological Review*, Vol. 64, No. 3 (1999), 356–80.

30 Anonymous US Army captain quoted in Michael Hirsh, "Blood and Honor," *Newsweek*, February 2, 2004.

31 Isaiah (Ike) Wilson III, "Thinking Beyond War: Civil-Military Operational Planning in Northern Iraq," unpublished paper, 2004, 46.

32 Col. Martin P. Schweitzer, US Army, Statement Before the House Armed Services Committee, Terrorism & Unconventional Threats Sub-Committee and the Research & Education Sub-Committee of the Science & Technology Committee, United States House of Representatives, 110th Congress, 2nd Session, Hearings on the Role of the Social and Behavioral Sciences in National Security, April 24, 2008.

33 Ibid.

34 Interview, 2008. Notes in possession of the author.

35 Interview, 2008. Notes in possession of the author.

36 Interview, 2008. Notes in possession of the author.

37 Interview, 2008. Notes in possession of the author.

38 Stephen Peter Rosen, "Military Effectiveness: Why Society Matters," *International Security*, Vol. 19, No. 4 (Spring 1995), 5–31.

39 Interview, 2006. Notes in possession of the author.

40 Derek J. Harvey, "A Red Team Perspective in the Insurgency in Iraq," in John J. McGrath (ed.), *An Army at War: Change in the Midst of Conflict*, Fort Leavenworth, KS: Combat Studies Institute Press, 2005.

41 Thanks to Michael V. Bhatia for this observation.

42 Frank Kitson, *Bunch of Five*, London: Faber & Faber, 1977, p. 283.

43 *Small Wars Manual* Fleet Marine Force Reference Publication 12-25, Sunflower University Press, July 1940, p. 15.

44 FM 3-24, p. 1-1; see also the section "Political Factors Are Primary," p. 1-123.

45 Thomas X. Hammes, "Rethinking the Principles of War: The Future of Warfare," in Anthony D. McIvor (ed.), *Rethinking the Principles of War*, Annapolis, MD: Naval Institute Press, 2005, p. 273.

46 For an excellent treatment of the Somalia crisis, see Robert F. Baumann and Lawrence A. Yates with Versalle F. Washington, *"My Clan Against the World": US and Coalition Forces in Somalia, 1992–1994*, Fort Leavenworth, KS: Combat Studies Institute Press, 2003.

47 US Department of Defense, JP 3-06, Doctrine for Joint Urban Operations, Washington, DC: Government Printing Office, September 16, 2002, III-10.

48 Kenneth Allard, *Somalia Operations: Lessons Learned*, Washington, DC: National Defense University Press, 1995, p. 95.

49 Harold E. Bullock, "Peace By Committee Command and Control Issues in Multinational Peace Enforcement Operations," thesis, School of Advanced Airpower Studies, Maxwell Air Force Base, AL, pp. 67, 93–4.

50 Tamara Duffey, "Cultural Issues in Contemporary Peacekeeping," *International Peacekeeping*, Vol. 7 (Spring 2000), 142–68.

51 Zinni, "Non-Traditional Military Missions, p. 268.

52 Ken Booth, *Strategy and Ethnocentrism*, New York: Holmes & Meier, 1979, p. 15.

53 Peter Morton, *Emergency Tour: 3 Para in South Armagh*, Wellingborough: Willaim Kimber and Co., 1989, p. 68.

54 Interview, 2006. Notes in possession of the author.

55 Booth, *Strategy and Ethnocentrism*, p. 98.

56 Rajiv Chandrasekaran, *Imperial Life in the Emerald City*, New York: Alfred A. Knopf, 2006, pp. 73–5.

57 Quoted in Michael R. Gordon and Bernard E. Trainor, *Cobra II: The Inside Story of the Invasion and Occupation of Iraq*, New York: Pantheon Books, 2006, p. 463.

58 Faleh A. Jabar, "Sheikhs and Ideologues: Deconstruction and Reconstruction of Tribes under Patrimonial Totalitarianism in Iraq, 1968–1998," in Faleh Jabar and Hosham Dawod (eds), *Tribes and Power: Nationalism and Ethnicity in the Middle East*, London: Saqi, 2003, pp. 69–110.

59 Michael Hirsh, "'If I Had to Do It Over Again': Condi Rice Admits the US Should have Understood Iraq Better," *Newsweek*, November 8, 2007.

60 The Islamic historian Ibn Khaldun (AD 1332–95) first noted the conflict between tribe and state. F. Rosenthal (ed. and trans.), *Ibn Khaldûn, The Muqaddimah*, Princeton, NJ: Princeton University Press, 1967, p. 124. See also Fred Donner, *The Early Islamic Conquests*, Princeton, NJ: Princeton University Press, 1981; Tom Nieuwenhuis, *Politics and Society in Early Modern Iraq*, Boston: Martinus Nijhoff, 1981; Chase F. Robinson, *Empire and Elites After the Muslim Conquest: The Transformation of Northern Mesopotamia*, New York: Cambridge University Press, 2000; M.A. Cook (ed.), *A History of the Ottoman Empire to 1730*, Cambridge: Cambridge University Press, 1976; Charles Tripp, *A History of Iraq*, Cambridge: Cambridge University Press, 2000; Dina Rizk Khoury, *State and Provincial Society in the Ottoman Empire: Mosul, 1540–1834*, Cambridge: Cambridge University Press, 1997; Hanna Batatu, *The Old Social Classes and the Revolutionary Movements of Iraq*, Princeton, NJ: Princeton University Press, 1978.

61 Interview, 2004. Notes in possession of the author.

62 The same mistake has arguably been made in Afghanistan: "The paradigm that has formed the backbone of the international effort since 2003—extending the reach of the central government—is in fact precisely the wrong strategy . . . Afghan identity is rooted in the woleswali: the districts within each province that are typically home to a single clan or tribe." (Thomas H. Johnson and M. Chris Mason, "All Counterinsurgency Is Local," *The Atlantic*, October 2008, available at: http://www.theatlantic.com/doc/200810/afghan.)

63 Clyde Kluckhohn, *Mirror for Man: The Relation of the Anthropology to Modern Life*, New York: Whittlesey House, 1949, p. 190.

64 Ibid., p. 172.

65 Petraeus, "Learning Counterinsurgency" 2.

66 Brig. Nigel Aylwin-Foster of the British Army identified the US emphasis on conventional warfare: "the US Army has developed over time a singular focus on conventional warfare, of a particularly swift and violent style, which left it ill-suited to the kind of operation it encountered as soon as conventional warfare ceased to be the primary focus. . ." (Nigel Aylwin-Foster, "Changing the Army for Counterinsurgency Operations," *Military Review*, Vol. 85, No. 6 (November/December 2005), 9.)

67 Andrew J. Bacevich, "The Petraeus Doctrine," *The Atlantic*, October 2008.

15 Ethics

Sarah Sewall

The purpose and the conduct of counterinsurgency have critical ethical dimensions that are central to its success or failure. Counterinsurgency's ends and means are intertwined and dynamic in any struggle to suppress rebellion. A counterinsurgent's efforts are shaped by the enemy's goals and tactics. Any state that intervenes on behalf of another government to fight insurgency is constrained by both its allies and enemies in maintaining ethical standards in choice and conduct of war. A foreign power faces two central conundrums when it conducts counterinsurgency abroad: it cannot guarantee the justness of its cause, and can only seek to ensure the justness of its military actions by assuming greater risk.

Classical counterinsurgency theory teaches that success hinges upon the legitimacy of the host nation government, and that popular support is the central prize in this regard. However, competing ethical constructs lie beneath the ideological, ethnic, religious, or socioeconomic divisions at issue in a struggle over political legitimacy. Assumptions and claims about morality and value permeate an insurgency and its suppression in unequal ways.

The counterinsurgent's *cause* must be perceived by the indigenous population as moral in a fundamental sense. Yet by definition, the counterinsurgent is—or, in the case of an intervening power, has aligned itself with—a government already judged as failing by the rebelling population. To this population, the counterinsurgent is compromised from the start by its reason for being—the defense of the flawed regime.

The cause may also matter to citizens of the foreign counterinsurgent. The intervening power may have different values than those of the partner host nation government; indeed national values rarely align perfectly. Yet even when an intervention stems from a realist assessment of national interests, the cause to which the foreign counterinsurgent commits must be perceived by its own population as not immoral.[1] If the nature of the defended regime diverges too greatly from the values of the allied counterinsurgent government, domestic support within the latter state is unlikely to prove sustainable.

In addition, the *conduct* of the struggle—its moral syntax—significantly shapes the outcome of counterinsurgency. Here, the burden on counterinsurgents is far higher than it is on insurgents. Counterinsurgents are responsible for securing citizens using the resources and armed forces of a state. This combination of greater authority and capability creates higher expectations and responsibilities for government(s) than rebels.

The host nation government (and the foreign counterinsurgency forces that support it) must physically protect citizens. They must avoid creating new dangers and grievances as they provide physical security. They must do so while confronting an enemy unburdened by these sensibilities and, worse, able to exploit them against the counterinsurgents.

Guerrillas violate established laws and norms as they prosecute their rebellion. They break rules in the very act of using violence to overthrow the existing order; beyond this, their violations in the conduct of war vary only by degree. The insurgent easily devolves from an outlaw challenging the state's monopoly of violence to also rejecting the laws of armed conflict established by states to constrain their use of violence. Given the insurgent's status as outsider, this progressive rejection of rules and standards costs relatively little.

Yet because of the different expectations of and responsibilities on the counterinsurgents, their departure from laws and norms costs them more. The predominantly Western version of counterinsurgency is a population-centric approach, which has now been enshrined in contemporary American military doctrine.[2] Pursuant to this doctrine, military efforts in counterinsurgency focus on civilian protection. The physical destruction of the insurgent—while a vital element of counterinsurgency—is largely incidental to winning the support of the civilian population. By this logic, civilian harm in any form undermines mission success.

Therefore the traditional ethical and existing legal norms of civilian protection support the broad goals of the counterinsurgent. Avoiding civilian harm effectively makes ethical military behavior an operational imperative. Actions that can be justified in the name of effectiveness appear consistent with the normative rules. In theory, then, utilitarianism and deontology make their peace in counterinsurgency.

Yet there is a catch. Insurgents not only impose greater direct costs on the civilian population; their strategies and tactics often encourage counterinsurgents to fight in ways that are harmful to civilians. The most straightforward way for the host nation and its allies to resolve this conundrum is to require that counterinsurgent forces assume greater risk in their conduct of war. This is the burden that the insurgent imposes on the established powers. The moral asymmetry of counterinsurgency ensures that the host nation and its external partners will often fail to be perceived as fighting justly even though they perceive themselves as assuming additional risk in order to fight well.

Ethical points of departure

The Western approach to the moral conundrums of war is embodied in what has come to be called the Just War Ethic (JWE). It is not my goal to trace its origins or complexities here, but the JWE provides a useful touchstone for any discussion about the ethics of counter-insurgency. It is also the logic from which the international law of armed conflict is derived, and as such it has acquired broader legitimacy over time.

First and foremost, just war logic concerns the toleration, not the abolition, of war.[3] In exchange for accepting the legitimacy of war, the JWE seeks to create boundaries and delineate its occurrence and practice.

Just war thinking clearly delineates between the morality of a decision to wage war and the means by which war is waged. The *jus ad bellum*, the logic of reasons for going to war, has its own particular considerations. The *jus in bello* evaluation of war gives a separate consideration to the manner of fighting, quite apart from the justness of the cause. Thus it is possible for contemporary theorist Michael Walzer to argue that a particular German officer can be considered to have fought ethically during World War II. Even if a party's purposes are fundamentally immoral, by this logic its conduct can comport with ethical expectations about restraint and honor in war.

The JWE emerged in a particular cultural and political context. Its roots are European and Judeo-Christian. Developed by theologians in independent religious institutions as a critique of political violence, just war reasoning eventually came to defend the state and the Westphalian order. It implicitly assumes a rough degree of equality in capability and reciprocity in conduct of the warring parties. It is inherently conservative, enshrining the right of a ruler to preserve the regime and the right of an interstate system to regulate itself through violence.

The JWE therefore seems inadequate for addressing critical questions about modern counterinsurgency. When are challenges to a government's claim to state sovereignty legitimate? At what point do enemy *jus in bello* violations relieve counterinsurgents of those ethical or legal strictures? What obligations do outside powers owe foreign citizens when fighting on behalf of their government? These questions are not simply about the adequacy of a legal regime or moral construct, because the rules have become embedded in the Western view of professional warrior conduct. Moreover, without these moral boundaries, there is little to distinguish the counterinsurgent from the guerrilla he opposes.

Yet, as will be argued below, upholding these distinctions and retaining moral clarity is extremely difficult and costly. For this reason, the *jus in bello* question of how to fight ultimately should affect the *jus ad bellum* choice of whether to fight a counterinsurgency at all. For if the choice of war is fundamentally compromised—particularly if the embattled host nation government lacks legitimacy, or refuses to take meaningful steps to regain it— then regardless of the foreign counterinsurgent's level of sacrifice, the cause may be lost.

This places a special burden on civilians who choose to commit their forces to fight on behalf of another nation's legitimacy. It also demands continual vigilance regarding the attitudes and actions of the host nation government; essentially a constant conditionality of external support. If the intervening power commits itself to the point that the host nation government can do no wrong, or the intervening power takes responsibility for success, then the external ally has turned itself into a hostage.

Counterinsurgency therefore hinges on the *jus ad bellum* choice as much as the *jus in bello* conduct. It is not just that counterinsurgency demands greater sacrifice; it is that the ultimate effectiveness of that sacrifice ultimately may depend more on the host nation government than on the conduct of the foreign nation. This burden of responsibility transcends the responsibilities of soldiers, yet they will bear its costs.

Difficulties of fighting well

The most glaring ethical challenges in counterinsurgency fall under the umbrella of "battlefield ethics"—the conduct of military operations. It is important to acknowledge that the application of violence in counterinsurgency is only part of the ethical landscape. Because counterinsurgency is so political in character, so invasive by design, and so complex, it raises countless other ethical questions. This chapter, though, is principally concerned with the military aspects of fighting counterinsurgency.

To be considered ethical, military operations must respect humanitarian principles including distinction, proportionality, and military necessity. Combatants must target only combatants and they must refrain from causing excessive civilian suffering even where pursuing legitimate military ends. Yet the application of these principles is often contested even in conventional conflicts between states. In counterinsurgency, the very meaning of the principles is thrown into question.

How does the requirement to distinguish between combatants and civilians apply to the young child who serves as a target "spotter," a woman who sews a suicide bomb vest, or an insurgent without a uniform or an identifiable chain of command? What is a proportionate use of force when the insurgent plans his operations to force counterinsurgents to cause excessive civilian harm? How should one judge military necessity in a fight that is predominantly political?

It is appropriate to consider insurgents responsible for the moral harms that their actions have indirectly caused. The guerrilla shares responsibility for civilians killed because he stored ammunition in a school, making it a legitimate target, or because the cell leader was sleeping surrounded by his family when the bomb dropped on his home. But counterinsurgent attempts to shift all moral blame onto the insurgent inevitably fall short.

From the insurgent's perspective, however, the moral equation looks different. Any moral claims used to justify targeting non-combatants dramatically depart from the ethical constructs adopted by states. The insurgent's cause alone may suffice to justify whatever means he uses, in a strictly utilitarian sense. In the act of rebellion, military necessity assumes an entirely different cast. Insurgents likely regard the JWE and its most highly articulated incarnation—the Law of Armed Conflict—as additional tools of oppression serving the existing political order. As a result, the insurgent does not see himself as bound by the norms of discourse and even behavior that have evolved among established states in the self-interested regulation of their common capacities for violence.

The resulting problems for the counterinsurgent are threefold. First, despite the insurgent's direct role in causing civilian harm, the counterinsurgent can be viewed as complicit in imposing that harm. Returning fire in the mosque, although perfectly justified by law and the JWE, will tarnish the counterinsurgent. When foreign bullets kill civilians the foreigners are seen as at least partly responsible, regardless of the circumstances. The relative contribution of the insurgent does not eliminate the ethical responsibilities of the counterinsurgent, and as a practical matter, the distinctions may be lost altogether in the eyes of the affected civilian population.

Second, the insurgent indirectly causes the counterinsurgent to kill civilians simply through the threat environment that the insurgent creates. The guerrilla's tactics exponentially increase the likelihood that counterinsurgents will mistake non-combatants for combatants. Because the insurgent won't identify himself, any human being is a potential combatant. No longer able to distinguish threats reliably, the counterinsurgent fears providing the benefit of the doubt to persons who appear to be civilians. Insurgents need not be anywhere in the vicinity to induce counterinsurgents to kill civilians inadvertently.

Third, the responsibility of the host nation government to provide security for the population means that civilian harm reflects poorly on the government, regardless of its specific causes. Through their failure to prevent insurgent activity, counterinsurgents are seen as indirectly responsible even for those civilian deaths directly caused by insurgents. Any civilian casualties disproportionately harm counterinsurgent forces. That is, after all, why the insurgent adopts such heinous tactics.

One might assume that such behavior undermines the insurgent's moral standing, and consequently his cause, much as it does for the counterinsurgent. Yet the insurgent's strategic goal of demonstrating government failure to provide security partially cushions the ethical blowback. In addition, the relative paucity of his means appears to shield the insurgent from some degree of moral accountability for his actions. The counterinsurgent, particularly the foreign counterinsurgent, generally has larger forces, better equipment, and advanced technology. Government forces see from afar or at night and can fire from long distances, sometimes without ever placing their own forces at risk, as in the use of unmanned aerial vehicles. Those sympathetic to the insurgent cause must ask how the insurgents could otherwise have a chance in the face of such power. Counterinsurgent capabilities also increase popular expectations that counterinsurgents can spare civilian harm, and that any failure to do so is purposeful.

This phenomenon is imperceptible to most Western observers steeped in the vocabulary of international humanitarian law. They see clear distinctions between collateral damage from a carefully planned air strike and the civilians that a suicide bomber kills in a marketplace. These distinctions may be irrelevant to the people affected by the carnage.

This is not to say that insurgents are immune to the counterproductive aspects of particular tactics that result in deaths of civilians. In fact, al-Qaeda in Iraq suffered from its focus on targeting civilians, which came to be seen by locals as anti-Iraqi. But because insurgent tactics have systemic effects on the overall conduct of war by all sides, the insurgents are shielded from bearing the full measure of accountability for civilian harm while the counterinsurgent bears more than his share.

Playing by the rules is therefore no panacea because the counterinsurgent is held responsible for the *effects* of his actions as well as those of the enemy. In the JWE and international law, intention is critical in parsing the ethical status of harm. It means something to have intended to harm only the enemy, not the civilian; it is a necessary, albeit not sufficient, aspect of fighting well. But these facts, however central to the counterinsurgent's judgments, offer little practical advantage in a counterinsurgency. The local population will judge the counter-insurgent efforts largely by their perceived impact. So the impact of civilian casualties—their effect on the confidence and support of the population—may be harmful operationally even if those casualties can be justified through Western ethical reasoning.

Responding to moral asymmetry

What is the solution, then, to this moral asymmetry? Fulfilling the traditional moral obligations in the face of an enemy that rejects them essentially requires the counterinsurgent to assume greater responsibility for civilian harm. In essence, the *operational* imperatives of counter-insurgency set the bar even higher than ethical reasoning demands for preventing, minimizing, and responding to civilian casualties. These heightened costs reflect the requirements of mission success—not normative niceties.

This dynamic is evident in the December 2006 US Army/Marine Corps Field Manual, *Counterinsurgency* (FM 3-24). The manual stresses the centrality of civilian protection and demands that counterinsurgent forces assume greater risk to achieve mission success. If civilian protection is mission-essential, the lives of foreign civilians effectively assume priority over the lives of counterinsurgents. Over the longer term, the requirement for greater risk assumption enhances both mission success and force protection.

This prioritization of protection of others—people outside the forces—is hardly unique to counterinsurgency. Secret Service agents subordinate their own lives to the protection of others when they take their oaths. Some military missions, such as the extraction of Americans from hostilities abroad (a non-combatant evacuation operation, or NEO), effectively privilege the lives of those being rescued over the safety of the soldiers assigned the mission. In these cases, protection of others is the mission, the very purpose of the professional. And the professional does not choose the nationality of those he protects. Still, a focus on protecting rather than destroying, and on protecting civilians rather than friendly forces, remains a radical departure from the dominant American military mindset.

The American military tradition has long emphasized the substitution of technology and firepower for manpower. The 1980s Weinberger-Powell doctrine of overwhelming force epitomized this approach. The American way of war did not eliminate risk to US armed forces. But US capabilities evolved to allow its forces to identify and attack targets from a distance that enemies could rarely match, dramatically altering the odds and risks of conventional combat. To illustrate the point, the US-led coalition killed some 20,000 Iraqi combatants during the 1991 Persian Gulf War,[4] while losing 246 coalition forces. While the evolution of military capabilities reduced US casualties, it also allowed American forces to reduce civilian casualties as well.

Civilian protection has long been considered a concern of the warrior, but it had never been preeminent. In the military vernacular, the mission comes first. The safety of the other men (and women) serving in uniform is also critical; they are a personal responsibility of commanders and a means to the end of accomplishing the mission. The civilian is obliquely embedded within the military hierarchy through the law of armed conflict and related training and education. But in the context of conventional war, the civilian did not feature prominently. In Cold War exercises focused on armies clashing on the German plains, the civilian was largely assumed away.

During the 1990s, the civilian began to take on increased prominence. The Law of Armed Conflict (LOAC) requires a minimum standard of non-combatant protection, but the US military started using technology and tactics to go beyond minimalist LOAC requirements, providing greater safety for civilians on the battlefield. After Operation Desert Storm, the US Air Force in particular began to look more closely at how the use of force affected industrial targets, and by extension civilians. Minimizing collateral damage became a recognized objective on the strategic air planning side, albeit one that sometimes competed with accomplishing the mission and with the safety of pilots. Increasing interest in ground operations in urban settings also expanded awareness of the civilian in war, and helped to insert the civilian directly into the Army's planning processes.

Sustained engagement in the crucible of counterinsurgency has pushed into the military mainstream a process that had already haltingly begun. Yet even in Iraq and Afghanistan, the US was slow to recognize the challenge it faced, and its responses have been largely reactive and driven by individual leaders. Whether these adaptations, including FM 3-24, will outlast current operations remains uncertain.

Operational aspects of minimizing harm

There are at least three aspects of minimizing civilian harm that deserve systemic attention as we examine the special challenges of counterinsurgency through the lens of contemporary American experience. These are: prevention, assessment, and response, considered in turn below. In my view, each aspect of addressing civilian harm is worthy of institutionalizing in military operations generally—although it is in counterinsurgency that their value is most easily recognized.

First, harm should be prevented. One of the more significant developments has been the widespread promulgation of escalation of force (EOF) measures, an overlay on the Rules of Engagement, to more carefully regulate the use of force. The EOF procedures were designed to address the challenge of distinguishing between those who intended harm and those who did not. They required a graduated use of force (the condensed version is to shout before shooting) in order to allow for determination of hostile status. They aimed to allow soldiers to gain control of a situation earlier, to essentially test the subjects with whom they were engaged, and to buy time to fully assess the situation before using deadly force. In essence, they sought to move military procedures toward policing procedures, with the goal of minimizing unintended harm. They aimed to reconcile force protection with civilian protection, although many debated whether they unduly restricted soldier's self-defense prerogatives.[5] It is noteworthy that a handbook for widespread use was not developed until July 2007.[6]

Significant changes in prevention of casualties often appear to have been driven or accelerated by a sensational event. One such incident was the accidental killing of the Italian intelligence agent Nicolas Calipari in March 2005. Escorting a rescued Italian journalist hostage to the airport, Calipari was shot dead as his vehicle was approaching a hastily assembled roadblock. The ensuing international controversy resulted in a military investigation that recommended changes to standard operating procedures, equipment packages, and unit training related to checkpoints.[7] This was a positive development. But given the numbers of Iraqi civilians that coalition forces had mistakenly killed in approaching vehicles, the real question was why it had taken so long to ensure a sensible common US approach toward checkpoints and roadblocks.

Over time, information about enemy tactics and adjustments for counterinsurgency warfare made its way into changes for preparing forces to fight. Unit commanders prepared different types of predeployment training focusing on EOF and scenarios involving civilians. A counterinsurgency academy was developed in Iraq to help new arrivals better understand their operating environment and the special demands of counterinsurgency. The national training centers also began to adapt, gradually phasing out the big armored scenarios and simulating the tactical dilemmas that soldiers and Marines would face, replete with Iraqi role-players. The trainers changed their metrics of success to include consideration of how military operations affected the civilians on the battlefield. Eventually, even the education side of military preparation for war began to adapt, moving counterinsurgency into core courses expected of graduates prepared to face the challenges of the twenty-first century.

Adaptation on the prevention side has occurred gradually and often unevenly. This is because the preparation and conduct of counterinsurgency is filtered through the lenses of individual field commanders who retain enormous latitude to respond to the changing combat environment. Thus it was often said in military circles that some battalion commanders and company commanders "got it" and others did not. The constant need to learn and improvise in counterinsurgency demanded individual latitude, but this did not necessarily ensure that leaders rose to the occasion. The role of leadership received greater attention after the military began to assess more systematically the actual behavior of forces in Iraq.[8]

Second, harm should be properly assessed. One of the most significant developments with regard to ethical challenges in counterinsurgency is the US military's willingness to evaluate its performance through data. Gradually, assessment of civilian harm—a task that American armed forces had specifically rejected for decades—has become an accepted element of mission assessment.

Data collection was standardized for a subset of incidents in which civilians are killed or wounded, as when in 2005 Lieutenant General John R. Vines, leader of Multi-National Force-Iraq (MNF-I), ordered the routine recording of the numbers of civilians killed at checkpoints and in other "escalation of force" incidents. The data were compiled across the theater and reviewed weekly as a means of identifying potential problems. Eventually, significant data points were being used to automatically trigger further inquiry.

Commanders saw these investigations as a means of understanding causality, allowing for corrective action or increased understanding of the incident. This approach made inquiry routine and decoupled the notion of investigation from the implication of criminal liability, much as a friendly fire investigation aims first and foremost to fix the problem rather than affix blame. In some cases, commanders were able to correlate suicide attacks and collateral damage incidents. Sometimes a particular leader or unit might be identified as requiring additional training. The data provided increased awareness of those time periods or cases in which additional restraint might be required, and allowed commanders to intervene as appropriate. The net result was a significant decrease in incidents of inadvertent civilian deaths in EOF incidents.[9]

This concrete assessment of civilian harm and affirmation of the need to focus efforts on reducing civilian casualties was only reinforced by a 2006 survey of Americans fighting in Iraq. Some 1600 soldiers and Marines were asked probing questions about their attitudes and actions toward civilians. Commanders were surprised by the relatively high percentage that seemed unable to internalize the practice of counterinsurgency as protecting the civilian population.

Almost 10 percent of American servicemen surveyed said they had mistreated civilians (by kicking them, damaging their possessions without cause, etc.). Less than half the troops interviewed even thought that civilians should be treated with dignity and respect, and less than half said they would report a team member's unethical behavior toward civilians. This assessment was revealing, particularly in suggesting a failure of military leaders to articulate the ethical requirements of counterinsurgency.[10]

General David H. Petraeus had just arrived in Baghdad as the commander of the MNF-I when the first battlefield ethics survey was released. He turned it into an opportunity to model and call for leadership, composing a letter to everyone in the theater. "This fight depends on securing the population, which must understand that we—not our enemies—occupy the moral high ground," he wrote.[11] "Seeing a fellow trooper killed by a barbaric enemy can spark frustration, anger, and a desire for immediate revenge," he empathized. "As hard as it might be, however, we must not let these emotions lead us—or our comrades in arms— to commit hasty, illegal actions . . . What sets us apart from our enemies . . . is how we behave."[12]

When General David H. Petreaus provided his highly anticipated assessment of Operation Iraqi Freedom in September 2007, the numbers of civilian casualties featured prominently as evidence of the success of the "surge."[13] Civilian casualty figures remain highly sensitive.[14] Yet after decades of insisting that the US military does not do "body counts," the change of attitude is important and hopeful. Quantifying actions and attitudes regarding non-combatants has proven a critical tool for commanders to monitor efforts and success in counterinsurgency.

Third, the response to harm should be the correct one. The fact of civilian harm is not the end of the matter, ethically or operationally. In addition to learning about the causes of the incident in order better to prevent collateral damage in the future, there is value in providing some form of amends for the harm itself.

US forces have used many different responses to defuse civilian anger in the event of collateral damage: providing medical care to the injured, aiding the affected community, offering apologies, ensuring proper burials, honoring the dead, and providing direct compensation to family survivors are all forms of making amends. Another potential form of redress is justice—the prosecution of wrongful death and injury. Military prosecutions are pursued only when initial investigations give rise to concerns about criminal action. Given the complexities of counterinsurgency, these prosecutions remain relatively rare and guilty verdicts rarer still. Yet even non-judicial amends remain surprisingly controversial.

Sensitivity to any admission of "guilt" has long been a barrier to providing official compensation to civilians on the battlefield, and has in turn impeded the language of apology. Although the United States has long provided financial compensation to civilians disrupted by routine peacetime or non-combat activities, the US military considers civilian harm in combat operations to be a separate case.[15] But such a process is not possible in the case of victims of an air strike against the wrong home.

In such a case, the military can offer victims *ex gratia* payments—a voluntary gesture of goodwill. Increasingly, US military leaders have used unit funds or the Commander's Emergency Response Program (CERP) funds to provide financial or other assistance in response to unintended civilian harm. Since these options are discretionary, their use has depended in large part upon the local commander. The same is true of whether a military leader decides to attend a funeral, evacuate a severely injured civilian, or build a school in response to acknowledged civilian harm.

Anecdotal evidence suggests that financial compensation, especially when combined with apology, may be the most effective route to reducing local anger toward counterinsurgent forces.[16] Yet different approaches to redress, including amounts of *ex gratia* payments, can breed frustration among the local population. Many observers have called for a more systematic and consistent approach to financial compensation. Indeed, a broader examination of the importance of redress and amends in counterinsurgency is in order.

Many challenges are associated with providing compensation of any kind. There is political resistance to appearing to take responsibility for deaths that may be directly or indirectly caused by illegal enemy actions. It is onerous and uncertain to corroborate or refute facts, seeking to determine truth. Redress consumes time and personnel that could be devoted to providing additional security. Further, amends are arguably not the job of the military at all. Yet many commanders see value in them, particularly during a protracted counterinsurgency.

This is not simply a matter of "buying off" local anger to make life easier for the unit, although the short-term instrumental benefits can be significant. There may be particular cultural reasons to provide financial or other compensation. Where the practice is deeply ingrained and highly ritualized, its absence is a grave insult in its own right, a second civilian "harm" from which the counterinsurgent must recover.

Because counterinsurgency is a predominantly political campaign, it demands a more proactive and consistent approach to redressing civilian harm. Civilian confidence and trust in the government and its allies is critical for success. Redress for unintended harm can help repair the damage when actions do not correspond with words. Making amends speaks to the true intent of the US military and its allies. Right intent is, after all, a key attribute to which counterinsurgents cling in the midst of the moral chaos in which they must operate. Redress is a means of attempting to make it visible to the victims and survivors.

There are other important reasons to take redress seriously, including the psychological health of individual soldiers and Marines and the cohesion and effectiveness of the unit. Collateral damage is by definition harm that combatants would have preferred to avoid. Knowingly killing innocent people, even when of necessity, is damaging to an individual. There is some evidence that post-traumatic stress disorder is correlated with the perception of having harmed a non-combatant.

Soldiers and Marines' sense of professionalism and honor is fundamentally undermined by a form of warfare in which the distinction between warrior and terrorist appears to slip away.[17] There are anecdotal accounts of grievous results when combatants return home without confidence in that distinction.[18] Since it violates a warrior's sensibility to kill the innocent, the conduct of counterinsurgency must take this into account in the field, not simply in mental health counseling back at home. Amends can be powerful for the individual who caused the harm as well as important to the victim and survivors.

Redefining warfare

When General Petraeus returned to Iraq for the third time as MNF-I commander, he predicted a tough fight as he sought to change the failing ground game. He directed the "surge" of additional US forces into Baghdad and he began implementing the tenets of the new counterinsurgency Field Manual that he had just published. Petraeus coordinated and rebalanced kinetic and non-kinetic activities and ensured that politics remained central in the fight. He supported proactive efforts to make amends another critical battlefield tool. But perhaps the critical variable in the strategy was a greater assumption of risk in both operational design and tactical conduct in order to protect the civilian population.

American casualties initially stayed high as the numbers of American forces increased and the operational strategy in Baghdad changed. But the relative stability that followed, and the associated reduction in US and civilian Iraqi casualties, affirmed the central premise behind greater risk assumption in counterinsurgency. A willingness to conduct operations differently reduced long-term risk to the force and strengthened the prospects for mission success.

This remains the nub of the ethical challenge and the most difficult aspect of institutional change. Stated too baldly, the demand to assume more risk—the notion that sacrifice of American combatant lives for foreign civilians is a military necessity—could paralyze troops and eventually undermine recruitment of an all-volunteer force. Yet without being stated fully and directly, the messages may not break through, even when the larger point is that short-term risk is the best route to assuring troop safety and mission accomplishment in the longer term.

The schoolhouse ought to be at the forefront of articulating this argument. Yet even here, the fundamental implications of counterinsurgency are often left vague. A chapter in a seminal Army book on professionalism struggles to make the difficult point about risk assumption, but stops short of clarity.[19] The case study, a common mode of teaching about the most difficult ethical dilemmas, by design leaves room for debate about the proper answer. Consider a case study about the incident in Haditha in which US forces killed 24 Iraqi civilians under highly questionable circumstances. A meaningful case study would consider the killings themselves, not just the alleged cover-up of the incident. It would explore issues of loyalty to soldiers, obligations to civilians and the meaning of professional honor. It would also rule out equivocation, for if the events at Haditha were not wrong, what is? Where organizations are seeking to change a culture, even-handed treatment risks being misconstrued as institutional ambivalence. Moreover, when incidents are explored on a case-by-case basis, larger patterns of activities and more important lessons can be lost entirely.

It may be impossible to quantify the vigilance, sacrifice, and empathy that counter-insurgency demands of its practitioners, but it is possible for the leaders of the armed forces to signal expectations. Military institutions send unmistakable messages through the choices about who to promote, how they train, and what they teach. Part of the solution lies in redefining what it means to be a warrior. Those who accept greater risk and show restraint on behalf of civilians should be celebrated, not suspect. They should not be accused of dereliction of duty if their calculated risks go sour. Instead they should receive medals and praise, just as honor is due the private who jumps on the grenade to save his fellow soldiers. This is the longer-term cultural challenge for the armed forces.

Counterinsurgency poses great and asymmetrical costs upon the counterinsurgent. It demands a willingness to evaluate one's own behavior closely, to accept greater risk in order to maintain an ethical keel, and to make amends when harms are inflicted. Without these actions, a civilian-centric counterinsurgency strategy is not sustainable as an operational matter because of the likelihood of alienating the indigenous population. It may not be sustainable as a political endeavor in a democracy where domestic political support may be a limited commodity. The ethical burden is forced upon the counterinsurgent by the enemy. But allies, too, can be a dangerous burden. Even the best-fought counterinsurgency will founder if the host nation government is illegitimate or unwilling to respond to the political realities of the insurgency.

The choice of war and the associated willingness to accept the risk are both ultimately political decisions, although they must be carried out by the military. And if the military has been hesitant, politicians, too, have been loath to accept the inherent costs and limits of counterinsurgency. A more complete military transformation will likely await clarity from political leaders about the priority of counterinsurgency in US military strategy. Let us hope that political leaders fully understand the implications of their choices.

Notes

1 An example would be the outrage within the United States about the Afghan government's passage of a law permitting marital rape. See, for example, Carlotta Gall and Sangar Rahimi, "Karzai Vows to Review Family Law," *The New York Times*, April 4, 2009.
2 The US Army/Marine Corps Field Manual, *Counterinsurgency* (FM 3-24).
3 Michael Walzer, *Just and Unjust Wars*, New York: Basic Books, 1977, p. 45.
4 Alastair Finlan, *The Gulf War 1991*, Oxford: Osprey Publishing, 2003, p. 85.
5 Kyndra Rotunda, "Denying Self-Defense to GIs in Iraq," *Christian Science Monitor*, March 2, 2007.
6 Escalation of Force Handbook, United States Army Center for Army Lessons Learned, July 21, 2007.
7 AR-15-6: Investigation into the shooting of Nicolas Calipari, an Italian intelligence officer, and the wounding of Guiliana Sgrena, an Italian journalist, Multi-National Force-Iraq, April 29, 2005.
8 See Sarah Sewall, "Leading Warriors in the Long War," in Robert Taylor, William E. Rosenbach and Erich B. Rosenbach (eds), *Military Leadership: In Pursuit of Excellence*, Boulder, CO: Westview Press, 2008.
9 Greg Jaffe, "U.S. Curbs Iraqi Civilian Deaths in Checkpoint, Convoy Incidents," *The Wall Street Journal*, June 6, 2006.
10 According to the 2006 Mental Health Advisory Team report released by the Army Medical Department, one third of Marines and one quarter of soldiers said their leaders did not tell them not to mistreat civilians. The follow-on survey in 2007 did not show appreciable change in any of the relevant indices. The 2008 survey is not available at the time of this writing. The reports may be found at http://www.armymedicine.army.mil/reports/mhat/mhat.html.
11 The letter was released May 10, 2007, available at http://www.centcom.mil/images/petraeus archive/08-%2010%20may%202007%20%20gen%20petraeus%20letter%20about%20values.pdf.
12 Ibid.
13 General Petraeus' report may be found at http://foreignaffairs.house.gov/110/pet091007.pdf.
14 See, for example, "Army officer arrested over 'leak,'" BBC News, February 4, 2009.
15 The Foreign Claims Act outlines the process for compensating foreign nationals who have suffered personal injury, death, or damage to property as a result of non-combat activities of the United States armed forces. 10 USC Sec. 2734.
16 For a detailed discussion of this issue in an Afghan context, see E.L. Gaston and Rebecca Wright, *Losing the People: The Costs and Consequences of Civilian Suffering in Afghanistan*, Washington, DC: Campaign for Innocent Victims in Conflict, 2009, pp. 31–47.
17 Surveys suggest a connection between exposure to violence, including the inadvertent killing of civilians, and mental health difficulties. See for example, C.W. Hoge et al., "Combat Duty in Iraq and Afghanistan, Mental Health Problems, and Barriers to Care," *The New England Journal of Medicine*, Vol. 351, No. 1 (July 1, 2004). The mental health impact of civilian harm upon combatants deserves greater study.
18 Scott Allen, "Rally's Veterans, Activists Seek to Avoid Glorifying War," *The Boston Globe*, May 27, 2008.
19 See Tony Pfaff, "Military Ethics in Complex Contingencies," in D.M. Snider and L.J. Matthews (eds), *The Future of the Army Profession*, Boston: McGraw-Hill, 2005.

16 Information operations

Andrew Exum

In Part II the operational aspects of counterinsurgency were covered, often in isolation of information operations. Contemporary US counterinsurgency doctrine, however, either considers information operations to be a separate line of operations within many or the "sheath" within which all lines of operation are woven. The past decade, in fact, has seen a rise in the degree to which counterinsurgents and guerrilla groups alike profess to take information operations seriously. Guerrilla groups, especially, have made effective use of the new media—the Internet and cell phone technology especially—to conduct what David Kilcullen has called "armed propaganda campaigns."

Counterinsurgent forces have been less effective with information operations. Much of this failure can be chalked up to the degree to which counterinsurgency forces are primarily comprised of military forces, for which the "war of ideas" comes less naturally than finding and killing the enemy. In neither Afghanistan nor Iraq, for example, have information operations ever realistically been made the "main effort" of an operation or strategy. Information operations, in the traditional view, are designed to support combat operations and not vice versa. The bulk of the counterinsurgent forces' resources and personnel are dedicated not to information operations but toward other lines of operation. This allocation of resources is at odds with contemporary doctrine such as The US Army/Marine Corps Field Manual, *Counterinsurgency* (FM 3-24).

The purpose of this chapter is to illustrate information operations in counterinsurgency. It does so by highlighting a typical problem: a disconnect between the counterinsurgent's theory and the insurgent's practice. The most elaborate doctrine and the most sophisticated debates on the subject are more likely to be found among Western counterinsurgent forces. They have the resources to invest in theory. Not so the insurgent: the most impressive and the most innovative *practical* use of information operations is, for several reasons, more likely to be observed among insurgents, not counterinsurgents. The chapter therefore first looks at the counterinsurgent's *theory* of information operations and second at the insurgent's *practice*—and eventually asks what the first can learn from the latter. For the purpose, one of the most sophisticated and nimble resistance groups is examined in more detail: Hezbollah, as it could be observed in southern Lebanon between 1985 and 2006. "The Party of God" first waged an effective counterinsurgency campaign against the State of Israel and its Lebanese allies between 1985 and 2000, and then against Israel in the July War of 2006. Counterinsurgent forces have as much to learn from Israel's failures in information operations as they do from Hezbollah's successes. Most ominously, though the campaign in southern Lebanon is relatively recent, insurgent forces have grown significantly more sophisticated as they have made better use of the new media than Hezbollah was able to do in the 1990s.

The counterinsurgent's theory

In this book, information operations are considered to be the efforts made by one side to shape the narrative of the conflict to increase an advantage over the adversary—and to inspire one's own constituents while demoralizing the other. A good example of information operations in action comes from a bemused George Orwell, describing what often passed for trench warfare in the Spanish Civil War:

> . . . the real weapon was not the rifle but the megaphone. Being unable to kill your enemy you shouted at him instead. . . . On the Government side, in the party militias, the shouting of propaganda to undermine the enemy morale had been developed into a regular technique. In every suitable position, usually machine-gunners, were told off for shouting duty and provided with megaphones. Generally they shouted a set piece, full of revolutionary sentiments which explained to the Fascist soldiers that they were merely the hirelings of international capitalism, that they were fighting against their own class, etc., etc., and urged them to come over to our side. This was repeated over and over by relays of men; sometimes it continued almost the whole night. There is very little doubt that it had its effect; everyone agreed that the trickle of Fascist deserters was partly caused by it. . . . Of course such a proceeding does not fit in with the English conception of war. I admit I was amazed and scandalized when I first saw it done. The idea of trying to convert your enemy instead of shooting him![1]

The primacy of psychological operations in warfare—not the presence of psychological operations—is what scandalized Orwell. Militaries exist, in what he called the "English conception of war," to find, fix, and destroy the enemy's fighting forces—not to shout at each another with megaphones. But as we shall see, while war might be an act of force designed to compel the enemy to act according to one's will, violence is not the only means that can be employed toward that end. Most of the time, though, psychological operations are used in conjunction with combat operations. David Galula describes the way in which the Front de Libération Nationale (FLN), an insurgent group, targeted the Algerian population with propaganda during France's war in Algeria in the 1950s. Combat operations were, he writes,

> accompanied by intensive propaganda, supported from the outside by broadcasts from Morocco, Tunisia, Egypt, Iraq, Albanian, Hungary, and Soviet Russia, the total of which exceeded by five to one the output in Arabic of the French stations in Algeria and Metropolitan France. It was impossible to jam effectively this volume . . . Taking advantage of the credulity of the rural population FLN agents circulated fantastic rumors: "Nasser's planes have killed thousands of French soldiers at such and such place"; "Russian (or Chinese) volunteers are ready for Tunisia"; "The French put poison in the milk they give our boys at school so as to make them impotent."[2]

To most practitioners either of insurgency or counterinsurgency warfare, and to the classic theorists upon whom they base their understanding of counterinsurgency warfare, information operations are synonymous with propaganda and psychological operations. Traditional counterinsurgency theory holds that, in a counterinsurgency campaign, the insurgent is assumed to possess an advantage in that he can freely spread lies to further his aims or to undermine support for the counterinsurgent.

"The insurgent," writes Galula, "is free to use every trick; if necessary, he can lie, cheat, exaggerate. He is not obliged to prove. He is judged by what he promises, not by what he does."[3] The counterinsurgent, meanwhile, must always make his aims "clearly known to the people."[4] He is not allowed to misrepresent his intentions or actions. This propaganda strategy can be accurately summed up by the words of an American commander in Afghanistan: "having a good story to tell, and always telling the truth."[5]

Often, insurgents and counterinsurgents end up telling their stories to the media—friendly, neutral, and hostile; "old" and "new." The media, writes Rupert Smith, is "the source of the context in which the acts in the theatre are played out." In more detail:

> they do not make up the facts, but it is they who express and display them. In the theatre of war those on the stage and watching in the stands judge actions in the theatre within this context, and it is up to the planners to ensure that the audience via the media always remembers that there are at least two producers and two companies on the stage—not a single, mixed-up large one. That is why establishing the context of the event and getting the story correct from the start is so important. To act effectively one is trying to gain a position where the majority of the audience and people on the stage are following your script in the context, and not that of the opponent. *If you are fighting for the will of the people, however many tactical successes you achieve they will be as naught if the people do not think you are winning.*[6]

Information operations, however, are not all about managing the narrative of a conflict—though that's certainly a big part of the effort. The insurgent and counterinsurgent are given both an obligation and an opportunity with respect to their own popular support and that of their enemy. One has an obligation to preserve one's own popular support while at the same time seeking to undermine the enemy's. An effective non-state actor also uses effective information operations to increase his own power while weakening his enemy—often without a shot having been fired. This can be done through propaganda designed to strengthen one's position with one's constituency as well as propaganda designed to weaken the will of the enemy populace. Hezbollah employed both types of propaganda in its war with Israel.

On one level, contemporary theorists and practitioners of counterinsurgency warfare seem to understand information operations and spend a great deal of time stressing their importance. "In a battle against insurgents," writes John Nagl,

> persuading fighters to surrender and provide information on their comrades is much more effective than killing them; persuading the masses of the people that the government is capable of providing essential services—and of defeating the insurgents—is just as important.[7]

In 2004, the commanding general of the 1st Marine Division operating in Iraq, later an author of FM 3-24, dictated that all of his division's operations—combat operations, the development of Iraqi security forces, the provision of essential services—was to be underpinned by effective information operations.[8] One illustration in FM 3-24 imagines the operational design of a counterinsurgency campaign as resembling a rope: the strands of the rope include combat operations, the training and equipment of host nation security forces, the provision of essential services, the improvement of local government, and economic development. Wrapping around all these lines of operations, however, is a sheath of information operations.[9]

At the same time, however, the term "information operations" is often invoked and frequently mentioned as important but is rarely defined and seldom discussed in detail.

Information operations are never satisfactorily defined in FM 3-24, for example: as Frank Hoffman has noted, the manual considered cutting edge in the field of counterinsurgency theory gives information operations short shrift. The doctrinal document, he wrote,

> admits that the "Information environment is critical" and that "interconnectedness" gives the adversary new capabilities, but stops short of offering more than general guidance. Something that is "critical" should merit more than three pages of succinct comments.[10]

But part of what vexes theorists and practitioners is the very definition of information operations as it is employed by most Western militaries. The official definition offered up by the US Department of Defense, for example, is awkward and bears little relevance to that which field commanders in Iraq and Afghanistan are describing—much less to what Nagl described above. Information operations are defined by the US Department of Defense as:

> the integrated employment of electronic warfare, computer network operations, psychological operations, military deception, and operations security, in concert with specified supporting and related capabilities, to influence, disrupt, corrupt, or usurp adversarial human and automated decision making while protecting our own.[11]

Conducting psychological warfare does not, necessarily, have anything to do with disrupting an enemy's communications or computer network. The US Department of Defense definition, though, is trying to be all things to all people, and this conflation of psychological operations with counter-network operations is a common mistake made by many other Western militaries, resulting in great confusion. On the one hand, the definition used by the US military has taken the way in which information operations are imagined by proponents of net-centric warfare (counter-network operations, disruption of computer systems) and on the other hand has taken the way in which information operations are imagined by practitioners of counterinsurgency warfare (psychological warfare, managing the message) and has thrown them together with little concern as to whether or not they belong together. It makes a fundamental difference if the target is a set of machines or a human community.

This confusion perhaps illustrates the degree to which information operations are both still being defined and is misunderstood among Western militaries and governments: a Wikipedia search for "information operations" informs us that information operations are "an evolving discipline within the military."[12] Just how quickly this discipline is evolving, though, can be discerned from the differences noted in the US Army Field Manual 3-0, *Operations*, printed in June 2001, and the latest edition of FM 3-0, printed in February 2008.[13] FM 3-0 is perhaps the most important document in the US Army because it defines, at a basic level, how the organization operates. The inclusion of "stability operations" as a core task alongside "offense" and defense" in 2008 was considered to be an earth-shaking event within the US Army.

In the 2001 manual, information operations are mentioned few times and mostly in reference to network-centric operations as opposed to psychological operations or strategic communication. The February 2008 edition, meanwhile, which incorporates lessons learned from the counterinsurgency campaigns being fought in Iraq and Afghanistan, dedicates an entire chapter to "information superiority," which it defines as "the operational advantage derived from the ability to collect, process, and disseminate an uninterrupted flow of information while exploiting or denying an adversary's ability to do the same."[14] So more serious thought and doctrine is being devoted toward information even as the definition continues to vex theorists and practitioners alike. For the purposes of this book, information operations are understood as *all efforts taken to manage the narrative of combat.*

Effective information operations tend to have a number of characteristics: they employ friendly media to shape narrative (television, radio, newspapers, Internet); set the conditions for what constitutes "success" at the enemy's expense; focus on the morale and loyalty of all sides of the conflict (friendly, enemy, neutral); effectively manage relations with external media; and they create "spectacles" that help shape public perceptions.

Information operations are, in one sense but not entirely, the creation of a narrative. Since an entrenched narrative can have a powerful impact upon operations and can shape perceptions, the establishment of a narrative is often contested. Varying narratives offered by competing sides compete for acceptance. The US military, for example, labeled the Islamist militants who contributed to the campaign of suicide bombings that collapsed the country's social infrastructure from 2003 until 2007 as "terrorists." The militants themselves, however, styled themselves as "the resistance"—to what they saw as an illegal, reprehensible American-led occupation of a Muslim nation. The degree to which the greater Arab public remained largely indifferent to the attacks—which, more often than not, killed Iraqi civilians rather than American soldiers—reveals the extent to which the militants succeeded in establishing their narrative among the Arabic-speaking public over that offered by the Americans.

Information operations are also the effort taken to demoralize the enemy—such as those efforts taken by Orwell's comrades in the hills of Spain or the leaflets dropped on the Iraqi Army prior to the US-led ground assault in 1991—and the effort taken to boost the spirits and resilience of one's own compatriots. Nagl describes the British and Malayan information operations between 1948 and 1960 as a largely psychological, media-based campaign that included everything from highly effective air-dropped leaflets to less effective jeep-mounted loudspeakers (he was himself supplied with something along these lines while fighting in Baghdad in 2003).[15]

The counterinsurgent's doctrine on information operations, in sum, is often devised by well-paid senior leaders in front of a computer screen in air-conditioned offices. It tends to be theory heavy, top down, input oriented, terminologically sophisticated, and focused on quantifiable measures of progress.

The insurgent's practice

The insurgent's practice of information operations is sharply different: unpaid activists and fighters innovate there and then, in the midst of fighting for the "resistance." It tends to be practice driven, bottom up, output oriented, improvised, and in touch with the community's feelings and grievances.

Between 1982 and 2000, Israel and its allies occupied a swath of land in southern Lebanon designed to prevent the area from being used as a staging ground for attacks on northern Israel. The military occupation was unsuccessful and ended with an Israeli withdrawal in May 2000. Israel's most deadly adversary during the 1990s was Hezbollah, a Shia militant group dedicated to armed "resistance" against the State of Israel. Much of Hezbollah's success, though, can be attributed to the way in which it "outfought" Israel along the line of information operations.

To understand Hezbollah's information operations, a brief look at the public affairs policies of Israel and its army is helpful. The Israel Defense Forces (IDF), usually focused on the military side of operations, have never been sophisticated with respect to strategic communication—this shortcoming was evident during both the 2006 war with Hezbollah and the preceding battles against Palestinian militants in the Gaza Strip. Israeli military planners never seriously saw themselves as being in a competition for the hearts and minds of the Lebanese population, although the IDF eventually improved their psychological operations, using airborne leaflets in an effort to dissuade the Lebanese from challenging Tel Aviv's "iron fist."[16] But if "having a good story to tell and always telling the truth" is the standard against which counterinsurgent information operations efforts are graded, the Israelis didn't always adhere to that rule. Following the April 1996 artillery barrage that killed over 100 Lebanese civilians in the town of Qana, for example, the Israeli response to inquiries about how such a disaster took place was inconsistent and muddled. As *The Economist* reported at the time:

> [D]id the Israeli gunners have aerial observation of the fall of shot? To begin with, Israel brushed aside the news, first reported by a British correspondent, the *Independent*'s Robert Fisk, that a remote-controlled aircraft had been videotaped over the scene, perhaps photographing the shelling. Then Israel agreed that the aircraft had indeed been there, but said it was on a different mission. Then, in a third variation, it said the drone arrived on the scene three minutes after the shelling stopped. Were there also two helicopter gunships airborne in the area? Israel at first said no; then later said yes.[17]

Israel's response to the Qana massacre of 1996 was no isolated episode. With alarming regularity, both the IDF and the rest of the Israeli government clumsily managed the narrative of the Israeli campaign in southern Lebanon and inefficiently countered the falsehoods spread by Israel's enemies. Like the US Army in Vietnam—famous for its "five o'clock follies" in which a cynical press corps came to distrust the official line presented by military spokespersons—the IDF mismanaged the press and too often failed to present a truthful initial narrative.

Israeli information operations efforts, though, were complicated in southern Lebanon by the Israeli media. Israel is an open society with a vibrant press. Hezbollah could in part control the message it wanted its constituents to hear through al-Manar, Hezbollah's own widely popular TV channel. But the IDF had to battle both the perceptions being created by Hezbollah and also the way in which the unpopular occupation of southern Lebanon was being treated in the Israeli press. Like a good guerrilla group, Hezbollah directed much of its efforts toward "softer" targets such as logistics convoys. Many of the Israeli soldiers killed, then, were not frontline combat troops, but rather reservists with families and civilian jobs. Israel is not a large country, and their loss was felt perhaps more acutely than the loss of younger, unmarried combat troops. Israeli television covered the deaths of reservists in such a way that they often asked the families of those killed to respond to the videos released by Hezbollah![18]

Democracies, in general, have a tougher time with information operations than non-state actors. Democracies are often constrained by laws prohibiting them from conducting anything that could be interpreted as a propaganda campaign aimed toward their own people. So there were very real limits to what the IDF could do to "sell" the occupation of southern Lebanon to their own people. Hezbollah faced no restraints in selling the resistance. Also, many militaries have classification mechanisms that keep military operations secret until days after their completion. So whereas Hezbollah could—and did—publicize its military operations immediately following their completion, the IDF were often forced to wait to acknowledge operations. The same went for casualties. The IDF, like most Western militaries, have a casualty notification procedure. Proper channels are observed to inform a family of the death of their son or daughter. Hezbollah hijacked this procedure, even broadcasting dead or dying Israelis on al-Manar.

In this environment, it should surprise no one that Israelis often watch al-Manar during times of conflict, or that the Israeli media use the channel as a source for their own reporting. By the time of the Grapes of Wrath campaign in 1996, for example, it was possible to write both that Hezbollah's rhetoric had grown "in menace and self-assurance" and that "it is no longer the Israeli government which 'advises' border residents to go down into the shelters, it is Hassan Nasrallah."[19]

Finally, by the late 1990s, the debate on Israel's continued presence taking place in the public sphere both depressed morale within the IDF and also offered a degree of aid and comfort to Hezbollah and its supporters. "If the public discussion of sensitive military issues goes beyond what is necessary," said the commander of the IDF's Northern Command in 1997 as withdrawal plans became an open topic of discussion in Israel, "it certainly has an effect on morale and on the feeling and decision not only of the Israel Defense Forces, but also of the other side."[20] Debates on the Israeli presence in Lebanon took place in the open; debates over Hezbollah's military activities took place in private. And while no Israeli would wish for an end to participatory democracy, this arrangement put Israel at a competitive disadvantage against Hezbollah.

Hezbollah's information operations can be divided into two separate activites—the effort aimed at undermining popular support within Israel for the Israeli occupation of Lebanon, and the effort aimed at solidifying Hezbollah's support from its own constituency in Lebanon.

Hezbollah uses a sophisticated mix of traditional and "new" media as part of its polished and expanding information operations. As of 2004, the organization operated four radio stations and five newspapers.[21] The official newspaper of Hezbollah, *al-Ahd*, has since been replaced by *al-Intiqad*, a journal edited by longtime Hezbollah media figure Ibrahim Moussawi. *Al-Intiqad* features a sharp Internet site that is often the first medium on which official party announcements and speeches feature.[22] In recent years, Hezbollah has grown steadily more sophisticated in its employment of new media—such as blogs and websites— to transmit the party's message. The crown jewel of Hezbollah's media operations, however, remains its television station, al-Manar.[23]

Al-Manar was founded in 1991 and today operates in professional offices in downtown Beirut. Ahmed Nizar Hamzeh described the station prior to the destruction of its offices in the 2006 July War:

> Although resistance fighters guard the station's five-storey building in the southern suburbs of Beirut, al-Manar has a corporate atmosphere with several hundred employees, a prayer room, a cafeteria, and several studios fitted with state-of-the-art editing and production suites.[24]

Al-Manar went off the air only briefly during the 2006 war. Israel bombed al-Manar's primary studios during the war, but the network continued to broadcast from alternate studios set up prior to the war. Today, following reconstruction, al-Manar is once again a professional news organization—albeit one in the control and at the service of a non-state actor frequently labeled a terrorist organization.

One of the founders of al-Manar, Nasser Akhdar, explained to researchers Dina Matar and Farah Dakhlallah that the station's primary concern was to communicate "the daily realities of the occupation of South Lebanon to Lebanese society and the heroic acts of resistance to the occupation in an effort to bolster the resilience of the Community of the Resistance in Lebanon." Accordingly, 40 percent of al-Manar's daily output in the 1990s was devoted to its coverage of events in southern Lebanon and insurgent attacks on Israel and its Lebanese allies.[25]

Hezbollah soon discovered, though, that its broadcasts had an effect not just on the Lebanese population but on the Israelis as well. "On the field, we hit one Israeli soldier," a Hezbollah official explained. "But a tape of him crying for help affects thousands of Israelis ... we realized the impact of our amateur work on the morale of the Israelis."[26] Hezbollah, which employs a small army of Hebrew linguists to monitor the Israeli media, soon learned that for Israeli news outlets broadcasting images of dead or dying Israeli soldiers was taboo. If a Lebanese outlet were to broadcast such images, though, and those images were then picked up by the international news wire services, the taboo was lifted. The cat was out of the bag, so to speak, and Israeli outlets began to rebroadcast the images most Israelis could watch anyway. Consequently, Hezbollah invested much effort and blood in videotaping their attacks on Israeli columns and positions. As soon as the attack had taken place, the cameramen would race back to Beirut to make sure footage of the attack went up on al-Manar in time for the next news cycle. Footage of these attacks had a galvanizing effect on a portion of the Israeli population but also fueled the growing movement against the war and occupation in Israel.

Timur Göksel, the UN's longtime spokesman in southern Lebanon, explained in 1993 that "Hezbollah knows they're not going to win the war on the battlefield, so they're not taking on Israel's military might on the ground. They're taking on the Israelis psychologically."[27] Hezbollah pressed their advantage. They understood, correctly, that the Israeli occupation of southern Lebanon was only possible so long as it was tolerated by the Israeli populace. Consequently, much of Hezbollah's propaganda was aimed not just at the Lebanese population but at Israelis as well. One of al-Manar's daily news broadcasts, even today, is in Hebrew. During the occupation, Hezbollah ran a constantly updated photo gallery of Israeli casualties with the phrase "Who's Next?" written in Hebrew at the end.[28] "We aren't doing this to show off," said one Hezbollah official. "We want to get into every [Israeli's] mind and affect Israeli public opinion."[29] When the occupation finally ended in 2000 as Israel and its Lebanese allies retreated back behind the "Blue Line" in humiliating and chaotic fashion, one UN official was moved to remark that "75 percent of Hezbollah's war against Israel was those videotapes."[30]

At the same time that Hezbollah was using its media against the Israelis, however, it was also using its media and information operations to build up its support at home, especially within the Shia community. In her study of the use of propaganda and spectacle by the Asad regime in Syria, Lisa Wedeen writes that:

> Politics is not merely about material interests but also about contests over the symbolic world, over the management and appropriation of meanings. Regimes attempt to control and manipulate the symbolic world, just as they attempt to control material resources or to construct institutions of enforcement and punishment.[31]

In the 1980s, Hezbollah was very much the upstart in southern Lebanon. Most of Hezbollah's leadership at the time hailed from the upper Bekaa Valley—not the south. Hezbollah knew, then, that in expanding into the south, it was on the turf of the Amal Movement, one of its rivals at the time. "When [Hezbollah] first came to the south, in 1984, 1985, they started by just hanging posters," recounts Timur Göksel. "When they started their fight with Amal, it was about who owned this electric pole. Who can put their poster on it."[32] The first clash between Hezbollah and Amal, then, was fought over symbols—who got to hang their poster where.

Eventually, Hezbollah began to eat into Amal's support in the south and capitalized on their gains in the southern suburbs of Beirut and the Bekaa Valley. Today, posters of martyrs and of Hezbollah leaders are to be found all over southern Lebanon. This propaganda serves a purpose. Hezbollah does not mourn or regret the deaths of its young men in combat with the Israelis—it celebrates their sacrifice.

Hezbollah has proven adept at providing new narratives for its constituency to follow depending upon the circumstances. It established a narrative for its constituents to follow in the 1990s when Hezbollah was fighting the Israelis; in 2000 when Hezbollah seized upon the Shebaa Farms controversy to retain its arms; in 2006 when its actions on July 12 brought much destruction upon Lebanon and the Shia especially; and in 2008 when it applied its arms to break political deadlock in Beirut.

Hezbollah stages a variety of spectacles designed to re-enforce its popularity with the Shia community of Lebanon. Hezbollah's military activities are shrouded in secrecy—even from its constituency. When Hezbollah first began its combat operations, for example, the people of southern Lebanon referred to them as "the invisible people."[33] A year after the 2006 war, Hezbollah opened a museum in the southern suburbs celebrating its victory and displaying arms both captured from the IDF and used against the IDF by Hezbollah fighters. The author visited this museum on a weekday to find it being visited by scores of Lebanese families in the same way that a military museum might be visited in the United States.

Following his assassination Hezbollah established a museum for Imad Mughniyeh in Nabatiyeh in 2008. Mughniyeh was considered a ruthless terrorist in the West, but in Nabatiyeh, fathers visited the museum with their sons and took in the displays erected by Hezbollah.[34] These displays allow Hezbollah to open up the secretive side of organization to the public, if only for a few weeks. Live displays and re-enactments serve the same purpose. In September 2008, for example, Hezbollah used 100 of its actual fighters to re-enact the battle in which Hadi Nasrallah, the son of secretary-general Hassan Nasrallah, was killed by Israeli soldiers.[35]

Hezbollah's information operations have two major effects on Hezbollah's relations with its constituency. First, as Matar and Dakhlallah argue, Hezbollah-supported media defines what it is to be Lebanese and Shia. Being Lebanese and Shia means, at the very least, supporting the armed resistance activities of Hezbollah. It is permissible for a Lebanese Shia to support another political party at the expense of Hezbollah—Amal, for example—but during the 1990s it was not permissible to speak out in opposition to the military campaign waged against the IDF in southern Lebanon, or to question Hezbollah's arms in the era that followed Israel's withdrawal in 2000.

It is important to note here, however, that Hezbollah's information operations do not threaten punitive action against those who speak out against the organization's arms and its armed activities. A Lebanese Shia who questions Hezbollah's authority—and some do—finds himself or herself against the odds of an established and powerful narrative. It is impressive how fast and how fundamentally Hezbollah is able to shape that narrative. Prior to 1999, for example, few in Lebanon had ever heard of the Shebaa Farms, a disputed border region seized from Syria by Israel in 1967. The lands historically belong to Lebanon, but are thought to have been an excuse Hezbollah seized upon when it appeared that Israel's withdrawal might have forced the organization's disarmament. When the speaker of Parliament Nabih Berri presented Lebanon's case to Israel and the UN, in fact, in 2000, he was unable to identify the farms himself on a map of Lebanon. Nonetheless, within a few years, few in the Shia communities of Lebanon would question Hezbollah's insistence upon both keeping its arms and launching cross-border raids into Israel (which provoked brutal responses from the Israelis) in order to liberate these farms—suddenly judged to be important for Lebanon's long-term well-being and sovereignty.

More recently, Hezbollah has made the case to its constituency that it is necessary to retain its arms due to the aggression of Lebanon's Sunni community. Although streetfighting which took place in May 2008 saw Hezbollah and its allies in the SSNP and Amal rout the ragtag militiamen of Saad Hariri's majority-Sunni Future Movement on the streets of Beirut, Hezbollah crafts a narrative for its constituents depicting the Shia of Lebanon as the permanent underdogs and in which, if it were not for Hezbollah's arms, the Shia would go back to being the forgotten sect of Lebanon. Hezbollah, in other words, is now playing on the domestic fears of its constituents rather than the need to defend Lebanon from Israeli aggression. Regardless, Hezbollah's strategy is working. Contrasting with the optimism that preceded Israel's 2000 withdrawal—in which several analysts confidently predicted Hezbollah would disarm and become a peaceful movement—few believe today that Hezbollah will give up its arms anytime soon.

This is not meant to argue, though, that Hezbollah gets it all right with respect to information operations. One of the more pervasive myths about Hezbollah—one that has largely taken root in the West following the 2006 war—is the myth that Hezbollah has been able to shape the way in which the foreign media have reported conflicts in Lebanon and between Hezbollah and Israel.[36] In reality, Hezbollah's performance with respect to its relations with the foreign press both during and following the 2006 war has been extremely poor. Hezbollah has enjoyed a great deal of success in shaping domestic opinion within Lebanon, and its the utilization of combat cameramen in the 1990s represents Hezbollah's greatest innovation. But the secretive and paranoid nature of Hezbollah has meant that they have never enjoyed a close relationship with the Western media. Whether this is for "security reasons" or simply because Hezbollah is dissatisfied with the way that it has been portrayed in the West, Hezbollah's failure to engage with the media of the West is not a component of savvy information operations.

Learning from the insurgent?

Insurgent groups tend to learn from the experiences of other insurgent groups. Exactly how tactics spread is a matter of greater debate. Political scientist Robert Pape argues that tactics like suicide bombing are adopted from Hezbollah by groups such as the Tamil Tigers and Hamas largely because they are perceived as being successful.[37] Insurgency scholars Michael Horowitz and Erin Simpson, meanwhile, argue that a functionalist explanation only goes so far toward describing the diffusion of tactics among insurgencies.[38] Horowitz and Simpson highlight the importance of close ties between groups, noting that suicide bombing is nowhere to be found in the insurgencies of Latin America yet has flourished as a tactic in the Middle East and South Asia.

One of Hezbollah's greatest innovations in the field of information operations—and perhaps one of its greatest innovations across all lines of operations—was the decision in the 1990s to include "combat cameramen" in combat operations. Accompanying Hezbollah guerrillas on ambushes of Israeli vehicles and soldiers, these cameramen—who often work with small, handheld video cameras—would race back to Beirut following the completion of operations in order to post footage of the attack on al-Manar.

The development of al-Manar suggests a bottom-up innovation in that its effectiveness against the Israeli public was not understood at the time of its launch. Indeed, the original goal of al-Manar as a television station and propaganda wing was to boost the spirits of those in the Lebanese population carrying the burden for Hezbollah's war against the Israeli occupation. When Hezbollah came to understand that al-Manar was having as much an effect on Israelis living south of the border as it was the Shia living in Lebanon, Hezbollah encouraged changes in the network's operations to take advantage of its psychological effect on Israelis. Combat cameramen—not unlike those who frequently accompany US military units into the field—began to follow Hezbollah ambush teams into combat. And what was first envisioned as a supporting effort became, in effect, the main effort of the operations.

In the same way that insurgent groups "borrow" tactics such as suicide bombing, insurgent groups in Iraq and Afghanistan have learned from the way in which Hezbollah used psychological warfare to great effect against the IDF and have applied such tactics to their resistance struggles against the American-led occupying armies.

In Iraq and Afghanistan, however, there are two key differences that must be noted. First, the enemy's propaganda has not been aimed to any great extent at undermining the support for the Iraq War in the United States or in allied nations. And second, whereas Hezbollah used traditional media—a television station, primarily, but also radio stations and newspapers—for its psychological operations, the insurgents in Iraq and Afghanistan have more often made use of the new media.[39] For Hezbollah, broadcasting a video of attacks against Israelis meant putting the video on television. But who needs al-Manar—or television in general—when you have the Internet and YouTube?

The most effective insurgent propaganda in Iraq has made use of the Internet, with slick sites such as BaghdadSniper.com. On BaghdadSniper, the viewer—who could be anywhere from Iraq to London to Indonesia—is greeted with the option of viewing the site in one of eight languages: English, Arabic, Urdu, Italian, French, Spanish, Chinese, or German. (But not Persian—this site is affiliated with the Sunni resistance groups.) Viewers can then watch videos of (alleged) attacks on US soldiers and Marines in Iraq by the anonymous "Baghdad Sniper."[40]

As interesting as the videos are, however, the claims made by the site are just as interesting. The site makes three main contentions. First, in harsher conditions than those in which the American soldiers and Marines operate, we out-perform the American soldiers. Second, unlike the Americans, we are moral—we never target innocent women or children, whereas the Americans often kill innocent civilians. Third, we the resistance have the technical and tactical know-how and skill to challenge the mighty American Army on the field of battle. One boast is particularly telling:

> Our snipers are superior to those in the US army. Our men have only minutes to stop, scope, shoot and retreat while American snipers always shoot from a safe place under American control. US snipers hit easy targets. *You hardly ever hear that they killed a fighter.* Our men only ever hit armed enemies.[41]

It is not in the character of a US Marine Corps sniper—among the world's most skillful— to brag about confirmed kills. But that is exactly what the Baghdad Sniper does because he understands the *claim* to have killed an American—and, better, a video showing the act—is more important than the act itself.

Conclusion

Information operations constitute the single most important line of operations in a successful insurgent campaign. Although combat operations are the base upon which other lines of operation are constructed, not even the combat operations themselves take precedence over information operations. In conventional thinking, information operations are a supporting effort. But Hezbollah has proved this wisdom wrong on both sides of the spectrum: on the one hand it has shown that combat operations themselves function in support of information operations, if planned concurrently; and on the other it has shown that information operations blur over into genuine political and social activities that serve its constituents in southern Lebanon.

Hezbollah's use of information operations represents an innovation that built upon the way in which media were traditionally used by Lebanese militias and political parties. In al-Manar first, and later through its use of the new media, Hezbollah used propaganda to not only spread word of its deeds within its natural constituency but to the adversary, producing a political effect unforeseen at the time of al-Manar's launch. The fact that Hezbollah's videos, statements, and claims had as much an effect on their adversary as their constituency was a pleasant surprise—and one on which Hezbollah quickly capitalized.

But while Hezbollah's decision to include combat cameramen on operations was a masterstroke, Hezbollah's overall information operations campaign perhaps receives more credit in Western political and military circles than it should. For while Hezbollah has enjoyed tremendous success crafting a narrative that its own constituency follows, much if not most of Lebanon remains wary of or hostile to Hezbollah's long-term political objectives and has a variety of conflicting opinions about Hezbollah's armed "resistance" campaign and its consequences for Lebanon. Also, Hezbollah has largely failed to alter the way in which it is perceived in the West. Part of this is due to poor press relations and media management, something the Palestinian groups that preceded Hezbollah in southern Lebanon arguably did much better.

Counterinsurgent force can derive many lessons from the Israeli experience in southern Lebanon. At the very least, the experiences of Israel in southern Lebanon instruct that information operations represent a contested space. If the insurgent force—rooted in and dependent upon popular support, just as counterinsurgent force is—can target the vulnerability of the counterinsurgent force among his population, so too can the counterinsurgent force target weaknesses in the popular support of the insurgent. Doing so, though, often means privileging information operations over combat operations—and the narrative of war over the act of war itself. This runs contrary to the strategic cultures of most Western militaries and calls for a rethink of the nature of war itself.

Notes

1 George Orwell, *Homage to Catalonia*, Orlando, FL: Harcourt, Inc., 1952, pp. 41–2.
2 David Galula, *Pacification in Algeria 1956–1958*, Santa Monica, CA: Rand Corporation, 1963 (2006), pp. 44–5.
3 David Galula, *Counterinsurgency Warfare: Theory and Practice*, New York: Praeger, 1964, p. 9.
4 Roger Trinquier, *Modern Warfare: A French View of Counterinsurgency*, Westport, CT: Praeger Security International, 2006, p. 41
5 David W. Barno, "Challenges in Fighting a Global Insurgency," *Parameters* (Summer 2006), 15–29.
6 R. Smith, *The Utility of Force: The Art of War in the Modern World*, London: Allen Lane, 2005, p. 400, emphasis original.
7 John A. Nagl, *Learning to Eat Soup with a Knife: Counterinsurgency Lessons fron Malaya and Vietnam*, Chicago: University of Chicago Press, 2005, p. 93.
8 FM 3-24, p. 4-8.
9 Ibid., p. 6-8.
10 F.G. Hoffman, "American Counterinsurgency Doctrine: Still Learning," in *Counterinsurgency and Human Rights*, The Carr Center for Human Rights Policy, Harvard University, Working Papers, Vol. 5, 2008.

11 JP 3-13, *Information Operations*, US Department of Defense, February 13, 2006.
12 Searched on 24 July 2008.
13 FM 3-0, *Operations*, US Department of Defense, June 2001 and FM 3-0, *Operations*, US Department of Defense, February 2008.
14 FM 3-0, *Operations*, February 2008, p. 7-1.
15 Nagl, *Learning to Eat Soup with a Knife*, pp. 93–5.
16 Julie Flint, "Force to Reckon With: The Hezbollah Factor," *Guardian*, July 9, 1987.
17 "The Qana Massacre. Why?," *The Economist*, May 11, 1996.
18 Author interview with Timur Göksel, Beirut, August 13, 2008.
19 David Hirst, "Return To The Bad Old Days: David Hirst in Beirut Reports on the Larger Significance of the Israeli Raids," *Guardian*, April 12, 1996.
20 Joel Greenberg, "Netanyahu Calls for End to 'Proxy War,'" *The New York Times*, January 31, 1997.
21 Ahmad Nizar Hamzeh, *In the Path of Hizbullah*, Syracuse, NY: Syracuse University Press, 2004, p. 58.
22 www.alntiqad.com.
23 Al-Manar first went on the air in June 1991. Only one complete study of the station has been written, which is Avi Jorisch's *Beacon of Hatred: Inside Hizbullah's al-Manar Television*, Washington, DC. The Washington Institute for Near East Studies, 2004. Jorisch's study mainly focuses on the hostile and antisemitic rhetoric to be found on al-Manar and was instrumental in al-Manar's designation as a terrorist organization by the US Dept of Treasury, available at https://www.washingtoninstitute.org/templateC04.php?CID=66. Since Jorisch's study, the literature on al-Manar has expanded. Dina Matar and Farah Dakhlallah have written of the way that al-Manar forms identity in the Shia community of Lebanon in "What It Means to Be Shiite in Lebanon: Al Manar and the Imagined Community of Resistance," *Westminster Papers in Communication and Culture*, Vol. 3, No. 2 (2006), 22–40, available at http://www.wmin.ac.uk/mad/page-1367.
24 Hamzeh, *In the Path of Hizbullah*, pp. 58–9.
25 Robert Fisk, "Television News is Secret Weapon of the Intifada," *Independent*, December 2, 2000.
26 As quoted both in *Jane's Foreign Report* and in Frederic M. Wehrey's excellent article on Hezbullah psychological operations against Israel, "A Clash of Wills: Hizbullah's Psychological Campaign Against Israel in South Lebanon," *Small Wars and Insurgencies*, Vol. 13, No. 3 (Autumn 2002), 53–74.
27 Wehrey, "A Clash of Wills," 53.
28 Ibid., 66.
29 Ibid.
30 Ibid.
31 Lisa Wedeen, *Ambiguities of Domination: Politics, Rhetoric, and Symbols in Contemporary Syria*, Chicago: University of Chicago Press, 1999, p. 30.
32 Author interview with Timur Göksel, Beirut, August 13, 2008. See also Flint, "Force to Reckon With."
33 Flint, "Force to Reckon With.": "The ordinary people of South Lebanon call the holy warriors of the Islamic Resistance 'the invisible people,' for the Israelis, they are an invisible enemy: they have no bases, no barracks, no identifiable offices, no arms depots."
34 See Robert F. Worth, "Hezbollah Shrine to Terrorist Suspect Enthralls Lebanese Children," *The New York Times*, September 2, 2008: "The presentation, which opened Aug. 15, is Hezbollah's most ambitious multimedia exhibit to date, meant to dramatize the group's bitter conflict with Israel on the second anniversary of their latest war. Schoolchildren pour in throughout the day, absorbing the carefully honed message of heroic resistance. At night, light and laser shows illuminate the weaponry and tanks, and overflow crowds have been keeping it open until after 1 a.m."
35 *L'Orient-Le Jour* and *as-Safir*, September 15, 2008: Hadi Nasrallah was killed in combat actions on September 13, 2008. Hassan Nasrallah was scheduled to deliver a public address that same day and memorialized his son, the other Hezballah fighters, and soldiers from the Lebanese Army in one of his best-remembered speeches. The son of a Lebanese political figure dying in combat was unprecedented and garnered Hassan Nasrallah much sympathy.
36 Marvin Kalb, "The Israeli–Hezbollah War of 2006: The Media as a Weapon in Asymmetrical Conflict," Harvard University Joan Shorenstein Center on the Press, Politics and Public Policy, Research Paper Series RWP07-012, February 2007.
37 See Robert Pape, *Dying to Win: The Strategic Logic of Suicide Terrorism*, New York: Random House, 2005.

38 See Michael Horowitz and Erin Simpson, "The Diffusion of Insurgency and Suicide Terrorism Strategies," paper prepared for the 2005 American Political Science Association Annual Meeting. Also, see Michael Horowitz, "The Diffusion of Suicide Terrorism," paper prepared for the Annual Meeting of the International Studies Association, San Francisco, CA, March 26–9, 2008. Both papers cited with permission of the authors.

39 It is important to note here that while the insurgents in Iraq have made greater use of the Internet, they have also used traditional media such as television. In the same way, Hezbollah has made more and more use of the Internet in its information operations. Thus, what we are seeing is perhaps a general move toward greater use of the Internet and less use of traditional media, though guerrilla groups will use both forms for some time to come.

40 http://www.baghdadsniper.net.

41 Ibid., emphasis added.

17 Civil-military integration

Michelle Parker and Matthew Irvine

Provincial reconstruction teams (PRTs) are a model of civil-military integration created to conduct stability operations in complex environments. The PRT concept has been used in both Afghanistan and Iraq and incorporated into modern counterinsurgency doctrine. The first provincial reconstruction team was inaugurated in December 2002, in the Afghan province of Gardez, by the United States. Quickly following the success of this new model, additional teams were placed in other Afghan provinces, Bamyian in January 2003, and Kunduz in February 2003. The concept of the PRT was exported to Iraq in November 2005.[1] As of March 2008, there were 26 PRTs in Afghanistan, led or co-led by 21 different nations,[2] and 31 different teams located in all 18 of Iraq's provinces.[3] The durability of the PRT concept and its adaptation to new challenges highlights the innovative benefits embodied in this critical test of civil-military integration.

This chapter provides a brief history of the evolution of the PRT model in Afghanistan from 2002 to 2006, and highlights many of the concept's unique benefits and challenges. Changing a military organizational model into an interagency team without any doctrine, clear lines of authority, or roadmap created a series of structural challenges for all parties involved. This chapter will point out five of these challenges in more detail. First, during the early development of the PRT concept, the lack of understanding from each agency and department's personnel of the other's mission, capabilities, culture, language, and operating style created many barriers to effectiveness. Second, coordinating and funding diverse policy objectives via projects requires a high degree of flexibility and cooperation among the personalities involved. Third, integration of military and civilian perspectives at all levels of decision making is necessary to ensure mission success and efficiency. Fourth, coordination between PRT efforts and external contributors such as local governments, non-governmental organizations (NGOs), and international institutions requires complex procedures for information sharing and policy synchronization. And finally, multinational and allied cooperation add another layer of administrative barriers to successful reconstruction efforts. Eventually, the model was expanded and adopted beyond its original goals and area.

Beginnings

While American counterinsurgency theory was inspired and triggered by the war in Iraq, the civil-military integration that evolved from the PRT model developed in Afghanistan. After initial combat operations began in Afghanistan in 2001, the mission quickly expanded to include stabilization efforts throughout the country. The US military sought to pacify the Afghan countryside by creating so-called coalition humanitarian liaison centers. These centers were small Special Forces bases located throughout Afghanistan, some of which included teams of Civil Affairs soldiers funding small-scale projects designed to win the support of the local population. The US Department of State and US Agency for International Development (USAID) were keenly interested in placing their own officers in these centers. The State Department wanted to increase its profile in the countryside, and USAID wanted to oversee existing programs and expand its operations. Civilians from both USAID and the State Department began rotating through the coalition humanitarian liaison centers in early 2002, while the agency and department were negotiating formal agreements with the Department of Defense. In August 2002, the US military command in Afghanistan and the State Department formalized the relationship in a memorandum of understanding,[4] and four months later, USAID signed a similar agreement.[5] Both agreements established a formal interagency relationship that allowed civilians to operate in conjunction with military forces in Afghanistan.[6]

However, in the early years of the war effort civilian and military development assistance and humanitarian aid was not fully integrated into a single decision-making and funding process. Effective coordination was dependent upon the personalities of the civilian field officers and military commanders involved. Some military officials worked closely with the USAID field officer to integrate projects and programs but others chose to operate independently. Military Civil Affairs officers had access to Department of Defense funding independent of State Department or USAID programs, and frequently embarked on projects without consulting their civilian counterparts despite operating in the same geographic area. To solve these conflicts and ensure coordination, military commanders at the liaison centers gave each province's development officer review authority over all military funded projects.[7]

Provincial reconstruction teams

The PRT grew out of the concept of the coalition humanitarian liaison center during a series of working groups at Bagram Airbase in Afghanistan in the summer of 2002. Various international NGOs, including the United Nations Assistance Mission to Afghanistan (UNAMA) were heavily involved in the discussions that shaped the PRT model. The Afghanistan Ministry of Interior ensured that it had a direct link into the teams and placed police colonels in each to advise foreigners and provide a link into the Afghan government.

From the start, PRTs were designed to be interagency, equally combining the three most critical instruments of US foreign engagement: development, diplomacy, and defense. Teams in Afghanistan were designed to operate by consensus rather than having military or civilian leadership. No agency or department was in command of any other on the PRT. The military was to provide security, life support, and transportation for the other instruments of power; however, the military did not have authority over policy, mission, funding, or activities. Each agency or department represented was intended to have an equal value and priority in shaping how to help extend the writ of the Afghan government in the province.

The model was also designed to be multinational, to counter the perception of the US as an occupying force. According to one Department of Defense official, "We want the PRTs to be international, not American, because Americans are combatants in the country, so it is hard to say 'We are doing this for your benefit,' but when you get the New Zealanders in Bamiyan, who is going to think about the Kiwi conspiracy to control central Afghanistan?"[8]

The first three PRTs, known as "pilot PRTs" were originally coalition humanitarian liaison centers that were transformed in part as showpieces for US allies interested in assisting the mission in Afghanistan. By the summer of 2003, the United Kingdom inaugurated the first non-US-led PRT in Mazar-I-Sharif; New Zealand took over the Bamyian mission, and later that year Germany began leading reconstruction efforts in Kunduz.

Control over the PRT program shifted from the original working group at Bagram Airbase to a formal executive steering committee in Kabul in 2003. The committee was designed to make decisions at the strategic level and send those decisions down both the civilian (Afghan and international) and military chains of command. This committee was made up of the ambassadors of troop-contributing nations, the Afghan minister of interior, and the commanding general of coalition military forces. Various other Afghan ministers attended the bimonthly meeting depending upon the issues on the agenda. In 2006, the military authority over the teams shifted to the NATO-led International Security Assistance Force (ISAF). With this change, ISAF prioritized the committee meetings to better coordinate PRT activities at the embassy and senior military levels and ensure that the Afghan government was involved in the process. Some examples of the issues the committee dealt with were the growing PRT role in counter-narcotics, the development of a PRT handbook, and salaries for the Afghanistan Ministry of Interior representatives.

Nonmilitary reconstruction and stabilization capabilities are required to achieve the greater goals of modern counterinsurgency doctrine. Counterinsurgency expert John Nagl argues:

> Defeating an insurgency requires winning the support of the population away from the insurgents, and unlikely as it seems, the "hierarchy of needs" propounded decades ago by humanistic psychologist Abraham Maslow is never more applicable than in a combat zone. After obtaining basic security, people want to live and work under the rule of law, with a chance for economic progress.[9]

PRTs were an instrumental first step in providing civilian expertise and resources to the host nation in an otherwise military effort. The flexibility and success of civilian members of PRTs highlight the enormous potential of the civilian assets of the US government. However, the tools and personnel available to the PRT and like efforts must be greatly expanded to assume a greater and more public role in stability and counterinsurgency efforts.

The early days of US PRTs were essentially a laboratory for the most tactical level interagency integration that the US has undergone since the Civil Operations and Revolutionary Development Support program in Vietnam (CORDS).[10] In 2003, there was no doctrine to explain the operational relationships between each representative. The only existing document that provided direction to a team came out six months after its inception. The US deputies committee issued the PRT Policy Guidance in June 2003. In a total of three pages it outlined the mission, general functions of military and civilian instruments, and resources available for PRTs. This directive placed the State Department as the policy lead among civilian agencies but otherwise chose not to place any department or agency in command.[11] It also required all PRT projects to be coordinated with the United Nations and the Afghan government.[12] This served as the only interagency guidance for nearly one and a half years.

By 2006, the model had changed significantly in most US PRTs. Initially the civilians had to convince the military of their added value to the mission in order to access resources such as transportation and security. Some military commanders understood that value quicker than others, so the rate at which real integration occurred differed depending on the personalities involved. Although the working relationship within each PRT remained personality dependent, a more integrated approach developed over time, with persistence and a growing understanding of what each element of power added to the mission. The concept of equality between civilians and the military commander, called the "command group" was codified in the ISAF PRT handbook that was issued in 2006. The command group determined the mission focus of the PRT by combining each agency or department's operating orders and integrating them on the ground. In the best circumstances, the command group jointly developed and executed a provincial stability plan.

Military support to civilians

From the outset, the general perception of Afghanistan's PRTs was that the military component of the mission was in charge. The army was responsible for providing all of the life support functions such as food, housing, security, transportation, and medicine.[13] This power imbalance was personality dependent: if the military commander of the team understood and acknowledged the importance of all missions, civilians had little trouble gaining support. However, if the commander determined the civilian effort was secondary to that of the military, then the civilians had to fight for access to resources, or sometimes even a seat at the table.[14]

When military commanders viewed civilian and military missions as equal, resources were sorted during a battle update briefing, a daily meeting at each PRT. At these briefings, each military and civilian section leader reviewed the day's events and reported future operations 24, 48, and 72 hours in advance, so all relevant actors could plan for resource needs. If multiple sections needed the same resource—transportation, for example—those competing for the resources were able develop solutions together. Such solutions included: shifting meetings earlier or later in the day or to a different day, meeting in the base rather than meeting outside, allowing civilians to ride in a contractor's vehicle or riding in convoys of other US military actors in the area.[15] Resource allocations were rarely a problem in the PRTs with the best interagency coordination.

In cases where military commanders did not support or understand the importance of the non-military mission, civilians were constantly required to justify why they needed access to resources. In some cases this adjustment worked well and both were able to function in their jobs. If the specific justification did not work, the civilians had to work around the commander or, in the most extreme circumstances, move to a more integrated PRT elsewhere.[16] As noted above, civilians frequently found others operating in the area and joined convoys headed to areas they needed to visit. In non-integrated PRTs civilians had to rely on other units and organizations as their primary source of transportation while in the integrated PRTs; the alternative transportation options were always a last resort. In secure areas, some civilians chose simply to drive themselves and forego force protection altogether.[17]

Some resources were divided between civilian and military budgets at the provincial level. Telecom and information technology were identified as civilian responsibilities in both agreements between the military and its civilian counterparts, the State Department and USAID. To meet this requirement USAID hired an information technology company to provide satellite Internet access for the civilians on each team. The Internet access was usually better than the military's, so some development officers would allow senior military officials access to the civilian system. Civilian officials also installed their own radios in their armored vehicles as an alternative form of communication to cell phones, satellite phones, and the military equipment.

Air transport was another challenge for civilians because military schedules remained in flux and it was difficult to assure a civilian seat on a helicopter. In 2004, USAID requested that the US Congress designate funds for an airline in that year's supplemental spending bill. With the funds, "PRT air" was initiated in late 2004, and additional funds were used to construct airstrips capable of landing a C130 cargo aircraft at each PRT base to provide a reliable transport option for all civilians working for the US government on teams, and USAID's implementing partners. According to some anecdotal reports, the US military was the most frequent user of the air service due to its reliability.

Coordination and funding

US PRTs had access to multiple funding mechanisms, controlled by either the Department of Defense or USAID. Each mechanism had different strengths and weaknesses. The teams with the best integration developed coordination methods to ensure they maximized each section's strength. Conversely, teams without strong integration tended to work on a variety of individual pet projects rather than developing a comprehensive approach to stabilize the province.

There are many examples of excellent interagency integration at the team level. US government leaders in Kabul and Bagram regarded the Jalalabad PRT as a prime example during the period of 2004–6.[18] Among PRTs in Afghanistan, the Jalalabad team saw tremendous unity of effort between both civilian and military components. The methods developed from the early Jalalabad cohorts were used as the basis for the best-practice recommendations in the ISAF PRT handbook. The Jalalabad team established a series of interagency project meetings, the first of which was project coordination. Once a week, the members of the command group plus the civil affairs team leaders met to update each other on the status of projects managed by the team. These meetings came out of necessity, because when any member of the team visited a village they would be asked about the status of the projects ongoing in the area, even if they were not managed by the specific personnel present. By having weekly coordination meetings, every team member was able to speak knowledgably about all concurrent projects. This unity of effort by the whole Jalalabad PRT helped maximize the effective use of its funding. When a maneuver unit was established in Jalalabad, its officers also attended the weekly meeting to ensure the PRT's projects were coordinated with the soldiers conducting combat operations.

The Jalalabad PRT viewed its available funds as taxpayer money rather than that of the Department of Defense or USAID. Shifting the view of ownership from those running the programs to the taxpayers allowed the project managers to act together as a team rather than in parallel. If any member of the team had a project idea, they would be able to bring it to a nomination board, which handled resource allocation. If a certain project was supported by the Afghan government and fit within the scope of the team's mission they would discuss and choose the best mechanism to fund it.

USAID funds were best used for complex projects that required difficult engineering work, large numbers of personnel, or technical training. The military's funds were best suited for local procurements or projects that needed to be completed rapidly. By focusing on the capabilities of the mechanisms rather than who owned them, it allowed the PRT to react to a wide variety of local needs.

Additionally, the funds were often used in partnership to balance civilian and military strengths and weaknesses. A simple example of this partnership occurred when the Afghan provincial governor asked the team to refurbish the open-sewer system of Jalalabad. The team's nomination board supported the project because it was a government-led initiative and fit within the scope of the team's stabilization plan. A USAID implementing partner was running an unskilled labor program in the city at the time, and could supply the personnel and low-level technical engineering expertise to clean and refurbish the sewers. The military used its Commander's Emergency Response Program (CERP) funds to procure local concrete that USAID's labor force would use to refurbish the sewers. In addition, the governor provided the director of public works funds to build and install concrete covers for the sewers. The UN provided demining support because the USAID-funded workers often found unexploded ordinance during the work. This project demonstrated coordination between the PRT, the Afghan government, and the UN.

Open meetings, in which anyone could raise an idea, brought members of the team together who would not normally engage on project-level issues. Such cooperation occurred at every level of the PRT. One example can be found when a medical officer knew that an NGO wanted to supply medical staff to a district, but it did not have a clinic so he raised that request in the meeting and the project was fully funded. Another example of integration in the Jalalabad team occurred when a force protection soldier found out that the neighborhood in which the team resided wanted a small park for the children and brought that request to the board. Open meetings allowed for the free flow of ideas and an efficient allocation of resources.

Civilian and military integration

In 2004, the US military expanded its field operations in Afghanistan by establishing regional brigade-sized commands and additional PRTs. The brigade headquarters, referred to as Regional Command East and Regional Command South, directly commanded the PRTs and maneuver forces in their respective area of operations. Regional Command East was based in Khost province and had command authority over the entire eastern part of Afghanistan, except in the areas directly adjacent to Bagram Airfield. Regional Command South was based in Kandahar and had command over Helmand, Kandahar, Uruzgan, and Zabul provinces. The civilian agencies provided advisors to the brigade commanders to ensure civil-military integration at all levels of decision making.

USAID created the position of regional development advisor to facilitate military-civilian integration at the regional level. This post was responsible for advising the commanding officer on USAID development programs, providing technical advice to the brigade's Civil Affairs office, working with the brigade's planners to incorporate development priorities in operations and to directly supervise USAID's field officers located in the teams.

The State Department created similar political advisor positions for the regional commanders, but unlike traditional advisors, who answer directly to the general officer for whom they work, these brigade-level advisors answered to the US Embassy in Kabul. The State Department initiative did not mirror the approach of USAID and the military in terms of command authority over their department's staff in PRTs; instead its officers held equal rank. The brigade-level political advisor, therefore, had to create personal relationships with the political officers on PRTs to ensure that he or she was kept fully informed.

In theory, the political advisors were able to work directly with the commander of a brigade or regiment; however, these civilians often faced the same challenge as those involved in the first PRTs. Civilians had to justify their positions to the brigade commander because no doctrine existed outlining the relationship between civilians and military headquarters. Integration was again personality dependent. In these early stages, civilians had to work their way into the decision-making meetings, briefings, and operational planning, and into advising the commander.

Multiple changes of military command frustrated the civilians who remained in their positions at the brigade level because their integration into the planning process did not automatically transfer to the incoming command. The lack of formal doctrine outlining the role and responsibility of the civilians required that they start over the education and relationship building with every command change.

In 2004, there was only one division-level command in Afghanistan, based at Bagram Airbase. The State Department had a traditional political advisor position for the major general in command, meaning that the advisor worked strictly for the general and did not take policy direction from the embassy in Kabul. The advisor, however, maintained a close informal relationship with the embassy. USAID stumbled into having a development advisor at the division command. The Parwan province PRT was based at Bagram Airbase, and the team's field program officer was occasionally called upon to answer questions that the division's general had about USAID programs. The program officer greatly impressed the commander, who requested that the agency reassign her to become his advisor. After this interim assignment, the USAID Civil-Military Office in Kabul determined that it was important to have its own officer working with division rather than at the base's PRT, and created a development advisor position for the division command.

The personal relationship between the commanding officer and the development advisor translated into access and influence for USAID in the Bagram Airbase headquarters. However, when that general completed his tour, his successor did not see the advisor position in the same light and moved it to the Civil Affairs Office. Because no doctrine existed to define the advisors' role, there was little civilians could do about the military change of focus. The lack of doctrine ensured that the role of the development advisor at Bagram Airbase remained personality dependent and continues to do so as this book goes to publication.

In May 2006, the authority for managing the Afghan campaign transferred from the US-led Operation Enduring Freedom to NATO's ISAF. A transition headquarters was established to manage the four-phase transfer of authority throughout the country to ISAF as it gained formal responsibility for the war effort in Afghanistan. The new ISAF mission and headquarters, named ISAF IX due to its sequencing in NATO's command rotation, set the tone of the future war effort by heavily emphasizing counterinsurgency efforts and civilian contributions.

The previous ISAF command had established the position of development advisor, but had never fully integrated the position into the military headquarters. The commanding general of ISAF IX, Sir David Richards, increased the role and responsibility of the development advisor by giving it a one-star equivalency, providing the needed gravitas to be effective in a corps command. He also wanted to ensure that the key donors were represented, so he requested an officer from the UK's Department for International Development and USAID to serve as "co-DEVADs" (development advisors).[19] USAID immediately placed a development advisor in the NATO headquarters in order to integrate its programs with the new international mission.[20] At this time, USAID was the largest donor in Afghanistan and its advisor was needed to integrate its programs into the greater NATO effort. Both advisors provided development expertise to all aspects of the headquarters including plans, information operations, civil-military affairs, engineers, operations, and intelligence. They worked to bring the civilian development community together with ISAF through meetings, briefings, and informal social activities at both the Kabul and PRT level.

The US State Department did not place a political advisor in the 2006 ISAF headquarters because it was a British-led operation and political advice was provided by the UK Ministry of Defence. Nonetheless, the US Embassy and ISAF agreed to create a billet for a US political advisor who worked informally with the other advisors at headquarters. This position was filled in late 2006, toward the end of the ISAF IX command.

Coordination between the civilian agencies and departments active in Afghanistan and the military command did not always occur. Neither the US Embassy nor USAID had an embedded military liaison or advisor to engage with senior military officers in country.

Although a defense attaché position existed in the embassy, it is not designed to coordinate operational military activities with the civilian US instruments operating in the field. The responsibility of integration rested entirely on the shoulders of those few civilians living on military bases as part of a PRT or as the advisor to a commanding officer.

External coordination

The PRTs were not the only development actors in Afghanistan. The United Nations Assistance Mission to Afghanistan (UNAMA) was instrumental in launching coordination meetings between the Afghan government and development organizations. UNAMA set up a monthly provincial coordination body,[21] chaired by the governor and attended by all of the ministerial representatives at the provincial level, some NGOs, international organizations, and the command group of the PRT. The meeting provided a forum to discuss the development plans for the province, and any critical issues that needed addressing. These coordination bodies were the precursors to provincial development committees, which were tasked with creating a provincial development plan.

The United Nations also helped establish technical working groups at the provincial level, which linked each Afghan ministry's provincial director with those working on projects associated with that ministry's field. Security, health, education, and water and sanitation were some examples of these groups. If the military wanted to build a school, they attended the education working group to ensure that the project did not conflict with others working on education in the province, and that it was on the government's priority list for schools.[22]

In addition to coordinating projects with the Afghan government's technical ministries and development actors in the area, the PRTs worked closely with provincial councils, the only democratically elected body in each province. Established in 2005, the provincial councils are the direct link between the government and the population. For example, the PRT in Jalalabad included the council in developing their provincial stability plan, which was used to fund projects throughout 2005. It was critical for the teams to partner with as many other actors in the province as possible, because leveraging each other's strengths and weaknesses allowed the province as a whole to move forward.

NATO and PRTs

By May 2006, 14 nations operated 25 PRTs in Afghanistan, all with no formal command and control authority tied to ISAF on the military side. Civilian political officers answered to their home nations, which were not necessarily each PRT's lead nation. For example, in 2005, the German-run Feyzabad team had both US and Croatian political advisors in addition to a German Ministry of Foreign Affairs representative. The US State Department officer reported to the US Embassy in Kabul, while serving as an advisor to the German PRT. Similar jurisdiction problems emerged with USAID personnel. USAID had had officers located in nearly every PRT since the model's inception, regardless of the host nation.[23] European development agencies were also represented in many of the PRTs, and like their political counterparts answered to their home nations rather than to a central coordinating body in Kabul. Often, they worked directly with ministries in Kabul because their office had no representation in the capital. Many non-US development agencies had a policy of working through the national government, which made creating a provincial-level stabilization plan extraordinarily difficult because the bulk of the funding went to the national government via trust funds or bilateral transfers.

ISAF developed a strategy to address the need for PRT coherence. At the strategic level, it focused on reinvigorating the executive steering committee and transforming it into a formal policy-making body. NATO worked with the United Nations to direct the weekly steering committee working group. The working group—comprised of embassy secretaries, UNAMA, development agencies working in PRTs, and the Afghanistan Ministry of Interior brigadier general in charge of PRTs—raised hot-button issues that the committee debated and coordinated policy for. In the end, the working group drafted the PRT-related policy that emerged from the executive steering committee.

The next level that needed attention was doctrine. Despite being operational for over three years and exported to Iraq, by May 2006 PRTs had no guiding doctrine. The executive steering committee requested that NATO create a PRT handbook to resolve the problem. The decision to have NATO issue the handbook was important for the handbook's legitimacy and influence. ISAF was the largest single international institution involved with the PRTs, and there was concern that it would be too difficult for civilians from individual countries to join together and write doctrine without clear authority. ISAF gave the task to the steering committee working group to ensure maximum civilian participation. The working group members volunteered to write different sections, and after multiple consultations with PRTs, endorsements by embassies and national capitals, and approval by the formal executive steering committee, ISAF issued the PRT Handbook (2nd edn) on October 31, 2006.[24]

Comprehensive training and information sharing was needed following the creation of the new PRT doctrine. NATO sought to ensure all command group members attended the same training on the ISAF PRT Handbook. A series of predeployment training classes for all NATO Command Group members was created to ensure total understanding of the role of PRTs. And finally, ISAF held quarterly PRT conferences where new issues were discussed and lessons learned were shared.

ISAF IX planners created a PRT helpdesk to assist those already in the field with logistical and procedural problems. This allowed those in PRTs to email or call the Kabul-based helpdesk to track down information needed in the field. For example, if the police in a province were not receiving salaries, team members could call the helpdesk and an ISAF Ministry of Interior liaison to find out why. The liaison was able to track down the information and report it back to officers in the field.

The final ISAF initiative was to develop an agreed set of metrics to measure the work of PRTs. The PRT working group coordinated with the embassies, development agencies, and the United Nations to develop a metrics questionnaire that allowed Headquarters to track overall team progress.

Some of these initiatives worked better than others. The civilian participants in the working group were engaged in writing the PRT Handbook and raising important issues for teams in the field. However, due to the nature of alliance warfare, the challenge of command and control remained present despite the best efforts at coherence. Effective coordination among the diverse civilian and military actors in the PRTs was always personality dependent, and no good bureaucratic solution was created. The handbook was considered a good start, but few changes have been made since its first publication and the extent to which it is used in predeployment training varies from nation to nation, despite centralized courses at NATO facilities.

Wider applications

The United States adapted the PRT model to Iraq in 2005. The new teams were tasked with political and economic development at the provincial level in an effort to build local institutional capacity on the heels of the centralized Ba'athist regime of Saddam Hussein. Over time two different forms of PRTs were deployed to Iraq: one civilian led and independent of military command, and the other embedded within military units and used to promote the goals of local counterinsurgency operations. Each of these models demonstrated the distinct characteristics of exclusive civilian and military leadership and the effects of stymied interagency cooperation.

The province-based PRTs were led by US State Department Foreign Service officers, marking a significant departure in structure from the Afghanistan model. These civilian teams remained independent of US military units operating in the same areas, possessing their own vehicles and dedicated movement security teams.[25] However, by 2007 US policy on the Iraq War was shifting to a heavier focus on counterinsurgency doctrine and the United States "created 14 new PRTs embedded with military brigades in Anbar Province and in and around Baghdad Province, so that both movement and perimeter security depended on the brigade."[26] Despite the different models, the personality driven civil-military cooperation of the PRT model was an important determinant of success due to the lack of strategic doctrine guiding the PRT effort in Iraq.[27]

In response to the demand for civilian participation in complex interagency reconstruction and stabilization operations such as Afghanistan and Iraq, the US State Department launched the Civilian Response Corps in 2008. This corps was an interagency effort to train and prepare non-military federal government personnel to deploy rapidly to emerging crisis areas.[28] In the corps, representatives of the US Department of State, Treasury, Agriculture, Commerce, Health and Human Services, Homeland Security, Justice, and USAID partnered to deploy resources on 48–72 hours notice. To avoid many of the interagency challenges inherent in the PRT concept, the State Department trained active and standby personnel from all eight participating agencies and departments together. A significant amount of the foundations training consisted of an introduction to USAID, the State Department and the Department of Defense. However, the civilian capacity to meet the needs of post-conflict reconstruction and stabilization operations remains nascent in 2009.

The eventual role of the corps has yet to be defined, but it has moved forward in developing capabilities to be deployed either with or without a military presence. In an article titled "Why Civilians Instead of Soldiers?," Corine Hegland observes that "building a system in which the military can depend on civilians to do civilian work requires a long-term investment in government."[29] The PRT was an early step toward this long-term investment, and many Civilian Response corps are alumni of the Afghanistan PRTs.

The PRT model developed in Afghanistan promoted the integration of the instruments of national power in an expeditionary setting. What began as a simple agreement between the military and two civilian entities that wanted to have officers gain visibility and design better programs in the country became an internationally championed method for approaching complex operations. This chapter is only a partial introduction to a topic that needs much more attention. As the US, NATO, and the UN are likely to engage in complex environments in the future, the use of combined civilian and military instruments of power will be more important.

Notes

1 US Secretary of State Condoleezza Rice, Speech at the Inauguration of Provincial Reconstruction Team in Ninawa Province, Iraq, November 11, 2005, available at http://iraq.usembassy.gov/iraq/2005 1111_rice_prt.html.

2   Twenty-six PRTs were established as of February 2008. Some PRTs were led by one nation, whereas others shared leadership between several nations. The countries leading or co-leading PRTs in Afghanistan included Australia, Belgium-Luxemburg, Canada, the Czech Republic, Denmark, Estonia, Germany, Hungary, Italy, Latvia, Lithuania, the Netherlands, New Zealand, Norway, Romania, South Korea, Spain, Sweden, Turkey, the United Kingdom, and the United States.

3   Provincial Reconstruction Teams (PRT) fact sheet, US Embassy/Iraq website, March 20, 2008, available at http://iraq.usembassy.gov/pr_01222008b.html.

4   Memorandum of Understanding Between Combined/Joint Task Force 180 and The US Department of State, August 15, 2002.

5   Memorandum of Understanding Between Combined/Joint Task Force 180 and US Agency for International Development, December 26, 2002.

6   Ibid.

7   Phone interview with Deborah Alexander, USAID Officer in 2002, March 4, 2008, Washington, DC.

8   Interview with Department of Defense official in the PRT directorate, October 28, 2003.

9   John A. Nagl, "The Expeditionary Imperative," *Wilson Quarterly*, Vol. 33, No. 1 (Winter 2009), 55–8.

10 For more information on CORDS, see: Richard A. Hunt, *Pacification: The American Struggle for Vietnam's Hearts and Minds*, Boulder, CO: Westview Press, 1995, pp. 82–132; Robert W. Komer, *Organization and Management of the New Model Pacification Program: 1966–1969*, Santa Monica, CA: RAND, 1970; Robert W. Komer, *Bureaucracy Does Its Thing: Institutional Constraints on U.S.-GVN Performance in Vietnam*, Santa Monica, CA: RAND, 1972; Thomas W. Scoville, *Reorganizing for Pacification Support*, Washington, DC: Center for Military History, 1982.

11 Originally, the deputies envisioned multiple US government civilian agencies participating in a PRT, including USAID, Department of State, US Dept of Agriculture, Dept of Health and Human Services, Dept of Justice, Dept of Education, etc. In reality, only the Dept of State, Dept of Agriculture, and USAID sent field staff to serve in Afghanistan-based PRTs, and often the State Department billet was not filled due to staffing issues so the State Department role did not become what the deputies had originally envisioned.

12 PRT Policy Guidance, Deputies Committee, June 2003.

13 Memorandum of Understanding Between Combined/Joint Task Force 180 and The US Department of State, August 15, 2002, and Memorandum of Understanding Between Combined/Joint Task Force 180 and US Agency for International Development, December 26, 2002.

14 To illustrate this point, Secretary Rumsfeld, Chairman of the Joint Chiefs of Staff Myers, and Ambassador Khalilzad visited the Jalalabad PRT two weeks after one of the authors (Parker) arrived in July 2004. The PRT military commander at the time determined that civilians did not need to participate in the briefing because it was a Department of Defense visit. He ordered his staff not to provide a seat at the table for USAID. The author disagreed with the military commander's decision, and as an equal part of the PRT chose to print her name card and add a seat to the table in the briefing room while the military commander greeted the VIPs at the landing zone, and was in the room waiting when the group entered. Secretary Rumsfeld spent much of the briefing quizzing the civilians on their activities and sharing his frustration in how few civilians were in the PRT. Although the military commander never mentioned the incident, USAID was included in all future briefings regardless of the visitor's affiliation.

15 Some military commanders allowed civilians to ride in US contractor's vehicles if they determined the environment was secure enough. The military commander was responsible for the civilian's security, so he or she was the final decision maker on how the civilians were allowed to travel.

16 This was a rare situation. From 2002 to 2007, there were only two cases of USAID field officers being reassigned to another PRT due to the lack of military support for the USAID mission.

17 USAID and the State Department purchased lightly and heavily armored SUVs to distribute to the field officers in PRTs. Most PRTs required their civilians to ride in military convoys, so although the civilians had their own vehicles, they were still required to be part of a convoy. Non-US PRTs had less oversight of the US civilians so some chose to drive themselves.

18 See Bob M. Perito, "The U.S. Experience with Provincial Reconstruction Teams in Afghanistan: Lessons Identified," Special Report No. 152, US Institute for Peace, October 2005; and see discussion by representatives Ileana Ros-Lehtinen, Todd Platts, and Steve Lynch at http://www.c-span archives.org/library/index.php?main_page=product_video_info&products_id=191137-1.

19 Other donors were approached for this position during ISAF IX and after, but only the Danish development agency supplied an officer to work in the headquarters. USAID continues to fill this position.
20 The ISAF IX Command Group consisted of all brigadier generals and above in rank and the senior civilians in headquarters, including the political advisor, the two development advisors, the deputy political advisor, the Prism cell (an internal think tank), and the NATO communications advisor.
21 These bodies had different names, depending on the province.
22 Some working groups were more effective than others, and much depended on the ministry's provincial representative. Some sectors had little or no local leadership, which made coordination very difficult, especially as the state was beginning to form. The descriptions here are merely to demonstrate some of the coordination mechanisms that existed, and not to comment on their effectiveness.
23 Some PRTs did not want USAID officers stationed on their bases for a variety of reasons, ranging from the logistics of human support (food, transport, housing) to more political reasons such as not wanting a US government official living on the base.
24 International Security Assistance Force, Provincial Reconstruction Team Handbook (2nd edn), October 31, 2006.
25 Jesse P. Pruett, "The Interagency Future: Embedded Provincial Reconstruction Teams in Task Force Marne," *Military Review* (September/October 2009), 55.
26 Henry L. Clarke, "Reconstructing Iraq's Provinces, One by One," *Joint Forces Quarterly*, No. 52 (1st Quarter 2009), 144.
27 Perito, "The U.S. Experience with Provincial Reconstruction Teams in Afghanistan": "The personal relationship between the DTL and the FOB commander strongly affects PRT operations."
28 See USAID website, "Civilian Response," available at http://www.usaid.gov/our_work/cross-cutting_programs/civilianresponse, accessed September 30, 2009. See also "Civilian Response Corps Launched," *Small Wars Journal*, July 16, 2008, available at http://smallwarsjournal.com/blog/2008/07/civilian-response-corps-launch-1/.
29 Corine Hegland, "Why Civilians Instead of Soldiers?," *National Journal* Vol. 39, No. 17 (April 28, 2007), 33.

18 Time

Austin Long

Time is a crucial factor in all forms of warfare, yet its role varies across the spectrum of conflict. At the high end of the spectrum—total or major conventional war—the role of time is succinctly captured in Civil War Commander Nathan Bedford Forrest's recipe for victory: "Get there first with the most men."[1] In other words, the key to winning battles was to employ maximal force in the shortest time possible, a dynamic which helped drive the tight mobilization schedules of the armies participating in World War I.[2] The advent of nuclear weapons and ballistic missiles compressed the time factor by orders of magnitude meaning an entire total war could potentially be concluded in a few hours, as Tom Lehrer comically noted ("I'll look for you when the war is over, an hour and a half from now") even as the same point was more grimly made by US military officers.[3]

In contrast, as one moves down the spectrum of conflict, the role of time changes. Wars characterized by the use of insurgency tend to be longer, as insurgents are dispersed within the population. The *median* length of insurgency appears to be between six and ten years.[4] Conventional wars, even very large ones, tend to be much shorter, with World War I lasting just over four years and World War II, six. One of the longest conventional wars of the twentieth century, the Iran–Iraq War, lasted only eight years; in contrast some insurgencies last in excess of two decades.

There are numerous reasons for this difference in duration of the two types of conflict but they can be reduced to differences in the actors and goals in the two categories. In major conventional war, the actors are nation-states and the goal is to defeat the fielded forces (and perhaps also to eliminate the ability to field additional forces) of the other side. In counterinsurgency, the actors are both nation-states and non-state actors, and the goal is to create or restore the monopoly of legitimate violence to the state. The latter goal is often more ambitious than the former, thus extending the duration of conflict.

The long duration of insurgency and counterinsurgency means that Forrest's equation is of less relevance. While it is still true of large-scale battles, these are much less common in counterinsurgency and often are of little importance to the overall outcome of the conflict. If major war is somewhat akin to a sprint, counterinsurgency is more like a marathon. In a marathon, time plays both a micro and macro role: the rhythm and pace of individual strides are important, yet an overall plan to run the course in a certain time is equally critical. So too in counterinsurgency does time play both a micro (tactical) and macro (strategic) role. Understanding and integrating these two aspects of time are vital to ensuring success in counterinsurgency.

Time at the tactical level

At the tactical level (meaning here the conduct of individual operations), the role of time is to establish routines or rhythms. Humans, like all animals, have natural biological rhythms; humans have also created social and technical artifacts that lead to additional rhythms.[5] These rhythms can be daily, weekly, monthly, or annual, depending on local factors. The term "battle rhythm" is used in the United States Army to capture many of these rhythms, defining it as "those events that a unit conducts on a recurring basis that facilitates setting the conditions for success."[6] While battle rhythm is not unique to counterinsurgency, it is of greater importance here than in more conventional warfare. This is due to both the longer overall duration of counterinsurgency and also because counterinsurgency operations are conducted in and among a civilian population that has many rhythms itself.

One of the most readily observable aspects of time at this level is the effect of day and night on rhythm. The typical description of day/night in counterinsurgency is that the government (i.e. the counterinsurgents) owns a given village or town during the day and the insurgents own the same area at night. Historically this has been due to the advantages conveyed by the cover of darkness to those operating covertly. In practice, the counter-insurgent will often attempt to contest control of the night, yet must also operate during the day. This can make for long operating hours.

Examples of day/night rhythm abound in practitioner descriptions of counterinsurgency. David Galula, a French company commander, described his company routine in Algeria in 1956 as beginning at 6:30 in the morning. After assembly, he would dispatch a daily convoy to battalion headquarters. He noted:

> We had been warned by Zone Headquarters that schedules and itinerary of convoys must be varied in order to avoid ambush. This was a fine idea, but in practice we had only one possible itinerary, and the distribution of food and supplies at the battalion command post took place in the morning at an hour that could not be changed because of various logistical imperatives at zone level . . . Lunch was around 12:30. Then the men rested until 2 p.m., most of them sleeping in anticipation of night watch and ambush . . . Once in a while I sent patrols out or went on operations during these hours just to show the rebels that we were not completely asleep. Our activity in the afternoon followed the same pattern as in the morning. Dinner was at about 6 p.m. During the night, ambushes went out. Sometimes I sent them simultaneously to different places, sometimes I spaced them at different hours.[7]

Galula's battle rhythm was thus driven by the demands of both higher headquarters logistics and insurgent activity. The day was given over to the former and the night the latter.

Marines operating in a Vietnamese village as part of a US-Vietnamese Combined Action Platoon (CAP) had a similar battle rhythm. Bing West describes the days of this unit as being given to digging in to reinforce its position and going into nearby hamlets to buy food, provide medical treatment to villagers, and other such mundane activities. At night, however, the unit sent out three or four patrols to hunt for insurgents.[8]

The advent of nearly ubiquitous night vision equipment in advanced militaries has altered the balance of day/night operations in counterinsurgency to some degree. Insurgents are no longer quite as safe in the dark when facing advanced counterinsurgents, who are in turn better able to use this time of day. This has lead to somewhat altered battle rhythm for US forces in both Afghanistan and Iraq.

In Afghanistan, US special operations forces operating under Combined Joint Special Operations Task Force Afghanistan (CJSOTF-A) established a battle rhythm similar to those seen in Algeria and Vietnam. Meetings and coordination took place in the morning and evening, leaving the middle of the day open.[9] However, rather than just sending out patrols, CJSOTF-A would conduct targeted operations such as raids at night. One example was Operation Princess in June 2004, which used ground and helicopter predawn assaults to capture insurgent leaders.[10] Night continues to be the preferred operating time for special operations forces.[11]

In Iraq, US battle rhythms in conventional units were often developed based in the interaction of local patterns of economic and social behavior, weather, insurgent activity, and US night-vision capabilities. For example, a common insurgent tactic was to emplace improvised explosive devices (IED) in the hours of predawn darkness. This time became a critical part of battle rhythm, which focused on having units in place and ready for counter-IED operations before this period began.[12]

Other operations were not so clearly tied to day/night per se, but rather to patterns of behavior of both the insurgents and the population. As indicated in Figure 18.1, in one region of Iraq, these patterns drove a considerable portion of the battle rhythm. Indirect fire (IDF) patterns indicated that insurgents would generally launch these attacks in the mornings (after dawn) and late afternoons. These patterns may have been in part due to the influence of available daylight for targeting, but more likely had to do with work patterns. Many insurgents also had business (legitimate or illegitimate) to conduct, so the period before and after business hours was a good time to launch an IDF attack. This was sometimes called "commuter jihad"

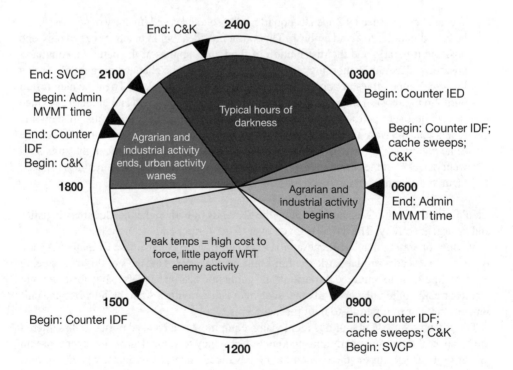

Figure 18.1 Iraq Unit Battle Rhythm, taken from an unclassified briefing from Multi-National Force-West

or "jihad on the way to work" by US officers. US battle rhythm for counter-IDF operations thus clustered around these two periods.[13]

This pattern of counter-IDF operations also fit in with the temperature gradient of Iraq. Midday temperatures during Iraqi summers frequently surpass 110 degrees Fahrenheit. Battle rhythm was therefore established to avoid major operations (unless critically time sensitive) during this time of day. Checkpoint operations, which required little movement once established, were the principal activity during this part of the day.

Patterns of local activity, weather, and US capabilities also interacted to push US administrative movement (e.g. logistics) to night and very early morning.[14] Few Iraqis were out at this time, meaning that convoys had clear roads and did not have to maintain the same vigilance about approaching civilian vehicles, which might be suicide vehicle-borne IEDs (SVBIEDs). Further, this period was cooler and therefore placed less strain on both personnel and vehicles.

In addition to the day/night cycle, other patterns influence tactical battle rhythm. In Afghanistan and Iraq, Islam plays a major role in daily and weekly battle rhythm. The Muslim call to prayer takes place five times daily and has some effect on when certain types of operations can take place. For example, meetings with the devout are often avoided around these times. More importantly, Friday is the Muslim holy day; many businesses close and individuals attend the mosque. Friday is thus frequently made a "low-tempo" day in the battle rhythm (at least in Afghanistan), as there are fewer opportunities to interact with the population.

The repetitious nature of battle rhythm can often have a deleterious effect on troop morale. In Iraq, this phenomenon of repetition has been termed "Groundhog Day," after the film in which the main character is forced to repeat the same day over and over again. The result of this phenomenon can range from complacency to frustrated (and potentially violent) outbursts. Tactical commanders have to be cognizant of this possibility and take steps to ameliorate it.[15]

Beyond the daily and weekly, other longer duration cycles also drive tactical considerations. Though generally not considered a part of battle rhythm, they are nonetheless routinely recurring. In Vietnam, the rice harvest (annual or semi-annual, depending on region) was a critical time as insurgents "taxed" the population for a portion of the rice in order to feed themselves. In August 1965, US forces south of Da Nang began operations, known as Operation Golden Fleece, to protect these harvests. Protection of the rice harvest soon became a major recurring element of US operations in Vietnam, serving to both hamper insurgent supply and to aid in "winning the hearts and minds" of the population.[16]

In Iraq, Islam is the source of several recurring patterns (beyond the daily and weekly) of tactical importance. The annual pilgrimage to Mecca, known as the Hajj, and the Shia observance of Ashura both require protection, as they involve major movements of large groups of the devout. US and Iraqi forces have annually conducted extensive security operations to protect observance of these religious activities.[17]

Weather is also a major component of these longer-term cycles. Southeast Asia experiences annual rainy seasons that can render movement along roads nearly impossible. This made warfare in the region a seasonal affair in many cases. For example, the war in Laos (1960–75) pitted relatively conventional forces from North Vietnam along with their Pathet Lao allies against US supported quasi-guerrilla units. US helicopter and fixed-wing aircraft gave these units mobility during the rainy season, while the numerically superior North Vietnamese were unable to move. While not strictly a counterinsurgency, as both combatant forces were at least semi-conventional, this weather-driven dynamic made the war in Laos tilt back and forth according to season, as the US-backed forces could seize key points during the rainy season but the North Vietnamese could reclaim them once the roads were passable again.[18]

Of course, war is not just about rhythm; it is broken up by engagements. Here time plays a critical role as well. Tactical engagements in counterinsurgency are often very brief; therefore time is at a premium.

The surprise attack is perhaps the tactical area where time is most precious, for both the initiator and the victim. Surprise attack from the insurgent side can be a mechanical ambush with an IED or other trap, a direct fire ambush, or a combination of the two (a "complex attack"). From the counterinsurgent, the surprise attack is usually a raid, with a specific target or targets.

For the initiator, success is strongly correlated with successful concealment or stealthy approach (to achieve surprise) combined with executing the operation at high speed. Together these two factors produce shock, and this in turn prevents an effective response by the victim. This is not a particularly new approach for some; it has long been a special operations force maxim.[19] John Boyd's OODA loop (observe, orient, decide, act) and theories of maneuver warfare also echo this point.

However, the need for speed and surprise applies to insurgent and counterinsurgent initiators in somewhat different ways due to the fundamental asymmetry of the two forces. For the insurgent, this combination allows an effective attack while minimizing the likelihood of a successful response from the counterinsurgent's often overwhelmingly superior firepower. For the counterinsurgent, this combination allows successful action against a target that is often highly mobile and able to blend into a population with ease if given time.

For the victim, the converse of the foregoing is true. If the victim is a counterinsurgent, time is at a premium because the initiator is likely to withdraw quickly if given time, particularly in the case of a mechanical ambush like a command-detonated IED. Relentless battle drills to make the response to contact as smooth, automatic, and rapid as possible are therefore crucial, as this will allow the counterinsurgent's firepower advantage to come into play. In contrast, the response to a raid for the insurgent is flight, concealment, or both. Given even a modest warning, a target can disappear (unless already under persistent surveillance), forcing the counterinsurgent to begin the painstaking process of gathering actionable intelligence again.

The foregoing is just a short summary of the wide variety of ways that time acts to set the pace of activity at the tactical level. Ultimately, however, tactics win battles but not wars. Strategy is required to convert tactical success into overall victory.

Time at the strategic level

At the strategic level (meaning here the overall structure and plan for the counterinsurgency), the role of time is more critical than at the tactical level: it has three principal effects, all having to do with the long duration of most counterinsurgency campaigns. The first is the impact of time horizons on appropriate organizational structures for conducting the war. The second is the impact on war planning for what can be called "third-party counterinsurgents," meaning those seeking to conduct or support counterinsurgency operations in a foreign country or territory. The third is a general maturation effect, as the long duration means that the very nature of the combatants and their conflict can change substantially over the course of the insurgency.

Creating the appropriate organizational structure for the conduct of war is central to strategic success. Organizational design involves making many trade-offs (level of centralization, layers of hierarchy, functional specialization, etc.), but the central one for warfighting is finding the optimal balance of temporal efficiency versus effectiveness. Temporal efficiency is the production of a given action (such as a tactical operation) with the lowest consumption of time. Effectiveness is the measure of how well that action achieves the intended end.

In major conventional wars, which combine relatively short duration and large scale, the appropriate organization is one which finds a balance between temporal efficiency and effectiveness. The pace of operations can often be very rapid, particularly with motorized and mechanized forces, so temporal efficiency is important. However, it is not so important that effectiveness of operations is meaningless.

The organizational design this environment favors is epitomized by the modern military unit and staff system, developed in the early part of the nineteenth century and perfected by the mid-twentieth. Functionally specialized subunits of a given military unit (e.g. battalion or division) handle different aspects of warfighting (e.g. intelligence, operations, logistics) in order to enable a single commander to make and execute decisions in a timely fashion. These decisions are then passed as orders to subordinate units, which then undertake the actual operation (or pass orders on to further subordinates, depending on the units and operations). The emphasis of the entire organization is on achieving timely and effective results, with timely being almost as important as effective. These organizations prefer a timely "80 percent solution" to a significantly slower but potentially more effective solution, as this is the optimal balance between temporal efficiency and effectiveness in the major conventional war environment.

Counterinsurgency, as noted earlier, is a different environment, with a much longer average length of conflict. This leads to both a much lower overall operational tempo and, therefore, less of a premium on temporal efficiency in most cases. The requirement for rapid, decisive action is sporadic in counterinsurgency, rather than nearly constant as in major conventional war.

At the same time, the need for effectiveness in action is greater in counterinsurgency. In major conventional war, the primary goal is the defeat of the forces of the enemy, which only requires being more effective than those opposing forces. In contrast, the formation or re-formation of a nation-state (the ultimate goal of counterinsurgency) involves significantly more than just a contest of military forces. It requires the formation of effective institutions, the training of personnel for the institutions, and the inculcation of some degree of loyalty to those institutions in the broader population.

The very structure of the counterinsurgency problem and the average lengthy duration of conflict combine to create a very different relationship between the need for temporal efficiency and effectiveness. Temporal efficiency is generally much less important in counterinsurgency than effectiveness, so organizational design for counterinsurgency should place a much greater premium on effectiveness than temporal efficiency. Put more simply, the organizational design for counterinsurgency should not be optimized for the timely 80 percent solution favored in major conventional war. Instead, it should seek effectiveness even if decisions are made more slowly.

The best example of organizational design for counterinsurgency is the British war committee system first utilized in Malaya. This system emerged from a hodge-podge of committees created between 1948 and 1950, as the insurgency in Malaya gathered momentum. The basic goal of the system was to ensure coordination of action between the military, the police, and civilian administrators. The initial haphazard committee structure was rationalized beginning in 1950 as part of the overall counterinsurgency plan created under the new director of operations (a senior civilian charged with coordinating counterinsurgency), Lieutenant General Harold Briggs (Retd).[20]

Briggs sought to effectively unify the security forces' actions with those of the civilian administrators, so he implemented a system of "war by committee," creating a pyramid of committees unifying the disparate actors. At the top was the Federal War Council. Its chairman was the high commissioner, a civilian and Briggs' superior. Additional members included Briggs, the chief secretary (a senior civilian administrator), the secretary of defense, the commissioner of police, and the senior ground and air force commanders. This committee set overall policy and allocated resources for the conflict.[21]

The next tier down in the system was the state war executive committee (SWEC), whose principal members were the senior civilian, police officer, and military officer in the state (a political subunit of Malaya as a whole). Other members could include representatives of non-governmental organizations such as the chief of the Planter's Association. There were a total of 11 SWECs, meeting in full session about once every two weeks. Each SWEC also had an operations subcommittee, generally more focused on security matters, which met more frequently (in one case meeting daily). The SWECs all reported up to the Federal War Council.[22]

The lowest tier was the district war executive committee (DWEC), which was more operationally focused than the SWEC. The principal membership was the district's senior civilian, the district police superintendent, and the battalion commander whose forces were present in the district (one battalion commander might have forces in multiple districts, so this would often be the commander's representative).[23] The DWECs fundamentally had the full panoply of powers of the state, and due to their committee structure ensured that these powers were not used at cross-purposes by different parts of the state apparatus. As Riley Sunderland summed up:

> The DWECs had very wide powers. They ordered police and military operations, controlled food supplies, and set curfews. They also maintained liaison among local agencies of government, which meant that the civil administrator could restrain the Security Forces from any proposed action likely to cause more ill will among the people than casualties among the terrorists, while the Security Forces could point out to the civil authorities the military implications of proposed local regulations.[24]

The war committee system thus ensured that actions taken were very likely to be effective from the perspective of counterinsurgency as a whole rather than just the military or civilian aspects. It did so by sacrificing some degree of the temporal efficiency that military officers trained for major conventional war were accustomed to. Briggs faced considerable resistance in implementing this system of war by committee, and at the conclusion of his 18-month term as director of operations the system had still not been perfected.

Briggs' successor, Sir Gerald Templer, was another retired general and it was to him that the task of perfecting the committee system would fall. Templer had the advantage of being given the position of both high commissioner and director of operations, as well as the power to issue orders to military units without reference to the regional headquarters for the Far East. His position, sometimes referred to simply as "Supremo," enabled him to enforce full compliance with the committee system by all government agencies.[25]

This system was, to say the least, highly abnormal for the military in particular. It essentially relegated not just the military's Far East command but also the division commanders to a role of support rather than command. Even brigade commanders functioned mostly as members of the SWEC rather than having a stand-alone brigade headquarters. Battalion commanders saw most of their companies parceled out to individual DWECs. The commander of the 17th Gurkha Division, whose unit provided most of the troops in Malaya, contented himself to routinely visiting the various SWECs and DWECs but had essentially no operational role.[26]

This system, however alien and cumbersome relative to the normal military way of operating, was highly successful in Malaya. By ensuring that all actions were taken in accord with the full framework of counterinsurgency rather than simply emphasizing military operations, the committee system achieved a high degree of effectiveness in operations even though the system was not optimal from the perspective of temporal efficiency. Although the war would take until the early 1960s to conclude fully, by 1954 the insurgency had been marginalized and by 1957 it had almost collapsed.

The British also used a committee system in conducting other counterinsurgency campaigns, though sometimes in a less formalized fashion. During the Dhofar insurgency in Oman, the British created a committee known as the Dhofar Development Committee to serve a function analogous to that of a SWEC in Malaya. It was headed by the senior civilian in Dhofar and included the brigade commander for the region.[27]

However, Dhofar lacked the infrastructure and civil service of Malaya, so there was no equivalent to the DWEC. Instead, that role was filled by civil action teams (CATs), which worked with the military to develop the various tribal areas in Dhofar. There was also no equivalent to the Federal War Council, as the sultan of Oman's autocratic rule and the small size of the state obviated the need for high-level coordination.[28]

In contrast to the British embrace of the committee system in Malaya and Oman, the United States has been less willing to utilize a similar organizational structure in counterinsurgency. In Vietnam, for example, the United States had no equivalent to a SWEC or a DWEC, despite the recommendations of both counterinsurgency doctrine and a major Army staff study of the counterinsurgency problem in that country. This latter study, known as "A Program for the Pacification and Long-Term Development of South Vietnam" (known by the acronym PROVN), was the most detailed attempt to design an appropriate organizational structure for counterinsurgency.[29]

PROVN's main organizational reform was to call for the designation of a "single manager" for counterinsurgency at each level of effort. At the senior level, PROVN recommended that the single manager be the US ambassador, who would be invested with powers roughly equivalent to that enjoyed by Templer in Malaya. At the province level, a senior US representative (SUSREP) would have authority for all US activity. The SUSREP would then work with his South Vietnamese counterpart, the province chief, who would be vested with similar authority.[30]

Unfortunately, PROVN was not well received by the US Army and its recommendations were not implemented.[31] Instead, after considerable prompting from the White House in 1966 and 1967, an organization known as Civil Operations and Revolutionary (later Rural) Development Support (CORDS) was created. CORDS pulled together the disparate civilian activities undertaken by US government agencies in South Vietnam under a single organization, headed by a civilian deputy to the senior US military officer in South Vietnam.[32]

CORDS was a step forward in coordinating actions on the civilian side, but it did little to address the balance of temporal efficiency and effectiveness. The US military still relied on the organizational design for major conventional war that was its standard. South Vietnam remained divided into four corps zones, with divisions, brigades, and battalions reporting up the chain of command. While this arrangement was temporally efficient, it did not ensure maximal effectiveness of operations in terms of the overall counterinsurgency campaign. US military operations were never restrained by US civilian agencies in the same way that British operations were and vice versa.

Despite different organizational designs for counterinsurgency, the British and US efforts were similar in that both were acting as third-party counterinsurgents (though this was not initially true of the British in colonial Malaya, negotiations for independence began early in the war and it was granted in 1957). Both therefore had to balance the commitment of resources to the counterinsurgency against the global interests of their nations and the need for domestic support of the campaign. This second requirement was particularly important for the British and Americans as both were democratic and therefore highly responsive to their respective populations. The emergence of strong domestic opposition to a campaign conducted by a democratic third-party counterinsurgent ultimately spells its end.[33]

The critical determinant of domestic support is the level of resource expenditure. Low levels of expenditure require corresponding low levels of resource extraction from the population in terms of both capital (through taxation) and labor (through a draft or volunteer recruitment). Low levels of extraction provoke low domestic opposition and therefore enable the conduct of a campaign of the length necessary for effective counterinsurgency. Put more simply, the lower the annual "burn rate" of resources, the longer the campaign can be sustained (another echo of the "counterinsurgency as marathon" analogy).

The British, partly by design and partly by virtue of limited total resources in the aftermath of World War II, had a very low burn rate in Malaya. Financially, most of the cost of the war was borne by Malaya itself. The British government expenditure in Malaya for the period 1948–60 has been estimated at roughly $235 million or about $2 billion in constant (2009) dollars. Most of this expenditure came in the period 1948–55, but the average annual burn rate was still less than $300 million in constant dollars. Even for the financially strained British this burn rate was sustainable.[34]

Similarly, British manpower demands were relatively low. At the peak of military deployments in 1952, there were 12 British battalions, comprising a little more than half of the total of about 22,000 combat troops in Malaya. These troops were supported by Gurkha and Commonwealth forces as well as by the growing Malayan Army and police force.[35]

In contrast, the US effort in Vietnam involved vast expenditure of both money and manpower. The Congressional Research Service estimated the total cost of Vietnam from 1965 to 1975 as slightly more than $670 billion in constant dollars. Total US military personnel peaked in 1969 at over 500,000 in South Vietnam.[36]

It is of course not entirely appropriate to compare these two very different conflicts, as the structure of the problem in South Vietnam was much more difficult than that in Malaya for a number of reasons; in particular the role of North Vietnam as a source of support to the insurgency. This drove the United States to invest ever-greater levels of resources into South Vietnam. However, it is nonetheless instructive in seeking to explain why the United States public lost patience with the war effort barely three years after the deployment of combat troops, while the British public was quiescent about the war in Malaya for the entire 12 years of the conflict.

It is also important to note that major opposition from both the public and in Congress to war in Vietnam did not begin until after the United States increased its "burn rate" by committing combat troops and incurring vast financial cost. Prior to 1965, opposition to US support to South Vietnam was muted. After the withdrawal of most US combat forces (and the draft that extracted these troops), opposition decreased, though it remained high enough that the US was unable to effectively support the government of South Vietnam against a North Vietnamese offensive in 1975.[37]

Other third-party counterinsurgency efforts by the two countries have required even less expenditure of resources. In the Dhofar campaign in Oman, the British government only provided a little over 500 advisors, who were seconded to the Sultan's Armed Forces (SAF) on detached duty or served on contracts to the Sultan. Similarly, British overall financial costs were low, with Oman shouldering most of the burden (with additional support from Iran and Jordan). The result was that the British support, in the words of historian Thomas Mockaitis, "produced few hostile questions from either major political party."[38]

The United States used a similar low "burn rate" approach in supporting the government of El Salvador in the 1980s. US military support was limited by a Congress wary of "another Vietnam," resulting in an official limit of 55 military advisors (though various bureaucratic tricks meant that the actual number of military personnel in El Salvador was usually somewhat higher). Further, the US costs of the war over the course of the decade were only about $12 billion in constant (2009) dollars.[39]

While some argue that the US approach in El Salvador did not result in an unambiguous victory for the government, this low-cost approach nonetheless kept political opposition to the strategy much lower than opposition to Vietnam. This limited opposition allowed the United States to maintain support for an entire decade, at the end of which negotiations produced an acceptable conclusion to the conflict (largely but not entirely due to the end of the Cold War). Moreover, this opposition to US support was in large part due to concerns about the Salvadorian government and military. The Salvadorian military had an atrocious record of human rights violation in the early 1980s, which at best saw only modest improvement during the remainder of the war.[40]

This pattern of lower levels of effort yielding longer periods of support for third-party counterinsurgents appears to be at least partly sustained in the recent conflicts in Iraq and Afghanistan. The high rate of resource consumption in Iraq, particularly in terms of manpower and casualties but also with fiscal expenditures of in excess of $10 billion per month in constant dollars, has at least contributed to the US electorate's desire to withdraw from the conflict, which in turn became a campaign promise of then candidate Barack Obama. In contrast, the US effort in Afghanistan has consumed much lower resource levels and, at least partly as a result, is still much more strongly supported by the electorate.[41]

This comparison should not be overdrawn, as the two wars began in very different contexts. Afghanistan began as an invasion in response to a terrorist attack on US soil and was thus widely supported from the beginning, while Iraq was a preventive war and enjoyed lower initial support. Yet this does suggest that the current plan to "surge" US forces into Afghanistan will have a very limited time in which to achieve success, as the increased resource consumption will begin to generate pressures to withdraw from that country as well.

Afghanistan and Iraq are also unusual in that both follow an invasion and regime change by the United States. This necessitated a significant commitment of US resources, at least initially, as there was no government to support in either country; the United States was required to build one in both cases. In contrast, the United States has been able to support counterinsurgency by the government of Pakistan using a less resource-intensive approach. US support to Pakistan during the period after September 11, 2001 has seen minimal opposition despite Pakistan's alleged ongoing support to terrorists and concerns about its involvement in nuclear proliferation. US support to Pakistan from fiscal year 2002 to fiscal year 2009 exceeded $14 billion in constant dollars, with minimal US personnel in the country.[42] This aid has undoubtedly increased the Pakistani government and military capabilities to some degree. However, insurgency and general lawlessness have nonetheless seemed to increase despite US support, particularly in western Pakistan.

These contrasting experiences with resource consumption and duration suggest that strategy may often be a Hobson's choice for third-party counterinsurgents. The annual resource levels needed to produce victory may often be greater than the willingness of the domestic audience to shoulder that burden. Extracting these greater levels of resources may therefore cause withdrawal before success can be achieved. The alternative is to commit politically acceptable levels of resources for a much longer period, knowing that this may merely be "buying time" as the resources are insufficient to ensure victory.

The long duration of insurgency has a third effect as the nature of a conflict and the belligerents can change substantially as counterinsurgency campaigns continue over the course of years. This process, which can be termed a maturation effect, can often complicate efforts to end the counterinsurgency. In other cases, however, it may create opportunities for the counterinsurgent that did not exist in the initial stages.

Colombia presents perhaps the most striking example of maturation effects over the course of decades. In the 1960s, following the Colombian civil conflict known as La Violencia (the Violence), a variety of leftwing groups began insurgent activity against the Colombian government, most notably the Revolutionary Armed Forces of Colombia (FARC). For the next two decades, these leftwing groups were relatively unsuccessful in expanding but were able to continue low-level insurgent activity.[43]

In the 1980s, the booming demand for cocaine in the United States led to an explosion of profits for coca growers and traffickers in Colombia. FARC began to tax these profits, greatly expanding its resources and capabilities. At the same time, the criminal cartels in Colombia grew into potential threats to the Colombian state, most exemplified by Pablo Escobar. Escobar used the enormous profits of the cocaine trade to either bribe or intimidate many state officials, as well as sponsoring various terrorist attacks to coerce the state. His death in 1993 (enabled by covert US assistance) ended that particular threat but not the cocaine trade, and FARC's involvement with the trade increased during this period. FARC's original leftwing motives also began to change or were diluted to some degree, as for many of the lower-ranking members the conflict itself had become integral both to their identities and to their livelihoods.[44]

In response to the growing capacity of FARC, various wealthy landowners and cocaine traffickers formed their own paramilitaries in the early 1990s. These groups would in 1997 form an umbrella organization known as the Autodefensas Unidas de Colombia (AUC) that served as a potent third force in the counterinsurgency campaign. US support to Colombian counternarcotics efforts also began to increase substantially in the late 1990s in an effort known as Plan Colombia. Though not intended to support counterinsurgency, Plan Colombia increased the capacity of the Colombian security forces and thus inherently increased their capability against FARC. Beginning in 2003, after a series of government offensives against FARC, the AUC accepted conditional amnesty and demobilization.[45]

The point of the foregoing is that over the course of four decades, insurgency in Colombia was marked by the appearance of new resources (cocaine), the emergence of new actors (the AUC and the drug cartels), changes in the nature of insurgents (FARC), changes in third-party counterinsurgent support (covert support against Escobar and Plan Colombia), and the disappearance of actors (the AUC). The long duration of the conflict has led to changes that would make it unrecognizable from the perspective of its origin in the 1960s. This maturation phenomenon, while not always as dramatic as in Colombia, is nonetheless common in long-lived counterinsurgency campaigns.

Maturation effects can occur more rapidly in some instances. In Iraq, the Sunni insurgency, unified in opposition to the United States in 2003–4, began to fragment in 2005. Nationalist and tribal elements of the insurgency turned against al-Qaeda in Iraq (AQI) and, after negotiations, sided with the United States against their former allies.[46] This shift radically altered the course of the conflict, bringing security to parts of Iraq, most notably Anbar province and Sunni parts of Baghdad, which had only a year before been incredibly violent.

Conclusion

An appreciation of both the tactical and strategic aspects of time in counterinsurgency is critical to an overall understanding of the course of a conflict. Temporal cycles of varying lengths drive tactical operations, from day-to-day patroling to major offensives and counter-offensives. The average length of counterinsurgency conflicts is sufficiently long that it requires an organizational approach and commitment of resources that is, from the perspective of analysts accustomed to conventional war, counterintuitive. Moreover, the nature of the conflict can change radically over time, as actors and resources emerge or disappear. Failure to incorporate these two aspects of time into counterinsurgency campaign planning, like attempting to run a marathon as a sprint, will ultimately doom the effort.

Notes

1   Quoted in Bruce Catton, *The Civil War*, Boston: Houghton Mifflin, 2005, p. 160.
2   Barbara Tuchman, *The Guns of August*, New York: Macmillan, 1962.
3   See Tom Lehrer, "So Long, Mom (A Song for World War III)" lyrics on "That Was The Year That Was" (1965) and David Alan Rosenberg, "A Smoking Radiating Ruin at the End of Two Hours: Documents on American Plans for Nuclear War with the Soviet Union, 1954–1955," *International Security*, Vol. 6, No. 3 (Winter 1981/2).
4   See James Fearon and David Laitin, "Ethnicity, Insurgency, and Civil War," *American Political Science Review*, Vol. 97, No. 1 (February 2003); and Martin Libicki, "Eighty-nine Insurgencies: Outcomes and Endings," in David C. Gompert, John Gordon IV, et. al., *War by Other Means: Building Complete and Balanced Capabilities for Counterinsurgency*, Santa Monica, CA: RAND, 2008.
5   See Dean V. Buonomano, "The Biology of Time Across Different Scales," *Nature Chemical Biology*, Vol. 3, No. 10 (September 2007).
6   See Center for Army Lessons Learned Newsletter 97–8, "Search and Attack! Tactics, Techniques and Procedures," Appendix B.
7   David Galula, *Pacification in Algeria, 1956–1958*, Santa Monica, CA: Rand Corporation, 1963, pp. 110–13.
8   Bing West, *The Village*, New York: Pocket Books, 2003, pp. 23–76.
9   Adrian Bogart, *One Valley at a Time*, Hurlburt Field, FL: Joint Special Operations University Press, 2006, p. 44.
10 Ibid., pp. 59–60.
11 See additional commentary in Sean Naylor, *Not A Good Day to Die: The Untold Story of Operation Anaconda*, New York: Berkley Books, 2005.
12 See Peter Mansoor, *Baghdad at Sunrise: A Brigade Commander's War in Iraq*, New Haven, CT: Yale University Press, 2008.
13 Figure 18.1 and discussion taken from an unclassified briefing from Multi-National Force-West.
14 Briefing with Maj. Gen. John Kelly, October 23, 2008, available at http://www.mnf-iraq.com/index.php?option=com_content&task=view&id=23225&Itemid=132.
15 See FM 22-51, Leaders' Manual for Combat Stress Control, Washington, DC: Headquarters, Department of the Army, 1994, Chapter 9.
16 Allan R. Millet, *Semper Fidelis: The History of the United States Marine Corps* (rev. edn), New York: The Free Press, 1991, pp. 570–1.
17 See for example, BBC News, January 19, 2008, available at http://news.bbc.co.uk/2/hi/middle_east/7197473.stm.

18 See Roger Warner, *Shooting at the Moon: The Story of America's Clandestine War in Laos*, South Royalton, VT: Steerforth Press, 1996; and Kenneth Conboy and James Morrison, *Shadow War: The CIA's Secret War in Laos*, Boulder, CO: Paladin Press, 1995.
19 William McRaven, *Spec Ops: Case Studies in Special Operations Warfare: Theory and Practice*, Novato, CA: Presidio Press, 1995, pp. 16–21.
20 Riley Sunderland, *Organizing Counterinsurgency in Malaya, 1948–1960*, Santa Monica, CA: Rand Corporation, 1964, pp. 30–6.
21 Ibid., pp.36–7.
22 Ibid., pp. 40–2.
23 Ibid., pp. 41–3.
24 Ibid., pp. 43–4.
25 Ibid., pp. 60–4.
26 Ibid., pp. 74–8.
27 Thomas R. Mockaitis, *British Counterinsurgency in the Post-Imperial Era*, New York: Manchester University Press, 1995, pp. 79–80.
28 Mockaitis, *British Counterinsurgency in the Post-Imperial Era*, pp. 77–9.
29 See Austin Long, *Doctrine of Eternal Recurrence: The US Military and Counterinsurgency Doctrine, 1960–1970 and 2003–2006*, Santa Monica, CA: Rand Corporation, 2008, for discussion of the content of US counterinsurgency doctrine; and US Department of the Army, A Program for the Pacification and Long-Term Development of South Vietnam (PROVN), March 1966.
30 PROVN, pp. 60–77.
31 See William Gibbons, *The US Government and the Vietnam War: Executive and Legislative Roles and Relationships*, Princeton, NJ: Princeton University Press, 1995, Part IV, pp. 201–12.
32 See Richard Hunt, *Pacification: The American Struggle for Vietnam's Hearts and Minds*, Boulder, CO: Westview Press, 1995.
33 See Gil Merom, *How Democracies Lose Small Wars: State, Society, and the Failures of France in Algeria, Israel in Lebanon, and the United States in Vietnam*, New York: Cambridge University Press, 2003; and Eliot Cohen, "Constraints on America's Conduct of Small Wars," *International Security*, Vol. 9, No. 2 (Autumn 1984).
34 Robert Komer, *The Malayan Emergency in Retrospect: Organization of a Successful Counterinsurgency Effort*, Santa Monica, CA: Rand Corporation, 1972, pp. 22–4.
35 Riley Sunderland, *Army Operations in Malaya, 1947–1960*, Santa Monica, CA: Rand Corporation, 1964.
36 Stephen Dagget, Costs of Major US Wars, Congressional Research Service report, July 2008.
37 John E. Mueller, *War, Presidents, and Public Opinion*, New York: Wiley, 1973.
38 Mockaitis, *British Counterinsurgency in the Post-Imperial Era*, p. 91.
39 Benjamin Schwarz, *American Counterinsurgency Doctrine and El Salvador: The Frustration of Reform and the Illusion of Nation Building*, Santa Monica, CA: Rand Corporation, 1991, p. v.
40 Ibid., pp. 22–34.
41 See Amy Belasco, The Cost of Iraq, Afghanistan, and Other Global War on Terror Operations Since 9/11, Congressional Research Service report, October 2008.
42 K. Alan Kronstadt, Direct Overt US Aid and Military Reimbursements to Pakistan, FY2002-FY2009, Congressional Research Service report, October 2008.
43 Nazih Richani, *Systems of Violence: The Economy of War and Peace in Colombia*, New York: State University of New York Press, 2002.
44 Angel Rabasa and Peter Chalk, *Colombian Labyrinth: The Synergy of Drugs and Insurgency and Its Implications for Regional Stability*, Santa Monica, CA: Rand Corporation, 2001. Mark Bowden, *Killing Pablo: The Hunt for the World's Greatest Outlaw*, New York: Atlantic Monthly Press, 2001.
45 Plan Colombia: Drug Reduction Goals Were Not Fully Met but Security Has Improved; US Agencies Need More Detailed Plans for Reducing Assistance, Government Accountability Office report, October 2008. Juan Forero, "Witness Ties Colombian General to Paramilitaries," *The Washington Post*, September 17, 2008.
46 Austin Long, "The Anbar Awakening," *Survival*, Vol. 50, No. 2 (April–May 2008), 67–94.

19 Counterinsurgency in context

Thomas Rid and Thomas Keaney

Counterinsurgency remains a moving target. One recent war gave rise to a new wave of counterinsurgency theory and practice. Another war consolidated some of the knowledge and the routines among the US land forces and their allies. But both wars are not over as this book goes to press, so the relevance of the lessons explored in these pages remains undetermined. Iraq appears to be headed into a more stable and more secure future than many expected possible in 2006 and 2007, and perhaps even a freer and more prosperous one. Afghanistan's future seems more uncertain. Yet, in both cases, it is uncertain how future historians will judge the outcome. It is important to note that the counterinsurgency methods developed and used in Iraq played an important role in turning the tide of that war. But for the time being and for the next several years, it is impossible to say if they laid the foundation for a more durable success. It is also very difficult to gauge if these promising new methods can be successfully applied and transplanted to other operational settings, much less to other regions and cultures. Any concluding statement therefore has to start by stressing modesty and limitations.

Several of these limitations apply to this book. The first is its narrow focus. *Understanding Counterinsurgency* has attempted to shed light on some basic doctrinal, operational, and strategic foundations of counterinsurgency. Various contributions highlighted the political and cultural aspects of war among the people; for instance the chapters on intelligence, culture, ethics, and governance. But the political aspects highlighted there were largely limited to the operational theater, to the field; and even that was necessarily done in an abstract, general fashion. The book therefore took a narrow view: it largely, and deliberately, ignored the vital context of counterinsurgency operations in the domestic political arena of the intervening power. Yet, it should be stressed that parliaments, the elected representatives of the people, in America but of course also in other democracies, are *part* of the larger war effort. War, in Clausewitz's timeless words, is a continuation of the political intercourse by other means, military means. These means are manned, equipped, funded, and psychologically supported by those who stayed behind. War, that is, is an expression of the national interest and the popular will, albeit perhaps the most extreme one. It cannot be separated from a nation's expression of its political goals.

For the practitioner as well as for the scholar of counterinsurgency, the consequences of Clausewitz's seemingly simple insight are profound; more profound than is often realized. In France, in the years after 1962, when Charles de Gaulle, one of the nation's greatest men, "lost" the war in Algeria, a number of veterans and scholars succumbed to the belief that the war *could have* been won, that the Plan Challe *could have* worked—had the political support at the home front not waned, had France not lost patience.

From this interpretation, it was only a short step to blame the media, the Left, or individual weak-kneed politicians and generals. The United States saw a comparable debate and reaction after the Vietnam War, although it was in many ways less vicious and destructive than France's. And to this day, both in France and in the United States, many people and some well-published scholars hold the view that these wars might have been victories, had the media reported differently, or had the military acted more forcefully. But even sophisticated and intellectually creative variants of the "stab in the back" thesis have a self-destructive and, at heart, an undemocratic bent. The metaphor itself is as seductive as it is conceptually misleading: the popular will cannot stab an army in the back—*it is its back*. National political support for any use of military force is one of the most fundamental elements of strategic reasoning, not something that is nice to have and unpleasant not to have. This caveat applies to all military operations that require a significant sacrifice—including counterinsurgencies.

A second limitation applies to the operational theater. Counterinsurgencies, as readers will be well aware at this point, are political struggles, not only in parliaments but also in theater. An insurgency needs a cause, a political objective, and a motivation that pulls in tempted potential supporters—that cause is, in David Galula's words, an insurgency's most valuable asset. Taking Galula seriously, therefore, means taking the granular origins of grievances very seriously: the local cultures, tribal or other loyalties, political systems, ideologies, faiths, beliefs, social dynamics, economic structures—even the languages, dialects, feelings, prejudices, and conspiracy theories—that dominate the setting in which an uprising may be brewing. Many of these details are endemic to one particular area, ethnic group, tribe, or clan, and cannot be generalized. But this book—in a way reflecting the counterinsurgency debate itself—has focused on the themes and subjects that can be generalized. Only an in-depth case-study design could have avoided this shortfall—and the case studies of such an approach would have to be current ones, not least for the significant influence of information technology on modern conflict; and preferably from Muslim countries, mostly for the significant influence of modern jihadi doctrine. Even a solid understanding of counterinsurgency methods and principles cannot replace the more critical understanding of local conditions.

This limitation relates to a third one: the odd relationship between counterinsurgency and counterterrorism. *Understanding Counterinsurgency* is of limited value to students who want to understand counterterrorism. Yet, both wars, the war in Iraq and the war in Afghanistan, were launched in reaction to the terrorist attacks of 9/11. Afghanistan was the temporary home of the planners; and Iraq was thought to be ready to pass on weapons of mass destruction to the next set of perpetrators. Counterinsurgency, therefore, from the start, had a counter-terrorism rationale. The most popular expression of this rationale is that Afghanistan must not again become a "safe haven" for jihadis with a global agenda; that it must not be used as a "launch pad" for terrorism against the United States and its allies. But the connection between counterinsurgency and counterterrorism is much more complex than such metaphors would have it appear.

Counterinsurgency, as one of the debate's common wisdoms has it, is a local affair. Consequently a counterinsurgency operation may be successful in a certain region—like, for instance, in al-Anbar province or in Helmand province in Afghanistan—without having any palpable effect on counterterrorism in Europe or the United States, simply because it is so regional. Conversely, counterterrorism operations may be successful in preventing attacks that are connected to an insurgency in some indirect way—the attackers may have trained in an Afghan camp in the past, or they may just have communicated with jihadis in the Afghan-Pakistani border region. In other words—assuming success—succeeding against an insurgency and succeeding against specific terrorists that are part of a wider, global ideological movement may be two different things. The assumption of failure might be even more instructive: it may be possible to avoid future terrorist attacks without succeeding in counterinsurgency, and it may be possible to succeed in counterinsurgency without avoiding future terrorist attacks. The book has not tackled this most fundamental problem.

Finally, a number of broader themes that have influenced today's debate on security and military policy need to be mentioned. One historical theme, perhaps the dominant one, is counterinsurgency's colonial heritage. Counterinsurgencies in the twenty-first century—and in an altogether different way even insurgencies in the twenty-first century—are connected to colonialism in several ways that should be kept strictly separated. One aspect is that concepts and tactics that were developed in Europe's imperial campaigns were instrumental in reorienting the US land forces as well as Europe's own forces. The "oil spot" or "ink blot"—its contemporary variety is also known as "clear, hold, build"—is a French idea that can easily be traced back to the 1890s.[1] Tactics and methods used by the British Empire on the deployment of local, indigenous forces had an important effect on contemporary operations.[2] Another aspect involves the jihadis' ubiquitous references to the colonial roots of their anti-Christian and anti-Western beliefs.

A second theme is the West's short memory. An untainted observer of the current wars and the doctrinal and operational reorientation of the armies fighting in the war would have to grapple with a certain amount of confusion. Such an observer may ask: Why were these historical lessons forgotten in the first place? A number of different reasons can explain the amnesia of large military organizations when it comes to their past counterinsurgency lessons. One is trauma—it is no surprise that an army shuns learning lessons from painful defeat. Not coincidentally did American officers study Galula in such detail, essentially examining a spectacularly traumatic and unsuccessful counterinsurgency of another country, France in Algeria. Another important reason for organizational forgetting is that the Cold War provided the relative convenience of a conventional enemy, and therefore the imperative of concentrating doctrine and forces that triggered and justified staggering investments in conventional fighting power. Even when engaged in unconventional counterinsurgency operations, such as Vietnam, the ultimate enemy—and the point of orientation—remained a conventional one, the USSR; although nuclear weapons and deterrence added another, altogether different, unconventional level. Another reason for an army's institutional inattention to the lessons of counterinsurgency, therefore, is money—a powerful driver of innovation and doctrinal orientation.

Third, a glance back into the past triggers the question of what the future has in store. Will counterinsurgency be the new template for future wars? The question cannot be answered in a scholarly way, as evidence is not available yet. But for political and psychological reasons that are already revealing themselves, it is unlikely that the United States or any of its allies will commit to an ambitious, large-scale war among the people any time soon. Much will depend on the outcome of Iraq and Afghanistan—and for this the next half-dozen years will be decisive. The price of being bogged down in two wars at the same time is coming to be perceived as high, perhaps prohibitively high—while the benefit of doing so remains more elusive and difficult to achieve than the proponents of military action or more military resources have been willing to concede.

Yet, it is probably safe to say that Afghanistan will not be the last major counterinsurgency that will entangle NATO's largest armies. Retaining some of the rich lessons in counterinsurgency, therefore, will be imperative—particularly if the United States and Europe should come to the conclusion that their present experiment with expeditionary wars among the people can be a template for the future. Such a shift of modern conflict, away from conventionally aligned armies on a set battlefield toward irregular warfare, affects western military force structure and doctrine as well as the orientation of opposing forces. Non-Western states and non-state actors threatened by the prospects of regime change or military attack are likely to adopt highly developed strategies of insurgency and irregular campaigns. The wars in Iraq and Afghanistan were fought for the most part against non-state actors waging loosely organized and weakly funded insurgencies. States lacking the financial and military resources to field conventionally dominant military forces are likely to adopt many of the remarkably successful unconventional tactics seen on the battlefield against American and Western forces. This adaptation brings about a whole new set of questions relating to counterinsurgency theory. How does a state-sponsored insurgency, trained and directed by a state or state-like actor, change the counterinsurgent playbook? The political realities of international relations may prevent direct interdiction against the state-sponsor and leave the Western force facing a well-equipped and well-funded opponent, determined to carry out the strategic mission of a nation-state through irregular warfare. Conflict will not remain static and Western militaries will undoubtedly have to adapt to an evolving foe. Stronger military challenges, weaving between traditional understandings of insurgency, terrorism, and conventional military opposition are likely to challenge NATO's large militaries to rethink the lessons currently being learned.

Part of that process of reflection, and another question that only future historians will be able to answer, is the changing role of civilians in these operations. Can and should civilians take over some of the responsibilities of counterinsurgency currently held by military forces? Will diplomatic and political roles be led by civilian personnel, or will the military continue to have to pick up the slack? Civilian government assets such as the State Department, USAID, and other agencies possess only a fraction of the resources available to their colleagues in arms, yet they have mission statements more directly in line with many of the goals and requirements of counterinsurgency. Substantial institutional change is required in order create permanent post-conflict reconstruction capabilities that play lead roles in future foreign engagements and counterinsurgency campaigns. Provincial reconstruction teams, state building and development assistance, and extensive strategic communications via public diplomacy are core components now handled in some capacity by the military command structure. This fundamental question of civilian capacity concerns all NATO countries— perhaps the Europeans even more than the United States.

But for America's allies, the hard questions start even earlier. What does a potential counter-insurgency "revolution" mean for them? During the 1990s, many European allies were concerned that they would not be able to fight jointly with America in a high-tech war. Counterinsurgency, although low-tech in many respects, has further aggravated this concern. A number of countries that are part of the Atlantic Alliance are not fully "interoperable" with the US land forces in counterinsurgency, not mainly for technical but primarily for political reasons. Their own governments might impose "caveats," in contemporary jargon, or red lines that their armies are not allowed to cross. Such lines could be troop levels, the use of certain tactics, regional restrictions, spending caps, or deeper rifts in the cultural underpinnings of the use of force. Some European countries, most notably Germany, are not fundamentally opposed to the use of military force any more. But there remains a gulf between America and Europe when it comes to the use of military force to further national security or national interests. America's warrior culture is more deeply rooted in the social and cultural fabric of the United States than many Europeans are able and willing to see. In counterinsurgency, that could mean that America is able to tolerate a level of risk, casualties, defense spending, and just violence that its European allies are unwilling to stomach. But anybody jumping to the conclusion that America perhaps retains something of a "heroic" character while Europe has entered a "post-heroic" age should pause. In counterterrorism, oddly, the opposite can be observed.

What does the "age of terror" have in store for Europe? Since 9/11, Europe has endured far more successful terrorist attacks than America and has foiled more near-attacks on its homeland. European countries, home to approximately 17 million people of Muslim origin, have far more Islamic extremists in their midst than the United States. Yet the vast majority of EU citizens do not see their way of life and their national security threatened by radical Islam, either in Europe nor from the far-flung places of the Middle East and South Asia. While America seems to be more "heroic" on the battlefield, Europeans appear to have more resilience at home. Perhaps because Europe has centuries of experience with its own religious extremisms, with vicious political ideologies, and with terrorism of many kinds, it sees the inherent limitations of radical Islam. The problem is not seen as an "insurrection" that is brewing in Europe's midst, or even in the Middle East, but as a vicious form of crime with an ideological component—impossible to solve, difficult to manage, but not an existential threat to "our way of life."

This observation has consequences for future counterinsurgency operations, and even for ongoing ones. To begin with, fewer Britons and Germans and French and Italians (in relative terms) supported the war in Iraq and Afghanistan than Americans did. Of this smaller share, a significant number supported the operation not because they firmly believed the wars had a counterterrorism effect, but for two other reasons: either because they firmly believed in the importance of a healthy transatlantic relationship (and therefore went to war to salvage the West from internal fissures, not from external threats); or because they firmly believed it was in the responsibility of the international community to help a country that had suffered so much, partly for reasons that can be found in Europe's own bloody colonial conflicts in these regions. They supported the war, in short, not for their narrow self-interest, but in the interest of a larger community. It may be concluded that Europe is less likely to support a future counterinsurgency operation than America—and if so, that the reasons for the support are likely to be markedly different.

Finally one much-neglected subject begs to be mentioned: emotion. Historically, military organizations developed routines and procedures that were designed to be stress resistant, even under fire, brutal attack, and prolonged hardship. Eighteenth-century armies had to be able to march closed ranks of identical soldiers into crackling enemy fire, to the rhythm of monotonous—almost mechanical—regimental drums. Out of necessity and functionality, modern industrial armies, even more so during the nineteenth and twentieth centuries, have gained a reputation for being orderly, drilled, straightforward, almost automated top-down organizations—the opposite of susceptible, sensitive, passionate, emotional. That cliché is only partly true. Proximity to violence and death in a combat zone has an effect, particularly in drawn-out counterinsurgencies against twenty-first-century insurgents. Roadside bombs and suicide attacks, the weapons of the weak, can have a disturbing impact—not just physically, but psychologically, and not just individually, but organizationally and even politically. In heavily contested areas, every movement, by foot or vehicle, becomes a nerve-wracking and risky activity. And if a bomb goes off, releasing the ubiquitous tension built up by that combustible blend of boredom and excitement, soldiers, in many cases, cannot react by returning fire— they can only absorb the blow, perhaps losing a friend, perhaps a leg, but with luck only an innocent mind. Deadly violence breathes life into notions that are, to many observers far from combat, bloodless and nearly devoid of meaning: courage is one of those words, but also risk, sacrifice, and loss. Those in the rear, especially senior officers, are close enough to *feel* what it means to be at the front, and give as much as they can and work as hard as they can to support the "kids" who take the brunt. And therein lies a danger. "War," Peter Paret pointed out, "is not only a complex social, organizational, technological and political reality, its ambiguous character engages emotion as well as reason."[3] It engages the rational as well as the irrational. But politicians, strategists, and generals tend to focus their thoughts and actions on the side of reason, on the instrumentality of force, and often neglect emotion—although they might become driven by it. "Once combat begins and people die, it may be difficult to remember the instrumentality of war," Paret wrote.[4] Sacrifice creates value. This observation gains particular weight in the kinds of confrontations that were the subject of this book—long, slow-moving, painful operations that offer few rewards, and often only brittle political success, if any at all, marred by inherent difficulties, such as corruption or political incompetence, dynamics that are almost entirely outside the control of the counterinsurgent forces. Understanding counterinsurgency also means understanding the emotional side and its ensuing risk: the higher the costs and the longer it takes, the higher the likelihood that war, in Paret's words, may change "from a tool of policy to a force that imposes—or seeks to impose—its own emotional demands."[5] These emotional demands make it both more difficult and more important to remember that wars are fought not to be won, but to gain a political objective beyond war.

Notes

1   Thomas Rid, "The 19th Century Origins of Counterinsurgency Doctrine," *Journal of Strategic Studies*, 2010, forthcoming.
2   Kimberly Marten, "The Same Old Mistake," *The New York Times*, September 3, 2009.
3   Peter Paret, *The Cognitive Challenge of War*, Princeton, NJ: Princeton University Press, 2009, p. 3.
4   Ibid.
5   Ibid, p. 4.

Suggested further reading

The reading list below is compiled from several sources. The most important points of orientation were the bibliography in the first draft of FM 3-24 (June 2006) as well as Abu Muqawama's—aka Andrew Exum's—COIN reading list. We amended these lists with a number of important contributions that, we think, are relevant for irregular warfare. The following reading list has short sections on theory, the nineteenth and twentieth centuries, the twenty-first century, and—in order to bridge the gap between the counterinsurgency and counterterrorism debates—on contemporary jihadi terrorism. Finally we recommend a few novels and films—these formats, or art more generally, fill an important gap and complement the academic literature on terrorism, insurgency, and counterinsurgency. Fiction is able to get across something that is difficult for how-to doctrines or even political philosophy: the emotion, what drives people, what they are willing to fight for, what a revolutionary movement is actually about, its cause. We would like to thank the readers of *Kings of War*, the blog of the Department of War Studies at King's College London, for their help in creating these lists.

The following list is far from comprehensive, complete, or authoritative. And it missed, we are sure, important contributions to the ongoing debate. Yet we hope it serves as a useful starting point for the interested reader.

Theory

Alwyn-Foster, Nigel. "Changing the Army for Counterinsurgency Operations." *Military Review,* 85, 6 (November/December 2005), 2–15.

Baker, Ralph O. "The Decisive Weapon." *Military Review*, 86, 3 (May/June 2006), 13–32.

Bulloch, Gavin. "Military Doctrine and Counterinsurgency: A British Perspective." *Parameters,* 26, 2 (Summer 1996), 4–16.

Callwell, Charles E. *Small Wars: Their Principles and Practice.* Lincoln: University of Nebraska Press, 1996. Reprint of *Small Wars: A Tactical Textbook for Imperial Soldiers.* London: Greenhill Books, 1890.

Chiarelli, Peter W. and Patrick R. Michaelis. "Winning the Peace: The Requirement for Full-Spectrum Operations." *Military Review,* 85, 4 (July/August 2005), 4–17.

Corum, James and Wray Johnson. *Airpower and Small Wars.* Lawrence: University Press of Kansas, 2003.

Fall, Bernard. *The Street without Joy.* Mechanicsburg, PA: Stackpole Books, 1964.

Galula, David. *Counterinsurgency Warfare: Theory and Practice.* London: Praeger, 1964.

Galula, David. *Pacification in Algeria 1956–1958* (MG-478-1). Santa Monica, CA: Rand Corporation, 1963 (2006).

Gray, Colin S. "Irregular Warfare: One Nature, Many Characters." *Strategic Studies Quarterly* (Winter 2007).

Guevara, Ernesto Che. *Guerilla Warfare.* New York: Classic House Books, 2009.

Gurr, Theodore. *Why Men Rebel*. Princeton, NJ: Princeton University Press, 1971.

Gwynn, Charles. *Imperial Policing*. London: Macmillan, 1939.

Hammes, T.X. *The Sling and the Stone*. Osceola: Zenith Press, 2004.

Hoffer, Eric. *The True Believer: Thoughts on the Nature of Mass Movements*. New York: Harper Classics, 1966.

Kitson, Frank. *Bunch of Five*. London: Faber, 1977.

Larteguy, Jean. *The Centurions*. New York: Dutton, 1962.

Lawrence, T.E. "The 27 Articles of T.E. Lawrence." *The Arab Bulletin*, 20 (August 1917).

Lawrence, T.E. *Seven Pillars of Wisdom: A Triumph*. New York: Anchor, 1991.

McCuen, John J. *The Art of Counter-Revolutionary War*. St. Petersburg, FL: Hailer Publishing, 2005.

Mack, Andrew. "Why Big Nations Lose Small Wars: The Politics of Asymmetric Conflict." *World Politics*, 27, 2 (1975).

Mao, Zedong. *On Guerilla Warfare*. London: Cassell, 1965.

Münkler, Herfried. *Der Wandel des Krieges. Von der Symmetrie zur Asymmetrie*. Weilerswist: Velbrück Wissenschaft, 2006.

Münkler, Herfried. *Die neuen Kriege*. Reinbek: Rowohlt, 2002.

O'Neill, Bard E. *Insurgency and Terrorism: From Revolution to Apocalypse*. Dulles, VA: Potomac Books, 2005.

Schelling, Thomas C. *Arms and Influence*. New Haven, CT: Yale University Press, 1966.

Schmitt, Carl. *The Theory of the Partisan*. New York: Telos Press, 2007.

Sepp, Kalev I. "Best Practices in Counterinsurgency." *Military Review,* 85, 3 (May/June 2005), 8–12.

Smith, Rupert. *The Utility of Force: The Art of War in the Modern World*. New York: Vintage Books, 2008.

Taber, Robert. *The War of the Flea*, Dulles, VA: Potomac Books, 2002.

Thompson, Robert. *Defeating Communist Insurgency: The Lessons of Malaya and Vietnam*, New York: Praeger, 1966.

Tomes, Robert. "Relearning Counterinsurgency Warfare." *Parameters*, 34, 1 (Spring 2004), 16–28.

Trinquier, Roger. *Modern Warfare: A French View of Counterinsurgency*. New York: Praeger, 1964.

US Army/Marine Corps Field Manual 3-24, *Counterinsurgency*. Chicago: University of Chicago Press, 2007.

US Army Field Manual 3-07, *Stability Operations*. Ann Arbor: University of Michigan Press, 2009.

US Marine Corps, *Small Wars Manual*. Washington: Government Printing Office, 1940.

Nineteenth and twentieth centuries

Asprey, Robert. *War in the Shadows: The Guerilla in History*. New York: William Morrow, 1994.

Begin, Menachim. *The Revolt: The Story of the Irgun*. New York: Steimatzky Agency Ltd, 1977.

Bugeaud, Thomas Robert and Weil, Maurice-Henri. *Œuvres militaires du Maréchal Bugeaud*. Paris: Baudouin, 1883.

Decker, Carl von. *Algerien und die dortige Kriegführung*. Berlin: F.-A. Herbig, 1844.

Ellis, John. *From the Barrel of a Gun: A History of the Guerrilla, Revolutionary, and Counterinsurgency Warfare from the Romans to the Present*. London: Greenhill, 1995.

Frémeaux, Jacques. *Les Bureaux arabes dans l'Algérie de la conquête*. Paris: Denoël, 1993.

Galliéni, Joseph-Simon. *Neuf ans a Madagascar*. Paris: Librairie Hachette, 1908.

Giap, Vo Nguyen. *People's War People's Army: The Viet Cong Insurrection Manual for Underdeveloped Countries*. Stockton, CA: University Press of the Pacific, 2001.

Gottmann, Jean. "Bugeaud, Galliéni, Lyautey: The Development of French Colonial Warfare," in Edward Mead Earle (ed.), *Makers of Modern Strategy*. Princeton, NJ: Princeton University Press, 1943, pp. 234–59.

Horne, Alistair. *A Savage War of Peace. Algeria 1954–1962*. New York: NYRB Classics, 1977 (2006).

Hosmer, Stephen T. and Sibylle O. Crane, *Counterinsurgency. A Symposium, April 16–20, 1962*. Santa Monica, CA: Rand Corporation, 1963.

Jackson, Mike. *Operation Banner*. Army Code 71842. London: British Army, 2006.

Krepinevich, Andrew F. *The Army and Vietnam*. Baltimore, MD: The Johns Hopkins University Press, 1988.

Laqueur, Walter. *Guerrilla. A Historical and Critical Study*, Vol. 4. Boston: Little, Brown, 1976.

Lawrence, T.E. *Seven Pillars of Wisdom*. Garden City, NY: Doubleday, 1935.

Linn, Brian McAllister. *The Philippine War, 1899–1902*. Lawrence: University Press of Kansas, 2002.

Lyautey, Hubert. *Du rôle colonial de l'armée*. Paris: Armand Colin, 1900.

McMaster, H.R. *Dereliction of Duty*. New York: Harper Perennial, 1998.

Marston, Daniel and Carter Malkasian (eds). *Counterinsurgency in Modern Warfare*. Oxford: Osprey Publishing, 2008.

Mathias, Grégor. *Les Sections administratives spécialisées en Algérie: entre idéal et réalité (1955–1962)*. Paris: L'Harmattan, 1998.

Mockaitis, Thomas R. *British Counter-Insurgency in the Post-Imperial Era*. Manchester: Manchester University Press, 1995.

Nagl, John A. *Learning to Eat Soup with a Knife: Counterinsurgency Lessons From Malaya and Vietnam*. Chicago: University of Chicago Press, 2005.

Paret, Peter. *French Revolutionary Warfare from Indochina to Algeria*, New York: Praeger, 1964.

Peng, Chin. *My Side of History*. New York: Media Masters, 2003.

Porch, Douglas. "Bugeaud, Galliéni, Lyautey: The Development of French Colonial Warfare," in Peter Paret (ed.), *Makers of Modern Strategy*. Princeton, NJ: Princeton University Press, 1986, pp. 376–407.

Race, Jeffrey. *War Comes to Long An: Revolutionary Conflict in a Vietnamese Province*. Berkeley: University of California Press, 1972.

Rashid, Ahmad. *Taliban*. New Haven, CT: Yale University Press, 2001.

Rid, Thomas. "Razzia. A Turning Point in Modern Strategy." *Terrorism and Political Violence*, 21, 4 (2009), 617–35.

Rid, Thomas. "The 19th Century Origins of Counterinsurgency Doctrine." *Journal of Strategic Studies*, 2010.

Short, Anthony. *The Communist Insurrection in Malaya, 1948–1960*. Crane: Russak, 1975.

Sullivan, Anthony Thrall. *Thomas-Robert Bugeaud, France and Algeria 1784–1849*. Hamden, CT: Archon, 1983.

West, Bing. *The Village*. New York: Pocket Books, 1972.

Twenty-first century

Biddle, Stephen. "Seeing Baghdad, Thinking Saigon." *Foreign Affairs*, March/April 2006.

Chandrasekaran, Rajiv. *Imperial Life in the Emerald City: Inside Iraq's Green Zone*. New York: Vintage, 2007.

Coll, Steve. *Ghost Wars*. New York: Penguin, 2004.

Crane, Conrad and W. Andrew Terrill. *Reconstructing Iraq*. Carlisle Barracks: Army War College, 2003.

Giustozzi, Antonio, (ed.), *Decoding the New Taliban: Insights from the Afghan Field*. New York: Columbia University Press, 2009.

Giustozzi, Antonio. *Empires of Mud: The Neo-Taliban Insurgency in Afghanistan 2002–2007*. New York: Columbia University Press, 2009.

Giustozzi, Antonio. *Koran, Kalashnikov, and Laptop. The Neo-Taliban Insurgency in Afghanistan*. New York: Columbia University Press, 2008.

Hoffman, Bruce. *Insurgency and Counterinsurgency in Iraq*. Santa Monica, CA: RAND, 2004.

Johnson, Thomas H. "The Taliban Insurgency and an Analysis of Shabnamah (Night Letters)." *Small Wars & Insurgencies*, 18, 3 (2007), 317–44.

Jones, Seth G. *In the Graveyard of Empires: America's War in Afghanistan*. New York: W.W. Norton & Company, Inc. 2009.

Kilcullen, David. "Anatomy of a Tribal Revolt." *Small Wars Journal*, August 29, 2007.

Kilcullen, David. "Countering Global Insurgency." *Journal of Strategic Studies* 28, 4 (August 2005), 597–617.

Kilcullen, David. "Twenty-Eight Articles: Fundamentals of Company Level Counterinsurgency." *Military Review*, 86, 3 (May/June 2006), 103–8.

Kilcullen, David. *The Accidental Guerrilla: Fighting Small Wars in the Midst of a Big One*. Oxford: Oxford University Press, 2009.

Krepinevich, Andrew F. "How to Win in Iraq." *Foreign Affairs*, 84, 5 (September/October 2005).

Long, Austin. "The Anbar Awakening," *Survival*, 50, 2 (2008), 67–94.

McCary, John A. "The Anbar Awakening: An Alliance of Incentives." *The Washington Quarterly*, 32, 1 (2009).

MacFarland, Sean and Niel Smith. "Anbar Awakens," *Military Review* (March/April 2008).

McFate, Montgomery. "Iraq: The Social Context of IEDs." *Military Review*, 85, 3 (May/June 2005).

Mackinlay, John. *The Insurgent Archipelago*. New York: Columbia University Press, 2009.

Packer, George. "The Lesson of Tal Afar." *The New Yorker*, April 10, 2006.

Packer, George. *Assassin's Gate: America in Iraq*. New York: Farrar, Straus and Giroux, 2005.

Peters, Gretchen. *Seeds of Terror: How Heroin Is Bankrolling the Taliban and al Qaeda*. New York: Thomas Dunne Books, 2009.

Petraeus, David. "Learning Counterinsurgency: Observations from Soldiering in Iraq." *Military Review,* 86, 2 (March/April 2006).

Rashid, Ahmed. *Descent into Chaos: The US and the Disaster in Pakistan, Afghanistan and Central Asia*. New York: Penguin Books, 2009.

Ricks, Thomas E. *Fiasco: The American Military Adventure in Iraq*. New York: Penguin Press, 2006.

Ricks, Thomas E. *The Gamble: General David Petraeus and the American Military Adventure in Iraq 2006–2008*. New York: Penguin Press, 2009.

Rid, Thomas and Marc Hecker. *War 2.0: Irregular Warfare in the Information Age*, Westport, CT: Praeger, 2009.

Rotmann, Philipp, David Tohn, and Jaron Wharton, "Learning Under Fire: Progress and Dissent in the US Military." *Survival*, 51, 4 (2009), 31–48.

Schmidle, Nicholas. *To Live or to Perish Forever*. New York: Henry Holt, 2009.

Semple, Michael. *Reconciliation in Afghanistan*. Washington, DC: United States Institute of Peace Press, 2009.

Ucko, David. *The New Counterinsurgency Era*. Washington, DC: Georgetown University Press, 2009.

Yingling, Paul. "A Failure in Generalship." *Armed Forces Journal* (May 2007).

Terrorism

Atkinson, Rick. "Left of Boom" (Series). *The Washington Post*, September 30, 2007.

Baum, Dan. "What the Generals don't know." *The New Yorker*, 80, 43 (2005), 42.

Beam, Louis. "Leaderless Resistance." *The Seditionist*, 12 (1992).

Bergen, Peter and Paul Cruickshank, "The Unraveling." *The New Republic* (2008).

Brachman, Jarret M. and McCants, William F. "Stealing Al Qaeda's Playbook," *Studies in Conflict & Terrorism*, 29, 4 (July 2006), 309–21.

Brown, Vahid. *Cracks in the Foundation*. US Military Academy, Combating Terrorism Center, 2007.

Cronin, Audrey Kurth. *How Terrorism Ends: Understanding the Decline and Demise of Terrorist Campaigns*. Princeton, NJ: Princeton University Press, 2009.

Hegghammer, Thomas. *Jihad in Saudi Arabia*. Cambridge: Cambridge University Press, 2010.

Hoffman, Bruce. "The Myth of Grass-Roots Terrorism. Why Osama bin Laden Still Matters." *Foreign Affairs*, May/June 2008.

Kepel, Gilles and Jean-Pierre Milelli. *Al-Qaeda in its own Words*. Cambridge, MA: Belknap Press, 2008.

Kepel, Gilles. *Jihad. The Trail of Political Islam*. London: I.B. Tauris, 2006.

Kimmage, Daniel. "The al-Qaeda Media Nexus." RFE/RL Special Report, 2008.

Kimmage, Daniel and Kathleen Ridolfo. "Iraqi Insurgent Media." RFE/RL Special Report, 2007.

Lewis, Bernard. *The Crisis of Islam: Holy War and Unholy Terror*. New York: Modern Library, 2003.

Lia, Brynjar. *Architect of Global Jihad: The Life of al-Qaida Strategist Abu Mus'ab al-Suri*. New York: Columbia University Press, 2008.

Musharbash, Yassin. *Die neue al-Qaida. Innenansichten eines lernenden Terrornetzwerks*. Köln: Kiepenheuer & Witsch, 2006.

Neumann, Peter and Brooke Rogers. *Recruitment and Mobilisation for the Islamist Militant Movement in Europe*. London: King's College London, 2008.

Roy, Olivier. *Globalised Islam: The Search for a New Ummah*. London: C. Hurst & Co., 2004.

Roy, Olivier. *The Politics of Chaos in the Middle East*, New York: Columbia University Press, 2008.

Sageman, Marc. *Leaderless Jihad: Terror Networks in the Twenty-First Century*. Philadelphia: University of Pennsylvania Press, 2008.

Sageman, Marc. *Understanding Terror Networks*. Philadelphia: University of Pennsylvania Press, 2004.

Steinberg, Guido. *Der nahe und der ferne Feind. Das Netzwerk des islamistischen Terrorismus*. München: Beck, 2005.

Stern, Jessica. "The Protean Enemy." *Foreign Affairs*, 82, 4 (2003).

Wright, Lawrence. "The Master Plan." *The New Yorker*, September 11, 2006.

Wright, Lawrence. "The Rebellion." *The New Yorker*, June 2, 2008.

Wright, Lawrence. *The Looming Tower. Al-Qaeda and the Road to 9/11*, New York: Alfred A. Knopf, 2006.

Fiction

A more detailed discussion of these 20 books—and more—can be found at http://kingsofwar.org.uk/2010/02/fiction.

Anderson, Kent, *Sympathy for the Devil*, 1987

Bolger, Daniel, *Feast of Bones,* 1990

Burdick, Eugene and William Lederer, *The Ugly American*, 1958

Forester, C.S., *Rifleman Dodd*, 1933

Greene, Graham, *The Quiet American*, 1955

Haldeman, Joe, *Forever Peace*, 1997

Hemingway, Ernest, *For Whom The Bell Tolls*, 1940

Hersey, John, *A Bell for Adano*, 1944

Kipling, Rudyard, *Kim*, 1901

Larteguy, Jean, *The Centurions*, 1960

Larteguy, Jean, *The Praetorians*, 1964

Lermontov, Mikhail, *A Hero of Our Time*, 1840

Levi, Primo, *If Not Now, When?* 1982

MacDonald Fraser, George, *Flashman*, 1969

Malraux, André, *Man's Fate*, 1933

Orwell, George, *Shooting an Elephant*, 1936

Roth, Robert, *Sand in the Wind*, 1973

Sterling, Bruce, *Distraction*, 1998

Tolstoy, Leo, *Hadji Murad*, 1912

Uris, Leon, *Trinity*, 1976

Films

A discussion and trailers to many of these films can be found at http://kingsofwar.org.uk/2010/02/films.

The Quiet American (1958, Joseph Mankiewicz)
Spartacus (1960, Stanley Kubrick)
Lawrence of Arabia (1962, David Lean)
La 317ème Section (1965, Pierre Schoendoerffer)
La battaglia di Algeri (1966, Gillo Pontecorvo)
Lost Command (1966, Mark Robson)
Army of Shadows (1969, Jean-Pierre Melville)
Cromwell (1970, Ken Hughes)
Soldier of Orange (1977, Paul Verhoeven)
Breaker Morant (1980, Bruce Beresford)
L'honneur d'un capitaine (1982, Pierre Schoendoerffer)
Full Metal Jacket (1987, Stanley Kubrick)
Michael Collins (1996, Neil Jordan)
No Man's Land (2001, Danis Tanović)
Bloody Sunday (2002, Paul Greengrass)
L'Ennemi intime (2007, Florent Emilio Siri)
Che (2008, Steven Soderbergh)
Waltz with Bashir (2008, Ari Folman)
Der Baader Meinhof Komplex (2008, Uli Edel, Bernd Eichinger)
The Hurt Locker (2009, Kathryn Bigelow)

Index

Afghan National Army 54, 166
Afghanistan 2, 13, 19, 22, 32–33, 46, 49–53, 100, 105, 132, 164–166, 178, 200, 231–239, 244, 251
air force 4, 31–32, 67, 103–108, 133, 210
Algerian War 21–25, 66, 84, 118, 217, 243–244, 257
al-Qaeda 1, 46, 70, 78–80, 97, 102, 105, 125, 141, 178, 195, 209, 253
Anbar Awakening 69, 81, 101, 142, 149,
army: France 11–12, 23–25, 190; Britain 28, 190; Germany 55–57; United States 59–60, 69, 75, 103–104, 134, 160–164, 167–168, 200, 233, 243,

blogs 2, 222, 261
Bugeaud, Thomas-Robert 3, 12–13, 26–27, 262–263
Bush, George W. 78, 81, 145, 197

Callwell, Charles 2, 28–39, 175
Centre de Doctrine d'Emploi des Forces (CDEF) 23
Chad 22
Challe Plan 20
Chechnya 76, 85
CIA 162–163, 254
Civil Operations and Revolutionary Development Support (CORDS)
Clausewitz, Carl von 8, 174–175, 186, 255
Coalition Provisional Authority (CPA) 178, 184, 199
Cold War 11, 22, 47, 64, 125, 129, 257.
colonial warfare 3, 11–16, 20–27, 31, 37, 76, 123, 250, 257, 262–263
counterterrorism 46–47, 128, 130–132, 137, 144, 256–259, 261
cyberspace 107

deterrence 23, 38, 108, 115, 118–119, 123, 161, 182, 257
drones 105–108, 221

El Salvador 59, 128, 133, 164, 176–178, 194, 251
emotions 31, 156, 212, 259–260,

FARC 105, 154, 252
Field Manual *Counterinsurgency* (FM 3-24) 4, 20–24, 59, 61, 65–69, 86, 103, 92–93, 100–104, 145, 160, 164, 167, 173, 184, 190–192, 197, 201–203, 209–210, 215–219, 227, 261–262
films 222–225, 245, 261–266,
Foreign Legion 14–17, 22,
Franco-Prussian War 12, 15, 22

Galliéni, Joseph-Simon, 3, 12–15, 26–27, 262–263
Galula, David 13, 16–17, 22–25, 34, 40, 61–62, 78, 145, 161, 175, 181, 182–183, 217, 243, 256–257
Gaulle, Charles de 19–22, 225
Gaza Strip 79, 120, 124, 221
Guevara, Che 75
Gwynn, Charles 3, 28–31, 33, 35, 37

Hamas 79, 120, 225
hearts and minds 18, 38, 82–83, 97, 101, 123, 221, 245
Hezbollah 7, 108, 120, 125, 218–227
human terrain 13–15, 24, 64, 90, 147, 189, 194–196
Huntington, Samuel 14, 22

improvised explosive devices (IED) 1, 52, 64, 106, 193, 244
Information Operations 6, 20, 61, 65, 77, 92, 107, 137, 161, 216–227, 236
insurgency 19, 30, 40, 63, 77–79, 94–95, 104, 132, 144–145, 177–179, 196, 225, 242–253,
interrogations 66, 118, 145
IRA 38
Iran 120, 125, 144, 147, 242, 251
Iraq, invasion of, 1–2, 59, 143, 178, 197, 251
Islam 80, 85, 193, 245, 259

Israel 25, 79, 108, 119–120, 124, 191, 216–227

Kabul 50, 55, 149, 151, 179, 232
Kader, Abd el- 12, 15
Kitson, Frank 3, 29, 34, 197
Korea 17, 137
Kosovo 22, 47–48, 104

Lacheroy, Charles, 16–18, 20, 26–27
Lebanon 108, 219–227
Libya 22, 120
Liddell Hart, Basil 89–90
Lyautey, Hubert 12–15, 24–27, 262–63

Madagascar 13–15
Malayan Emergency 3, 28–39, 83, 119, 122,
    135, 145, 154, 176–177, 182, 187, 220,
    247–250, 262
Mao, Tse-Tung 17–18, 39, 161
Marine Corps 4, 61, 63, 68, 87–99, 141,
    162–167, 192–200
Marxism 18

Napoleon 12–15, 114, 190
NATO 2–3, 13, 46–53, 133–134, 136–138, 166,
    232, 237–239, 258
Northern Ireland 28–40, 197–198
novels 261, 265

Obama, Barack 129, 251
oil spot method 13–15, 19, 24, 257
Oman 28, 30–36, 249, 251
Organisation de l'armée secrète (OAS) 17, 22

Pakistan 68, 78, 106, 132, 143, 196, 251–252,
    256
Petraeus, David x, 20, 22, 25, 59–70, 81–83,
    179, 189, 212–213, 220
Philippines, Philippine war (1899–1902) 76, 87,
    176
piracy 12
provincial reconstruction teams (PRTs) 7, 147,
    156, 182, 230–239, 258
psychological operations (PSYOPS) 36, 83, 131,
    137, 217–219, 226
public affairs 220

quadrillage 19

Ramadi 80–81, 141
Reagan, Ronald 177
religion 62, 68, 83, 190, 193, 205–206, 245, 259
Russia 76, 108, 129, 217

al-Sadr, Muqtada 82, 103, 147, 153
safe haven 4, 75, 78, 82, 88–94, 107, 123 143,
    178, 182, 192, 256
Salan, Raoul 20
September 11, 2001, 1, 108, 256, 259
Shia 1, 80, 143–144, 147, 193, 220, 223–226,
    245
Somalia: battle of Mogadishu 47–48, 129, 148,
    162, 198,
State Department 63, 68, 147, 153, 163, 176,
    179, 181, 183–185, 231–239, 258
suicide bombings 1, 52–53, 120–121, 144–145,
    193, 207, 209–211, 220, 225–226, 245, 259
Sunni 77–81, 144, 173, 193

Taliban 53–54, 57, 68, 78, 100, 105–107, 132,
    143–144, 149, 178, 197
targeted killings 4, 18, 75, 77, 82
Templer, General Sir Gerald 37, 83, 135, 177,
    248, 249
terrorism 18, 38, 50, 66, 79, 82, 84, 132, 136,
    161, 168, 256–259
Thompson, Sir Robert, 3, 29, 33, 175
trauma 17, 26, 213, 257
Trinquier, Roger 16–17, 24–27, 61, 71, 227, 262

United Nations 47, 54, 76, 124, 130–131,
    147–148, 178, 198, 231–238
USAID 63, 176, 147, 182–184, 230–239, 258

Vietnam War 43, 59, 76–79, 117–118, 162–164,
    175–176, 243–245, 249–251

Westmoreland, William 116, 162–163, 175, 192
World War II 3, 12, 16–17, 47–48, 92, 114, 128,
    152, 175, 201, 206, 242, 250

Yemen 3, 29, 36, 39, 40
Yugoslavia 48, 57